distributer
or
Sponsor = underwriter

- A prospectus in use for more than nine months
cannot contain info more than 16 months old (p.98)

Act of 1933 Associated with
- new issues
- underwriting
- registration statement
- prospectus
- primary mkt

Regulation T - regulates the extension of credit to
customers by B/D
Regulation U - regulates the extension of credit
to customers by Banks or other lenders

Act of
Regulation D - under 1933
- allows offer + sale of sec. to accredited
investors + no more than 35 non-accredited
investors w/o registration
- These transactions are called Private Placement

Series 6
Investment Company Products/Variable
Contracts Limited Representative Exam

License Exam Manual

2nd Edition

Funds that comply w/ Subchapter M
are known as regulated Investment
companies

$1 mill net worth + $200,000
income in 2 yrs or good
prospects of meeting $300,00 that
yr (as a married couple)

ERISA - regulates private sector plans only
(corporations) - not gov't (fed or state workers)

Disputes

- between member firms / associated persons
+ less than $25000 is simplified industry arbitration

- dispute between a member + customer or member goes to
simplified arbitration $25,000 - no hearing
↳ less than

- MRV + AWC used for Code of Procedure violations,
not disputes

firm commitment - underwriter acts as principal.

-aka - negotiated underwriting contract
competitive bid arrangement

Standby underwriting

- underwriter agrees to buy all
shares that remain unsold

IRA ineligable
Investments
- collectibles
- Life Insurance
- Muni Bonds
- covered call writing is permissable

ineligable
Investment Practices
- Short Sales of stock
- spec. option strategies
- Margin Acct trading

All B/D registered w/ SEC must
be SIPC members except:

1) B/D handling only mutual funds + UIT
2) B/D "   " var. annuities + insurance
3) investment advisors

To join SIPC - must by a Fidelity Bond
of atleast $25,000 - to protect against
employee loss or theft of customer securities

KAPLAN FINANCIAL

p.276

Plan companies - buy fund shares
from an underwriter + hold them in a
trust for an individual purchasing the shares
under a periodic payment plan

p. 282 - review Classes / duration / prices

D1153867

At press time, this edition contains the most complete and accurate information currently available. Owing to the nature of license examinations, however, information may have been added recently to the actual test that does not appear in this edition. Please contact the publisher to verify that you have the most current edition.

This publication is designed to provide accurate and authoritative information in regard to the subject matter covered. It is sold with the understanding that the publisher is not engaged in rendering legal, accounting, or other professional services. If legal advice or other expert assistance is required, the services of a competent professional should be sought.

We value your input and suggestions. If you found imperfections or incorrect information in this product, please let us know by sending an email to **errata@kaplan.com**.

We are always looking for ways to make our products better to help you achieve your career goals.

SERIES 6 INVESTMENT COMPANY PRODUCTS/VARIABLE CONTRACTS LIMITED REPRESENTATIVE EXAM, 2ND EDITION
©2006, 2007 DF Institute, Inc. All rights reserved.

Published by DF Institute, Inc.

Printed in the United States of America.

ISBN: 1-4195-1603-5

PPN: 3606-0226

07 08 10 9 8 7 6 5 4 3 2 1
J   F   M A M J J A S O N D

Contents

U N I T   2   **Product Information: Investment Company Securities and Variable Contracts   87**

UNIT 3　Securities and Tax Regulations　167

UNIT 4　Marketing, Prospecting, and Sales Presentations　253

Series 6 Introduction

INTRODUCTION

Thank you for choosing this exam preparation system for your educational needs and welcome to the Series 6 License Exam Manual. This manual has applied adult learning principles to give you the tools you'll need to pass your exam on the first attempt.

Some of these special features include:

■ exam-focused questions and content to maximize exam preparation;

■ an interactive design that integrates content with questions to increase retention; and

■ integrated Drill & Practice exam preparation tools to sharpen test-taking skills.

Why do I need to pass the Series 6 exam?

The National Association of Securities Dealers (NASD) or another self-regulatory organization requires its members and employees of its members to pass a qualification exam to become registered as an Investment Company Products/Variable Contracts Limited Representative. You must pass the Series 6 exam to be qualified to sell investment company securities and variable contracts.

Are there any prerequisites?

There are no prerequisite exams to pass before sitting for the Series 6 exam.

What is the Series 6 exam like?

The Series 6 is a 135-minute, 100-question exam administered by the NASD. It is offered as a computer-based exam at Prometric testing centers around the country.

What score must I achieve to pass?

You need a score of at least 70% on the Series 6 exam to pass and become eligible for registration as an Investment Company Products/Variable Contracts Limited Representative.

What topics will I see on the exam?

The questions you will see on the Series 6 exam do not appear in any particular order. The computer is programmed to select a new, random set of questions for each exam taker, selecting questions according to the preset topic weighting of the exam. Each Series 6 candidate will see the same number of questions on each topic, but a different mix of questions. The Series 6 exam is divided into six critical function areas:

	# of Questions	% of Exam
Securities Markets, Investment Securities, and Economic Factors	8	8%
Product Information: Investment Company Securities and Variable Contracts	26	26%
Securities and Tax Regulations	23	23%
Marketing, Prospecting, and Sales Presentations	18	18%
Evaluation of Customers	13	13%
Opening and Servicing Customer Accounts	12	12%

When you complete your exam, you will receive a printout that identifies your performance in each area.

PREPARING FOR THE EXAM

How is the License Exam Manual organized?

The License Exam Manual consists of Units and Unit Tests. In addition to the regular text, each Unit also has some unique features designed to help with quick understanding of the material. When an additional point will be valuable to your comprehension, special notes are embedded in the text. Examples of these are included below.

TAKE NOTE   These highlight special or unusual information and amplify important points.

TEST TOPIC ALERT   Each Test Topic Alert! highlights content that is especially likely to appear on the exam.

EXAMPLE   These give practical examples and numerical instances of the material just covered and convert theory into practice.

You will also see Quick Quizzes, which will help ensure you understand and retain the material covered in that particular section. Quick Quizzes are a quick interactive review of what you just read.

In addition, HotSheets for each Unit summarize the key points in bullet-point format. For your convenience and use as review notes, these HotSheets are located at the end of the book on perforated pages.

The book is made up of Units organized to explain the material that the NASD has outlined for the exam.

If your study packet included a Drill & Practice CD-ROM, this CD includes a large bank of questions that are similar in style and content to those you will encounter on the exam. You may use it to generate tests by a specific topic or create exams that are similar in difficulty and proportionate mixture to the exam.

If you prefer to complete written tests, the Practice Final Tests will provide similar practice. The questions on the print tests are included in the CD. Devote a significant amount of your study time to the completion of practice questions and review of rationales on the CD and/or the Practice Final Tests.

Your study packet may also include Mastery Exams. They are designed to simulate the actual NASD exam. You will not receive rationales, but your scores will be tracked and you will receive a diagnostic report that identifies topics for further review.

What topics are covered in the course?

The License Exam Manual consists of six Units, each devoted to a particular area of study that you will need to know to pass the Series 6. Each Unit is divided into study sections devoted to more specific areas with which you need to become familiar.

The Series 6 License Exam Manual addresses the following topics:

Unit	Topic
1	Securities Markets, Investment Securities, and Economic Factors
2	Product Information: Investment Company Securities and Variable Contracts
3	Securities and Tax Regulations
4	Marketing, Prospecting, and Sales Presentations
5	Evaluation of Customers
6	Opening and Servicing Customer Accounts

How much time should I spend studying?

Plan to spend approximately 40–60 hours reading the material and carefully answering the questions. Spread your study time over the 4–5 weeks before the date on which you are scheduled to take the Series 6 exam. Your actual time may vary depending on your reading rate, comprehension, professional background, and study environment.

What is the best way to structure my study time?

The following schedule is suggested to help you obtain maximum retention from your study efforts. Remember, this is a guideline only, because each individual may require more or less time to complete the steps included.

Step 1. Read a Unit and complete the Unit Test. Review rationales for all questions whether you got them right or wrong (2–3 hours per Unit).

Step 2. On the Drill & Practice CD-ROM, create and complete a test for each topic included under that Unit heading. For best results, select the maximum number of questions within each topic. Carefully review all rationales. Do an additional test on any topic on which you score under 60%. After completion of all topic tests, create a 50-question test comprising all Unit topics. Repeat this 50-question test until you score at least 70% (4–6 hours).

TAKE NOTE   Do not be overly concerned with your score on the first attempt at any of these tests. Instead, take the opportunity to learn from your mistakes and increase your knowledge.

Step 3. When you have completed all the Units and their Unit Tests, on the Drill & Practice CD-ROM, complete at least 5 of the 100-question exams. Complete as many as necessary to achieve a score of at least 80–90%. Create and complete additional topic tests as necessary to correct problem areas (10–20 hours).

Step 4. If your study packet includes Mastery Exams, then you are ready for the challenge of completing an exam that is designed to simulate the actual NASD exam. The Mastery Exams are full-length exams that present you with questions from the topics covered based on their weighting and emphasis on the actual exam. You will not receive rationales for the answers you select, nor will you receive immediate feedback if you answered a particular question right or wrong as you take the Mastery Exam. You should complete the Mastery Exam while observing the time limits for the actual exam. Upon completing the Mastery Exam, you will receive a diagnostic report that identifies topics for further review (3–4 hours per Exam).

Do I need to take all of the Practice Final Tests?

The Practice Final Tests assess the knowledge you need to answer the questions on the exam. By completing the Practice Final Tests and checking your answers against the rationales, you should be able to pinpoint areas of difficulty. Review any questions you miss, paying particular attention to their rationale. If any subjects still seem troublesome, go back and review the section(s) covering those topics.

How well can I expect to do?

The exams administered by the NASD are not easy. You must display considerable understanding and knowledge of the topics presented in this course to pass the exam and qualify for registration.

If you study diligently, complete all sections of the course, and consistently score at least 85% on the tests, you should be well prepared to pass the exam. However, it is important for you to realize that merely knowing the answers to our questions will not enable you to pass unless you understand the essence of the information behind the question.

SUCCESSFUL TEST-TAKING TIPS

Passing the exam depends not only on how well you learn the subject matter, but also on how well you take exams. You can develop your test-taking skills—and improve your score—by learning a few test-taking techniques:

- Read the full question

- Avoid jumping to conclusions—watch for hedge clauses

- Interpret the unfamiliar question

- Look for key words and phrases

- Identify the intent of the question

- Memorize key points

- Use a calculator

- Beware of changing answers

- Pace yourself

Each of these pointers is explained below, including examples that show how to use them to improve your performance on the exam.

Read the full question

You cannot expect to answer a question correctly if you do not know what it is asking. If you see a question that seems familiar and easy, you might anticipate the answer, mark it, and move on before you finish reading it. This is a serious mistake. Be sure to read the full question before answering it—questions are often written to trap people who assume too much.

Avoid jumping to conclusions—watch for hedge clauses

The questions on NASD exams are often embellished with deceptive distractors as choices. To avoid being misled by seemingly obvious answers, make it a practice to read each question and each answer twice before selecting your choice. Doing so will provide you with a much better chance of doing well on the exam.

Watch out for hedge clauses embedded in the question. (Examples of hedge clauses include the terms *if, not, all, none,* and *except*.) In the case of *if* statements, the question can be answered correctly only by taking into account the qualifier. If you ignore the qualifier, you will not answer correctly.

Qualifiers are sometimes combined in a question. Some that you will frequently see together are *all* with *except* and *none* with *except*. In general, when a question starts with *all* or *none* and ends with *except*, you are looking for an answer that is opposite to what the question appears to be asking.

Interpret the unfamiliar question

Do not be surprised if some questions on the exam seem unfamiliar at first. If you have studied your material, you will have the information to answer all the questions correctly. The challenge may be a matter of understanding what the question is asking.

Very often, questions present information indirectly. You may have to interpret the meaning of certain elements before you can answer the question. Be aware that the exam will approach a concept from different angles.

Look for key words and phrases

Look for words that are tip-offs to the situation presented. For example, if you see the word *prospectus* in the question, you know the question is about a new issue. Sometimes a question will even supply you with the answer if you can recognize the key words it contains. Few questions provide blatant clues, but many do offer key words that can guide you to selecting the correct answer if you pay attention. Be sure to read all instructional phrases carefully. Take time to identify the key words to answer this type of question correctly.

Identify the intent of the question

Many questions on NASD exams supply so much information that you lose track of what is being asked. This is often the case in story problems. Learn to separate the story from the question.

Take the time to identify what the question is asking. Of course, your ability to do so assumes you have studied sufficiently. There is no method for correctly answering questions if you don't know the material.

Memorize key points

Reasoning and logic will help you answer many questions, but you will have to memorize a good deal of information. The HotSheets summarize some of the most important key points for memorization.

Use a calculator

For the most part, the NASD exams will not require the use of a calculator. Most of the questions are written so that any math required is simple. However, if you have become accustomed to using a calculator for math, you will be provided with one by the testing center staff.

Avoid changing answers

If you are unsure of an answer, your first hunch is the one most likely to be correct. Do not change answers on the exam without good reason. In general, change an answer only if you:

■ discover that you did not read the question correctly; or

■ find new or additional helpful information in another question.

Pace yourself

Some people will finish the exam early and some do not have time to finish all the questions. Watch the time carefully (your time remaining will be displayed on your computer screen) and pace yourself through the exam.

Do not waste time by dwelling on a question if you simply do not know the answer. Make the best guess you can, mark the question for *Record for Review*, and return to the question if time allows. Make sure that you have time to read all the questions so that you can record the answers you do know.

THE EXAM

How do I enroll in the exam?

To obtain an admission ticket to an NASD exam, your firm must file an application form and processing fees with the NASD. To take the exam, you should make an appointment with a Prometric Testing Center as far in advance as possible of the date on which you would like to take the exam.

You may schedule your appointment at Prometric, 24 hours a day, 7 days a week, on the Prometric secure Website at **www.prometric.com**. You may also use **www.prometric.com** to reschedule or cancel your exam, locate a test center, and get a printed confirmation of your appointment. To speak with a Prometric representative by phone, please contact the Prometric Contact Center at 1-800-578-6273.

What should I take to the exam?

Take one form of personal identification with your signature and photograph as issued by a government agency. You cannot take reference materials or anything else into the testing area. Calculators are available upon request. Scratch paper and pencils will be provided by the testing center, although you cannot take them with you when you leave.

Additional trial questions

During your exam, you may see extra trial questions. These are potential exam-bank questions being tested during the course of the exam. These questions are not included in your final score and you will be given extra time to answer them.

Exam results and reports

At the end of the exam, your score will be displayed, indicating whether you passed. The next business day after your exam, your results will be mailed to your firm and to the self-regulatory organization and state securities commission specified on your application.

Periodically, new editions of this License Exam Manual are published to reflect improvements, regulatory changes, and modifications to testable content. Kaplan Financial publishes *TestAlerts!* to update existing editions with changes that have been incorporated in new editions. The *TestAlerts!* are available at no charge at **www.kaplanfinancial.com**. Click on *View Securities TestAlerts!* to access them.

We encourage you to check this Website before taking your exam to be sure you have the latest testable information.

After you review the *TestAlert!*, you may wish to upgrade to the next edition, but keep in mind that any new material and major changes will be found in the *TestAlert!*.

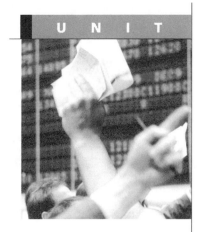

1

Securities Markets, Investment Securities, and Economic Factors

This Unit encompasses a wide discussion of different types of securities, the markets in which they trade, and basic economics. Though fewer questions are asked in this Unit than in other Units, the securities industry fundamentals discussed here will be important for success in future sections. Be sure to acquire a sound understanding of the differences between equity and debt securities and the marketplaces in which they trade.

The Series 6 exam will include eight questions on the topics covered in this Unit. ■

When you have completed this Unit, you should be able to:

- **describe** the basic features of equity and debt;

- **name** five types of preferred stock and their unique features;

- **discuss** the inverse relationship between bond prices and yields;

- **compare** and contrast the different types of marketable government securities;

- **describe** the two basics categories of municipal bonds;

- **list** and describe common money market instruments;

- **discuss** fundamental option positions;

- **identify** the four phases and key characteristics of the business cycle;

- **list** the four major interest rates in the United States; and

- **explain** currency exchange rates and their effects on business.

WHAT IS A SECURITY?

A **security** is an investment instrument that represents either ownership (equity) interest in a company or a creditor relationship (through a debt obligation) with a company. Equity is most commonly represented by the various forms of stock. Debt is most commonly represented by bonds and notes. Instruments that give enhanced access to securities, such as rights, warrants, and options, are also considered securities.

FUNCTION AND REGULATION OF SECURITIES

Business enterprises raise money for their operations by selling, or issuing, stocks or bonds to the public in what is called a **primary offering**. Firms that specialize in providing advice on raising capital to such companies and in handling the offering of their securities to the public are known as **investment bankers**. An investment banker can either (1) function as a **broker** in the sales and collect a **commission** or (2) function as a **principal** in the sales, actually purchasing the securities from the issuer and collecting a **markup** upon sale to the public.

Once issued in a primary offering, securities typically trade between investors in what are known as **secondary transactions**. These trades take place on stock exchanges, in the over-the-counter (OTC) market, or, in the case of some securities, both. Exchange-listed securities, like those listed on the New York Stock Exchange (NYSE), are priced by auction on the trading floor. Brokerage houses purchase the securities for their customers through specialists at the lowest available **asked** or **offering price** (established by open outcry), or they sell securities for their customers, through specialists, at the highest available **bid price**.

Because there is no centralized trading location, over-the-counter securities, on the other hand, are priced not by open outcry at an auction, but by negotiation. Within this market, regulated by the **National Association of Securities Dealers (NASD)**, broker/dealers called **market makers** maintain inventories of OTC securities and sell to other broker/dealers out of their inventory for their asked or offering price, or they buy from other broker/dealers for their inventory at their bid price. Thus, market makers serve as a source for securities that customers wish to buy through their broker/dealers and as a repository for securities that customers wish to sell through their broker/dealers. It is important to remember that market makers buy and customers sell at the bid price and that market makers sell and customers buy at the asked price. Competition among market makers ensures the customer of the lowest asked price available if he is buying or the highest bid price available if he is selling.

The NASD is a self-regulatory organization (SRO), reporting to the Securities and Exchange Commission, to which broker/dealers in the OTC market belong. The following terms have specific meanings to the NASD.

IMPORTANT DEFINITIONS IN THE SECURITIES INDUSTRY

Associated Person (AP) of a Member

An associated person is any employee, manager, director, officer, or partner of a member broker/dealer or another entity (issuer, bank, etc.) or any person controlling, controlled by, or in common control with that member.

Broker

(1) A broker includes: an individual or a firm that charges a fee or commission for executing buy and sell orders submitted by another individual or firm; (2) the role of a brokerage firm when it acts as an agent for a customer and charges the customer a commission for its services; and (3) any person engaged in the business of effecting transactions in securities for the accounts of others that is not a bank.

Customer

A customer is any individual, person, partnership, corporation, or legal entity that is not a broker, dealer, or municipal securities dealer—that is, the public.

Dealer

(1) A dealer includes: the role of a brokerage firm when it acts as a principal in a particular trade. A firm acts as a dealer when it buys or sells a security for its own account and at its own risk, then charges the customer a markup or markdown; and (2) any person engaged in the business of buying and selling securities for their own account, either directly or through a broker, that is not a bank.

Member

A member of the NASD is any individual, partnership, corporation, or legal entity admitted to membership in the NASD.

Security

Under the act of 1934, any note, stock, bond, investment contract, variable annuity, profit-sharing or partnership agreement, certificate of deposit, option on a security, or other instrument of investment is commonly known as a security.

Equity and Debt

Equity in a company is perhaps the most visible and widely accessible means by which wealth is created. Individual investors become owners of a publicly traded company by buying stock in that company (**common stock**). In so doing, they can participate in the company's growth over time.

SECURITIES AND BUSINESS

Stock represents equity or ownership in a company, and bonds are a loan to a company. A company discloses the composition of its total capitalization—debt and equity—by publishing a balance sheet. The **balance sheet** summarizes the company's:

- **assets**—what the company owns: cash in the bank, accounts receivable (money it is owed), investments, property, inventory, etc.;

- **liabilities**—what the company owes: accounts payable (current bills it must pay), short-term and long-term debt and other obligations; and

- Net worth, or shareholders' **equity**—the excess of the value of assets over the value of liabilities.

A company's **net worth** is computed by subtracting all liabilities from the value of total assets. This computation is summarized by the basic balance sheet equation and may be represented two different ways:

$$\text{Assets} - \text{liabilities} = \text{net worth,}$$
$$\text{or}$$
$$\text{Assets} = \text{liabilities} + \text{net worth.}$$

A company's **total capitalization** is its net worth plus its long-term debt. Companies can be categorized according to this value as large cap, mid cap, or small cap. Here is a typical categorization:

Category	Total Capitalization
Large cap	Over $5 billion
Mid cap	$500 million to $5 billion
Small cap	Less than $500 million

QUICK QUIZ 1.1

Match the following terms with the appropriate description below.

A. Dealer
B. Associated person
C. Member
D. Broker

_C_   1. The NASD permits only firms to become one of these.

_D_   2. Compensated by a commission in securities transactions.

_A_   3. Compensated by a markup/markdown in securities transactions.

_B_   4. Someone controlling or controlled by a member firm.

Quick Quiz answers can be found at the end of the Unit.

Terms and Concepts Checklist

✓

- ☐ Security
- ☐ Equity
- ☐ Debt
- ☐ Small cap, mid cap, large cap
- ☐ Assets
- ☐ Liabilities
- ☐ Net worth

✓

- ☐ Broker
- ☐ Dealer
- ☐ Associated person
- ☐ Customer
- ☐ Primary offering
- ☐ Secondary transaction

EQUITY SECURITIES

This section discusses the following equity securities:

- Common stock

- Preferred stock

- Related equity securities

Corporations may issue two types of stock: common stock and preferred stock. When speaking of stock, people generally refer to common stock.

COMMON STOCK

A company issues **common stock** as its primary means of raising business capital. Investors who buy the stock buy a share of ownership in the company's net worth. Whatever a business owns (its assets) less its creditors' claims (its liabilities) belongs to the business owners (its stockholders).

TAKE NOTE   An individual's stock ownership represents his proportionate interest in a company. If a company issues 100 shares of stock, each share represents an identical $\frac{1}{100}$ (or 1%) ownership position in the company. A person who owns 10 shares of stock owns 10% of the company; a stockholder with 50 shares of stock owns 50% of the company.

Each share of common stock entitles its owner to a portion of the company's profits and dividends and an equal vote on directors and other important matters. Most corporations are organized in such a way that their common stockholders regularly vote for and elect candidates to a board of directors to oversee the company's business. By electing a board of directors, stockholders have some say in the company's management but are not involved with the day-to-day details of its operations.

Common stock can be classified in four ways: authorized, issued, treasury, and outstanding.

Authorized Stock

As part of its original charter, a corporation receives authorization from the state to issue, or sell, a specific number of shares of stock. Often, a company sells only a portion of the authorized shares, raising enough capital for its foreseeable needs. The company may sell the remaining **authorized shares** in the future or use them for other purposes. Should the company decide to sell more shares than are authorized, it must amend its charter through a stockholder vote that approves more shares.

Issued Stock

Once authorized, **issued stock** can be distributed to investors. As already stated, when a corporation issues or sells fewer shares than the total number authorized, it normally reserves the unissued shares for future needs, including:

- raising new capital for expansion;

- paying stock dividends;

- providing stock purchase plans for employees or stock options for corporate officers;

- exchanging common stock for outstanding convertible bonds or preferred stock; or

- satisfying the exercise of outstanding stock purchase warrants.

Authorized but unissued stock does not carry the rights and privileges of issued shares (such as voting rights and the right to receive dividends) and is not considered in determining a company's total capitalization.

Treasury Stock

Treasury stock is stock a corporation has issued and subsequently repurchased from the public. The corporation can hold this stock indefinitely or can reissue or retire it. A corporation could reissue its treasury stock to fund employee bonus plans, distribute it to stockholders as a stock dividend or, under certain circumstances, redistribute it to the public in an additional offering. Treasury stock does not carry the rights of outstanding common shares, such as voting rights and the right to receive dividends.

TEST TOPIC ALERT

Treasury stock:

■ was outstanding stock before it was repurchased by the issuer;

■ has no voting rights;

■ does not receive dividends; and

■ can be reissued or retired.

A corporation buys back its stock for a number of reasons, such as to:

■ increase earnings per share;

■ have an inventory of stock available to distribute as stock options, fund an employee pension plan, etc.; or

■ use for future acquisitions.

Outstanding Stock

Outstanding stock includes any shares that a company has issued but has not repurchased—that is, investor-owned stock.

TEST TOPIC ALERT

Expect to see a question on outstanding stock similar to the following:
ABC company has authorized 1 million shares of common stock. It issued 800,000 shares one year ago. It then purchased 200,000 shares for its treasury. How many shares of ABC stock are outstanding?

The solution requires you to know a basic formula:

Issued stock – Treasury stock = Outstanding stock; thus,

800,000 – 200,000 = 600,000.
ABC company has 600,000 shares of common stock outstanding.

This question illustrates another point about NASD exams. The question gives the number of shares of authorized stock, but this information is unnecessary. Many questions give more information than you need. The Series 6 exam requires you to know concepts well enough that you can determine both what is and what is not essential to solving a problem.

Common Stock Values

Market Value

The most familiar measure of a stock's value is its **market price**, or **current market value (CMV)**. It is the price investors must pay to buy the stock. Market value is influenced by a company's business prospects and the consequent effect on supply (the number of shares available to investors) and demand (the number of shares investors want to buy).

Although a stock's market price is the most meaningful measure of its value, other measures include par value and book value.

Par Value

For investors, a common stock's **par value** is meaningless. It is an arbitrary value the company gives the stock in its articles of incorporation, and it has no effect on the stock's market price. If a stock has been assigned a par value for accounting purposes, such as $1 or $.01, it is usually printed on the face of the stock certificate.

When the corporation sells stock, the money received exceeding par value is recorded on the corporate balance sheet as **capital in excess of par**, also known as **paid-in surplus**, **capital surplus**, or **paid-in capital**.

Book Value

$$= \frac{\text{Tot Assets} - \text{Tot. Liab}}{\# \text{ SO}}$$

$$= \frac{TL}{\# \text{SO}}$$

A stock's **book value** per share is a measure of how much a common stock-holder could expect to receive for each share if the corporation were liquidated. Most commonly used by fundamental analysts, the book value per share is the difference between the historical value of a corporation's tangible assets and liabilities, divided by the number of shares outstanding. The book value per share can (and usually does) differ substantially from a stock's market value.

TEST TOPIC ALERT

The three methods of common stock valuation do not result in the same amount.

- Par value = an arbitrary accounting value

- Book value = current hypothetical liquidation value of a share

- Market value = supply and demand price (most familiar to investors)

QUICK QUIZ 1.2

Match the following items to the appropriate description below:
   A.   Outstanding stock
   B.   Authorized stock
   C.   Book value
   D.   Par value

_B_   1.   Number of shares that a corporation is permitted to issue

_D_   2.   Dollar amount assigned to a security by its issuer

_C_   3.   Hypothetical net worth of each share of common stock

_A_   4.   Equity securities in the hands of the public

The Rights of Stock Ownership

Because common stockholders are owners of a company, they have certain rights that protect their ownership interests.

Voting Rights

Common stockholders exercise control of a corporation by electing a board of directors and by voting at annual meetings on important corporate policy matters, such as:

■ issuance of convertible securities or additional common stock; or

■ substantial changes in the corporation's business, such as mergers or acquisitions; and

■ election of board of directors.

Shareholders do not vote on anything that has to do with dividends, such as when they are declared and how much they will be. Shareholders do vote on stock splits, membership on the Board of Directors, and issuance of additional securities like common stock and convertible bonds.

Calculating the Number of Votes

A stockholder can cast one vote for each share of stock owned for each item on the ballot. Depending on the company's bylaws and applicable state laws, a stockholder may have a **statutory** or **cumulative vote**.

Statutory Voting. Statutory voting allows a stockholder to cast one vote per share owned for each item on a ballot, such as seats on the board of directors. A board candidate needs a simple majority to be elected.

Cumulative Voting. Cumulative voting allows stockholders to allocate their votes in any manner they choose. Cumulative voting may be advantageous for small shareholders by giving them a greater opportunity to offset the votes of large shareholders by combining all their shares on a single seat.

 EXAMPLE   An investor owns 100 shares of stock in the ABC Company. An election of the board of directors is coming up, and several candidates are running to fill three seats. The investor thus has a total of 300 votes—100 for each seat. Under **statutory voting**, he would allocate 100 votes to each of the three candidates he prefers. Under **cumulative voting**, he could, if he wished, allocate all 300 of his votes to a single candidate for just one of the seats.

Proxies. Most stockholders find it difficult to attend the annual stockholders' meeting and so vote on company matters by means of a **proxy**, a form of absentee ballot. Once returned to the company, a proxy is cancelled if the stockholder attends the meeting, authorizes a subsequent proxy, or dies.

Preemptive Rights. When a corporation raises capital through the sale of additional common stock, it may be required by law or its corporate charter to offer the securities to its common stockholders before the general public; this is known as an **antidilution provision**. Stockholders then have a **preemptive right** to buy enough newly issued shares to maintain their proportionate ownership in the corporation.

TAKE NOTE

Preemptive rights give investors the right to maintain a proportionate interest in a company's stock.

EXAMPLE

ABC, Inc., has 1 million shares of common stock outstanding. Shareholder X owns 100,000 shares of ABC common stock, or 10%. If ABC issues an additional 500,000 shares, Shareholder X will have the opportunity to buy 50,000 of those shares.

Limited Liability. Stockholders cannot lose more than the amount they have paid for a corporation's stock. **Limited liability** protects stockholders from having to pay a corporation's debts in bankruptcy.

TEST TOPIC ALERT

Limited liability means that a shareholder of common stock cannot lose more than was invested—a shareholder can lose the original value of his stock only.

Inspection of Corporate Books. Stockholders have the right to receive annual financial statements and obtain lists of stockholders. Inspection rights do not include the right to examine detailed financial records or the minutes of directors' meetings.

Residual Claims to Assets. If a corporation is liquidated, the common stockholder, as owner, has a residual right to claim corporate assets after all debts and other security holders have been satisfied. The common stockholder is at the bottom of the liquidation priority list. This makes common stock the most junior security.

Bullish and Bearish Stock Positions

Generally, and throughout this course, we assume an investor buys or owns shares of stock with the intent of selling them at a higher price at some point in the future—buy low now, sell high later. An investor who buys shares is considered **long** the stock, and is bullish—that is, expects the stock to increase in price.

An investor may also sell shares he has borrowed, with the intent of buying them back at a lower price in the future for return to the owner (sell high now, buy back low later). Such a transaction, known as a **short sale**, involves borrowing shares to sell that the investor must eventually replace. An investor who sells borrowed shares is **short** the stock until he buys and returns the shares to the lender, and is bearish—that is, expects the stock to go down in price.

Benefits of Owning Common Stock

Investors generally expect to receive capital growth, income, or both from common stock investments.

Growth

An increase in the market price of shares is called **capital appreciation**. Historically, owning common stock, with its associated capital appreciation, has provided investors with high real returns compared to other types of investments.

TAKE NOTE   Buying low and selling high is one of the main objectives of stock investors. When this is accomplished, investors have capital gains. If the investor sells the stock at the higher price, the investor has a realized gain and must pay taxes on the gain. If the investor does not sell the stock, the investor has an unrealized gain, which is not taxed. Capital gains are taxable only when they are realized.

Income

Many corporations pay regular quarterly cash dividends to stockholders based upon the company's earnings. A company's dividends may increase over time as profitability increases. Dividends, which can be a significant source of income for investors, are the other main reason many people invest in stocks.

TAKE NOTE   A company that earns $1 per share may elect to pay a portion of those earnings to shareholders in dividends. As earnings increase over time, the company may increase its dividend as well. Investors who receive dividends must generally pay 15% dividend tax. (Until recently, investors paid ordinary income taxes on dividend income.) The IRS makes no exceptions for individuals, but corporations receive a 70% exclusion on dividend income.

EXAMPLE   Ten years ago, an investor bought 100 shares of ABC Corp. for $20 per share, for a total investment of $2,000. At the time, the company's business was profitable, earning $3 per share of which it paid $1 per share in dividends to shareholders and reinvested the rest in growing the business. Ten years later, after moderate but consistent growth, the company earns $12 per share and pays $4 in dividends per share. The stock price has consistently increased with the earnings growth and now sells for $80 per share ($8,000 total value for our investor's 100 shares). The investor has had to pay income taxes each of the past 10 years on the dividend income he received but will only have to pay capital gain taxes if he sells the stock. If he sold the stock now, his taxable capital gain would be $60 per share ($80 current value – $20 original cost = $60 capital gain).

Risks of Owning Stock

Regardless of their expectations, investors have no assurances that they will receive the returns they expect from their investments.

Market Risk

The chance that a stock will decline in price at a time that the investor needs the money is a risk of owning common stock. A stock's price fluctuates daily as perceptions of the company's business prospects change and affect the actions of buyers and sellers. An investor has no assurance that he will be able to recoup the investment in a stock at any point in time.

A long investor's losses are limited to his total investment in a stock. A short seller's losses are theoretically unlimited because there is no limit to how high a stock's price may climb.

Decreased or No Income

Another risk of stock ownership is the possibility of dividend income decreasing or ceasing entirely if the company has business reverses.

Low Priority at Dissolution

If a company declares bankruptcy, holders of its bonds and preferred stock have priority over common stockholders. A company's debt and preferred shares are senior securities. Common stockholders have only residual rights to corporate assets upon dissolution.

TAKE NOTE   Common shareholders are last in line when a corporation's assets are liquidated, so common stock is often called the most junior security.

QUICK QUIZ 1.3

1. Which of the following represent ownership (equity) in a company?

   I.   Corporate bonds
   II. Common stock
   III. Preferred stock
   IV. Mortgage bonds

   A. I and II
   B. I and III
   C. II and III
   D. III and IV

2. Which of the following statements describe Treasury stock?

    I.   It has voting rights and is entitled to a dividend when declared.

    II.   It has no voting rights and no dividend entitlement.

    III. It has been issued and repurchased by the company.

    IV.   It is authorized but unissued stock.

    A.   I and III

    B.   I and IV

    C.   II and III

    D.   II and IV

3. Stockholders' preemptive rights include the right to

    A.   serve as an officer on the board of directors

    B.   maintain proportionate ownership interest in the corporation

    C.   purchase Treasury stock

    D.   examine the corporation's books

4. At the annual meeting of ABC Corporation, 5 directors are to be elected. Under the cumulative voting system, an investor with 100 shares of ABC would have a total of

    A.   100 votes to be cast for each of 5 directors

    B.   500 votes to be cast in any way the investor chooses for 5 directors

    C.   500 votes to be cast for each of 5 directors

    D.   100 votes to be cast for only 1 director

5. Cumulative voting rights

    A.   benefit the large investor

    B.   aid the corporation's best customers

    C.   give preferred stockholders an advantage over common stockholders

    D.   benefit the small investor

6. What is the basic formula of the balance sheet?

    A.   Assets = liabilities − net worth

    B.   Assets + liabilities = net worth

    C.   Assets = net worth

    D.   Assets = liabilities + net worth

7. All of the following are potential benefits of stock ownership EXCEPT

    A.   dividends

    B.   growth

    C.   guaranteed income

    D.   voting rights

PREFERRED STOCK

Preferred stock is an equity security because it represents ownership in the corporation. However, it does not normally offer the appreciation potential associated with common stock.

Like a bond, preferred stock is usually issued as a fixed-income security with a fixed dividend. Its price tends to fluctuate with changes in interest rates rather than with the issuing company's business prospects unless, of course, dramatic changes occur in the company's credit quality or financial risk. Unlike common stock, most preferred stock is nonvoting and maintains no preemptive rights.

Although preferred stock does not typically have the same growth potential as common stock, preferred stockholders generally have two advantages over common stockholders.

- When the board of directors declares dividends, owners of preferred stock receive their dividends before common stockholders can be paid.

- If a corporation goes bankrupt, preferred stockholders have a priority claim over common stockholders on the assets remaining after creditors have been paid.

Because of these features, preferred stock appeals to investors seeking income and safety.

TAKE NOTE   Preferred stock has preference over common stock in payment of dividends and in claim to assets in the event the issuing corporation goes bankrupt.

Fixed Rate of Return. A preferred stock's **fixed dividend** is a key attraction for income-oriented investors. Normally, a preferred stock is identified by its annual dividend payment stated as a percentage of its par value, which is usually $100. (A preferred stock's par value is meaningful, unlike that of common stock.) A preferred stock with a par value of $100 that pays $6 in annual dividends is known as a 6% preferred. The dividend of preferred stock with par value other than $100 is stated in a dollar amount, such as a $6 no-par preferred.

The stated rate of dividend payment causes the price of preferred stock to act like the price of a bond: prices and interest rates have an inverse relationship.

EXAMPLE   Consider a 6% preferred. If interest rates are at 8% and you want to sell your preferred, you will have to sell at a discounted price. Why would a buyer pay full value for an investment that is not paying a competitive market rate? But if interest rates fall to 5%, the 6% preferred will trade at a premium. Because it is offering a stream of income above the current market rate, it will command a higher price.

TAKE NOTE   When interest rates rise, the preferred price falls. Conversely, when interest rates fall, the preferred stock's price rises. This exact relationship occurs in bonds and is known as the **inverse relationship** between price and interest rates.

Adjustable-Rate Preferred. Some preferred stocks are issued with adjustable, or variable, dividend rates. Such dividends are usually tied to the rates of other interest rate benchmarks, such as Treasury bill and money market rates, and can be adjusted as often as semiannually.

Limited Ownership Privileges. Except for rare instances, preferred stock does not have voting or preemptive rights.

TEST TOPIC ALERT

Preferred stock represents ownership in a company like common stock, but its price is sensitive to interest rates—just like the price of a bond.

No Maturity Date or Set Maturity Value. Although it is a fixed-income investment, preferred stock, unlike bonds, has no preset date at which it matures and no scheduled redemption date or maturity value.

Categories of Preferred Stock

Separate categories of preferred stock may differ in the dividend rate, profit participation privileges, or other ways. All, however, maintain a degree of preference over common stock. One or several of the features described below may characterize issues of preferred stock.

Straight (Noncumulative)

Straight preferred has no special features beyond the stated dividend payment. Missed dividends are not paid to the holder. The year's stated dividend must be paid on straight preferred if any dividend is to be paid to common shareholders.

TAKE NOTE

Preferred stock with no special features is known as **straight preferred**.

Cumulative Preferred

Buyers of preferred stock expect fixed dividend payments. The directors of a company in financial difficulty can reduce or suspend dividend payments to both common and preferred stockholders. With cumulative preferred, dividends in arrears are made up.

TAKE NOTE

Any special feature attached to preferred, such as a cumulative feature, has a price. The cost for such a benefit is less dividend income. Cumulative preferred typically has a lower stated dividend than straight preferred (less risk equals less reward).

All dividends due to cumulative preferred shareholders accumulate on the company's books until the corporation can pay them. When the company can resume full payment of dividends, cumulative preferred stockholders receive their current dividends plus the total accumulated dividends—dividends in arrears—before any dividends may be distributed to common or other straight preferred stockholders. Therefore, cumulative preferred stock is safer than straight preferred stock.

TEST TOPIC ALERT	The exam is likely to include a question on cumulative preferred stock.

EXAMPLE	RST Corp. has both common stock and cumulative preferred stock outstanding. Its preferred stock has a stated dividend rate of 5% (par value $100). Because of financial difficulties, no dividend was paid on the preferred stock last year or the year before. If RST wishes to declare a common stock dividend this year, RST is required to first pay how much in dividends to the cumulative preferred shareholders?
	RST must pay missed dividends to cumulative preferred (as well as the current dividend) before dividends are paid on common stock. RST must pay $5 for the year before last, $5 for last year, and $5 for this year, for a total of $15.
	For noncumulative preferred stock outstanding, the answer would have been $5. Only the current year dividend would need payment before common because noncumulative preferred is not entitled to dividends in arrears.

Convertible Preferred

A preferred stock is **convertible** if the owner can exchange each preferred share for shares of common stock. The price at which the investor can convert is a preset amount and is noted on the stock certificate. Because the value of a convertible preferred stock is linked to the value of the issuer's common stock, the convertible preferred's price fluctuates in line with the common.

Convertible preferred is often issued with a lower stated dividend rate than nonconvertible preferred because the investor may have the opportunity to convert to common shares and enjoy capital gains. In addition, the conversion of preferred stock into shares of common increases the total number of common shares outstanding, which decreases earnings per common share and may decrease the common stock's market value. When the underlying common stock has the same value as the convertible preferred, it is said to be at its parity price.

EXAMPLE	XYZ Company's convertible preferred stock, with a par value of $100 and a conversion price of $20, can be exchanged for five shares of XYZ common stock ($100 ÷ $20 = 5). This is true, no matter what the current market value of either the preferred or the common stock. Thus, if an investor bought the preferred for $100 per share and the common stock rises in price eventually to more than $20 per share, the preferred stockholder could make a capital gain from converting.

Participating Preferred

In addition to fixed dividends, **participating preferred stock** offers owners a share of corporate profits that remain after all dividends and interest due other securities are paid. The percentage to which participating preferred stock participates is noted on the stock certificate.

If a preferred stock is described as "XYZ 6% preferred participating to 9%," the company could pay its holders up to 3% in additional dividends in profitable years, if the board so declares.

Callable Preferred

Corporations often issue **callable**, or **redeemable**, **preferred**, which a company can buy back from investors at a stated price after a specified date. The right to call the stock allows the company to replace a relatively high fixed dividend obligation with a lower one.

When a corporation calls a preferred stock, dividend payments and conversion rights cease on the call date. In return for the call privilege, the corporation usually pays a premium exceeding the stock's par value at the call, such as $103 for a $100 par value stock.

Callable preferred stock is unique because of the risk that the issuer may buy it back and end dividend payments. Because of this risk, callable preferred has a higher stated rate of dividend payment than straight, noncallable preferred.

Issuers are likely to call securities when interest rates are falling. Like anyone, an issuer would prefer to pay a lower rate for money. Issuers call securities with high rates and replace them with securities that have lower fixed rate obligations.

Below are several test points on preferred stock:

1. Which of the following types of preferred stock typically has the highest stated rate of dividend (all other factors being equal)?

    A. Participating
    B. Straight
    C. Cumulative
    D. Callable

    Answer: D. When the stock is called, dividend payments are no longer made. To compensate for that possibility, the issuer must pay a higher dividend.

2. Of straight and cumulative preferred, which would you expect to have the higher stated rate?

    A. Straight
    B. Cumulative

    Answer: A. Cumulative preferred is safer, and there is always a risk-reward trade-off. Because straight preferred has no special features, it will pay a higher stated rate of dividend.

1. Which of the following types of preferred stock is most influenced by the price of an issuer's common stock?

    A. Participating
    B. Straight
    C. Convertible
    D. Callable

Dividends

Dividends, both common and preferred, are distributions from a company's profits to its stockholders. Investors who buy stock are entitled to dividends only when the company's board of directors votes to make such distributions. Stockholders are automatically sent any dividends to which their shares entitle them.

TAKE NOTE

Dividends are never guaranteed to shareholders. This distribution of corporate profits is made only when declared by the BOD.

Cash Dividends. Cash dividends are normally distributed by check if an investor holds the stock certificate or are automatically deposited to a brokerage account if the shares are held in street name—that is, held in a brokerage account in the firm's name to facilitate payments and delivery. Dividends are usually paid quarterly and taxed as dividend income in the year they are received.

Stock Dividends. If a company uses its cash for business purposes rather than to pay cash dividends, its board of directors may declare a **stock dividend**. This is typical of many growth companies that invest their cash resources in research and development. Under these circumstances, the company issues shares of its common stock as a dividend to its current stockholders. A stock's market price per share declines after a stock dividend, but the company's total market value remains the same.

Stock Splits. A company will sometimes change the number of outstanding shares by means of a stock split. The total value of the outstanding stock must be the same before and after the split. Thus if the XYZ Corporation did a 2-for-1 stock split, an investor who owned 100 XYZ shares worth $20 per share before the split would own 200 shares worth $10 per share after the split. If the company did a 1-for-2 reverse split, an investor with 100 shares worth $20 per share before the split would own 50 shares worth $40 per share after the split. Note that although the individual share value changes as a result of a split, the total value of the stock remains the same. Since they change the trading characteristics of a stock, shareholder approval must be obtained for stock splits.

TAKE NOTE

Stock dividend distributions are not taxed when received. There are no tax consequences incurred until the investor chooses to liquidate the shares and realize his gains or losses.

Calculating Dividend Yield/Current Yield

The **dividend yield** is the annual dividend (four times the quarterly dividend) divided by the current price of the stock. A stock's dividend yield may also be referred to as its **current yield**.

TEST TOPIC ALERT

You might be asked to calculate dividend yield on the exam.

$$\frac{\text{Annual dividend}}{\text{Current market value of the stock}}$$

EXAMPLE

RST stock has a current market value of $50. Total dividends paid during the year were $5. What is the dividend yield? The solution is found by dividing $5 by $50. The yield is 10%.

Be alert for a slightly tricky approach to this question. The question might state that RST has a current market value of $50. The most recent quarterly dividend paid was $1.25. What is the dividend yield?

The solution is found by annualizing the dividend (multiplying by 4) first. $1.25 × 4 = $5. $5 ÷ $50 = a 10% dividend yield—remember to use *annual* dividends in calculating yield.

TEST TOPIC ALERT

You may see a question that asks about the priority of dividend payments made by a corporation. The order of payment is as follows:

1. Dividends in arrears paid to cumulative shares

2. Stated dividends paid to all preferred shares

3. Common dividend and participating excess dividend paid

Return on Investment

An investment's **total return** is a combination of the dividend income and price appreciation or decline over a given period of time.

TEST TOPIC ALERT   Know how to calculate total return, or yield, for the exam.

Total Return on Investment

Total return is comprised of the yield and growth from an investment.

EXAMPLE   A common stock purchased for $20 with an annual dividend of $1 is sold after one year for $24. The total return on the investment is $5, $1 in dividends plus $4 in capital appreciation. The total return, then, is 25% ($5 ÷ $20 = 25%).

Transferability of Ownership

The ease with which stocks and other securities can be bought and sold contributes to the smooth operation of the securities markets. When an investor buys or sells a security, the exchange of money and ownership requires little or no additional action on his part.

The Stock Certificate

A stock certificate is evidence of ownership for the shares of a corporation a person owns. The vast majority of stock transactions are for **round lot** numbers of shares (share amounts evenly divisible by 100). **Odd lot** transactions are share amounts of fewer than 100 shares, such as 4 or 99. Individual stock certificates may be issued for any number of shares.

EXAMPLE   An investor who buys 100 shares of ABC, Inc., would receive one certificate for 100 shares.

Stock certificates identify the company's name, number of shares, and investor's name, among other things. Each certificate is printed with the security's CUSIP number (an identification or tracking number).

Negotiability

Shares of stock are negotiable; that is, a stockholder can give, transfer, assign, or sell shares he owns with few or no restrictions.

Match the following items to the appropriate description below.

A. 100
B. Preemptive right
C. Current yield
D. Quarterly

_D_   1. Typical frequency of dividend payment on common stock

_A_   2. Number of shares in a standard trading unit of stock

_B_   3. Stockholders may maintain proportionate ownership by purchasing newly issued shares before they are offered to the public

_C_   4. Annualized dividend divided by current market price

AMERICAN DEPOSITARY RECEIPTS

American depositary receipts (ADRs), also known as American depositary shares (ADSs), facilitate the trading of foreign stocks in US markets. An ADR is a negotiable security that represents a receipt for shares of stock in a non-US corporation, usually from one to 10 shares. ADRs are bought and sold in the US securities markets like stock.

TAKE NOTE

ADRs allow domestic investors to buy foreign securities more easily. Many investors include foreign issues in their portfolios for diversification.

Rights of ADR Owners

Actual share certificates of the foreign company are held by a US depository bank. The investor purchases the ADR with US dollars, receives dividends through the bank in US dollars, and may sell the ADR on the open market for US dollars, but the bank actually votes on the shares and receives preemptive rights. If rights are issued, the bank would normally sell them and distribute the proceeds to the ADR holders.

It is important to remember that the stock represented by the ADR is originally traded in a foreign currency, and that dividends are initially paid by the foreign company in that currency; the dividends are simply exchanged for dollars before being passed on to the ADR holder. Thus, ADR holders face not only the normal business risks characteristic of stock ownership, but currency risks as well, should the foreign currency decline in value.

The ADR holder also has the right to exchange his ADRs for the actual foreign share certificates.

TEST TOPIC ALERT

The following question identifies nearly all of the testable points on ADRs:

Which of the following statements about ADRs is TRUE?

A. Owners of ADRs have voting rights.
B. ADRs allow foreign investors to buy domestic issues of stock.
C. Owners of ADRs receive dividends in foreign currency.
D. ADR owners are subject to currency risk.

Answer: D. Owners of ADRs face currency risk. The exchange rate between the foreign currency of the ADR issuer and the US dollar causes the dividend payment to rise and fall in dollar value. Owners of ADRs have no preemptive rights or voting rights. ADRs allow domestic investors to purchase foreign issues, not the reverse. ADR owners receive dividends in dollars.

QUICK QUIZ 1.6

1. ADRs are used to facilitate the

   A. foreign trading of domestic securities
   B. foreign trading of US government securities
   C. domestic trading of US government securities
   D. domestic trading of foreign securities

2. The owner of an ADR is likely to receive which of the following?

   A. Dividends
   B. Capital gains or losses
   C. Both dividends and capital gains or losses
   D. Neither dividends nor capital gains or losses

TRACKING EQUITY SECURITIES

Common and preferred stock prices are listed in the financial sections of daily newspapers and in other financial publications. A stock's market price is quoted in whole dollars, also known as **points**, plus fractions of a dollar expressed in cents.

TAKE NOTE

The exam will probably ask you to determine the cost of a round lot of stock in whole dollars from its quoted price.

EXAMPLE

If ABC stock is quoted at 83.10, how much does the investor pay for 100 shares? For the price of a round lot, multiply by 100 (move the decimal point two places to the right). The investor will pay $8,310 for a round lot of ABC stock.

TAKE NOTE

Calculators are available at the test center, but do not expect a lot of math. Typically, the entire exam has fewer than five calculations.

NYSE Composite Transactions

New York Stock Exchange Composite Prices

Tuesday, September 14, 2004

52 Weeks High	Low	Stock	Div	Yld %	PE Ratio	Sales 100s	High	Low	Last	Chg
80	40	ABCorp	.75	1	12	3329	78	71	73	- 1.50
8.38	6.50	ACM IncFd	1.01	12.4	...	178	8.25	8.13	8.13	- .13
42.63	26.88	ALFA	2.40	5.6	12	x 1265	42.63	41.25	42.63	+1.25
35	24.63	Anchor	1.48	4.9	36	1960	30	29.75	30	+ .25
27.25	25	ANR pf	2.67	10.3	...	6	26	26	26	...
6	1.88	ATT Cap wt	...	...	...	20	5.88	5.75	5.75	- .25
22.75	14	AVEMCO	.40	1.9	17	6	21.50	21.38	21.50	...
84.25	40	BrlNth	2.20	3.7	13	2701	59.38	58.25	58.75	+ .50
4.75	.50	Brooke rt	...	...	...	26	4.63	4.63	4.63	...
7	2.50	CV REIT	.25	4.0	...	10	6.38	6.25	6.25	...
3.13	2.25	CalifREIT	.40	13.9	...	3	2.88	2.88	2.88	...
39.38	17.88	Circus wi	...	...	...	14	39.25	38.88	39.25	+ .63
82.50	39.63	Dsny	.32	.6	17	6211	53.75	52	53.25	+1.25
38.38	19.50	Febar	.24	.9	13	z 1454	28	26.88	27.38	+ .25
8.75	3.63	Navistr	...	...	...	6484	4.50	4.13	4.25	...

EXPLANATORY NOTES

High-Low: High-low numbers are the highest and lowest prices for the stock in the last 52 weeks, not including yesterday's trading.
Stock: Stocks are listed alphabetically, by the company's full name (not by its abbreviation). Company names that are made up of initials appear at the beginning of the letter's list.
Div: Current annual dividend rate paid on stock, based on the latest quarterly or semiannual declaration, unless otherwise footnoted.
PE Ratio: Closing price of the stock divided by the company's earnings per share for the latest 12-month period reported. No P/E shown for stocks with no profit or for preferred stocks.
Last: The price at which the stock was trading when the exchange closed for the day.
Chg: The loss or gain for the day, compared with previous session's closing price. No change at the close is indicated by ... mark.

pf: Preferred stock. Dividends paid to preferred shareholders take precedence over those on common stock. **rt:** Rights. **wi:** When and if issued. Stock may be authorized but not yet issued; it may be a new issue; or it may have been split. **wt:** Warrant. The right to buy a set number of shares at a specific price and until a certain date. **x:** Ex-dividend, meaning the seller of the stock, not the buyer, receives the latest declared dividend. **z:** Sales total is given in full, not in hundreds.

* This sample comprises formats, styles, and abbreviations from a variety of currently available sources and has been created for educational purposes.

Exchange-Listed Stocks

The illustration is an example of an NYSE composite transactions listing as it might be printed in *The Wall Street Journal*. These consolidated stock tables, which present the most complete information available, report activity for the previous business day.

Nasdaq

Over-the-counter (OTC) stocks that have national interest are listed on the **National Association of Securities Dealers Automated Quotation System (Nasdaq).** Quotes for these securities can be found on a quote machine, a computer that facilitates OTC trading. Listings for more frequently traded Nasdaq securities may appear in *The Wall Street Journal*. The listing shows the stock name, its dividend, its sales volume for the day in round lots, the execution price of the day's last transaction, and the net change in price from the previous day's last transaction.

Nasdaq National Market Stocks

OTC stocks with very high national interest are included in the **Nasdaq National Market (NNM)**. Although these securities may be eligible for listing on an exchange, the companies have chosen to trade OTC instead. NNM issues contain information similar to that supplied for exchange-listed securities.

Stocks of smaller companies that are included in the Nasdaq system comprise the **Nasdaq Capital Market**.

EXAMPLE   Intel is a well-known company that does not list its stock on an exchange. It is a Nasdaq National Market stock.

Non-Nasdaq

Thousands of securities trade in the OTC market that are not part of Nasdaq. These securities are termed non-Nasdaq securities and trade on the over-the-counter bulletin board (OTCBB) or the Pink Sheets.

RIGHTS AND WARRANTS

In addition to issuing stock, a company can issue securities that allow the owner to buy its stock under certain conditions. A company can issue rights to existing stockholders that allow the owner to buy stock at a favorable price for a short period of time. A company can issue warrants, normally in conjunction with the issue of another security, that allow the holder to buy the stock at a set price (higher than at time of issue) for a long period of time.

Rights

Preemptive rights allow existing stockholders to maintain their proportionate ownership in a company by buying newly issued shares before the company offers them to the general public. A **rights offering** allows stockholders to purchase common stock below the current market price. The rights are valued separately from the stock and trade in the secondary market during the subscription period. A stockholder who owns rights may:

- exercise the rights to buy stock by sending the rights certificates and a check for the required amount to the rights agent;

- sell the rights and profit from their market value (rights certificates are negotiable securities); or

- let the rights expire and lose their value.

Approval of Additional Stock

The board of directors must approve decisions to issue additional stock through a rights offering. If the additional shares will increase the stock outstanding beyond the amount authorized in the company charter, the stockholders must vote to amend the charter.

Characteristics of Rights

Once a rights offering has been issued, the rights may be bought or sold in the secondary market just as stock is bought and sold. If the holder of a right does not sell it, the holder may exercise it to buy the stock specified in the right or let it expire.

Subscription Right Certificate. A subscription right is a certificate representing a short-term (typically 30 to 45 days) privilege to buy additional shares of a corporation. One right is issued for each common stock share held by the investor.

Terms of the Offering. The terms of a rights offering are stipulated on the subscription right certificates mailed to stockholders. The terms describe how many new shares a stockholder may buy, price, the date new stock will be issued, and a final date for exercising the rights. The stock is often offered to rights holders at a discount.

Standby Underwriting. If the current stockholders do not subscribe to all the additional stock, the issuer may offer unsold shares to a broker/dealer in a standby underwriting. A standby underwriting is done on a **firm commitment** basis, meaning the broker/dealer or underwriter buys all unsold shares from the issuer and then resells them to the general public.

Warrants

A **warrant** is a certificate granting its owner the right to buy securities from the issuer at a specified price, normally higher than the market price when issued. Unlike a right, a warrant is usually a long-term instrument, giving the investor the choice of buying shares at a later date at the exercise price.

Origination of Warrants

Warrants are usually offered to the public as *sweeteners* (inducements) in connection with other securities, such as debentures or preferred stock, to make the securities more attractive; such offerings may be bundled as units.

Warrants may be *detachable* or *nondetachable* from other securities. If detachable, they trade in the secondary market in line with the common stock's price. When first issued, a warrant's exercise price is set well above the stock's market price. If the stock's current market price increases, the owner can exercise the warrant and buy the stock at the exercise price or sell the warrant in the market.

Comparison of Rights and Warrants

Rights	Warrants
Short term	Long term
Exercisable below market value	Exercisable above market value
May trade with or separate from the common stock	May trade with or separate from the units
Offered to existing shareholders with preemptive rights	Offered as a sweetener for another security
One right issued per share outstanding	Number issued is determined by corporation

---

TEST TOPIC ALERT

Rights: Short-term instruments, exercise price is below market price; issued to current shareholders only

Warrants: Long-term instruments; exercise price is above market price at time of issue; used as sweeteners with issues of more speculative corporate bonds; also, warrants are not entitled to dividends

Rights and **warrants** may be traded in the secondary market

---

QUICK QUIZ 1.7

1. Which of the following statements regarding warrants is TRUE?

    A. Warrants are offered to current shareholders only.
    B. Warrants have longer terms than rights.
    C. Warrants do not trade in the secondary market.
    D. At the time of issuance, the exercise price of a warrant is typically below the market price of the underlying stock.

2. Which of the following statements about rights is TRUE?

    A. Common stockholders do not have the right to subscribe to rights offerings.
    B. Preferred stockholders do not have the right to subscribe to rights offerings.
    C. Rights are long-term instruments.
    D. The exercise price of rights is greater than the current market price of the stock at the time of issuance.

OPTIONS

An **option** is a contract that establishes a price and time frame for the purchase or sale of a particular investment instrument. Two parties are involved in the contract: one party receives the right to exercise the contract to buy or sell the underlying security; the other is obligated to fulfill the terms of the contract.

Calls and Puts

Listed option contracts are issued in standardized formats by the Options Clearing Corporation (OCC) and traded on the Chicago Board Options Exchange. (CBOE) or another exchange. Because the CBOE and other exchanges provide forums to trade, and the OCC stands behind option contracts in the event of a firm's failure, options are easily tradable.

There are two basic types of option contracts: calls and puts.

- A **call option** gives the buyer the right to call (buy) a security away from someone. You can buy that right for yourself, or you can sell that right to someone else.

- A **put option** gives the buyer the right to put (sell) a security to someone. You can buy that right for yourself, or you can sell that right to someone else.

Each stock option contract covers 100 shares (a round lot) of stock to be traded at a specific price before a specific date. An option's cost is called the **premium**. Premiums are quoted in dollars per share. Each contract covers 100 shares.

EXAMPLE   A premium of $3 means $3 for each share × 100 shares, or $300.

Exercise Prices

An option's **exercise** or **strike price** is the price at which the option owner is entitled to buy or sell the underlying security and the price at which the option seller has agreed to sell or buy the security.

Leverage

Option contracts provide investors with leverage: a relatively small cash outlay allows an investor to control an investment that would otherwise require a much larger sum. If a stock is currently $20 per share, 100 shares would cost $2,000, but a call on 100 shares might cost only $200 to $300.

TAKE NOTE   Options require a strategy of opposites. Buyers always do the opposite of sellers. If you know what the buyer of an option does, you can always figure out what the seller does.

EXAMPLE   **In a call:** the buyer of the call has the right to buy; the seller of the call has the obligation to sell.

In a put: the buyer of the put has the right to sell; the seller of the put has the obligation to buy.

TEST TOPIC ALERT   The exam will have very few questions about options. You should be well prepared if you know the information in the following tables.

Buyer vs. Seller in an Option Contract

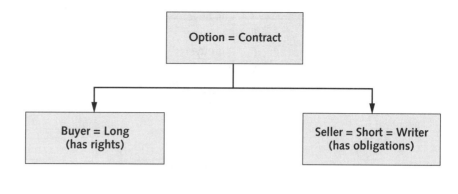

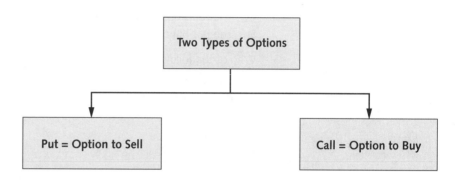

The following table identifies the market attitude of each option position. The upward arrow denotes a bullish investor who profits when the market goes up; a downward arrow denotes a bearish investor who profits when the market goes down. Each quadrant identifies an option position.

	Buy = Long	**Sell = Short**
Call	Right to Buy ↑	Obligation to Sell ↓
Put	Right to Sell ↓	Obligation to Buy ↑

Upper left quadrant: Buying a call (Long call position)	**Upper right quadrant:** Selling a call (Short call position or call writer)
An investor long a call is bullish and has the right to buy stock.	An investor short a call is bearish and has the obligation to sell stock.
Lower left quadrant: Buying a put (Long put position)	**Lower right quadrant:** Selling a put (Short put position or put writer)
An investor long a put is bearish and has the right to sell stock.	An investor short a put is bullish and has the obligation to buy stock.

Be prepared to answer the following questions.	
Which options positions are bearish?	Long put, short call
Which options positions are bullish?	Long call, short put
Which positions buy stock at exercise?	Long call, short put
Which positions sell stock at exercise?	Long put, short call
Which positions have rights?	Long call, long put
Which positions have obligations?	Short call, short put

QUICK QUIZ 1.8

1. Who of the following are bearish?

    I.   Call buyer
    II. Call writer
    III. Put buyer
    IV. Put writer

    A. I and III
    B. I and IV
    C. II and III
    D. II and IV

2. Upon exercise of an option, who of the following would buy stock?

    A. The call buyer because he is obliged to.
    B. The put seller because he is obliged to.
    C. The call seller because he elects to.
    D. The put buyer because he elects to.

3. Who of the following have acquired an obligation?

    I.   Call buyer
    II. Call writer
    III. Put buyer
    IV. Put writer

    A. I and III
    B. I and IV
    C. II and III
    D. II and IV

Terms and Concepts Checklist

✓

- ☐ Common stock
- ☐ Authorized
- ☐ Issued
- ☐ Treasury
- ☐ Outstanding
- ☐ Market value (CMV)
- ☐ Par value
- ☐ Book value
- ☐ Statutory voting
- ☐ Cumulative voting
- ☐ Exchange listed
- ☐ OTC

✓

- ☐ Preferred stock
- ☐ Fixed income
- ☐ Straight preferred
- ☐ Cumulative preferred
- ☐ Callable preferred
- ☐ Convertible preferred
- ☐ Participating preferred
- ☐ Adjustable rate preferred
- ☐ ADR
- ☐ (Preemptive) rights
- ☐ Warrant
- ☐ Option

✓

- ☐ Bull, bullish
- ☐ Bear, bearish
- ☐ Cash dividends
- ☐ Dividend yield
- ☐ Stock dividends
- ☐ Growth
- ☐ Investment risk
- ☐ Return on investment
- ☐ Exercise price
- ☐ Leverage
- ☐ Long or short call
- ☐ Long or short put

DEBT SECURITIES

So far, we have been discussing equity securities, those that confer actual ownership in a company upon its holder. These securities, as we have seen, take the form of common and preferred stock. A second major form of security, **debt securities**, can be issued not only by corporations, but by federal, state, or local governmental bodies as well. Corporate debt instruments can be secured or unsecured. A debt instrument issued by a state or local government takes the form of a municipal bond or note. A debt instrument issued by the federal Treasury takes the form of a Treasury bill, note, or bond. A debt instrument issued to fund a government-sponsored enterprise takes the form of an agency issue.

Bonds, whether issued by corporations, municipalities, the US government, or its agencies, are **debt securities**. As the borrower, the issuer promises to repay the debt on a specified date and to pay interest on the loan amount.

Because the interest rate the investor receives is set when the bond is issued, it is a **fixed-income security**. Individual bonds usually have a face (or par) value of $1,000.

TEST TOPIC ALERT   An investor who buys stock in a company is an owner or has equity in the company. An investor who buys bonds is owed money by the issuer. Bondholders are creditors of the issuer. Like any other borrower, the bond issuer pays interest for the use of the money to the bondholder.

CHARACTERISTICS OF BONDS

Unlike stockholders, bondholders have no ownership interest in the issuing corporation or voice in management. As creditors, bondholders receive preferential treatment over common and preferred stockholders if a corporation files for bankruptcy. Because creditor claims are settled before the claims of stockholders, bonds are considered senior securities. Therefore, stockholder interests are subordinate to those of bondholders.

Issuers

Corporations issue bonds to raise working capital or funds for capital expenditures such as plant construction or equipment and other major purchases. Corporate bonds are commonly referred to as funded debt. Funded debt is any long-term debt payable in five years or more.

The federal government is the nation's largest borrower and the most secure credit risk. Treasury bills (maturities of six months or less), notes (one- to 10-year maturities), and bonds (10- to 30-year maturities) are backed by the full faith and credit of the government and its unlimited taxing powers.

Municipal securities are the debt obligations of state and local governments and their agencies. Most are issued to raise capital to finance public works or construction projects that benefit the general public.

TAKE NOTE Generally, bonds issued by the federal government are the safest, followed by municipal bonds, then corporate bonds. Because corporate bonds are the riskiest, they provide the highest potential income to investors.

The Trust Indenture Act of 1939

The Trust Indenture Act requires corporate bonds of $5 million or more to be issued under a **trust indenture**, a legal contract between the bond issuer and a trustee representing bondholders. The face of a bond certificate mentions the trust indenture, but it is not automatically supplied to bondholders. The trust indenture specifies the issuer's obligation and the bondholders' rights and also identifies the trustee.

The Trustee

The Trust Indenture Act of 1939 requires a corporation to appoint a **trustee**—usually a commercial bank or trust company—for its bonds. The trustee ensures compliance with the covenants of the indenture and acts on behalf of the bondholders if the issuer defaults.

Exemptions. Federal and municipal governments are exempt from the Trust Indenture Act provisions, although municipal revenue bonds are typically issued with a trust indenture to make them more marketable.

Interest

Both the interest rate an issuer pays its bondholders and the timing of payments are set when a bond is issued. The interest rate, or coupon, is calculated from the bond's par value. Par value, also known as face value, is normally $1,000 per bond, meaning each bond will be redeemed for $1,000 when it matures. Interest on a bond accrues daily and is paid in semiannual installments over the life of the bond.

The final interest payment is made when the bond matures, and it is normally combined with repayment of the principal amount.

TEST TOPIC ALERT Be prepared to solve a question similar to the following:

An investor buys an ABC J&J 8s of '09. What will the investor receive at maturity of the bond? To solve the problem, decode the bond quote first:

ABC: The issuer of the bond; it is a corporate bond.

J&J: The bond pays semiannual interest on January and July 1 each year. The interest dates are six months apart (an M&S bond would pay interest on March and September 1).

8s: The bond pays a stated rate of interest of 8% annually, paid in two installments of $40. This is known as the coupon or nominal or stated rate of interest.

'09:   The investor will receive the principal at the bond's maturity in 2009.

Now back to the original question. The investor will receive the full principal plus the last semiannual interest payment when the bond matures.

Bond principal:	$1,000	
Semiannual interest:	40	(Annual interest is $80 per thousand; the
Total at maturity:	$1,040	semiannual interest is $40.)

Maturities

On the maturity date, the loan principal is repaid to the investor. Each bond has its own maturity date. The most common maturities fall in the five- to 30-year range.

Bond Certificates

All bond certificates contain basic information including the following:

- Name of issuer

- Interest rate and payment date

- Maturity date

- Call features

- Principal amount (par value)

- CUSIP number for identification

- Dated date—the date that interest starts accruing

- Reference to the bond indenture

Registration of Bonds

Bonds are registered to record ownership should a certificate be lost or stolen. Tracking a bond's ownership through its registration has been common in the United States only since the early 1970s.

Coupon (Bearer) Bonds

Though rare today, in past years most bonds were issued in **coupon**, or **bearer**, form. Issuers kept no records of purchasers, and securities were issued without an investor's name printed on the certificate. Because coupon bonds are not registered, whoever possesses them can collect interest on and either sell or redeem the bonds.

Interest coupons are attached to bearer bonds, and holders collect interest by clipping the coupons and delivering them to an issuer's paying agent. Individual coupons are payable to the bearer. When a bond matures, the bearer delivers it to the paying agent and receives his principal. No proof of ownership is needed to sell a bearer bond. Even though bearer bonds are not issued today, the term *coupon* is still used to describe interest payments received by bondholders.

Registered Bonds

The most common form of bond currently issued is the **registered bond**. When a registered bond is issued, the issuer's transfer agent records the bondholder's name. The buyer's name appears on the bond certificate's face.

Fully Registered. When bonds are **registered** as to both principal and interest, the transfer agent maintains a list of bondholders and updates this list as bond ownership changes. Interest payments are automatically sent to bondholders of record. The transfer agent transfers a registered bond whenever a bond is sold by cancelling the seller's certificate and issuing a new one in the buyer's name. Most corporate bonds are issued in fully registered form.

Registered as to Principal Only. Principal-only registered bonds have the owner's name printed on the certificate, but the coupons are in bearer form.

When bonds registered as to principal only are sold, the names of the new owners are recorded (in order) on the bond certificates and on the issuer's registration record. Like bearer bonds, bonds registered as to principal only are no longer issued.

Book-Entry Bonds

Book-entry bond owners do not receive certificates. Rather, the transfer agent maintains the security's ownership records. The names of buyers of both registered and book-entry bonds are recorded (registered), but the book-entry bond owner does not receive a certificate—the registered bond owner does. The trade confirmation serves as evidence of book-entry bond ownership. Most US government and municipal bonds are available only in book-entry form.

TEST TOPIC ALERT

The exam might ask you in what form a bond must be for an investor to receive interest and principal payments by mail. Bonds must be fully registered—the issuer must have the name of the investor entitled to both principal and interest payments on his ownership list. New bonds are issued only in registered form or book-entry form.

Remember that bonds are senior to stock, meaning they must be paid first. Thus, bond interest must be paid before stock dividends may be paid. Similarly, just as preferred stock is senior to common stock, secured bonds are senior to unsecured bonds (debentures), which are in turn senior to subordinated debt. The general order thus described may be illustrated with the other obligations of a company by means of the priority of payment upon liquidation.

Liquidation

In the event a company goes bankrupt, the hierarchy of claims on the company's assets are as follows.

1. Unpaid wages

2. IRS, state, and county (taxes)

3. Secured debt (bonds and mortgages)

4. Unsecured liabilities (debentures) and general creditors

5. Subordinated debt

6. Preferred stockholders

7. Common stockholders

TEST TOPIC ALERT   Be ready for a question on liquidation priority. Secured debt is safest, followed by unsecured bonds and general creditors, then subordinated debt. Common stock is always last in line. Bonds are frequently called senior securities because of their priority in this hierarchy.

Pricing

Once issued, bonds are bought and sold in the secondary market at prices determined by market conditions.

Par, Premium, and Discount

Bonds are issued with a face, or par, value of $1,000. **Par** represents the dollar amount of the investor's loan to the issuer, and it is the amount repaid when the bond matures. The par value of bonds is $1,000; the par value of preferred stock is $100.

TEST TOPIC ALERT   When a bond's price is above $1,000 it is trading at a premium. When a bond's price is below $1,000 it is trading at a discount.

In the secondary market, bonds can sell for any price—at par, below par (at a *discount*), or above par (at a *premium*). The two primary factors affecting a bond's market price are the issuer's financial stability and overall trends in interest rates. If an issuer's credit rating remains constant, interest rates are the only factor that affects the market price.

Bond quotes are commonly stated as percentages of par. A bid of 100 means 100% of par, or $1,000. A bond quote of 98⅛ means 98⅛% (98.125%) of $1,000, or $981.25.

Sample Corporate Bond Pricing

A Price of:	Means . . .		Or . . .
92	92% of	$1,000	$ 920.00
93⅛	93⅛% of	$1,000	$ 931.25
94¼	94¼% of	$1,000	$ 942.50
95⅜	95⅜% of	$1,000	$ 953.75
96½	96½% of	$1,000	$ 965.00
97⅝	97⅝% of	$1,000	$ 976.25
98¾	98¾% of	$1,000	$ 987.50
99⅞	99⅞% of	$1,000	$ 998.75
100	100% of	$1,000	$1,000.00
105	105% of	$1,000	$1,050.00

Bond price changes are quoted in newspapers in points. One point is 1% of $1,000 (or $10), and ¼ point is $2.50. The minimum variation for most corporate bond quotes is ⅛ (.125%, or $1.25).

TEST TOPIC ALERT   It is important to remember that one bond point is equal to $10 and one stock point is equal to $1.

TAKE NOTE   Just like preferred stock, bond prices are inversely affected by interest rates. As interest rates fall, bond prices rise; as interest rates rise, bond prices fall. This inverse relationship affects any fixed income security.

Bond Price/Yield Relationship

Rating and Analyzing Bonds

Rating services, such as Standard & Poor's and Moody's, evaluate the credit quality of bond issues and publish their ratings. Standard & Poor's and Moody's rate both corporate and municipal bonds and base their bond ratings primarily on an issuer's creditworthiness—that is, the issuer's ability to pay interest and principal as they come due.

In the following chart, two of the major rating services' criteria are compared:

Bond Ratings

Standard & Poor's	Moody's	Interpretation
Bank-grade (investment-grade) bonds		
AAA	Aaa	Highest rating. Capacity to repay principal and interest judged high.
AA	Aa	Very strong. Only slightly less secure than the highest rating.
A	A	Judged to be slightly more susceptible to adverse economic conditions.
BBB	Baa	Adequate capacity to repay principal and interest. Slightly speculative.
Speculative (noninvestment-grade) bonds		
BB	Ba	Speculative. Significant chance that issuer could miss an interest payment.
B	B	Issuer has missed one or more interest or principal payments.
C	Caa	No interest is being paid on bond at this time.
D	D	Issuer is in default. Payment of interest or principal is in arrears.

TEST TOPIC ALERT

You might be asked to choose the bond with the highest rating. Ratings are like reports cards—the more As, the better.

EXAMPLE

Which of the following bonds is considered to be the safest?
A.   A rated mortgage bond
B.   Baa rated equipment trust certificate
C.   AA rated unsecured debenture
D.   B rated funded debt

Answer: C. The safest of the bonds listed is the AA rated unsecured debenture. You don't need to be concerned with the type of bond; the rating takes into account all features of the security when rating the credit risk.

Comparative Safety of Debt Securities

Relationship of Rating to Yield

Generally, the higher a bond's rating, the lower its yield. Investors will accept lower returns on their investments if their principal and interest payments are safer. Bonds with low ratings due to the issuer's financial condition pay higher rates because of the risks to principal and interest associated with such uncertainties.

Qualitative Analysis. In addition to financial statistics, qualitative factors such as an industry's stability, the issuer's management, and the regulatory climate may be considered when bonds are rated.

Types of Debt Securities

US Government and Agency Securities

The highest degree of safety is in securities backed by the full faith and credit of the US government. Such securities include:

- US Treasury bills, notes, and bonds, and Series EE, HH, and I bonds;
- New Housing Authority bonds (NHAs); and
- Securities of the Government National Mortgage Association (GNMA or Ginnie Mae).

Issues of Agency-Like Organizations

The second highest degree of safety is in securities issued by government-sponsored corporations, although the US government does not back the securities. These organizations include:

- Federal Farm Credit Banks (FFCBs);
- Federal Home Loan Mortgage (Freddie Mac); and
- Federal National Mortgage Association (FNMA or Fannie Mae).

Municipal Issues

Generally, the next level of safety is in securities issued by municipalities. **General obligation bonds (GOs),** backed by the taxing power of the issuer, are usually safer than revenue bonds. Revenue bonds are backed by revenues from the facility financed by the bond issue.

Corporate Debt

Corporate debt securities cover the spectrum from very safe (AAA corporates) to very risky (**junk bonds**). Corporate bonds are backed, in varying degrees, by the issuing corporation.

Usually, these securities are ranked from safe to risky, as follows:

1. Secured bonds
2. Debentures
3. Subordinated debentures
4. Income bonds

However, these rankings serve only as a general guideline.

Liquidity

Liquidity is the ease with which a bond or any other security can be sold. Many factors determine a bond's liquidity, including:

- quality;

- rating;

- maturity;

- call features;

- coupon rate and current market value;

- issuer; and

- existence of a sinking fund (an account to insure payment of principal).

TAKE NOTE   The terms *liquidity* and *marketability* are synonymous. Know that either term refers to how quickly a security can be converted into cash.

Maturity

The longer the term to maturity, the greater the risk to bondholders. Bonds with longer terms to maturity experience greater fluctuation in price, or **volatility**, than short-term bonds. Short-term interest rates, however, fluctuate more than long-term interest rates.

TAKE NOTE   Long-term bonds fluctuate more in price, but short-term interest rates fluctuate more than long-term interest rates.

Debt Retirement

The schedule of interest and principal payments due on a bond issue is known as the **debt service**.

Redemption

When a bond's principal is repaid, the bond is redeemed. **Redemption** usually occurs on the maturity date.

Sinking Fund. To facilitate the retirement of its bonds, a corporate or municipal issuer sometimes establishes a **sinking fund** operated by the bonds' trustee. The trust indenture often requires a sinking fund, which can be used to call bonds, redeem bonds at maturity, or buy back bonds in the open market.

To establish a sinking fund, the issuer deposits cash in an account with the trustee. Because a sinking fund makes money available for redeeming bonds, it can aid the bonds' price stability.

Calling Bonds

Bonds are often issued with a call feature or provision. A call feature allows the issuer to redeem a bond issue before its maturity date, either in whole or in part (in-whole or partial calls). The issuer does this by notifying bondholders that it will redeem the bonds at a particular price on a certain date.

Call Premium. The right to call bonds for early redemption gives issuers flexibility in their financial management. In return, an issuer usually pays bondholders a premium, a price higher than par, known as a **call premium**. Various municipal bonds, corporate bonds, and preferred stocks are callable at some point over their terms.

Advantages of a Call to the Issuer. Callable bonds can benefit issuers in several ways.

- If general interest rates decline, the issuer can redeem bonds with a high interest rate and replace them with bonds with a lower rate.

- An issuer can call bonds to reduce its debt any time after the initial call date.

- The issuer can replace short-term debt issues with long-term issues, and vice versa.

- The issuer can call bonds as a means of forcing the conversion of convertible corporate securities.

Term bonds, which all mature on the same date, are generally called by random drawing. Serial bonds, which are issued with a sequence of maturities, are usually called in reverse order of their maturities, because longer maturities tend to have higher interest rates. Calling the long maturities lowers the issuer's interest expense by the largest amount.

If a bond issue's trust indenture does not include a call provision, the issuer normally can buy bonds in the open market, known as **tendering**, to retire a portion of its debt.

Call Protection. Bonds are called when general interest rates are lower than they were when the bonds were issued. Investors, therefore, are faced with having to replace a relatively high fixed-income investment with one that pays less; this is known as **call risk**.

A newly issued bond normally has a **call protection period** of five or 10 years to provide some safety to investors. During this period, the issuer cannot call any of its bonds. When the call protection period expires, the issuer may call any or all of the bonds, usually at a premium. A call protection feature is an advantage to bondholders in periods of declining interest rates.

Callable bonds generally have slightly higher coupons than comparable noncallable bonds because of the increased risk to investors.

TEST TOPIC ALERT

1. Under what economic circumstances do issuers call bonds?

    Bonds are typically called when interest rates are declining. Consider the issuer's side: would you want to pay more interest for the use of money than you need to?

2. Investors who purchase callable bonds face what types of investment risk?

    Call risk is the risk that the bonds will be called and the investor will lose the stream of income from the bond. Remember that bonds don't pay interest after they have been called. The call feature also causes reinvestment risk. If interest rates are down when the call takes place, what likelihood does the investor have of reinvesting the principal received at a comparable rate?

    Both call risk and reinvestment risk apply to callable bonds.

3. Which of the following would an investor prefer in a bond she is purchasing?
    A. A long call protection period when interest rates are high
    B. A long call protection period when interest rates are low
    C. A short call protection period when interest rates are high
    D. A short call protection period when interest rates are low

    Answer: A. Investors want to lock in the highest possible rate of interest for the longest period of time. During the call protection period the issuer cannot call the bonds away.

Refunding Bonds

Refunding is the practice of raising money to call a bond. Specifically, the issuer sells a new bond issue (with a lower rate) to buy back an old bond issue (with a higher rate). Refunding, like a call, can occur in full or in part. Generally, an entire issue is refunded at once. Refunding is common for bonds approaching maturity because an issuer may not have enough cash to pay off the entire issue. Or, it may choose to use its cash for other needs.

TAKE NOTE

Refunding can be thought of as issuer refinancing. Homeowners are familiar with this: when interest rates drop, it makes sense to replace a high-interest mortgage with a new mortgage at a more competitive rate. An issuer can accomplish the same thing by refunding.

QUICK QUIZ 1.9

Match the following terms to the appropriate description below.
    A. Call protection
    B. Premium
    C. Debt service
    D. Sinking fund

_D_ 1. Account established so that an issuer has the money to redeem its bonds

_A_ 2. Contractual promise stating that the bond issue is not callable for a certain period of time

_C_   3. The schedule of interest and principal payments due on a bond issue

_B_   4. Difference between the higher price paid for a bond and the bond's face amount at issue

BOND YIELDS

A bond's **yield** expresses the cash interest payments in relation to the bond's value. Yield is determined by the issuer's credit quality, prevailing interest rates, time to maturity, and call features. Bonds can be quoted and traded in terms of their yield as well as their price, expressed as a percentage of par dollar amount.

Comparing Yields

Because bonds most frequently trade for prices other than par, the price discount or premium from par is taken into consideration when calculating a bond's overall yield. You can look at a bond's yield in several ways.

Nominal Yield

A bond's **coupon rate**, or **nominal yield**, is set at issuance and printed on the face of the bond.

Nominal yield is a fixed percentage of the bond's par value.

EXAMPLE   A coupon of 6% indicates the bondholder is paid $60 in interest annually until the bond matures.

TAKE NOTE   Recognize that different names exist for a bond's nominal yield. It can be called the coupon rate, the fixed rate, or the stated rate of the bond. The nominal rate of interest will always be paid to the bondholder, regardless of whether the bond's price changes.

Current Yield

Current yield (CY) measures a bond's annual interest relative to its market price, as shown in the following equation:

Annual interest ÷ market price = current yield

Bond prices and yields move in opposite directions: as a bond's price rises, its yield declines, and vice versa. When a bond trades at a discount, its current yield increases; when it trades at a premium, its current yield decreases.

Yield to Maturity

A bond's **yield to maturity (YTM)** reflects the annualized return of the bond if held to maturity. In calculating yield to maturity, the bondholder takes into account the difference between the price paid for a bond and par value.

If the bond's price is less than par, the discount amount increases the return. If the bond's price is greater than par, the premium amount decreases the return.

Relationship Between Bond Prices and Yields to Maturity

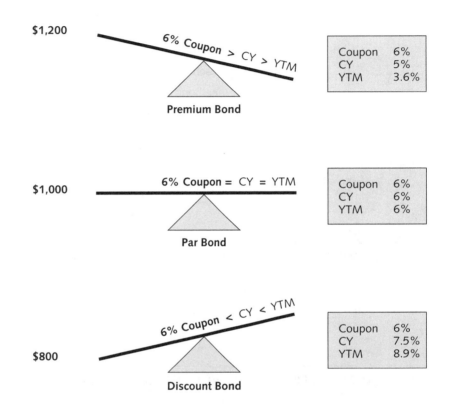

EXAMPLE

What is the current yield of a 6% bond trading for $800?

Current yield (CY) = annual interest ÷ current market price

Find the solution as follows: $60 ÷ $800 = 7.5%. Note that this bond is trading at a discount. When prices fall, yields rise. The current yield (7.5%) is greater than the nominal yield (6%) when bonds are trading at a discount.

EXAMPLE

What is the current yield of a 6% bond trading for $1,200? Find the solution as follows: $60 ÷ $1,200 = 5%. This bond is trading at a premium. Price is up, so the yield is down. The current yield (5%) is less than the nominal yield (6%) when bonds are trading at a premium.

The diagram below is effective in helping master the relationships in bond yields. Be sure to understand the inverse relationship between price and yield.

Inverse Bond/Yield Relationship Chart

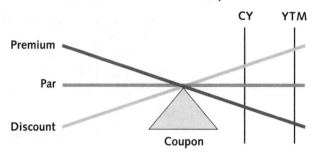

Follow the lines on the chart to identify these concepts:

1. When bonds are at par, coupon and current yield are equal. (The point of intersection on the CY line is neither higher nor lower than the coupon on the line that represents par.)

2. When bonds are at a premium, the CY is less than the coupon. (The point of intersection on the CY line is below the coupon on the line that represents premium.)

3. When bonds are at a discount, the CY is greater than the nominal yield. (The point of intersection on the CY line is above the coupon on the line that represents discount.)

You can also compare a bond's yield to maturity to its coupon and current yield.

TAKE NOTE   When a bond is trading at a premium, its YTM is less than its current yield. The point of intersection on the YTM line is below the current yield on the line that represents premium. Use the chart to keep these important relationships in mind. When you take the Series 6 exam, draw this chart for reference on a piece of scratch paper.

QUICK QUIZ 1.10   Match the following terms with the appropriate description below.

A. Premium
B. Discount
C. Par

_B_ 1. YTM is greater than coupon.

_A_ 2. CY is less than coupon.

_B_ 3. YTM is greater than CY.

_C_ 4. YTM is equal to nominal.

_B_ 5. CY is less than YTM.

_A_ 6. YTM is less than coupon.

_C_ 7. YTM is equal to CY.

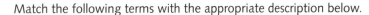

Match the following terms with the appropriate description below.

A. Nominal yield
B. Investment grade
C. Book entry
D. Current yield
E. Yield to maturity

__E__ 8. Percentage return reflecting the annualized return of the bond if held to maturity

__A__ 9. Stated on the face of the bond certificate

__D__ 10. Annual interest divided by today's market price

__C__ 11. Bondowner's name stored in records kept by the issuer or transfer agent

__B__ 12. Bonds rated BBB/Baa or above

QUICK QUIZ 1.11

1. A new bond contains a provision that it cannot be called for five years after the date of issuance. This call protection would be most valuable to a recent purchaser of the bond if interest rates are

   A. falling
   B. rising
   C. stable
   D. fluctuating

2. What is the calculation for determining the current yield on a bond?

   A. Annual interest ÷ par value
   B. Annual interest ÷ current market price
   C. Yield to maturity ÷ par value
   D. Yield to maturity ÷ current market price

3. A customer purchased a 5% US government bond yielding 6%. A year before the bond matures, new US government bonds are being issued at 4%, and the customer sells the 5% bond. The customer probably

   I. bought it at a discount
   II. bought it at a premium
   III. sold it at a discount
   IV. sold it at a premium

   A. I and III
   B. I and IV
   C. II and III
   D. II and IV

4. Which yield to maturity would be higher?

   A. 10% nominal yield bond with a premium price
   B. 10% nominal yield bond with a discount price
   C. 10% nominal yield bond with a price at par
   D. 10% current yield bond with a price at par

5. In a comparison of long-term bonds with short-term bonds, all of the following are characteristics of long-term bonds EXCEPT

   A. they usually have higher yields than short-term bonds
   B. they usually provide greater liquidity than short-term bonds
   C. they are more likely to be callable
   D. they will fluctuate in price more than short-term bonds in response to interest rate changes

6. When interest rates are falling or rising, the price fluctuations of which of the following will be the greatest?

   A. Short-term bonds
   B. Long-term bonds
   C. Money market instruments
   D. Common stock

CORPORATE BONDS

Corporate bonds are issued to raise working capital or capital for expenditures such as plant construction and equipment purchases.

Types of Corporate Bonds

The two primary types of corporate bonds are **secured** and **unsecured**. Other types of bonds are also discussed in this section: guaranteed bonds, income bonds, and zero-coupon bonds.

Secured Bonds

A bond is secured when the issuer has identified specific assets as collateral for interest and principal payments. A trustee holds the title to the assets that secure the bond. In a default, the bondholder can lay claim to the collateral.

Mortgage Bonds. **Mortgage bonds** have the highest priority among all claims on assets pledged as collateral. While mortgage bonds, in general, are considered relatively safe, individual bonds are only as secure as the assets that secure them and are rated accordingly. Mortgage bonds are normally issued by utilities.

Collateral Trust Bonds. **Collateral trust bonds** are usually issued by corporations that own securities of other companies as investments. A corporation issues bonds secured by a pledge of those securities as collateral. The trust indenture usually contains a covenant requiring that a trustee hold the pledged securities. Collateral trust bonds may be backed by one or more of the following securities:

- stocks and bonds of partially or wholly owned subsidiaries;

- another company's stocks and bonds;

- installment payments or other obligations of the corporation's clients; or

- US Treasuries.

Equipment Trust Certificates. Railroads, airlines, trucking companies, and oil companies use **equipment trust certificates** (or **equipment notes** and **bonds**) to finance the purchase of capital equipment. Title to the newly acquired equipment is held in trust, usually by a bank, until all certificates have been paid in full. Because the certificates normally mature before the equipment wears out, the amount borrowed is generally less than the full value of the property securing the certificates.

Senior vs. Subordinated Debt

Secured bonds are said to be senior to unsecured bonds. This simply means that the claims of senior debt are honored before those of subordinated debt.

TAKE NOTE   Holders of secured bonds do not have access to any of the other assets of the corporation in a liquidation.

Unsecured Bonds

Unsecured bonds have no specific collateral backing and are classified as either debentures or subordinated debentures.

Debentures. **Debentures** are backed by the general credit of the issuing corporation, and a debenture owner is considered a general creditor of the company. Debentures are below secured bonds and above subordinated debentures and preferred and common stock in the priority of claims on corporate assets.

Subordinated Debentures. The claims of **subordinated debenture** owners are junior to the claims of other general creditors. Subordinated debentures generally offer higher income than either straight debentures or secured bonds due to their subordinate, therefore riskier, status, and they often have conversion features. Subordinate debentures are often referred to as high-yield or junk bonds.

Guaranteed Bonds

Guaranteed bonds are backed by a company other than the issuer, such as a parent company. This effectively increases the issue's safety.

Income Bonds

Income bonds, also known as **adjustment bonds,** are used when a company is reorganizing and coming out of bankruptcy. Income bonds pay interest only if the corporation has enough income to meet the interest payment and the board of directors declares a payment. Because missed interest payments do not accumulate for future payment, these bonds are not suitable investments for customers seeking income.

TAKE NOTE   Unsecured bonds and debentures are interchangeable terms. Both refer to bonds that have no specific collateral backing. Subordinated debentures are designated as junior in claim to other debentures. As a result of this higher risk, subordinated debentures pay higher interest.

Zero-Coupon Bonds

Bonds are normally issued as fixed-income securities. **Zero-coupon bonds** are debt obligations that do not make regular interest payments. Instead, zeros are issued at a deep discount from their face value. The difference between the discounted purchase price and the full face value at maturity is the return (accreted interest) the investor receives. The price of a zero-coupon bond reflects the general interest rate climate for similar maturities.

Zero-coupon bonds are issued by corporations, municipalities, and the US Treasury and may be created by broker/dealers from other types of securities.

Advantages and Disadvantages of Zero-Coupon Bonds. A zero-coupon bond requires a relatively small investment—perhaps $100 to $200 per bond—and matures at $1,000. They offer investors a way to speculate on interest rate moves. Because they sell at deep discounts and offer no cash interest payments to the holder, zeros are substantially more volatile than traditional bonds; their prices fluctuate wildly with changes in interest rates. Moreover, the longer the time to maturity, the greater the volatility. When interest rates change, a zero's price changes much more as a percentage of its market value than an ordinary bond's price.

Taxation of Zero-Coupon Bonds. Although zeros pay no regular interest income, an investor who owns taxable (government or corporate) zeros owes income tax each year on the amount by which the bonds have accreted, just as if the investor had received it in cash. The income tax is due regardless of the direction of the market price. Because the annual interest is not prorated in equal amounts, the bond issuer must send each investor an Internal Revenue Service (IRS) Form 1099 annually showing the amount of interest subject to taxation.

TEST TOPIC ALERT   If asked which security has no reinvestment risk, look for a zero. This is because there are no semiannual interest payments to reinvest. Also, buying a zero is the only way to lock in a rate of return.

When the exam asks you to select an investment that provides for a certain dollar amount in the future, zeros are a good choice because investors know they will receive the face amount at maturity.

EXAMPLE   A suitability question asks what you would recommend to a couple who wishes to have $100,000 available in a college education fund in 10 years. Choose a zero coupon.

Convertible Bonds

Convertible bonds are corporate bonds that may be exchanged for a fixed number of shares of the issuing company's common stock. Because they are convertible into common stock, convertible bonds pay lower interest rates than nonconvertible bonds and often trade in line with the common stock. They are bonds with fixed interest payments and maturity dates, so convertible bonds are less volatile than common stock. Issuers add convertible features to bonds or preferred stock to make these issues more marketable.

Investor Considerations

Since convertible bonds offer the safety of the fixed-income market and the potential appreciation of the equity market, they provide investors with several advantages.

- As a debt security, a convertible debenture pays interest at a fixed rate and is redeemable for its face value at maturity, provided the debenture is not converted. As a rule, interest income is higher and surer than dividend income on the underlying common stock. Similarly, convertible preferred stock usually pays a higher dividend than does common stock.

- If a corporation experiences financial difficulties, convertible bondholders have priority over common stockholders in the event of a corporate liquidation.

- In theory, a convertible debenture's market price tends to be more stable during market declines than the underlying common stock's price. Current yields of other competitive debt securities support the debenture's value in the marketplace.

- Because convertibles can be exchanged for common stock, their market price tends to move upward if the stock price moves up. For this reason, convertible securities are more volatile in price during times of steady interest rates than are other fixed-income securities.

Conversion of a senior security into common stock is not considered a purchase and a sale for tax purposes. Thus, the investor incurs no tax liability on the conversion transaction.

Calculating Conversion Parity

Parity is the state of a convertible bond (or preferred stock) when its price is equal to the market price of the underlying stock. It means that two securities are of equal dollar value.

The following formulas calculate the parity prices of convertible securities and their underlying common shares:

$$\frac{\text{Market price of the bond}}{\text{Conversion ratio (\# of shares)}} = \text{Parity price of common stock, or}$$

Market price of common × conversion ratio = Parity price of convertible.

TEST TOPIC ALERT

On the Series 6, there will probably be a question on the parity concept.

EXAMPLE

RST convertible bond has a conversion price of $50. If the bond is currently trading for $1,200, what is the parity price of the underlying common stock?

Method 1

Par value: $1,000
Conversion price: $50
Conversion ratio: 20 (1,000 ÷ 50 = 20 shares)

The parity stock price is found by dividing the $1,200 market price by 20 shares. The parity price of the underlying common stock is $60.

Method 2

Par value: $1,000
Conversion price: $50
Conversion ratio: 20 (1,000 ÷ 50 = 20 shares)

A second method to determine parity is by using percentages. In this example, the bond is trading at 20% above face value (1,200 − 1,000) ÷ 1,000 = 20%); therefore, the stock should be trading at 20% above the conversion price ($50 × 120% or 1.2 = $60) or $60.

EXAMPLE

RST convertible bond has a conversion price of $50. If the current market value of the underlying common stock is $40, what is the parity price of the bond?

Par value: $1,000
Conversion Price: $50
Conversion Ratio: 20 (1,000 ÷ 50 = 20 shares)

To calculate parity price of the bond multiply the current market value of the common stock by the conversion ratio. The parity price of this bond is $800 ($40 × 20 = $800).

Duration is another useful tool in bond calculations. Most convenient with interest-paying bonds, it is a measure of the amount of time a bond will take to pay for itself. Each interest payment is taken to be part of a discounted cash flow, so there is more to the calculation than simply adding up the interest payments. For the Series 6, remember that duration is often used to assess the volatility of a bond in response to interest rate changes—the longer the duration, the greater the volatility, and thus risk, in an environment of changing interest rates. Remember also that the duration of an interest-paying bond is always shorter than the time to its maturity because of the interest payments. By way of comparison, the duration of a zero-coupon bond is always equal to the time to its maturity because there is only one payment—the one made when the bond matures.

QUICK QUIZ 1.12

Match the following items to the appropriate description below.

A.   Zero-coupon bonds
B.   Parity
C.   Guaranteed bonds
D.   Subordinated debenture

_D_   1.   Claims are junior to those of other creditors

_C_   2.   Party other than the issuing corporation promises to maintain payments of principal and interest

_B_   3.   Dollar amount at which a convertible security is equal in value to its corresponding stock

_A_   4.   Investor receives Form 1099 and reports interest for taxation even though no interest income has been received

Match the following items to the appropriate description below.

A.   Collateral trust bond
B.   Income bond
C.   Mortgage bond
D.   Convertible bond

_C_   5.   Debt obligation secured by a property pledge

_D_   6.   Debenture that can be exchanged for common stock at specified prices or rates

_A_   7.   Secured bond backed by stocks or bonds of another issuer

_B_   8.   Interest payment must be declared by issuer's board of directors

9.   ABC, Inc., has filed for bankruptcy. Parties will be paid off in which order?

I.   Holders of secured debt
II.   Holders of subordinated debentures
III.   General creditors
IV.   Preferred stockholders

A.   I, III, II, IV
B.   III, I, II, IV
C.   I, II, III, IV
D.   IV, I, II, III

10. Moody's Bond Page lists the following:

GMAC ZR '12 54¼

Ogden 5s '93 78⅞

The annual interest on 50 Ogden bonds is

A. $93

B. $500

C. $930

D. $2,500

11. Which of the following statements regarding convertible bonds is NOT true?

A. Coupon rates are usually higher than nonconvertible bond rates of the same issuer.

B. Convertible bondholders are creditors of the corporation.

C. Coupon rates are usually lower than nonconvertible bond rates of the same issuer.

D. If the underlying common stock should decline sharply, the bonds will sell at a price based on their inherent value as bonds, disregarding the convertible feature.

12. A bond is convertible to common stock at $20 per share. If the market value of the bond is $800, what is the parity price of the stock?

A. $12

B. $16

C. $25

D. $40

13. A convertible bond is purchased at a discount and is convertible at $125. What is the conversion ratio?

A. 2

B. 8

C. 12

D. 20

TRACKING CORPORATE BONDS

Bonds are listed in newspapers and other financial publications such as *Barron's* and *The Wall Street Journal*.

EXAMPLE   Alabama Power 9s 2010 (AlaP): The description of its 9s 2010 bond indicates that the bond pays 9% interest and matures in the year 2010. The current yield is given as 8.9%, which indicates that the bond is selling at a premium. The "Vol" (volume, or sales) column states how many bonds traded the previous day (the day being reported). In this case, 18 bonds, or $18,000 par value, were traded in Alabama Power 9s 2010. The next three columns explain the high, low, and closing prices for the day.

Corporate Bond Quotations

New York Exchange Bonds

Quotations as of 4 pm Eastern Time
Friday, August 20, 2004

Corporation Bonds
Volume $45,198,000

Bonds	Cur Yld	Vol	High	Low	Close	Net Chg
AForP 5s 30r	9.6	50	52 1/4	51 7/8	52	+3/4
AbbtL 7 5/8s 09	7.6	21	99 3/4	99 3/4	99 3/4	...
Advst 9s 08	cv	72	103 1/2	103	103	...
AetnLf 8 1/8s 07	8.5	15	95 3/4	95 3/4	95 3/4	−1
AirbF 7 1/2s 11	cv	32	114	112	114	+1
AlaP 9s 2010	8.9	18	100 3/4	100 5/8	100 3/4	+1/4
AlaP 8 1/2s 09	8.6	13	98 3/8	98 3/8	98 3/8	−3/8
AlaP 8 7/8s 11	8.5	65	102 7/8	102 1/2	102 1/2	−3/8
AlldC zr 12	...	10	91 1/2	91 1/8	91 1/2	−1/8
viAmes 7 1/2s 14f	cv	79	15 1/2	14 3/4	15	+1
Ancp 13 7/8s 12f	cv	10	91	89 3/8	91	+2

EXPLANATORY NOTES

Yield is current yield. **cld:** Called. **cv:** Convertible bond. **dc:** Deep discount. **f:** Dealt in flat. **m:** Matured bonds, negotiability impaired by maturity. **na:** No accrual. **r:** Registered. **zr:** Zero coupon. **vi:** In bankruptcy or receivership or being reorganized.

This sample comprises formats, styles, and abbreviations from a variety of currently available sources and has been created for educational purposes.

For AlaP, the high was 100¾, the low was 100⅝, and the bonds closed at (last trade) 100¾. Net change (the last column) refers to how much the bond's closing price was up or down from the previous day's close. AlaP 9s of 2010 closed up ¼ of a point, or $2.50. AlaP closed yesterday at 100½ (100¾ − ¼).

Note that the Allied Chemical (AlldC) zr bonds have ellipses in the current yield column; these are zero-coupon bonds that do not pay interest.

TEST TOPIC ALERT   You might be asked to determine the price of a bond from a bond quote; 1 bond point = $10. If the bond's quote is 105, its price is $1,050.

If a bond is quoted at 97⅝, find its price in three steps:

1. 97 × 10 = $970

2. ⅝ = .625 × 10 = $6.25

3. $970 + $6.25 = $976.25

US GOVERNMENT AND AGENCY SECURITIES

The US Treasury Department determines the quantity and types of government securities it must issue to meet federal budget needs. The marketplace determines the interest rates those securities will pay. In general, the interest that government securities pay is exempt from state and municipal taxation but is subject to federal taxation.

The federal government is the nation's largest borrower as well as the best credit risk. Interest and principal on securities issued by the US government are backed by its full faith and credit, which is based on its power to tax.

Most government securities are issued in book-entry form, meaning no physical certificates exist.

Nonmarketable government securities are also known as EE and HH (double E and double H) savings bonds.

Marketable Government Securities

Treasury debt securities are classified as bills, notes, and bonds to distinguish an issue's term to maturity.

Treasury Bills (T-Bills)

T-bills are short-term obligations and, unlike most other debt securities, are issued at a discount from par. The difference between the issue price and par value at maturity is the investor's return. Rather than making regular cash interest payments, the return on a T-bill is the difference between the price the investor pays and the par value received when the bill matures.

EXAMPLE

An investor buys a T-bill for 975 ($975) and receives $1,000 when the bill matures in six months. The $25 difference ($1,000 – $975) is the investor's return.

Maturities and Denominations. Treasury bills are issued in denominations of $1,000 to $1 million and, although there have been one-year maturities in the past, currently T-bills mature in four, 13, or 26 weeks. T-bills with 13- and 26-week maturities are auctioned weekly.

Pricing. Once they are issued, T-bill bid and ask quotes in the secondary market are stated in terms of the annualized interest rates that the discount from par value will yield.

EXAMPLE

Note the following quote:

US Treasury Bills

Mat. Date	Bid	Ask
12/15	5.00	4.90

The bid and ask quotes represent discounts from the par value. The higher interest rate (5.00%) bid will result in a lower dollar price paid for the bill than the ask interest rate (4.90%). In other words, an investor that sells ten 6-month T-bills ($10,000 par value) at the bid of 5.00 would receive 10,000 – 5% ($500, but since it is for 6 months, half that amount or $250) or $9,750. An investor that buys ten 6-month T-bills at the ask of 4.90 would pay $10,000 – 4.90% ($490, again, since it is half a year, half that amount or $245), or $9,755.

Treasury Notes (T-Notes)

Unlike Treasury bills, **T-notes** pay interest every six months.

Maturities and Denominations. Issued in denominations of $1,000 to $1 million, T-notes are intermediate-term bonds maturing in one to 10 years. T-notes mature at par, or they can be refunded. If a T-note is refunded, the government offers the investor a new security with a new interest rate and maturity date as an alternative to a cash payment for the maturing note. Bondholders may always request their principal in cash.

Pricing. T-notes are issued, quoted, and traded in $\frac{1}{32}$ of a percentage of par. A quote of 98.24, which can also be expressed as 98-24 or 98:24, on a $1,000 note means that the note is selling for $98\frac{24}{32}$% of its $1,000 par value. In this instance, .24 designates $\frac{24}{32}$ of 1%, not a decimal. A quote of 98.24 equals 98.75% of $1,000, or $987.50.

EXAMPLE

A Bid of ...	Means ...	Or...
98.01	$98\frac{1}{32}$% of $1,000	$980.3125
98.02	$98\frac{2}{32}$% of $1,000	$980.6250
98.03	$98\frac{3}{32}$% of $1,000	$980.9375
98.10	$98\frac{10}{32}$% of $1,000	$983.1250
98.11	$98\frac{11}{32}$% of $1,000	$983.4375
98.12	$98\frac{12}{32}$% of $1,000	$983.7500

Treasury Bonds (T-Bonds)

T-bonds are long-term securities that pay interest every six months.

Maturities and Denominations. Treasury bonds are issued in denominations of $1,000 to $1 million and mature in 10 years or more.

Pricing. T-bonds are quoted exactly like T-notes.

Callable. Some Treasury bonds have optional call dates, ranging from three to five years before maturity. The Treasury department must give bondholders four months' notice before calling the bonds.

Marketable Government Securities: T-bills, T-notes, and T-bonds

Type	Maturity	Pricing	Form
T-bill	30 to 180 days (four to 26 weeks); short term	Issued at discount; priced on discount basis	Book entry
T-note	One to 10 years; intermediate-term	Priced at percentage of par	Book entry
T-bond	Usually 10 to 30 years; long term	Priced at percentage of par	Book entry

Treasury Receipts

Brokerage firms can create **Treasury receipts** from US Treasury notes and bonds. Broker/dealers buy Treasury securities, place them in trust at a bank, and sell separate receipts against the principal and coupon payments. The Treasury securities held in trust collateralize the Treasury receipts. Unlike Treasury securities, Treasury receipts are not backed by the full faith and credit of the US government.

EXAMPLE

To illustrate how Treasury receipts are created, consider a $1,000 10-year Treasury note with a 6% coupon as 21 separate payment obligations. The first 20 are the semiannual $30 interest payment obligations until maturity. The 21st is the obligation to repay the $1,000 principal at maturity. An investor may purchase a Treasury receipt for any of the 20 interest payments or the principal repayment.

TAKE NOTE

Each Treasury receipt is priced at a discount from the payment amount, like a zero-coupon bond.

STRIPS. In 1984, the Treasury department entered the zero-coupon bond market by designating certain Treasury issues as suitable for stripping into interest and principal components. These securities are known as **STRIPS (Separate Trading of Registered Interest and Principal of Securities)**. The securities underlying Treasury STRIPS are the US government's direct obligation.

TEST TOPIC ALERT

STRIPS are backed in full by the US government—receipts are not. Both are zero-coupon instruments.

Nonmarketable Government Securities

Nonmarketable government securities include Series EE and Series HH bonds. These bonds are nontransferable—that is, they are not bought and sold between investors. They are purchased from the Treasury Department and can be redeemed only by the purchaser or a beneficiary. Series EE and Series HH bonds are exempt from state and local taxation but are subject to federal taxation.

Series EE bonds are bought at a discount and can be redeemed for the face value at maturity. Series EE bonds are issued at 50% of their face value in denominations from $50 to $10,000. The bonds can be redeemed before maturity but will receive a lower rate of return. The tax on accrued interest can be paid annually or deferred until the bonds mature. Tax can be deferred further by trading EE bonds for HH bonds.

Series HH bonds can be purchased only by trading in matured Series EE bonds. Series HH bonds pay semiannual interest, come in denominations of $500 to $10,000, and mature in 10 years, although the investor can redeem them at face value at any time.

The US Treasury has been issuing Series I bonds since 1998. Their purpose is to help protect a US government securities holder from inflation. They have denominations ranging from $50 to $10,000 and are issued at face value. For I bonds, interest accrues monthly and compounds semiannually. This feature enables investors to protect against loss of purchasing power from inflation. Interest and income tax is not paid until the bond is redeemed. Series I bonds can be purchased from a broker/dealer or bank directly, but Series EE cannot be exchanged for Series I bonds.

TEST TOPIC ALERT

EE and I bonds pay no current interest. EE are sold at a discount, and the interest accrues and is paid upon maturity. I bonds are purchased at face value, and the monthly interest accrues and is paid upon redemption of the bond. Series HH bonds pay monthly interest but are no longer issued. None of these bonds can be traded in the secondary market.

Agency Issues

Certain federal government agencies may also issue debt securities to finance their public sector operations. It is important to note that, except for Ginnie Mae, agency debt obligations have an implicit backing of the government, not the direct backing. Because of this difference in government backing, the interest rate paid by agency issues is higher than that paid by Treasury securities.

Yields and Maturities. Agency issues have higher yields than direct obligations of the federal government but lower yields than corporate debt securities. Their maturities range from short to long term. Agency issues are quoted as percentages of par (97 means 97% of $1,000 par value, or $970) and trade actively in the secondary market.

Backing. Agency issues are backed by revenues from taxes, fees, or interest income from lending activities. They may also be backed by collateral, such as cash or US Treasury securities, by a US Treasury guarantee, or in the case of Ginnie Mae, by the full faith and credit of the government.

Taxation. Interest on government agency issues is sometimes exempt from state and local income taxes but is always subject to federal income tax.

TAKE NOTE

Interest income from Fannie Mae, Freddie Mac, and Ginnie Mae securities is taxed at the federal, state, and local levels.

Government National Mortgage Association (Ginnie Mae)

The Government National Mortgage Association (GNMA or Ginnie Mae) is a government-owned corporation that supports the Department of Housing and Urban Development. Ginnie Maes are backed by the full faith and credit of the government.

Types of Issues. GNMA buys Federal Housing Administration (FHA) and Department of Veteran Affairs (VA) mortgages and auctions them to private lenders, which pool the mortgages to create pass-through certificates for sale to investors. Thus, monthly interest and principal payments from the pool of mortgages pass through to investors. Like the principal on a single mortgage, the principal represented by a GNMA certificate constantly decreases as the mortgages in the pool are paid down.

TAKE NOTE

Unlike a traditional bond that pays interest every six months and returns an investor's principal in one lump sum at maturity, Ginnie Maes pay interest and return a portion of principal to investors each month.

GNMA pass-throughs pay higher interest rates than comparable Treasury securities, yet are guaranteed by the federal government. GNMA also guarantees timely payment of interest and principal. Because GNMAs are backed directly by the government, risk of default is nearly zero. The price, yield, and maturities of Ginnie Maes in the secondary market fluctuate in line with general interest rate trends.

The primary risk in Ginnie Maes has to do with changes in interest rates in general. If interest rates fall, homeowners tend to pay off their mortgages early, which accelerates the certificate maturities. If interest rates rise, certificates may mature more slowly.

GNMAs are issued in minimum denominations of $25,000. Because few mortgages last the full term, yield quotes are based on a 12-year prepayment assumption (i.e., a mortgage balance should be prepaid in full after 12 years of normally scheduled payments).

Taxation. Interest earned on GNMA certificates is taxable at the federal, state, and local levels.

TEST TOPIC ALERT

Of agency securities, GNMAs are the most testable.
Important points to remember:

■ Ginnie Maes are the only agency security backed in full by the US government

■ Ginnie Mae issues pass-through certificates

■ Investors receive interest and principal on a monthly basis; investors buy Ginnie Maes to satisfy income objectives

■ Yields on Ginnie Maes are slightly higher than on Treasuries

■ Ginnie Maes are subject to interest rate and prepayment risk

Agency-Like Organizations

Federal Home Loan Mortgage Corporation (Freddie Mac, FHLMC)

Freddie Mac is a public corporation whose stock trades on the NYSE. It was created to promote the development of a nationwide secondary market in mortgages by purchasing residential mortgages from financial institutions and packaging them into mortgage-backed securities for sale to investors.

Federal National Mortgage Association (Fannie Mae, FNMA)

Fannie Mae is a publicly held corporation that provides mortgage capital. FNMA purchases conventional and insured mortgages from agencies such as the FHA and the VA. The securities it creates are backed by FNMA's general credit, not by the US government. FNMA stock also trades on the NYSE.

TAKE NOTE

Ginnie Mae is the only agency that is backed by the US government. Freddie Mac, Fannie Mae, and other agencies are backed by their own issuing authority. Freddie Mac and Fannie Mae are publicly owned and traded, but Ginnie Mae is fully owned by the US government.

Collateralized Mortgage Obligations (CMOs)

Collateralized mortgage obligations (CMOs) are mortgage-backed securities like the pass-through obligations Ginnie Mae and Fannie Mae issue. CMOs pool a large number of mortgages, usually on single-family residences. A pool of mortgages is structured into maturity classes called **tranches**. CMOs are issued by private sector financing corporations and by government-sponsored corporations such as FNMA and FHLMC. The chief risk with all mortgage-backed securities is refinancing risk.

CMO Characteristics

Because mortgages back CMOs, they are considered relatively safe. However, their susceptibility to interest rate movements and the resulting changes in the mortgage repayment rate mean CMOs carry several risks.

The rate of principal repayment varies.

■ If interest rates fall and homeowner refinancing increases, principal is received sooner than anticipated, and fewer interest payments are made.

■ If interest rates rise and refinancing declines, the CMO investor may have to hold his investment longer than anticipated, although he does receive more interest payments.

Yields. CMOs yield more than Treasury securities and normally pay investors interest and principal monthly. Principal repayments are made in $1,000 increments to investors in one tranche before any principal is repaid to the next tranche.

Taxation. Interest from CMOs is subject to federal, state, and local taxes.

Liquidity. An active secondary market exists for CMOs, but the market for CMOs with more complex characteristics may be limited or nonexistent. Certain tranches of a given CMO may be riskier than others, and some CMOs or certain tranches carry the risk that repayment of principal may take longer than anticipated (called **extension risk**).

Denominations. CMOs are issued in $1,000 denominations.

Suitability. Some varieties of CMOs may be particularly unsuitable for small or unsophisticated investors because of their complexity and risks. Customers may be required to sign a suitability statement before buying high-risk classes.

Real Estate Mortgage Investment Conduits

Real Estate Mortgage Investment Conduits (REMICs) are another mortgage-backed pass-through investment vehicle. These are more flexible than CMOs, in that issuers separate mortgage pools into different risk classes, as well as different maturity classes. Interests may be senior or junior and may be regular (a debt instrument, yielding income) or residual (essentially an equity instrument). All returns are taxed as ordinary income.

TAKE NOTE

CMOs and REMICs are mortgage-backed corporate securities. The term *pass-through certificate* is associated with both. Both are subject to taxation at all levels.

QUICK QUIZ 1.13

Match the following items to the appropriate description below.

   A. Treasury bill
   B. GNMA pass-through certificate
   C. Collateralized mortgage obligation
   D. Separate Trading of Registered Interest and Principal of Securities (STRIPS)

_D_   1. Zero-coupon bond issued and backed by the Treasury Department

_A_   2. Marketable US government debt with a maturity of less than one year

_B_   3. Security representing an interest in a pool of mortgages that is guaranteed by the full faith and credit of the US government

_C_   4. Mortgage-backed corporate security that attempts to return interest and principal at a predetermined rate

   5. CMOs are backed by

     A. mortgages
     B. real estate
     C. municipal taxes
     D. full faith and credit of US government

6. The term *tranche* is associated with which of the following investments?

    A. FNMA
    B. CMO
    C. GNMA
    D. SLMA

7. REMICs differ from CMOs in that REMICs

    A. are not mortgage-backed
    B. are not pass-through type investment vehicles
    C. have high- as well as low-risk pools of mortgages
    D. are not issued by corporations

MUNICIPAL BONDS

Municipal securities are considered second only to US government and US government agency securities in terms of safety. The degree of safety varies among issues and among municipalities; the safety of a municipal issue is generally based on the municipality's financial strength.

Municipal bonds pay interest semiannually. The interest payment schedule is set when the bonds are issued.

Tax Benefits

The federal government does not tax the interest from debt obligations of municipalities, but any capital gains from municipal transactions are taxable. This tax-advantaged status of municipal bonds allows municipalities to pay lower interest rates on their bond issues.

Municipal securities are more appropriate for investors in high tax brackets than those in low tax brackets because the amount of tax savings for high tax-bracket investors is larger.

Calculating Tax Benefits

In comparing a corporate with a municipal bond, the tax-equivalent yield (TEY) gives the equivalent yield of a corporate bond to that of a municipal bond; the tax-free equivalent yield (TFEY) gives the equivalent yield of a municipal bond to that of a corporate bond.

TEY: (Municipal yield) ÷ (1 – investor tax rate %) = Equivalent corporate yield

TFEY: (Corporate yield) × (1 – investor tax rate %) = Equivalent municipal yield

EXAMPLE

Two investors, one in a 15% tax bracket and one in a 30% tax bracket, consider purchasing $10,000 worth of a new municipal bond with a 7% coupon. Comparable corporate bonds are currently being issued at 8.5%.

The investor in the 15% tax bracket would receive a tax-equivalent yield of 8.2%. To calculate this, divide 7% by (100% minus his tax rate of 15%), or 7% divided by 85% (.85), which equals 8.2%. The municipal bond would not be a good choice for this investor because he could get a higher rate of return by investing in corporates.

EXAMPLE

If the investor chooses a corporate bond paying $85 a year, he would pay taxes of $12.75 per bond ($85 × 15%), leaving him with $72.25 after taxes, which is more than $70.00 tax free.

The investor in the 30% tax bracket would receive a tax-equivalent yield of 10% (7% divided by 100% minus his 30% tax rate, or 7% divided by 70% = 10%). He would receive a higher after-tax yield from the municipal bond.

EXAMPLE

If the investor chooses a corporate bond paying $85 a year, he would pay taxes of $25.50 ($85 × 30%), leaving him with $59.50 after taxes, which is less than $70.00 tax free.

TEST TOPIC ALERT

The most important point about municipal debt is that interest earned on these securities is generally exempt from federal taxation. It is most suitable for high tax-bracket investors and generally unsuitable for investors in low tax brackets or within retirement plans.

General Obligation Bonds (GOs)

GOs are also known as full faith and credit bonds because the interest and principal payments are backed by the full faith and credit of the issuer. GOs are used to raise funds for municipal capital improvements that benefit the entire community—public schools or a courthouse, for instance. These facilities typically do not produce revenues.

Sources of Funds

GOs are backed by a municipality's taxing power. Bonds issued by states are backed by income taxes, license fees, and sales taxes. Bonds issued by towns, cities, and counties are backed by property taxes, license fees, fines, and all other municipal revenue sources. School, road, and park districts may issue municipal bonds backed by property taxes.

Revenue Bonds

Revenue bonds can be used to finance any municipal facility that generates enough income to support its operations and debt service.

Sources of Revenue

The interest and principal payments of revenue bonds are payable to bond-holders only from the specific earnings and net lease payments of revenue-producing facilities such as:

- utilities (water, sewer, electric);
- housing;
- transportation (airports, toll roads);
- education (college dorms, student loans);
- health (hospitals, retirement centers); and
- industrial (industrial development, pollution control).

Debt service payments do not come from general or real estate taxes and are not backed by the full faith and credit of the municipality.

Special Revenue Bonds

A municipality issues **industrial development revenue bonds (IDRs or IDBs)** to construct facilities or purchase equipment, which is then leased to a corporation. The municipality uses the money from lease payments to pay the principal and interest on the bonds. The ultimate responsibility for the payment of principal and interest rests with the corporation; therefore, the bonds carry the corporation's debt rating.

Technically, industrial revenue bonds are issued for the benefit of a corporation. Under the Tax Reform Act of 1986, the interest on these bonds is usually taxable because the act reserves the tax exemption for public purpose bonds.

Legal Opinion

Attached to every bond certificate (unless the bond is specifically stamped *ex-legal*) is a **legal opinion** written and signed by the bond counsel, an attorney specializing in tax-exempt bond offerings. The legal opinion states that the issue conforms with applicable laws, the state constitution, and is tax free at the federal level.

QUICK QUIZ 1.14

True or False?

_F_   1. Municipal securities are issued by federal and state governments.

_T_   2. Capital gains from the profitable sale of municipal securities are not exempt from taxation.

_F_   3. Municipal revenue bonds are generally backed by taxes collected by the municipality.

_T_   4. The interest on IDRs is typically taxable at the federal level.

__T__   5.   Bonds issued by school, road, and park districts are examples of GOs.

__T__   6.   Municipals generally pay less interest than corporate issuers.

THE MONEY MARKET

In the financial marketplace, a distinction is made between the capital market and the money market. The capital market serves as a source of intermediate- to long-term financing usually in the form of equity or debt securities with maturities of more than one year.

The money market, on the other hand, provides very short-term funds to corporations, municipalities, and the US government. Money market securities are debt issues with maturities of one year or less.

TAKE NOTE   The money market is the source for short-term financing, while the capital market is the source for medium- to long-term financing. Money market funds are short-term, liquid debt obligations.

Money Market Instruments

Money market instruments provide businesses, financial institutions, and governments a means to finance their short-term cash requirements.

Liquidity and Safety

Money market instruments are debt securities with short-term maturities, typically one year or less.

Because they are short-term instruments, money market securities are highly liquid. Money market securities also provide a relatively high degree of safety because most issuers have high credit ratings.

Money market securities issued by the US government and its agencies include the following:

■   Treasury bills that trade in the secondary market

■   Treasury and agency securities with remaining maturities of less than one year

■   Federal National Mortgage Association short-term discount notes

■   Short-term discount notes issued by various smaller agencies

Money market portfolios that include municipal securities are considered tax-exempt money market instruments.

Corporations and banks have a number of ways to raise short-term funds in the money market, such as:

■   bankers' acceptances (time drafts);

- commercial paper (prime paper);

- negotiable certificates of deposit;

- federal funds; and

- brokers' and dealers' loans.

Banker's Acceptance (BA)

A **banker's acceptance (BA)** is a short-term time draft with a specified payment date drawn on a bank—essentially a postdated check or line of credit. The payment date of a BA is normally between one and 270 days.

American corporations use bankers' acceptances extensively to finance international trade—that is, a BA typically pays for goods and services in a foreign country. They are issued at a discount and mature at par.

Commercial Paper

Corporations issue short-term, unsecured **commercial paper,** or **promissory notes,** to raise cash to finance accounts receivable and seasonal inventory gluts. Commercial paper interest rates are lower than bank loan rates. Commercial paper maturities range from one to 270 days, although most mature within 90 days. Commercial paper is issued at a discount from face value.

Typically, companies with excellent credit ratings issue commercial paper. The primary buyers of commercial paper are money market funds, commercial banks, pension funds, insurance companies, corporations, and nongovernmental agencies.

Certificates of Deposit (CDs)

Nonnegotiable CDs. Most investors are familiar with the CD time deposits that have set maturities and fixed interest rates and are offered by banks and savings and loans. Banks offer **nonnegotiable CDs** with maturities ranging from 30 days to 10 years or more. Banks may issue nonnegotiable CDs for small or large amounts, which are insured by the Federal Deposit Insurance Corporation (FDIC) for up to $100,000.

Nonnegotiable CDs are not traded in the secondary market and are not money market securities.

Negotiable CDs. Negotiable CDs (jumbo CDs) are time deposits banks offer. They have minimum face values of $100,000, but most are issued for $1 million or more. A negotiable CD is an unsecured promissory note guaranteed by the issuing bank.

Most negotiable CDs mature in one year or less, with the maturity date often set to suit a buyer's needs. Because the CDs are negotiable, they can be traded in the secondary market before their maturity and are considered money market securities.

TEST TOPIC ALERT

Know the features of each money market instrument listed below.

Banker's Acceptance

■ Time draft or letter of credit for foreign trade

■ Maximum maturity of 270 days

Commercial Paper

■ Issued by corporations

■ Unsecured promissory note

■ Maximum maturity of 270 days

Negotiable CDs

■ Issued by banks

■ Minimum face value of $100,000

■ Mature in one year or less

QUICK QUIZ 1.15

1. All of the following are money market instruments EXCEPT
   A. Treasury bills
   B. municipal notes
   C. commercial paper
   D. newly issued Treasury bonds

2. The maximum maturity of commercial paper is how many days?
   A. 90
   B. 180
   C. 270
   D. 360

3. Which of the following statements regarding negotiable CDs are TRUE?
   I. The issuing bank guarantees them.
   II. They are callable.
   III. Minimum denominations are $1,000.
   IV. They can be traded in the secondary market.
   A. I and II
   B. I and IV
   C. II and III
   D. III and IV

4. Commercial paper is
   A. a secured note issued by a corporation
   B. a guaranteed note issued by a corporation
   C. a promissory note issued by a corporation
   D. none of the above

5.   Which money market instrument finances imports and exports?

   A.   Eurodollars
   B.   Bankers' acceptances
   C.   ADRs
   D.   Commercial paper

Terms and Concepts Checklist

✓	✓	✓
☐ Bond	☐ Sinking Fund	☐ Negotiable CD
☐ Par, premium, discount	☐ Trust Indenture Act	☐ Interest
☐ Coupon yield	☐ Trustee	☐ Maturity
☐ Current yield	☐ Secured bond	☐ Liquidation priority
☐ Yield to maturity	☐ Mortgage bond	☐ Bond rating
☐ Inverse relationship	☐ Collateral trust certificate	☐ Liquidity
☐ Note	☐ Equipment trust certificate	☐ Call
☐ Fixed income security	☐ Debenture	☐ Call protection
☐ Agency issues	☐ Subordinated debenture	☐ Call premium
☐ Redemption	☐ Zero coupon bond	☐ Coupon
☐ Refunding	☐ Convertible bond	☐ Fully registered
☐ Duration	☐ Conversion price	☐ Registered as to principal only
☐ T-bills, T-notes, T-bonds	☐ Conversion ratio	☐ Book entry
☐ Treasury receipts	☐ Conversion parity	☐ GNMA
☐ STRIPS	☐ Senior, junior security	☐ Agency-like organization
☐ Municipal bond	☐ IDR, IDB	☐ FNMA
☐ GO bond	☐ Legal opinion	☐ FHLMC
☐ Revenue bond	☐ Money market	☐ CMO
☐ TEY	☐ Banker's acceptance	☐ REMIC
☐ TFEY	☐ Commercial paper	

ECONOMIC FACTORS

Economics is the study of supply and demand. When people want to buy an item that is in short supply, the item's price rises. When people do not want an item that is in plentiful supply, the price declines. This simple notion—the foundation of all economic study—is true for bread, cars, clothes, stocks, bonds, and money. Economic activity reflects the overall health of a country's economy. Economists attempt to measure and predict the economy's cycles and the effect on various industries and corporations.

The economic climate has an enormous effect on the condition of individual companies and the securities markets. A company's earnings and business prospects, business cycles, changes in the money supply, Federal Reserve Board (FRB) actions, and a host of complex international factors affect securities prices and trading.

GROSS DOMESTIC PRODUCT (GDP)

A nation's annual economic output, all of the goods and services produced within it, is known as its **gross domestic product (GDP)**. The US GDP includes personal consumption, government spending, gross private investment, foreign investment, and the total value of exports.

Price Levels

When comparing the economic output of one period with that of another, analysts must account for changes in the relative prices of products that have occurred during the intervening time. Economists adjust GDP figures to constant dollars rather than compare actual dollars. This allows economists and others who use GDP figures to compare the actual purchasing power of the dollars instead of the dollars themselves.

Consumer Price Index (CPI)

The most prominent measure of general price changes is the **Consumer Price Index (CPI)**. The CPI measures the rate of increase or decrease in a range of consumer prices (e.g., food, housing, transportation, medical care, clothing, electricity, entertainment, and services).

Inflation

Inflation is a general increase in prices. Mild inflation can encourage economic growth because gradually increasing prices tend to stimulate business investments. High inflation reduces the buying power of a dollar and hurts the economy. Gold prices usually rise during periods of high inflation. Increased inflation drives up interest rates of fixed-income securities, which drives down bond prices. Decreases in the inflation rate have the opposite effect: as inflation declines, bond yields decline and prices rise.

If . . .	And . . .	Then . . .	Thus . . .
inflation increases	interest rates go up	bond prices go down	bond yields go up
inflation decreases	interest rates go down	bond prices go up	bond yields go down

Deflation

Though rare, deflation is a general decline in prices. Deflation usually occurs during severe recessions when unemployment is on the rise.

Business Cycles

Periods of economic expansion are historically followed by periods of economic contraction in a pattern called the **business cycle**. Business cycles go through four stages:

- Expansion

- Peak

- Contraction (decline)

- Trough

- Repeat

Expansion is characterized by increased business activity—increasing sales, manufacturing, and wages—throughout the economy. For a variety of reasons, an economy can grow for only so long, and will reach its upper limit, or **peak**. When business activity declines from its peak, the economy is **contracting**.

Depressions occur when the GDP declines for six consecutive quarters, or 18 months. When business activity stops declining and levels off, it is known as a **trough**. According to the US Commerce Department, the economy is in a **recession** when a decline in real output of goods and services (the GDP) lasts for six months or more.

TEST TOPIC ALERT   Know the order of the four phases of the business cycle: expansion, peak, contraction, and trough.

TAKE NOTE   Inflation causes purchasing power risk. Today's dollars can buy fewer goods tomorrow. A **constant dollar adjustment** must be made to compare dollars from year to year that have been affected by inflation.

The Four Stages of the Business Cycle

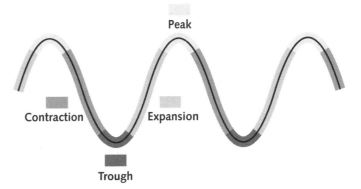

In the normal course of events, some industries or corporations prosper as others fail. So to determine the economy's overall direction, economists consider many aspects of business activity.

Expansions are characterized by:

- increases in industrial production;

- bullish (rising) stock markets;

- rising property values;

- increased consumer demand for goods and services;

- increasing GDP; and

- low unemployment.

Downturns in the business cycle tend to be characterized by:

- rising numbers of bankruptcies and bond defaults;

- higher consumer debt;

- bearish (falling) stock markets;

- rising inventories (a sign of slackening consumer demand in hard times);

- decreasing GDP; and

- high unemployment.

ECONOMIC POLICY

The **Federal Reserve Board** (the Fed) conducts monetary policy by influencing the money supply, which in turn affects interest rates and the economy. The government conducts fiscal policy by influencing the economy through its powers to tax and spend.

Monetary Policy

Most people think of money as cash in their pockets. Economists take a much broader view and include loans, credit, and an assortment of other liquid instruments. To a monetarist, the rate of expansion or contraction of the money supply is the most important element in determining economic health. The Federal Reserve Board determines monetary policy.

Because the FRB determines how much money is available for businesses and consumers to spend, its decisions are critical to the US economy. The FRB affects the money supply through its use of three policy tools:

- changes in reserve requirements;

- changes in the discount rate (on loans to member banks); and

- open-market operations (buying and selling Treasury securities).

Reserve Requirements

Commercial banks must deposit a certain percentage of their depositors' money with the Federal Reserve. This is known as the **reserve requirement**. All money deposited by commercial banks at Federal Reserve Banks, including money exceeding the reserve requirement, is called federal funds.

When the Fed raises the reserve requirement, banks must deposit more funds with the Fed and, thus, have less money to lend. Reducing the reserve requirement has the opposite effect.

To compensate for shortfalls in its reserve requirement, a bank may borrow money directly from the Fed at its discount rate, or it may borrow the excess reserves (federal funds) from another member bank. The interest rate that banks charge each other for such loans is called the federal funds rate.

The federal funds rate fluctuates daily and is the most volatile interest rate in the economy. A rising rate usually indicates that member banks are more reluctant to lend their funds and, therefore, want a higher rate of interest in return. A higher rate usually results from a shortage of funds to lend and probably indicates that deposits, in general, are shrinking. A falling federal funds rate usually means that the lending banks are in competition to loan money and are trying to make their own loans more attractive by lowering their rates. A lower rate often results from an excess of deposits.

Discount Rate. The Fed can also adjust the money supply by raising or lowering the **discount rate**, the interest rate the Fed charges its members for short-term loans. Lowering the discount rate reduces the cost of money to banks, which increases the demand for loans. Raising the discount rate increases the cost of money and reduces the demand for loans.

Open-Market Operations

The Fed buys and sells US government securities in the open market to expand and contract the money supply. The **Federal Open Market Committee (FOMC)** was created to direct the FRB's open market operations. When the FOMC buys securities, it increases the supply of money in the banking system, and when it sells securities, it decreases the supply of money in the banking system.

When the Fed wants to expand (or loosen) the money supply, it buys securities from banks. The banks receive direct credit in their reserve accounts. The increase of reserves allows banks to make more loans and effectively lowers interest rates. Thus, by buying securities, the Fed pumps money into the banking system, expanding the money supply.

When the Fed wants to contract (or tighten) the money supply, it sells securities to banks. Each sale is charged against a bank's reserve balance. This reduces the bank's ability to lend money, which tightens credit and effectively raises interest rates. By selling securities, the Fed pulls money out of the system, contracting the money supply.

When the Fed buys securities, bank excess reserves go up; when the Fed sells securities, bank excess reserves go down. When the Fed buys, it expands the money supply; when the Fed sells, it contracts the money supply. Because most of these transactions involve next-day payment, the effects on the money supply are immediate, making open market operations the Fed's most efficient tool.

Fiscal Policy

Fiscal policy refers to legislative decisions of Congress and the President, which can include increases or decreases in:

- federal spending;

- money raised through taxation; and

- federal budget deficits or surpluses.

Fiscal policy is based on the assumption that the government can control the levels of unemployment and inflation by adjusting overall demand for goods and services. Through its fiscal policies, increasing or decreasing taxes, and spending, the government can:

- reduce the rate of inflation by reducing aggregate demand for goods and services if price levels are excessive; or

- increase the rate of inflation by increasing aggregate demand if low inflation is causing unemployment and economic stagnation.

Economic Policy and the Stock Market

Fiscal and monetary policies have considerable influence on the market. If the FRB eases interest rates, the money supply increases, making credit easier to obtain and increasing overall liquidity.

Similarly, lower tax rates can stimulate spending because they leave more spendable dollars in the hands of individuals and businesses. Like easier credit, lower tax rates are bullish for the stock market. Raising taxes has the opposite effect; it reduces the amount of money available to businesses and consumers for spending and investment.

Because the political process determines fiscal policy, it takes time for conditions and solutions to be identified, negotiated, and implemented; fiscal policy is considered an inefficient way to solve short-term economic problems.

Interest Rates

The cost of doing business is closely linked to the cost of money; the cost of money is reflected in **interest rates**. The money supply, general economic conditions, and inflation levels within the economy determine the level of interest rates. The level of a specific interest rate can be tied to one or more benchmark rates, such as those described below.

Discount Rate

The **discount rate** is the rate the New York Federal Reserve Bank (FRB) charges for short-term loans to member banks. The discount rate indicates the direction of FRB monetary policy: a decreasing rate indicates an easing of FRB policy; an increasing rate indicates a tightening of FRB policy. This rate is set by the Fed.

Federal Funds Rate

The **federal funds rate** is the rate banks charge each other for overnight loans of $1 million or more. It is considered a barometer of the direction of short-term interest rates, which fluctuate constantly. The federal funds rate is listed in daily newspapers. It is a market rate of interest, heavily influenced by actions of the Fed.

Broker Call Loan Rate

The **broker loan rate** is the interest rate banks charge broker/dealers on money they borrow to lend to margin account customers. The broker loan rate is also known as the **call loan rate** or **call money rate**. The broker loan rate usually is a percentage point or so above other short-term rates. Broker call loans are callable on 24 hours' notice.

Prime Rate

The **prime rate** is the interest rate that large US money center commercial banks charge their most creditworthy corporate borrowers for unsecured loans. Each bank sets its own prime rate, with larger banks generally setting a rate other banks use. Banks lower their prime rates when the Fed eases the money supply and raise rates when the Fed contracts the money supply.

Interest Rate Summary

Interest rates reflect the cost of money and, therefore, the cost of doing business. The key interest rates include the following.

■ **Federal funds rate**—Interest rate charged on reserves traded among member banks for overnight use in amounts of $1 million or more; changes daily in response to the borrowing banks' needs

■ **CD rate**—Bank rate offered on nonnegotiable CDs; considered the least volatile of the rates listed

■ **Prime rate**—Base rate on corporate loans at large US money center commercial banks; the prime rate changes when banks react to changes in FRB policy

■ **Discount rate**—Charge on loans to depository institutions by the New York Federal Reserve Bank (FRB)

■ **Call money rate**—Charge on loans to brokers with stock as collateral

International Monetary Factors

Fiscal and monetary policy are not the only influences on the economy. In today's global marketplace, international monetary factors include the balance of payments and currency exchange rates.

Balance of Payments

The flow of money between the United States and other countries is known as the **balance of payments**. The balance of payments may be a surplus (more money flowing into the country than out) or a deficit (more money flowing out of the country than in). A deficit may occur when interest rates in another country are high as money flows to where it will earn the highest return.

The largest component of the balance of payments is the balance of trade—the export and import of merchandise. On the US credit side are sales of American products to foreign countries. On the debit side are US purchases of foreign goods that cause US dollars to flow out of the country. When debits exceed credits, a deficit in the balance of payments occurs; when credits exceed debits, a surplus exists.

Currency Exchange Rates

Exchange rates among world currencies have a profound effect on profitability in international trade and, of course, on individuals, mutual funds, and others that invest in that trade. Importers profit if their own currency becomes stronger relative to other currencies. If the US dollar strengthens in value from 1.3 Swiss francs to 1.4, then goods priced in Swiss francs will look cheaper to a US importer of Swiss goods. Exporters, on the other hand, profit if their own currency becomes weaker. If the US dollar weakens in value from 1.3 Swiss francs to 1.2, then goods priced in US dollars look less expensive to Swiss buyers and a US exporter will be able to sell more.

TAKE NOTE   Importers like their own currency to be strong (or, similarly, foreign currencies to be weak). Exporters like their own currency to be weak (or, similarly, foreign currencies to be strong).

TEST TOPIC ALERT
- The FRB sets the discount rate, not the federal funds rate.
- A change in the reserve requirement has a multiplier effect on the money supply.
- Open market operations are the most frequently used tool of the FRB.

    Fiscal Policy:
- Actions of Congress and the President
- Government spending and taxation

Monetary Policy:

■ Policy of the Federal Reserve Board (FRB)

■ Discount rate

■ Reserve requirement (most drastic)

■ Open market operations (most frequently used)

QUICK QUIZ 1.16

1. When the FOMC purchases T-bills in the open market, which of the following scenarios are likely to occur?

   I.   Secondary bond prices will rise
   II. Secondary bond prices will fall
   III. Interest rates will rise
   IV. Interest rates will fall

   A. I and III
   B. I and IV
   C. II and III
   D. II and IV

2. Which of the following situations could cause a fall in the value of the US dollar in relation to the Japanese yen?

   I.   Japanese investors buying US Treasury securities
   II. US investors buying Japanese securities
   III. Increase in Japan's trade surplus over that of the United States
   IV. General decrease in US interest rates

   A. I, II and III
   B. I and IV
   C. II and III
   D. II, III and IV

3. Disintermediation is most likely to occur when

   A. money is tight
   B. interest rates are low
   C. margin requirements are high
   D. the interest ceilings on certificates of deposit have been raised

4. To tighten credit during inflationary periods, the Federal Reserve Board can take any of the following actions EXCEPT

   A. raise reserve requirements
   B. change the amount of US government debt held by institutions
   C. sell securities in the open market
   D. lower taxes

5. The effective federal funds rate is the

   A. daily average rate charged by the largest money center banks
   B. daily rate charged by Federal Reserve member banks
   C. weekly average rate charged by the largest money center banks
   D. weekly average rate charged by national Federal Reserve member banks

6. Which of the following interest rates is considered the most volatile?

   A. Discount rate
   B. Federal funds rate
   C. Prime rate
   D. LIBOR

Terms and Concepts Checklist

✓

- ☐ GDP
- ☐ Business cycle
- ☐ Expansion, peak, contraction, trough
- ☐ CPI
- ☐ Inflation
- ☐ Fiscal policy
- ☐ Monetary policy
- ☐ Balance of payments
- ☐ Currency exchange rates

✓

- ☐ FRB
- ☐ Reserve requirement
- ☐ Discount rate
- ☐ FOMC
- ☐ Open market operations
- ☐ Federal funds rate
- ☐ Broker call loan rate
- ☐ Prime rate
- ☐ Constant dollar adjustment

HOTSHEETS

For your convenience, Unit HotSheets summarizing the key points are located at the end of the manual on perforated pages.

UNIT TEST

97.375

1. Which of the securities listed below is issued without a stated rate of return?

   A. Treasury bond
   B. Treasury bill
   C. Preferred stock
   D. Treasury note

2. Which of the following statements describing current yield is TRUE?

   A. The terms *current yield* and *total return* are identical.
   B. Current yield is calculated by dividing the current market price of an investment into its annual interest or dividend.
   C. Current yield compares an investment's current price to its price at the end of the previous year.
   D. Current yield can be used to express the income return on a bond but not on a stock or a mutual fund.

3. Where are securities that are NOT listed on an exchange traded?

   A. Only through INSTINET
   B. On the over-the-counter market
   C. On a regional exchange in the same state where the security was issued
   D. All securities must be listed in order to trade publicly

4. Which of the following types of preferred stock may pay a single dividend that is greater than the dividend stated on the face of the certificate?

   I. Straight
   II. Cumulative
   III. Convertible
   IV. Participating

   A. I and II
   B. I and III
   C. II and III
   D. II and IV

5. An investor purchased a corporate bond for 97⅜. If the bond is sold for 99⅜, the investor has a profit of

   99.375

   A. $.20
   B. $2
   C. $20
   D. $200

6. The Federal Open Market Committee is concerned with rising inflation. To counteract this concern the FOMC should

   A. increase the reserve requirement
   B. sell US Treasury securities in the open market
   C. increase the federal funds rate
   D. increase the discount rate

7. All of the following types of securities trade in the secondary market EXCEPT

   A. debentures
   B. open-end investment company shares
   C. closed-end investment company shares
   D. municipal bonds

8. Which of the following are characteristics of a corporate zero-coupon bond?

   I. The bond pays interest on a semiannual basis.
   II. The bond is purchased at a discount from its face value.
   III. The investor has locked in the rate of return.
   IV. The bond interest is taxed each year on an as-earned basis.

   A. I and II
   B. I and III
   C. II and III
   D. II, III and IV

9. Which of the following statements about bid and asked prices are TRUE?

    I. Market makers buy at the bid and sell at the asked.
    II. Market makers buy at the asked and sell at the bid.
    III. Customers buy at the bid and sell at the asked.
    IV. Customers buy at the asked and sell at the bid.

    A. I and III
    B. I and IV
    C. II and III
    D. II and IV

10. Which of the following provides the right to buy a corporation's stock for the longest period of time?

    A. Warrant
    B. Long put
    C. Long call
    D. Preemptive right

11. An investor owns 100 shares of common stock in ABC Corporation. ABC Corporation allows for statutory voting in board of directors elections. If there are 5 positions to be voted on for the board, the investor has

    A. 500 votes for each of the positions
    B. a total of 500 votes which may be cast in any manner
    C. 100 votes for each of the 5 positions
    D. 20 votes for each of the 5 positions

12. Which of the following would be considered money market instruments?

    I. A Treasury bond with 11 months to maturity
    II. 10 shares of preferred stock sold within 270 days
    III. An American depository receipt (ADR) held for less than 1 year
    IV. A $200,000 negotiable certificate of deposit

    A. I and III
    B. I and IV
    C. II and III
    D. III and IV

13. Which of the following are characteristics of general obligation (GO) municipal bonds?

    I. They are backed by the revenue generated from the facility that was built with the proceeds of the bond issue.
    II. Interest paid is tax free at the federal level.
    III. They are issued by agencies of the federal government.
    IV. They are backed by the taxing power of the issuing municipality.

    A. I and III
    B. I and IV
    C. II and III
    D. II and IV

14. A convertible corporate bond that has an 8% coupon yielding 7.1% is available but may be called some time this year. Which feature of this bond would probably be least attractive to your client?

    A. Convertibility
    B. Coupon yield
    C. Current yield
    D. Near-term call

15. All of the following statements about preferred stock and bonds are true EXCEPT

    A. they are both debt instruments
    B. they both have a fixed rate of return
    C. they are both senior to common stock at the dissolution of a corporation
    D. the prices of both are directly influenced by interest rates

16. Which of the following statements about collateralized mortgage obligations (CMOs) are TRUE?

    I. CMOs are backed by the US government.
    II. CMOs are financial institution-sponsored pools of mortgages.
    III. CMOs are exempt from taxation at the federal level.
    IV. CMOs cannot include municipal issues.

    A. I and III
    B. I and IV
    C. II and III
    D. II and IV

17. Which of the following statements regarding Ginnie Maes are TRUE?

   I. They are not taxable at the state level.
   II. They are directly backed by the federal treasury.
   III. The minimum purchase at issue is $1,000.
   IV. Investors receive a monthly check representing both interest and a return of principal.

   A. I and III
   B. I and IV
   C. II and III
   D. II and IV

18. An investor owns a 9% convertible bond issued by the XYZ Corporation, a subsidiary of the ABC Corporation. The bond is convertible at $25. This investor may convert the bond into

   A. 4 shares of common stock of the ABC Corporation
   B. 4 shares of common stock of the XYZ Corporation
   C. 40 shares of common stock of the ABC Corporation
   D. 40 shares of common stock of the XYZ Corporation

19. Importers enjoy the greatest profits when

   A. their own currency is strong and foreign currencies are weak
   B. their own currency is strong and foreign currencies are strong
   C. their own currency is weak and foreign currencies are weak
   D. their own currency is weak and foreign currencies are strong

20. If the Swiss franc has depreciated relative to the US dollar, then goods produced in

   I. Switzerland become less expensive in the United States
   II. Switzerland become more expensive in the United States
   III. the United States become less expensive in Switzerland
   IV. the United States become more expensive in Switzerland

   A. I and III
   B. I and IV
   C. II and III
   D. II and IV

ANSWERS AND RATIONALES

1. **B.** Treasury bills are not issued with a stated coupon rate. Instead, they are sold through auctions at a discount to their par value of $1,000. They then mature to their face amount and the discount represents the interest earned. Treasury bonds and Treasury notes are issued with a stated rate of interest, and interest is paid semiannually. Preferred stock has a stated rate of dividend; however, it is not guaranteed. The stated rate of dividend is only paid if declared by the board of directors.

2. **B.** Current yield is calculated by dividing the annual income distribution from an investment (interest for bonds and dividends for stock or mutual funds) by the current market value (price) of the security. The current return calculation does not factor price movement over time or reinvestment of distributions, and thus does not express an investment's total return.

3. **B.** Securities not listed on an exchange are traded on the over-the-counter market. INSTINET is used by institutional investors for fourth-market trades. The location of the issue has no bearing on whether the issue is listed on a regional exchange.

4. **D.** Cumulative preferred stockholders have the right to receive skipped dividends of the corporation and can receive a dividend in arrears plus the current year's dividend. Participating preferred stockholders have the right to receive a share of the common dividend.

5. **C.** This investor has a profit of two points, or $20. Bond points are worth $10 each. The actual dollar prices of the bonds are computed as follows: 97⅜ = 970 + 3.75 (⅜ of $10) = $973.75; 99⅜ = 990 + 3.75 = $993.75.

6. **B.** The FOMC buys and sells US Treasury securities to impact the money supply. To counteract inflation, the FOMC needs to remove dollars from the money supply. By selling US Treasury securities, the FOMC requires payment which removes money from the economy, causing interest rates to rise. The FOMC does not set the reserve requirement or the discount rate; these are tools of the Federal Reserve Board (FRB). The federal funds rate is determined by market supply and demand of excess reserves between banks.

7. **B.** Open-end investment company shares (mutual funds) are available in the primary market only. There is no secondary trading of mutual fund shares. Shares are redeemed by the issuing fund.

8. **D.** Zero-coupon bonds are bought at a discount from their face value. The investor has locked in a rate of return because the maturity value of the bond is known at the time of purchase. A corporate zero-coupon bond pays no interest each year but is taxed as if it did.

9. **B.** Customers buy stock at the asked price, which means that market makers must sell at the asked price. Customers sell to market makers at the bid price, which is the price that a market maker will pay to buy the customer's stock. Remember that customers buy at the ask. Then remember that market makers do the opposite and easily solve questions like this.

10. **A.** A warrant allows an investor a long-term right to buy an issuer's stock. The expiration period of a warrant is generally 5 years. Long calls are options that give the holder the right to buy stock, but typically expire within 9 months. Preemptive rights are short-term rights to buy stock and usually expire within 30–45 days. Long puts are rights to sell.

11. **C.** Statutory voting allows investors 1 vote for each share of stock they own per open-director position. This investor has 100 votes for each of the 5 voting positions on the board of directors.

12. **B.** Money market securities are high grade and liquid debt securities with less than 1 year to maturity. Preferred stock and ADRs are equity securities. The T-bond with less than 1 year to maturity and a negotiable CD are money market instruments.

13. **D.** General obligation bonds are backed by the full faith and credit (and taxing authority) of the issuing municipality. The interest that is paid on municipal bonds is exempt from taxation at the federal level. Municipal revenue bonds are backed by revenues generated from the use of the facility. Municipal bonds are issued by government levels other than the federal government.

14. **D.** The near-term call would mean that no matter how attractive the bond's other features, the client may not have very long to enjoy them.

15. **A.** Preferred stock is an equity instrument because it represents an ownership interest in a corporation. However, because of its fixed dividend rate, the price of preferred stock (like the price of bonds) is directly influenced by changes in interest rates. Debt securities and preferred stock are senior to common stock in corporate dissolutions.

16. **D.** CMOs are financial institution-sponsored mortgage pools and are not backed by the US government. Like other corporate instruments, they are subject to taxation at all levels. Regulations prohibit CMOs from including municipal issues.

17. **D.** Government National Mortgage Association (GNMA) pass-through certificates are directly backed by the federal treasury. Each monthly check is part interest, part principal. The minimum purchase at issue is $25,000 and the interest portion of the check is taxable at both the federal and the state level.

18. **D.** To calculate the number of shares that a bond is convertible into, divide the bond's par value ($1,000) by the conversion price ($25). Because the bond was issued by the XYZ Corporation, this bond is convertible into 40 shares of XYZ Corporation's common stock.

19. **A.** If domestic currency is strong, then foreign currencies are weak by comparison and vice versa. Importers, who order foreign goods, would like those goods to be priced as low as possible, which is another way of saying they would like the foreign currency to be weak and their own currency to be strong.

20. **B.** If the Swiss franc falls in value relative to the US dollar, goods produced by the United States become more expensive in Switzerland. Goods produced in Switzerland become less expensive in the United States.

QUICK QUIZ ANSWERS

Quick Quiz 1.1

1. **C.**

2. **D.**

3. **A.**

4. **B.**

Quick Quiz 1.2

1. **B.**

2. **D.**

3. **C.**

4. **A.**

Quick Quiz 1.3

1. **C.** Owning either common or preferred stocks represents ownership (or equity) in a corporation. The other two choices represent debt instruments. Clients purchasing corporate or mortgage bonds are considered lenders, not owners.

2. **C.** Treasury stock is stock a corporation has issued but subsequently repurchased from investors in the secondary market. The corporation can either reissue the stock at a later date or retire it. Stock that has been repurchased by the corporation has no voting rights and is not entitled to any declared dividends.

3. **B.** Preemptive rights enable stockholders to maintain their proportionate ownership when the corporation wants to issue more stock. If a stockholder owns 5% of the outstanding stock and the corporation wants to issue more stock, the stockholder has the right to purchase enough of the new shares to maintain a 5% ownership position in the company.

4. **B.** With cumulative voting rights, this investor may cast 500 votes for the 5 directors in any way the investor chooses.

5. **D.** The cumulative method of voting, like the statutory, gives an investor 1 vote per share owned, times the number of directorships to be elected. For instance, if an investor owns 100 stock shares, and there are 5 directorships to be elected, the investor will have a total of 500 votes. Under cumulative voting, however, the stockholder may cast all of his votes for 1 candidate, thereby giving the small investor more voting power.

6. **D.** The basic formula of the balance sheet is assets = liabilities + net worth. By the same algebra, a company's shareholder equity can be calculated as such: net worth = assets − liabilities.

7. **C.** Although stocks often pay regular dividends, they are not guaranteed. If the board decides the company cannot afford to pay a dividend this quarter, no dividend will be paid.

Quick Quiz 1.4

1. **C.** Because convertible preferred shares can be exchanged for common shares, its price can be closely linked to the price of the issuer's common and is less influenced by changes in interest rates.

Quick Quiz 1.5

1. **D.**

2. **A.**

3. **B.**

4. **C.**

Quick Quiz 1.6

1. **D.**   ADRs are tradable securities issued by banks, with the receipt's value based on the underlying foreign securities held by the bank.

2. **C.**   An ADR represents ownership of a foreign corporation. The ADR holder receives a share of the dividends and capital appreciation (or capital loss) when sold.

Quick Quiz 1.7

1. **B.**   Warrants are issued with long-term maturities. They may be used as sweeteners in an offering of the issuer's preferred stock or bonds. Warrants are not offered only to current shareholders. The exercise price of a warrant is always above the market price of the stock at the time of issue.

2. **B.**   Preferred stockholders have no right to maintain a percentage of ownership when new shares are issued (no preemptive rights). However, they do receive preference in dividend payment and company liquidation.

Quick Quiz 1.8

1. **C.**   The call writer expects the stock to decrease in price, and that the call will therefore not be exercised. This permits him to keep the premium. The put buyer thinks the stock will go down in price, and thus reserves to himself the right to sell it at the higher put strike price.

2. **B.**   The put seller has sold another investor the right to sell stock to him at the put strike price. Thus, if the put is exercised, he will be obliged to buy the stock.

3. **D.**   The call seller is obliged to sell stock, and the put seller is obliged to buy stock, should the option be exercised.

Quick Quiz 1.9

1. **D.**
2. **A.**
3. **C.**
4. **B.**

Quick Quiz 1.10

1. **B.**
2. **A.**
3. **B.**
4. **C.**
5. **B.**
6. **A.**
7. **C.**
8. **E.**
9. **A.**
10. **D.**
11. **C.**
12. **B.**

Quick Quiz 1.11

1. **A.**   Call protection is most valuable to a purchaser when interest rates are falling. Bonds tend to be called in a falling interest rate environment.

2. **B.**   Annual interest ÷ current market price = current yield.

3. **B.**   The customer purchased the 5% bond when it was yielding 6%, therefore at a discount. The customer sold the bond when other bonds of like kind, quality, and maturity were yielding 4%. The bond is now at a premium because the 5% coupon is attractive to other investors. The customer, therefore, made a capital gain on the investment.

4. **B.**   With the same nominal yield, the discount bonds will generate higher yields. In addition to the interest payments received on an ongoing basis, the investor receives the amount of the discount at maturity.

5. **B.**   Long-term bonds are not as liquid as short-term obligations.

6. **B.** Long-term debt prices fluctuate more than short-term debt prices as interest rates rise and fall. Common stock prices are not directly affected by interest rates.

Quick Quiz 1.12

1. **D.**

2. **C.**

3. **B.**

4. **A.**

5. **C.**

6. **D.**

7. **A.**

8. **B.**

9. **A.** The order in a liquidation is as follows: wages, the IRS (and other government agencies), secured debt holders, unsecured debt holders, general creditors (in most cases, unsecured debt holders are given a slight priority over all but the largest creditors), holders of subordinated debt, preferred stockholders, and then common stockholders.

10. **D.** Ogden 5s means 5% bonds. Five percent of $1,000 par = $50 interest per bond annually. For 50 bonds, the annual interest is $2,500.

11. **A.** Coupon rates are not higher; they are lower because of the value of the conversion feature. The bondholders are creditors, and if the stock price falls, the conversion feature will not influence the bond's price.

12. **B.** The calculations are: $1,000 ÷ $20 = 50 shares for one bond. $800 bond price ÷ 50 shares = $16 parity price.

13. **B.** $1,000 par ÷ $125 conversion price = 8 shares per bond.

Quick Quiz 1.13

1. **D.**

2. **A.**

3. **B.**

4. **C.**

5. **A.** CMOs are collateralized by mortgages on real estate. They do not own the underlying real estate, so they are not considered to be backed by it.

6. **B.** Collateralized mortgage obligations are a type of mortgage-backed security. A CMO issue is divided into several tranches, which set priorities for payments of principal and interest.

7. **C.** Unlike CMOs, which are uniformly highly rated, REMICs contain several classes of debt.

Quick Quiz 1.14

1. **F.** Municipal securities are issued by state and local governments.

2. **T.** Capital gains from the profitable sale of municipal securities are not exempt from taxation.

3. **F.** Revenue bonds are self-supporting and are backed by income from the use of the facility. GOs are backed by taxes.

4. **T.** The interest on IDRs is typically taxable at the federal level.

5. **T.** Bonds issued by school, road, and park districts are examples of GOs.

6. **T.** Municipals generally pay less interest than corporate issuers.

Quick Quiz 1.15

1. **D.** Newly issued Treasury bonds have a minimum maturity of 10 years. Money market instruments have a maximum maturity of one year.

2. **C.** Commercial paper is normally issued for a maximum period of 270 days.

3. **B.** Negotiable certificates of deposit are issued primarily by banks and are backed by, or guaranteed, by the issuing bank.

4. **C.** Commercial paper is a short-term promissory note issued by a corporation.

5. **B.** Bankers' acceptances are used in international trade to finance imports and exports. Euro-dollars and ADRs are not money market instruments.

Quick Quiz 1.16

1. **B.** When the Federal Open Market Committee purchases T-bills in the open market, it pays for the transaction by increasing the reserve accounts of member banks, the net effect of which increases the total money supply and signals a period of relatively easier credit conditions. Easier credit means interest rates will decline and the price of existing bonds will rise.

2. **D.** Increased foreign investment in the United States (I) would raise the US dollar's relative value. A decrease in US interest rates (IV) would chase money out of the United States and increase the foreign currency's relative value.

3. **A.** Disintermediation is the flow of deposits out of banks and savings and loans into alternative, higher paying investments. It occurs when money is tight and interest rates are high because these alternative investments may then offer higher yields than S&Ls and banks. However, when interest rates are low, investors may prefer to keep their money in banks and S&Ls.

4. **D.** To curb inflation, the Fed can sell securities in the open market, thus changing the amount of US government debt institutions hold. It can also raise the reserve requirements, discount rate, or margin requirements. The Fed has no control over taxes, which are raised or lowered by Congress.

5. **B.** The federal funds rate reflects the rate charged by member banks lending funds to member banks that need to borrow funds overnight to meet reserve requirements.

6. **B.** The federal funds rate is the interest rate that banks with excess reserves charge other banks that are associated with the Federal Reserve System and that need overnight loans to meet reserve requirements. Because the federal funds rate changes daily, it is the most sensitive indicator of interest rate direction.

2

Product Information: Investment Company Securities and Variable Contracts

Investment company products offer a diversified portfolio of securities, professional management, and reduced transaction costs. Because of these attractive features, they are very popular with investors. Mutual funds, one form of investment company, currently manage trillions of dollars for investors.

Insurance companies also offer products, known as variable contracts, that are classified as securities. Variable annuities are a popular retirement instrument that may invest in mutual funds or may invest directly in individual securities for the purpose of funding a customer's retirement. Variable life insurance, a comparatively new product, permits a customer to assume some of the investment risk inherent in insurance coverage in order to obtain inflation protection for his contract's death benefit.

The Series 6 exam will include 26 questions on the topics covered in this Unit. ■

When you have completed this Unit, you should be able to:

- **list** the three types of investment companies defined by the Investment Company Act of 1940;

- **compare** the characteristics of open- and closed-end management companies;

- **recognize** the situations that require a majority vote of outstanding shares;

- **identify** five significant roles in the operation of an investment company;

- **describe** unique features and benefits of mutual fund shares;

- **explain** contractual plans under the Investment Company Act of 1940 and the Investment Company Act Amendments of 1970;

- **list** the similarities between variable annuities and mutual funds;

- **explain** the phases of the annuity contract;

- **determine** fluctuations in monthly payouts based on separate account performance compared to AIR;

- **differentiate** the features of traditional whole life, variable life, and universal variable life policies; and

- **assess** the impact of AIR on variable life death benefit and cash value accumulation.

INVESTMENT COMPANY OFFERINGS

An **investment company** is a corporation or trust that pools investors' money and then invests that money in securities on their behalf. By investing these pooled funds as a single large account jointly owned by every investor in a company, the investment company management attempts to invest and manage funds for people more efficiently than the individual investors could themselves. Additionally, it is expected that a professional money manager should be able to outperform the average investor in the market.

INVESTMENT COMPANY PURPOSE

Like corporate issuers, investment companies raise capital by selling shares to the public. Investment companies must abide by the same registration and prospectus requirements imposed by the Securities Act of 1933 on every other issuer. Investment companies are subject to regulations regarding how their shares are sold to the public, and they are regulated by the **Investment Company Act of 1940**.

TYPES OF INVESTMENT COMPANIES

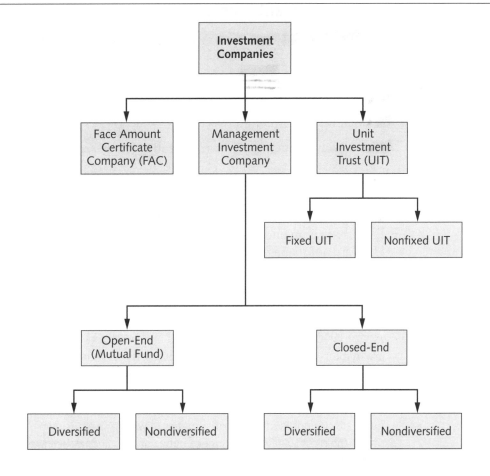

The Investment Company Act of 1940 classifies investment companies into three broad types: face-amount certificate companies (FACs), unit investment trusts (UITs), and management investment companies.

Face-Amount Certificate Companies (FACs)

A **face-amount certificate (FAC)** is a contract between an investor and an issuer in which the issuer guarantees payment of a stated (face amount) sum to the investor at some set date in the future. In return for this future payment, the investor agrees to pay the issuer a set amount of money either as a lump sum or in periodic installments. If the investor pays for the certificate in a lump sum, the investment is known as a **fully-paid face-amount certificate**.

Issuers of these investments are **face-amount certificate companies**. Very few face-amount certificate companies operate today because tax law changes have eliminated their tax advantages.

TEST TOPIC ALERT   You will see no more than one or two questions involving face-amount certificate companies on the Series 6 exam. Face-amount certificate companies:

■ pay a fixed rate of return;

■ do not trade in the secondary market but are redeemed by the issuer; and

■ are classified as investment companies.

Unit Investment Trusts (UITs)

A **unit investment trust (UIT)** is an investment company organized under a trust indenture. A UIT functions as a holding company for its investors. Unit investment trusts do not:

■ have boards of directors;

■ employ investment advisers; or

■ actively manage their own portfolios (trade securities).

UIT managers typically purchase other investment company shares or government and municipal bonds. They then sell **redeemable shares,** also known as **units** or **shares of beneficial interest**, in their portfolio of securities. Each share is an undivided interest in the entire underlying portfolio. Because UITs are not managed, all proceeds must be distributed when any securities in the portfolio are liquidated.

A UIT may be fixed or nonfixed. A **fixed UIT** typically purchases a portfolio of bonds and terminates when the bonds in the portfolio mature. A **nonfixed UIT** purchases shares of an underlying mutual fund. Under the Investment Company Act of 1940, the trustees of both fixed and nonfixed UITs must maintain secondary markets in the units to guarantee liquidity to shareholders.

TAKE NOTE   A UIT is very similar to a mutual fund—up to a point. Both fixed UITs and mutual funds are comprised of a pool of securities in which investors own a proportionate share. The most significant difference between UITs and mutual funds is that mutual funds actively trade their portfolios and a portfolio manager gets paid a fee to meet the objectives of the fund.

UIT portfolios usually are not traded; they are fixed trusts. The advantage to the investor is that they own a diversified interest but do not pay a management fee—the biggest expense of mutual fund ownership. The downside is that the UIT portfolio is not traded in response to market conditions.

TEST TOPIC ALERT

- ■ UITs are not actively managed; there is no board of directors or investment adviser.

- ■ UIT shares (units) are not traded in the secondary market; they must be redeemed by the trust.

- ■ UITs are investment companies as defined under the Investment Company Act of 1940.

Management Investment Companies

The most familiar type of investment company is the **management investment company**, which actively manages a securities portfolio to achieve a stated investment objective. A management investment company is either closed-end or open-end. Both closed- and open-end companies sell shares to the public in an initial public offering; the primary difference between them is that a closed-end company's initial offering of shares is limited (it closes after a set number of shares have been sold) and an open-end company is perpetually offering new shares to the public (it is continually open to new investors).

Closed-End Investment Companies

A **closed-end investment company** will raise capital for its portfolio by conducting a common stock offering, much like any other publicly traded company that raises capital to invest in its business. In the initial offering, the company registers a fixed number of shares with the SEC and offers them to the public with a prospectus for a limited time through underwriters. Once all the shares have been sold, the fund is closed to new investors. Many times, a fund elects to be a closed-end company because the sector in which it intends to invest has a limited amount of securities available. Closed-end investment companies may also issue bonds and preferred stock or exchange-traded funds (ETFs).

Closed-end investment companies are often called **publicly traded funds**. After the stock is sold in the initial offering, anyone can buy or sell shares in the secondary market (i.e., on an exchange or OTC) in transactions between private investors. Supply and demand determine the **bid price** (price at which an investor can sell) and the **ask price** (price at which an investor can buy). Closed-end fund shares may trade above (at a premium to) or below (at a discount to) the shares' net asset value (NAV).

EXAMPLE

The ABC New York Municipal Bond Fund issued 25 million shares of stock priced at $20 per share, raising a total of $500 million. When all of the shares were sold, the fund closed to new investors. The fund manager then invested the proceeds of the offering in tax-exempt bonds issued by the state of New York. Although the shares have a net asset value of about $20 per share, an investor that decides to sell may receive $19 per share (possibly more or less) when the shares trade at a discount to their net asset value.

Open-End Investment Companies

Unlike a closed-end fund, an **open-end investment company (mutual fund)** does not specify the exact number of shares it intends to issue but registers an open offering with the SEC. With this registration type they can raise an unlimited amount of investment capital by continuously issuing new shares. Conversely, when investors want to sell their holdings in a mutual fund, the fund itself redeems those shares at their current NAV, which reduces the total value of the fund by the value of the shares redeemed. The offering of new shares never closes because the number of shares the company can offer is unlimited.

EXAMPLE   The ABC Growth & Income Fund was established in 1972. In its first month, the fund sold 1 million shares to the public. Because of the fund's investment performance, investors have continued to invest with the fund and, over 30 years later, the fund has 2 billion shares outstanding. If the fund shares have a net asset value of $20 per share (for a total fund value of $40 billion) and an investor redeems 1,000 shares, it will reduce the total value of the fund by $20,000 and the total shares outstanding by 1,000. There is no effect on the NAV per share for the remaining shareholders.

Any person who wants to invest in the company buys shares directly from the company or its underwriters at the **public offering price (POP)**. A mutual fund's POP is the net asset value (NAV) per share plus a sales charge. A mutual fund's NAV is calculated by deducting the fund's liabilities from its total assets. NAV per share is calculated by dividing the fund's NAV by the number of shares outstanding.

The shares an open-end investment company sells are **redeemable securities**. When an investor sells shares, the company redeems them at NAV. For each share redeemed, the company sends the investor money for the proportionate share of the company's net assets. Therefore, a mutual fund's capital shrinks when investors redeem shares but the NAV per share does not fall.

Comparison of Open-End and Closed-End Investment Companies

	Open-End	Closed-End
Capitalization	Unlimited; continuous offering of shares	Fixed; single offering of shares
Issues	Common stock only; no debt securities; permitted to borrow	May issue common, preferred, and debt securities
Shares	Full or fractional	Full only
Offerings and Trading	Sold and redeemed by the fund only; continuous primary offering; must redeem shares	Initial primary offering; secondary trading OTC or on an exchange; does not redeem shares
Pricing	NAV + sales charge; selling price determined by formula in the prospectus	CMV + commission; price determined by supply and demand
Shareholder Rights	Dividends (when declared); voting	Dividends (when declared); voting; preemptive
Ex-Date	Set by BOD	Set by the exchange or NASD

TAKE NOTE   You are likely to see 3 to 4 questions on the Series 6 exam that require understanding the features of a closed-end company. Think in terms of what would be true for any corporate security and examine the following chart.

Where do shares of closed-end companies trade?		In the secondary market
What types of securities can closed-end companies issue?		Common stock, preferred stock, and bonds
Can fractional shares be purchased?	Like corporations:	Only full shares can be purchased
When must a prospectus be used?		Only in the IPO (no prospectus is given when the shares are purchased in a secondary market transaction)

NOT INVESTMENT COMPANIES

Hedge Funds. These funds are a type of equity security with similarities to a mutual fund (we will study mutual funds in detail in this Unit). The difference is that the hedge fund does not register with the SEC, and it requires that its buyers be accredited investors. Such funds are free to adopt far riskier investment policies than those open to ordinary mutual funds, such as arbitrage strategies and massive short positions during bearish markets. Hedge funds are indirectly available to ordinary investors through mutual funds called funds of hedge funds.

Exchange-Traded Funds (ETFs). This type of fund, also an equity security, invests in a specific group of stocks in deliberate mimicry of a particular index, such as the S&P 500. In this way, an ETF is similar to an index mutual fund. The difference is that the exchange-traded fund trades like a stock on the floor of an exchange and, in this way, is similar to a closed-end investment company. The investor can take advantage of price changes that are due to the market, rather than just the underlying value of the stocks in the portfolio. Expenses tend to be lower than those of mutual funds as well because the charge for buys and sells is simply the commission one pays for any trade.

QUICK QUIZ 2.1   Determine whether each statement describes an open-end or a closed-end company. Write **O** for open-end and **C** for closed-end.

_C_ 1. Trades in the secondary market

_O_ 2. Investors may purchase fractional shares

_C_ 3. Can issue common stock, preferred stock, and bonds

_C_   4.   Are sold with prospectus during IPO only

_C_   5.   Issues a fixed number of shares

_O_   6.   Ex-date is set by the board of directors

_O_   7.   Do not trade in the secondary market; shares are redeemable

_C_   8.   Price is set by supply and demand

_O_   9.   Usually called mutual funds

_O_   10. Selling price usually includes a sales charge

Quick Quiz answers can be found at the end of the Unit.

Diversified and Nondiversified

Diversification provides risk management that makes mutual funds popular with many investors. However, not all investment companies feature diversified portfolios.

Diversified

Under the Investment Company Act of 1940 a **diversified investment company** is one that meets the requirements of the 75-5-10 test:

■   At least 75% of the fund's total assets must be invested in securities issued by companies other than the investment company itself or its affiliates.

■   The 75% must be invested in such a way that:

— no more than 5% of the fund's total assets are invested in the securities of any one issuer, and

— the fund may not own more than 10% of the outstanding voting securities of any one issuer.

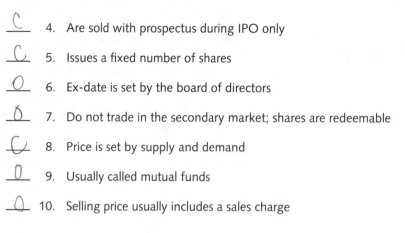

TEST TOPIC ALERT   Remember, for testing purposes, the 5% and 10% limitations are part of the 75% invested. There are no conditions attached to the remaining 25%.

Nondiversified

A **nondiversified investment company** does not meet the 75-5-10 test. An investment company that specializes in one industry is not necessarily a nondiversified company. Some investment companies choose to concentrate their assets in an industry or a geographic area, such as health care stocks, technology stocks, or South American stocks; these are known as **specialized funds** or **sector fund**s.

An investment company that invests in a single industry can still be considered diversified provided it meets the 75-5-10 test.

TEST TOPIC ALERT

Both open- and closed-end companies can be diversified or nondiversified.

QUICK QUIZ 2.2

1. Which of the following are covered under the Investment Company Act of 1940?

    I.   Unit investment trusts
    II. Face-amount companies
    III. Open-end management companies
    IV. Closed-end management companies

    A. I and II
    B. I and III
    C. II and IV
    D. I, II, III and IV

2. Which of the following investment companies has no provision for redemption of outstanding shares?

    A. Open-end company
    B. Closed-end company
    C. Unit investment trust
    D. Mutual fund

3. Which of the following statements regarding the investment practices of diversified management companies are TRUE?

    I.   They can own no more than 5% of the voting stock of a single company.
    II. No more than 5% of their assets are invested in any one company.
    III. They can own no more than 10% of the voting stock of any one company.
    IV. If they own more than 25% of a target company, they do not vote the stock.

    A. I and II
    B. I and III
    C. II and III
    D. III and IV

4. According to the Investment Company Act of 1940, an investment company with a fixed portfolio, redeemable shares, and no management fee is a

    A. face-amount certificate company
    B. management company
    C. unit investment trust
    D. closed-end investment company

5. Which of the following statements are TRUE regarding open-end, but not closed-end, investment companies?

    I.   They can make continuous offerings of shares provided the original registration statement and prospectus are periodically updated.
    II. They can be listed on registered national exchanges.
    III. They always redeem their shares.
    IV. They can issue only common stock.

    A. I and II
    B. I and III
    C. I, III and IV
    D. II and IV

Terms and Concepts Checklist

✓	✓
☐ Investment company	☐ Unit, share
☐ Face amount certificate company	☐ Continuous primary offering
☐ Unit investment trust	☐ Public offering price
☐ Fixed trust	☐ Exchange traded fund
☐ Management company	☐ Hedge fund
☐ Open-end investment company	☐ 75-5-10 test
☐ Closed-end investment company	☐ Diversified
	☐ Nondiversified

INVESTMENT COMPANY REGISTRATION

A company must register with the SEC as an investment company if:

■ the company is in the business of investing in, reinvesting in, owning, holding, or trading securities; or

■ 40% or more of the company's assets are invested in securities (government securities and securities of majority-owned subsidiaries are not used in calculating the 40% limitation).

A company must meet certain minimum requirements before it may register as an investment company with the SEC. An investment company cannot issue securities to the public unless it has:

■ private capitalization (**seed money**) of at least $100,000 of net assets;

■ 100 investors; and

■ clearly defined investment objectives.

If the investment company does not have 100 shareholders and $100,000 in net assets, it can still register a public offering with the SEC if it can meet these requirements within 90 days of registration.

The company must clearly define an investment objective under which it plans to operate. Once defined, the objective may be changed only by a majority vote of the company's outstanding shares.

Open-End Companies

The Act of 1940 requires open-end companies to:

■ issue no more than one class of security; and

■ maintain a minimum asset-to-debt ratio of 300%.

Because open-end investment companies may issue only one class of security (common stock), they may borrow from banks provided their asset-to-debt ratio is not less than 3:1—that is, debt coverage by assets of at least 300%, or no more than one-third of assets from borrowed money.

TAKE NOTE

Mutual funds may borrow money from banks but not from investors. Borrowing money from investors is like issuing bonds, and only closed-end companies may issue bonds. When borrowing money from the bank, the fund must have at least $3 of total assets for every $1 borrowed.

TEST TOPIC ALERT

Be cautious of questions that ask about the asset-to-debt ratio described above. If a question specifically asks about the *asset-to-debt ratio,* the answer to the question is 3:1, or 300%. But, if it asks about the *debt-to-asset ratio*, the correct answer would be 1:3, or 33%.

SEC REGISTRATION AND PUBLIC OFFERING REQUIREMENTS

Investment companies must file registration statements with the SEC, provide full disclosure, and generally follow the same public offering procedures required of other corporations when issuing securities. In filing for registration, an investment company must identify:

■ the type of management investment company it intends to be (e.g., open- or closed-end);

■ plans the company has to raise money by borrowing;

■ the company's intention, if any, to concentrate its investments in a single industry;

■ plans for investing in real estate or commodities;

■ conditions under which investment policies may be changed by a vote of the shares;

■ the full name and address of each affiliated person; and

■ a description of the business experience of each officer and director during the preceding five years.

Because an investment company is a corporate issuer, it is subject to the Act of 1933's full and fair disclosure rules, just like any other corporation. A registration statement, which includes the prospectus, must be filed with the SEC before securities may be sold to the public.

In filing for registration, an investment company must identify the overall investment intentions of the fund as well as background information on affiliated persons, officers, and directors.

Continuous Public Offering Securities

The SEC treats the sale of open-end investment company shares as a continuous public offering of shares, which means all sales must be accompanied by a prospectus. The financial information (**statements**) in the prospectus must be current. A prospectus in use for more than nine months cannot contain information more than 16 months old.

Three important points regarding the investment company prospectus:

- Mutual funds must always be sold with a prospectus because they are continuous primary offerings. New securities must always be sold with a prospectus.

- Closed-end funds must be sold with a prospectus in their IPO only. When they are trading in the secondary market, closed-end funds need not be sold with a prospectus.

- Financial information in a prospectus in use for more than nine months can be no more than 16 months old. The Act of 1933 requires that information disclosed to an investor is reasonably current.

Purchasing Mutual Fund Shares on Margin

Because a mutual fund is considered a continuous primary offering, Regulation T of the Federal Reserve Board prohibits the purchase of mutual fund shares on margin. **Margin** is the use of money borrowed from a bank through a brokerage firm to purchase securities. Mutual fund shares may be used as collateral in a margin account, however, only if they have been held fully paid for more than 30 days.

In margin accounts, investors borrow money from banks through broker/dealers to purchase securities. Broker/dealers acquire funds to loan by pledging customer securities to the bank as collateral. Mutual funds may be used in this way but cannot be purchased using borrowed funds. Mutual funds are considered new issues, and rules prohibit the purchase of new issues on margin.

REGISTRATION OF INVESTMENT COMPANY SECURITIES

After filing as an investment company under the Act of 1940, the investment company must register with the SEC any securities it intends to sell. The registration of shares takes place under the Securities Act of 1933.

Registration Statement and Prospectus

The registration statement an investment company must file consists of two parts. **Part 1** is the prospectus that must be furnished to every person to whom the company offers the securities. Part 1 is also called an **N1-A prospectus** or a **summary prospectus**.

Part 2 is the document containing information that need not be furnished to every purchaser but must be made available for public inspection. Part 2 is called the **statement of additional information (SAI)**.

The prospectus must contain any disclosure that the SEC requires. The fact that all publicly issued securities must be registered with the SEC does not mean that the SEC in any way approves the securities. For that reason, every prospectus must contain a disclaimer similar to the following on its front cover:

These securities have not been approved or disapproved by the Securities and Exchange Commission nor has the Commission passed on the accuracy or adequacy of this prospectus. No state has approved or disapproved this offering. Any representation to the contrary is a criminal offense.

TAKE NOTE	Investors who purchase mutual funds must receive a prospectus no later than the time of solicitation. They do not automatically receive the SAI; this supplementary information is available upon request from the fund.

TEST TOPIC ALERT	As with any other security, the SEC does not approve mutual funds for sale; they merely acknowledge that they can be released for sale as they contain sufficient disclosure for an investor to make an informed investment decision.

RESTRICTIONS ON OPERATIONS

The SEC prohibits a mutual fund from engaging in the following activities unless the fund meets stringent disclosure and financial requirements:

- Purchasing securities on margin

- Selling securities short

- Participating in joint investment or trading accounts

- Acting as distributor of its own securities (except through an underwriter)

- Selling uncovered options

The fund must specifically disclose these activities, and the extent to which it plans to engage in these activities, in its prospectus.

TAKE NOTE

Short selling is a securities industry practice that involves selling shares that are not owned. Investors borrow shares from the broker/dealer by putting up collateral in a margin account. The borrowed shares are sold with the hope that their market price will fall. If the market price does fall, the short seller can buy back the borrowed shares at a lower price to repay the broker/dealer. The difference in the price at which the shares are sold and the lower price at which they are bought to repay the broker/dealer is the investor's profit. But if the price goes up, the potential for loss is unlimited.

Investors usually buy low and sell high for a profit; a short sale involves the same steps in a different order. In a short sale, investors sell high and buy low.

TEST TOPIC ALERT

The exam may ask which mutual fund trading activities may be prohibited by the SEC. The correct answer choices include margin account trading, short selling, and naked (uncovered) options trading strategies. Covered option transactions are permissible, but naked strategies are considered too risky.

Shareholder Right to Vote

Before any change can be made to a fund's published bylaws or objectives, shareholder approval is mandatory. In voting matters, it is the majority of shares voted for or against a proposition that counts, not the majority of people voting. Thus, one shareholder holding 51% of all the shares outstanding can determine a vote's outcome.

The changes that require a majority vote of the shares outstanding include:

- issuing or underwriting other securities;

- purchasing or underwriting real estate;

- making loans;

- changing subclassification (e.g., from open-end to closed-end or from diversified to nondiversified);

- changing sales load policy (e.g., from a no-load fund to a load fund);

- changing the nature of the business (e.g., ceasing business as an investment company);

- changing investment policy (e.g., from income to growth or from bonds to small capitalization stocks); and

- changes in fees or auditors.

In addition to the right to vote on these items, shareholders retain all rights that stockholders normally possess.

TEST TOPIC ALERT   When answering questions, discern between shares voting and shareholders voting in mutual fund matters. A majority vote of the outstanding shares is required to approve such actions as sales load or investment company objectives changes.

QUICK QUIZ 2.3   True or False?

_F_   1. Mutual funds are generally prohibited from using covered options strategies.   F

_F_   2. A majority vote of the outstanding shareholders is required to change the   T
investment objectives of a mutual fund.

_F_   3. Mutual fund shares may be purchased on margin but cannot be used as   F
collateral in margin accounts.

_T_   4. Open-end companies must have 100 shareholders and $100,000 of assets   T
before they can operate as an investment company.

_T_   5. Mutual funds are required to file registration statements with the SEC   T
before shares are sold to the public.

_F_   6. Mutual funds make continuous secondary offerings of securities.   F

_F_   7. Open-end investment companies must maintain a 3:1 debt-to-asset ratio.   F

_F_   8. Closed-end companies are generally considered mutual funds.   F

Terms and Concepts Checklist

✓   ✓

☐ Prospectus   ☐ Affiliated person
☐ Registration statement, N1A   ☐ Shareholder voting rights
   prospectus, summary prospectus   ☐ Purchase on margin
☐ Statement of additional information   ☐ Short sale
   (SAI)   ☐ Uncovered call

MANAGEMENT OF INVESTMENT COMPANIES

Five parties work together to help an investment company operate: a board of directors, an investment adviser, a custodian, a transfer agent, and an underwriter.

BOARD OF DIRECTORS

Like publicly owned corporations in general, a management investment company has a CEO, a team of officers, and a board of directors (BOD) to serve the interests of its investors. The officers and directors deal with policy and administrative matters. They do not manage the investment portfolio. As with other types of corporations, the shareholders of an investment company elect the BOD to make decisions and oversee operations.

A management investment company's board of directors pulls together the different parts of a mutual fund. The BOD:

- defines the type of funds to offer (e.g., growth, income, sector);

- defines the fund's objective; and

- approves/hires the transfer agent, custodian, and investment adviser.

Organizational Structure of a Fund

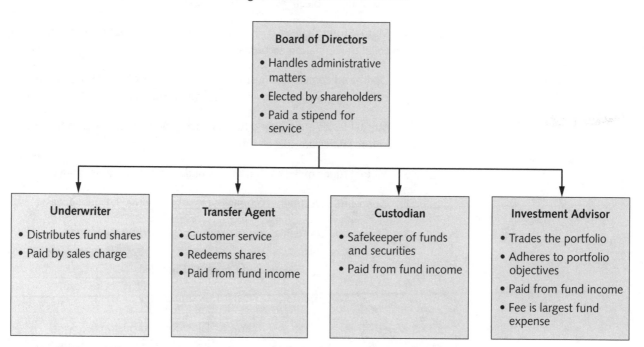

The Act of 1940 restricts who may sit on an investment company's board of directors. At least 40% of the directors must be independent or noninterested persons. **Noninterested persons** are only connected with the investment company in their capacity as director. A noninterested person is not connected with the investment company's investment adviser, transfer agent, or custodian bank. This means that no more than 60% of the board members may be interested persons, including attorneys on retainer, accountants, and any persons employed in similar capacities with the company.

Also, no individual who has been convicted of a felony of any type or a misdemeanor involving the securities industry may serve on a BOD, nor may anyone who has been either temporarily or permanently barred from acting as an underwriter, a broker, a dealer, or an investment company by any court.

INVESTMENT ADVISER

An investment company's BOD contracts with an **investment adviser** or portfolio manager to invest the cash and securities in the fund's portfolio, implement investment strategy, and manage the portfolio's day-to-day trading. Advisers must adhere to the objectives stated in the fund's prospectus and cannot transfer the responsibility of portfolio management to anyone else.

The investment adviser earns a management fee, which is paid from the fund's income. This fee is typically a set annual percentage of the portfolio asset value. In addition, an investment adviser who consistently outperforms a specified market performance benchmark can usually earn an incentive bonus.

An investment company cannot contract with an investment adviser who has been convicted of a securities-related felony unless the SEC has granted an exemption. In addition, an investment company cannot lend money to its investment adviser.

TEST TOPIC ALERT

Some facts and responsibilities of mutual fund's investment adviser:

- Trades the portfolio to meet the investment objectives, but cannot change them

- Is given an initial two-year contract by the BOD, but the contract is subject to annual approval by the BOD or a majority vote of outstanding shares

- Fee is the largest single management expense associated with fund ownership and is a percentage of the assets managed

- Must inform shareholders of the tax status of fund distributions

- Responsibilities cannot be transferred to a third party

- Must be registered with the SEC according to the Investment Advisers Act of 1940

CUSTODIAN

To protect investor assets, the Act of 1940 requires each investment company to place its securities in the custody of a bank or a stock exchange member broker/dealer. The bank or broker/dealer performs an important safekeeping role as **custodian** of the company's securities and cash and receives a fee for its services. Often, the custodian handles most of the investment company's clerical functions.

The custodian may, with the consent of the investment company, deposit the securities it is entrusted to hold in one of the systems for the central handling of securities established by the NASD or NYSE. These systems make it easier to transfer securities. Once securities are placed in the system, most transfers can be accomplished with a simple bookkeeping entry rather than physical delivery of the securities.

Once an investment company designates a custodian and transfers its assets into the custodian's safekeeping, the custodian must:

■ keep the investment company's assets physically segregated at all times;

■ allow withdrawal of assets only under SEC rules; and

■ restrict access to the account to certain officers and employees of the investment company.

TEST TOPIC ALERT

The custodian:

■ is generally a commercial bank;

■ is the safekeeper of the assets of the fund;

■ periodically audits the fund's assets to assure that they are properly accounted for; and

■ is paid a fee from the income of the fund.

TRANSFER AGENT (CUSTOMER OR SHAREHOLDER SERVICES AGENT)

The **transfer agent's** functions include:

■ issuing, redeeming, and cancelling fund shares;

■ handling name changes for the fund;

■ sending customer confirmations and fund distributions; and

■ recording outstanding shares for proper distribution.

The transfer agent can be the fund custodian or a separate service company. The fund pays the transfer agent a fee for its services.

TEST TOPIC ALERT

The transfer agent:

■ issues and redeems shares and handles other customer service work; and

■ is paid a fee from the income of the fund.

UNDERWRITER

A mutual fund's **underwriter**, often called the **sponsor** or **distributor**, is appointed by the board of directors and receives a fee for selling and marketing the fund shares to the public. The open-end investment company sells its shares to the underwriter at the current NAV, but only as the underwriter needs the shares to fill customer orders.

The underwriter is prohibited from maintaining an inventory of open-end company shares. The underwriter is compensated by adding a sales charge to the share's NAV when it makes sales to the public.

In general, a mutual fund may not act as its own distributor or underwriter. However, there is an exception to this rule for no-load and 12b-1 funds.

TEST TOPIC ALERT

In general, a fund cannot act as its own underwriter, but a fund may act as its own underwriter under Section 12b-1 of the Act of 1940. Many funds today follow this section. Section 12b-1 distribution fees are very common. Fund underwriters:

- are also called the sponsors or distributors;

- must be NASD member firms;

- cannot inventory mutual fund shares; and

- are compensated from the sales charge.

TAKE NOTE

All parties that work together in the operation of a mutual fund are paid from the income of the fund except the underwriter. The underwriter's compensation comes from sales charges.

INFORMATION DISTRIBUTED TO INVESTORS

Investors must be provided with specific information when purchasing and tracking mutual funds.

Prospectus

The **prospectus** must be distributed to an investor before or during any solicitation for sale. The prospectus contains information on the fund's objective, investment policies, sales charges and management expenses, and services offered. It also discloses one-, five-, and 10-year performance histories.

Statement of Additional Information (SAI)

While a prospectus is always sufficient for the purpose of selling shares, some investors may seek additional information not found in the prospectus. This additional information is not necessarily needed to make an informed investment decision but may be useful to the investor.

Mutual funds and closed-end funds are required to have a **statement of additional information (SAI)** available to investors upon request without charge. Investors can obtain a copy by calling or writing to the investment company, via a company Website, contacting a broker that sells the investment company shares, or contacting the SEC.

The SAI affords the fund an opportunity to have expanded discussions on matters such as the fund's history and policies. It will also typically contain the fund's consolidated financial statements, including:

- the balance sheet;

- a statement of operations;

■ an income statement; and

■ a portfolio list at the time the SAI was compiled.

Financial Reports

The Act of 1940 requires that shareholders receive financial reports at least semiannually. One of these must be an audited annual report. The reports must contain:

■ the investment company's balance sheet;

■ a valuation of all securities in the investment company's portfolio as of the date of the balance sheet (a portfolio list);

■ the investment company's income statement;

■ a complete statement of all compensation paid to the board of directors and to the advisory board; and

■ a statement of the total dollar amount of securities purchased and sold during the period.

In addition, the company must send a copy of its balance sheet to any shareholder who requests one in writing between semiannual reports.

Additional Disclosures

The SEC requires the fund to include the following in its prospectus or annual reports:

■ A discussion of factors and strategies that materially affected its performance during its most recently completed fiscal year

■ A line graph comparing its performance to that of an appropriate broad-based securities market index

■ The name(s) and title(s) of the person(s) primarily responsible for the fund portfolio's day-to-day management

---

TAKE NOTE

Keep the financial reports of the fund and shareholder account statements separate. The fund must distribute financial reports to shareholders semiannually. The annual report must be audited; semiannual reports can be unaudited.

Account statements are typically sent monthly to shareholders with active accounts, or quarterly to inactive accounts.

QUICK QUIZ 2.4

1. The custodian of a mutual fund usually
   A. approves changes in investment policy
   B. holds the cash and securities of the fund and performs clerical functions
   C. manages the fund
   D. markets the fund to the public

2. Investment company financial statements are sent to shareholders
   A. monthly
   B. quarterly
   C. semiannually
   D. annually

3. The role of a mutual fund's underwriter is to
   A. hold the fund's assets and perform clerical responsibilities
   B. determine when dividends should be distributed
   C. market shares
   D. provide investment advisory services

4. To change the name of a recently married shareholder on her registered shares of the fund, the shareholder should contact
   A. the custodian
   B. the transfer agent
   C. her registered representative
   D. the investment adviser

5. Typically, the largest single expense of a mutual fund is the
   A. custodian fee
   B. registration fee
   C. management fee
   D. brokerage fee

Terms and Concepts Checklist

✓

- ☐ Board of directors
- ☐ Interested persons
- ☐ Noninterested persons
- ☐ Financial reports
- ☐ Disclosures

✓

- ☐ Investment adviser
- ☐ Custodian
- ☐ Transfer agent
- ☐ Underwriter, sponsor, distributor
- ☐ Section 12b-1

CHARACTERISTICS OF MUTUAL FUNDS

A mutual fund is a pool of investors' money invested in various securities as determined by the fund's objective. Mutual funds have several unique characteristics as detailed in this section.

THE MUTUAL FUND CONCEPT

A mutual fund must redeem shares at the NAV. Unlike other securities, mutual funds offer guaranteed marketability: there is always a willing buyer for the shares. Mutual funds, then, are **redeemable securities**.

Each investor in the mutual fund's portfolio owns an undivided interest in the portfolio. All investors in an open-end fund are mutual participants; no one investor has a preferred status over any other investor because mutual funds issue only one class of common stock. Each investor shares mutually with other investors in gains and distributions derived from the investment company portfolio.

Each investor's participation in the fund's performance is based on the number of shares owned. Mutual fund shares may be purchased in either full or fractional units, unlike corporate stock, which may only be purchased in full units. Because mutual fund shares can be fractional, the investor can think in terms of dollars rather than number of shares owned.

An investment company portfolio is elastic. Money is constantly being invested or paid out when shares are redeemed. The mutual fund portfolio's value and holdings fluctuate as money is invested or redeemed and as the value of the securities in the portfolio rises and falls. The investor's account value fluctuates proportionately with the mutual fund portfolio's value.

TEST TOPIC ALERT

Other mutual fund characteristics include the following.

- A professional investment adviser manages the portfolio for investors.

- Mutual funds provide diversification by investing in different companies.

- A custodian holds a mutual fund's shares to ensure safekeeping.

- Most funds allow a minimum investment, often $500 or less, to open an account and they allow additional investment for as little as $25.

- An investment company may allow investments at reduced sales charges by offering breakpoints through larger deposits, a letter of intent, or rights of accumulation.

- An investor retains voting rights similar to those extended to common stockholders, such as the right to vote for changes in the BOD, approval of the investment adviser, changes in the fund's investment objective, changes in sales charges, and liquidation of the fund.

- Many funds offer automatic reinvestment of capital gains and dividend distributions without a sales charge.

- An investor can liquidate a portion of his holdings without disturbing the portfolio's balance or diversification.

- Tax liabilities for an investor are simplified because each year the fund distributes a 1099 form explaining taxability of distributions.

- A fund may offer various withdrawal plans that allow different payment methods at redemption.

■ Funds may offer reinstatement provisions that allow investors who withdraw funds to reinvest up to the amount withdrawn within 30 days with no new sales charge. This provision must be in the prospectus and is available one time only.

Comparison of Common Stock and Mutual Fund Shares

Common Stock	Mutual Fund Shares
Dividends from corporate profits	Dividends from net investment income
Price of stock determined by supply and demand	Price of share determined by forward pricing—the next price calculated as determined by the fund's pricing policy
Traded on an exchange or the OTC market	Purchased from and redeemed by the investment company; no secondary trading
Sold in full shares only	Can purchase full or fractional shares
First security issued by a public corporation	Only security issued by a mutual fund
Carries voting rights	Carries voting rights
May carry preemptive rights	Does not carry preemptive rights
Ex-dividend: 2 business days before record date as set by the SRO	Ex-dividend: typically the day after record date as set by the BOD

QUICK QUIZ 2.5

True or False?

___F___ 1. Mutual fund shareholders own a divided interest in the fund's portfolio.

___T___ 2. A mutual fund shareholder's account value fluctuates proportionately with the mutual fund's portfolio value.

___T___ 3. The mutual fund's investment adviser is offered a 2-year initial contract that is subject to annual approval.

___F___ 4. The transfer agent holds the mutual fund's assets for safekeeping.

___T___ 5. Mutual funds issue only one class of common stock.

___F___ 6. The reinstatement provision allows reinvestment of withdrawn funds within 60 days at no load.

___T___ 7. To open an account, most funds require a minimum investment.

___F___ 8. Mutual fund shareholders are allowed to vote on the frequency of dividend distributions.

PRICE OF MUTUAL FUND SHARES

Mutual fund shares are priced as a fraction of the net assets of the mutual fund company. To calculate the value of a fund share, start with the total assets of the fund and subtract out the liabilities:

Total Assets − Liabilities = Net Assets (NA) of the fund.

Then, divide the Net Assets of the fund by the number of shares outstanding to get the Net Asset Value per share (NAV) of the fund:

$$\frac{\text{Net Assets}}{\text{Shares Outstanding}} = \text{NAV}.$$

EXAMPLE

The ABC fund has total assets of $100 million and $5 million in liabilities. If it has 10 million shares outstanding, what is its NAV per share?

Net Assets: $100 million − $5 million = **$95 million**, and
NAV: $95 million ÷ 10 million shares outstanding = **$9.50 per share.**

The NAV of a fund share is the amount the investor receives upon redemption. It must be calculated at least once per business day. A typical fund calculates its NAV at 4:00 pm every business day, since that is when the New York Stock Exchange closes. The price that the customer receives is the next NAV calculated after receipt of his redemption request. The customer thus never knows exactly what he will get for his fund shares. This practice is known as **forward pricing**.

The purchase price of a fund share is called the **public offering price**, or **POP**. For the class of fund shares known as **front-end loaded** funds, it is simply the NAV, plus an additional charge called the **sales charge**. The sales charge is paid to the fund's underwriter as compensation for marketing the shares. As we will see, sales charges can be levied at the time of purchase (front-end load), at the time of redemption (back-end load), taken from the investor's account as an ongoing quarterly charge (level load or 12b-1 fee), or there can simply be no sales charge (no-load).

Changes in NAV

The NAV can change daily because of changes in the market value of a fund's portfolio. Any of the events in the following chart may change a fund's NAV per share.

Changes in NAV

Increases	Decreases	Does not change
Market value of securities increases	Market value of securities declines	Manager buys or sells securities
Fund receives dividends	Fund distributes dividends	Fund issues shares
Fund receives interest	Fund distributes capital gains	Fund redeems shares
Liabilities decline	Liabilities increase	

TEST TOPIC ALERT

Expect to see questions similar to the following:

Under which of the following circumstances does NAV per share decrease?

I. Portfolio securities decrease in value.
II. Dividends are distributed from the portfolio to shareholders.
III. New shares are issued.
IV. Shares are redeemed.

The correct choices are I and II. NAV per share decreases when the portfolio securities decline in value or when an income distribution is made from the portfolio to the shareholders. NAV does not change when shares are issued or redeemed. When shares are purchased, new money paid to the fund is offset by a greater number of shares outstanding; when shares are redeemed, the decrease in portfolio assets is offset by a decrease in shares outstanding.

SALES CHARGES

The NASD prohibits its members from assessing sales charges in excess of 8.5% of the POP on customers' mutual fund purchases. However, members selling mutual fund contractual plans may not assess sales charges in excess of 9% of the POP over the life of a fund. Mutual funds are free to charge lower rates and most do, provided they specify those rates in the prospectus.

TAKE NOTE

A mutual fund's maximum sales charge is based on the POP—not the NAV. The maximum load for mutual fund shares is 8.5% of the POP, unless sold through a contractual plan. The maximum sales charge for contractual plans is 9% of the POP over the life of the fund.

Most funds today charge somewhat lower sales loads. 5 to 6% is a typical maximum load for equity funds; 4 to 5% is a typical maximum load for bond funds.

Closed-End Funds

After the initial public offering, closed-end funds do not have a sales charge embedded in the share price. In the secondary market, an investor pays a brokerage commission (in an agency transaction) or pays a markup or markdown (in a principal transaction). Closed-end funds may trade at a premium (above) or discount (below) relative to their NAV.

Open-End Funds

All sales commissions and expenses for an open-end fund are embedded in the POP or other fees. Sales expenses include commissions for the managing underwriter, dealers, brokers, and registered representatives, as well as all advertising and sales literature expenses. Mutual fund distributors use three different methods to collect the fees for the sale of shares.

■ Front-end loads (difference between POP and NAV)

■ Back-end loads (contingent deferred sales loads)

■ 12b-1 sales charges (asset-based fees)

Front-End Loads

Front-end sales loads are the charges included in a fund's public offering price. The charges are added to the NAV at the time an investor buys shares. Front-end loads are the most common way of paying for the distribution services a fund's underwriter and broker/dealers provide.

EXAMPLE   An investor deposits $10,000 with a mutual fund that has a 5% front-end load. The 5% load amounts to $500, which is deducted from the invested amount. In this example, $9,500 is invested in the fund's portfolio on the investor's behalf.

Back-End Loads

A **back-end sales load (contingent deferred sales charge or CDSC)** or redemption fee is charged if and when an investor redeems mutual fund shares. The sales load, a declining percentage charge that is reduced annually (e.g., 6% the first year, 5% the second, 4% the third, etc.), is applied to the proceeds of any shares sold in that year. The back-end load is usually structured to drop to zero after an extended holding period, such as six or seven years. The sales load schedule is specified in a fund's prospectus.

TAKE NOTE   With a back-end load, when an investor deposits $10,000 in a mutual fund, the full $10,000 is invested in the portfolio on the investor's behalf. The sales load is deducted only if the investor withdraws the money before the CDSC expires. This type of sales charge is intended to discourage frequent trading in mutual fund accounts. Many back-end load funds also have 12b-1 fees.

12b-1 Asset-Based Fees

Mutual funds cannot act as distributors for their own fund shares except under **Section 12b-1** of the Investment Company Act of 1940. Named after the SEC rule that allows them, 12b-1 fees are deducted each quarter from a mutual fund's assets to cover the costs of marketing and distributing the fund to investors. Like sales charges, 12b-1 fees can be used to compensate registered representatives. The fee is deducted quarterly as a flat dollar amount or as a percentage of the fund's average total NAV. If a mutual fund has adopted a 12b-1 plan, the board of directors must review the expenditures made under the plan at least annually. The fee is disclosed in the fund's prospectus. Requirements for 12b-1 fees include the following.

■ The percentage of net assets charged must be reasonable. 12b-1 fees may not exceed .75% of a fund's net assets per year.

■ The fee must reflect the anticipated level of distribution services.

Approval. The 12b-1 plan must be approved initially and reapproved at least annually by a majority of the outstanding shares, the board of directors, and those directors who are noninterested persons.

Termination. The 12b-1 plan may be terminated at any time by a majority vote of the noninterested directors and a majority vote of outstanding shares.

Misuse of No-Load Terminology. A fund that has a deferred sales charge or an asset-based 12b-1 fee of more than .25% of average net assets may not be described as a no-load fund. To do so violates the NASD's Conduct Rules; the violation is not alleviated by disclosures in the fund's prospectus.

TEST TOPIC ALERT

Expect at least three questions about 12b-1 fees and know the following points.

- 12b-1 fees are quarterly charges that are reviewed annually.

- To implement 12b-1 fees approval requires three votes: a majority of the outstanding shares, the full board, and the noninterested members of the board.

- Termination requires two votes: a majority of the outstanding shares and the noninterested members of the board.

- Charges covered by 12b-1 fees include advertising, sales literature, and prospectuses delivered to potential customers, not fund management expenses.

- In general, funds that have 12b-1 fees are not no-load funds (note the exception for 12b-1s that charge .25% or less of average net assets).

- Under NASD rules, the maximum 12b-1 charge is .75%.

Computing the Sales Charge Percentage

When the NAV and the POP are known, the sales charge percentage can be determined.

$$\text{POP (\$10.50)} - \text{NAV (\$10)} = \text{sales charge dollar amount (\$.50)}$$

$$\frac{\text{Sales charge dollar amount (\$.50)}}{\text{POP (\$10.50)}} = \text{sales charge percentage (4.8\%)}$$

If the dollar amounts for the NAV and sales charges are specified, the formula for determining the POP of mutual fund shares is:

$$\text{NAV (\$10)} + \text{sales charge dollar amount (\$.50)} = \text{POP dollar amount (\$10.50)}$$

A mutual fund prospectus must contain a formula that explains how the fund computes the NAV and how the sales charge is added. The sales charge is always based on the POP, not on the NAV.

If the dollar amount of the NAV and the sales charge percent are specified, the formula to determine POP is to divide the NAV by 100% minus the sales charge percentage.

$$\frac{\text{NAV (\$10)}}{100\% - \text{sales charge percentage (4.8\%)}} = \text{POP (\$10.50)}$$

Because of the sales charge, mutual funds should be recommended for long-term investing.

EXAMPLE

NAV = $20 and POP = $21.00. What is the sales charge percentage?
The sales charge percentage is calculated by finding the sales charge amount ($21.00 – $20.00) and dividing by the POP. Remember, sales charge is a percentage of the POP, not the NAV.

$$\$1.00 \div \$21.00 = 4.8\% \text{ (when rounded)}$$

Assume a NAV of $20 and a sales charge of 5%. What is the POP?
POP is found by dividing the NAV by 100% minus the sales charge percentage.

$$\$20 \div .95 = \$21.05$$

In determining the POP when provided with the NAV, the answer has to be more than the NAV. If such a question has only one choice with a higher POP than the NAV, the correct answer should be immediately apparent.

TEST TOPIC ALERT

Although there are several computations reviewed in this Unit, the exam is more concerned with your understanding of formulas than with actual calculations. The entire exam may include no more than two to five computations. Practice calculations to assure an understanding of the formulas. Also note that the POP may not be greater than 8.5% over the NAV for an open-end fund.

INVESTMENT OBJECTIVES

Once a mutual fund defines its objective, the portfolio is invested to meet it. The objective must be clearly stated in the mutual fund's prospectus and can only be changed by a majority vote of the fund's outstanding shares.

TEST TOPIC ALERT

The exam may include up to 10 situational questions asking you to recommend a type of security to meet customer investment objectives.

Stock Funds

Common stock is normally found in the portfolio of any mutual fund that has growth as a primary or secondary objective. Bonds, preferred stock, and blue-chip stocks are typically used to provide income to mutual funds with income objectives.

Growth Funds

Growth funds invest in stocks of companies whose businesses are growing rapidly. Growth companies tend to reinvest all or most of their profits for research and development rather than pay dividends. Growth funds are focused on generating capital gains rather than income.

Blue-chip or **conservative growth funds** invest in established and more recognized companies to achieve growth with less risk. Generally these companies have fairly large capitalization. These funds are sometimes called **large-cap funds** (capitalization of more than $10 billion).

Aggressive growth funds are sometimes called **performance funds**. These funds are willing to take greater risk to maximize capital appreciation. Some of these funds invest in newer companies with relatively small capitalization (less than $5 billion capitalization) and are referred to as **small-cap funds. Mid-cap funds** are somewhat less aggressive and have capitalization of between $5 and $10 billion.

Investment style in growth funds can also be weighted toward capitalization, where companies are expected to continue to perform well in business and their stock to continue to grow in price, versus valuation, where undervalued companies are expected to perform better than the reports indicate, and thus their stock to increase in price.

Income Funds

An **income fund** stresses current income over growth. The fund's objective may be accomplished by investing in the stocks of companies with long histories of dividend payments, such as utility company stocks, blue-chip stocks, and preferred stocks.

Option income funds invest in securities on which options can be written and earn premium income from writing options. They may also earn capital gains from trading options at a profit. These funds seek to increase total return by adding income generated by the options to appreciation on the securities held in the portfolio.

Growth and Income Funds

A **growth and income fund** (**combination fund**) may attempt to combine the objectives of growth and current yield by diversifying its stock portfolio among companies showing long-term growth potential and companies paying high dividends.

Specialized (Sector) Funds

Many funds attempt to specialize in particular economic sectors or industries. Usually, the **specialized (sector) funds** have a minimum of 25% of their assets invested in their specialties. Sector funds offer high appreciation potential, but may also pose higher risks to the investor. Examples include gold funds (gold mining stock), technology funds, and utility funds. **Precious metals funds**, a type of sector fund, are mostly international in scope. They invest almost exclusively in the stock of mining companies involved in extracting precious and strategic metals. Their portfolios may contain a minor percentage of investments in bonds or other sectors, but the percentages of precious metal company stocks tend to be in the high nineties.

Special Situation Funds

Special situation or **value funds** buy securities of companies that may benefit from a change within the companies or in the economy. Takeover candidates and turnaround situations are common investments.

Blend/Core Funds

Blend/core funds are stock funds with a portfolio composed of a number of different classes of stock. Such a fund might include both blue-chip stocks and high-risk/high-potential return growth stocks or both growth stocks and value stocks. The purpose is to allow investors to diversify their equity holdings and maximize their growth returns while owning just a single stock fund. Customers, however, must understand that diversification is just one of a number of risk management strategies and that blend/core funds share the risks common to other equity funds.

Index Funds

Index funds invest in securities to mirror a market index, such as the S&P 500. An index fund buys and sells securities in a manner that mirrors the composition of the selected index. The fund's performance tracks the underlying index's performance. Turnover of securities in an index fund's portfolio is minimal. As a result, an index fund generally has lower management costs than other types of funds.

Foreign Stock Funds

Foreign stock funds, invest mostly in the securities of companies that have their principal business activities outside the United States. Long-term capital appreciation is their primary objective, although some funds also seek current income.

International funds invest in the securities of foreign countries, while **global** or **worldwide funds** invest in the securities of US and foreign countries.

Balanced Funds

Balanced funds, also known as hybrid funds, invest in stocks for appreciation and bonds for income. In a balanced fund, different types of securities are purchased according to a formula the manager may adjust to reflect market conditions.

EXAMPLE   A balanced fund's portfolio might contain 60% stocks and 40% bonds.

Asset Allocation Funds

Asset allocation funds split investments between stocks for growth, bonds for income, and money market instruments or cash for stability. Fund advisers switch the percentage of holdings in each asset category according to the performance (or expected performance) of that group.

EXAMPLE

A fund may have 60% of its investments in stock, 20% in bonds, and the remaining 20% in cash. If the stock market is expected to do well, the adviser may switch from cash and bonds to stock. The result may be a portfolio of 80% in stock, 10% in bonds, and 10% in cash. Conversely, if the stock market is expected to decline, the fund may invest heavily in cash and sell stocks.

Dual-Purpose Funds

Dual-purpose funds are closed-end funds that meet two objectives: investors seeking income purchase income shares and receive all the interest and dividends the fund's portfolio earns. Investors interested in capital gains purchase the gains shares and receive all gains on portfolio holdings. The two types of shares in a dual fund are listed separately in the financial pages. They are not to be confused with exchange-traded funds, discussed in Unit 1, which meet the technical definition of closed-end funds but are designed to track a particular index. Both dual-purpose and exchange-traded funds are priced by the market rather than by the value of the shares in their portfolios.

Bond Funds

Bond funds have income as their main investment objective. Some funds invest solely in investment-grade corporate bonds. Others, seeking enhanced safety, invest only in government issues. Still others pursue capital appreciation by investing in lower-rated bonds for higher yields.

Corporate Bond Funds

Investors seeking high current income choose **corporate bond funds**. Because of their increased credit risk, these funds provide higher yields to investors than do government and municipal bond funds.

Tax-Free (Tax-Exempt) Bond Funds

Tax-exempt funds invest in municipal bonds or notes that produce income exempt from federal income tax. **Tax-free funds** can invest in municipal bonds and tax-exempt money market instruments.

US Government and Agency Security Funds

US government funds purchase securities issued by the US Treasury or an agency of the US government, such as Ginnie Mae. Investors in these funds seek current income and maximum safety. Ginnie Mae funds yield slightly more than government securities funds. Because Ginnie Mae funds are pools of home mortgages, they are susceptible to prepayment risk when interest rates fall and homeowners refinance their mortgages.

Funds of Funds

A **fund of funds** is a type of mutual fund that invests solely in other mutual funds. These funds' strategies and objectives necessarily reflect the strategies of the underlying mutual funds that make up their portfolios, and they can be pure growth, pure income, or a mixture of two or more objectives. They are not to be confused with funds of hedge funds.

Funds of Hedge Funds

Though hedge funds are available only to accredited investors, there are registered mutual funds available to ordinary investors that invest in hedge funds. Not surprisingly, they are called **funds of hedge funds**. They can diversify among several hedge funds and thus give ordinary investors indirect access to hedge fund investments. Funds of hedge funds to some extent share the benefits (and risks) of hedge funds and have much lower initial investment requirements, but they also have some peculiar disadvantages. For instance, the shares are neither traded nor readily redeemable unless the fund itself offers to redeem them. Thus, such an investment cannot be liquidated readily. Expenses and risks also tend to be significantly higher than those of other types of mutual funds. Any recommendations to customers must include full coverage of these drawbacks.

Money Market Funds

Money market funds are usually no-load, open-end mutual funds that serve as temporary holding tanks for investors who are most concerned with liquidity. **No-load** means investors pay no sales or liquidation fees. A fund manager invests the fund's capital in money market instruments that pay interest and have short maturities. Interest rates on money market funds are not fixed or guaranteed and change often, and the interest these funds earn is computed daily and credited to customers' accounts monthly. Many funds offer check-writing privileges; however, checks normally must be written for amounts of $500 or more. The largest expense to investors is the management fee.

The NAV of money market funds is set at $1 per share. Although this price is not guaranteed, a fund is managed in order not to "break the buck," regardless of market changes. Thus, the price of money market shares does not fluctuate in response to changing market conditions; what fluctuates is yield.

Restrictions on Money Market Funds

SEC rules limit the investments available to money market funds and require certain disclosures to investors. Restrictions include the following.

■ The front cover of every prospectus must prominently disclose that an investment in a money market fund is neither insured nor guaranteed by the US government and that an investor has no assurance the fund will be able to maintain a stable NAV. This statement must also appear in all literature used to market the fund.

■ Investments are limited to securities with remaining maturities of no more than 13 months, with the average portfolio maturity not exceeding 90 days.

■ Investments are limited to eligible securities determined to have minimal risk. Eligible securities are defined as those rated by nationally recognized rating organizations (Standard & Poor's, Moody's, etc.) in one of the top two categories (no more than 5% of the portfolio may be in the second tier of ratings). Comparable unrated securities must adhere to the definition of safety as provided by the rating organizations.

Beta

One characteristic of note for money market funds is their low beta coefficient. Beta is a means of measuring the volatility of a security or portfolio in comparison with the market as a whole. A beta of 1 indicates a security's price will move in direct correlation with the market. A beta greater than 1 indicates a security is more volatile than the market, and a beta less than 1 indicates that a security will be less volatile than the market.

Remembering the money market fund portfolio restrictions discussed previously such as the limitation to invest in short term, minimal risk securities and the ability to peg the NAV at $1 per share, it becomes apparent that little correlation exists between the movements of the market and the share prices of these portfolios.

TAKE NOTE

For suitability questions on the exam, first determine the customer's primary objective. In general, the following basic rules apply.

Investors interested in:	should invest in:
growth	stock funds
income	bond funds
safety of principal	government bond funds
immediate liquidity	money market funds
tax relief	municipal bond funds
maximizing current income	corporate bond funds

Other Recommendation Considerations

The secondary objective of investors must also be taken into account.

- Investors who are interested in aggressive growth should invest in technology stock funds or stock funds investing in new companies with new ideas. Aggressive funds or small-cap funds are usually most suitable for younger investors who have high risk tolerance.

- Investors seeking growth but are more conservative should consider balanced growth funds, which are likely to be large-cap funds. These funds are not as speculative as smaller cap and aggressive funds.

- Investors who are interested in income but want safety of principal should invest in a government bond fund.

- Investors seeking the highest possible income with little concern for risk should invest in a corporate bond fund.

- High tax bracket investors seeking income should invest in a municipal bond fund.

- Investors seeking safety of principal with high liquidity should consider a money market fund.

- Investors who wish to invest in a portfolio that mirrors the performance of the stock market should consider an index fund.

Investor Objective	Recommendation
Preservation of capital; safety	Government securities or Ginnie Maes
Growth	Common stock or common stock mutual funds
Balanced or moderate growth	Blue-chip stocks
Aggressive growth/speculation	Technology stocks or sector funds
Income	Bonds—but not zero-coupons
Tax-free income	Municipal bonds or municipal bond funds
High-yield income	Corporate bonds or corporate bond funds
Equity income	Preferred stock and utility stocks
Liquidity	Money market funds (DPPs, CDs, real estate, annuities not considered liquid)
Keep pace with inflation	Stock portfolio

Strategies

Many things influence a portfolio's makeup, including personal and market factors.

EXAMPLE   A portfolio of securities appropriate for a 25-year-old unmarried man may not be appropriate for a 45-year-old married man with two children in college or a 65-year-old woman facing retirement.

Quantitative Risk Management

Portfolio managers use a variety of financial information about the markets, securities, interest rates, current economic conditions, and the companies and industries themselves in which they invest in an effort to manage risk. Quantitative risk management can be top-down, that is, based on general market conditions, interest rates, and price trends in the general economy to guide portfolio purchases and sales. It can also be bottom-up, that is, based on direct assessments of a stock's performance in a universe of 3,000 or more stocks and the characteristics of the company of investment interest itself. It is important to remember that risk cannot be eliminated, only managed.

Defensive Strategies

Defensive investment strategies may have growth or income as an objective, but safety of principal tends to be the top priority. Such portfolios often are invested in blue-chip stocks with moderate or low volatility and AAA or government bonds.

Aggressive Strategies

Aggressive investment strategies attempt to maximize investment returns by assuming higher risks. Such strategies include selecting highly volatile stocks, buying securities on margin, and using put and call option strategies.

Balanced Strategies

Most investors adopt a combination of aggressive and defensive strategies when making decisions about the securities in their portfolios. A balanced, or mixed, portfolio holds securities of many types.

QUICK QUIZ 2.6

Match the investment objective with the most suitable recommendation.

A. Balanced fund
B. Aggressive growth fund
C. Specialized fund
D. Blue-chip stock fund

___D___ 1. Desires capital growth with minimal risk

___B___ 2. Wishes to maximize capital gains quickly with high risk tolerance

___A___ 3. Wishes to diversify securities and is conservative

___C___ 4. Wishes to invest in medical technology and is not risk averse

Match the objective with the type of fund.

A. Conservative growth fund
B. Money market fund
C. Small-cap fund
D. Balanced fund

D   5. Capital gains/income/lower risk

A   6. Capital gains/low risk

B   7. Liquidity/low risk

C   8. Capital gains/higher risk

Match the objective with the type of fund.

    A. Government bond fund
    B. Large-cap fund
    C. Asset allocation fund
    D. Hedge fund

C   9. Capital gains/income/lower risk

D   10. Growth/high risk

B   11. Growth/low risk

A   12. Income/low risk

Match the description with the type of fund.

    A. Ginnie Mae fund
    B. Special situation fund
    C. Asset allocation fund
    D. Index fund

C   13. Purchase variety of assets to achieve capital gains, income, diversification

D   14. Mimic stock market indexes to achieve performance comparable to the market overall

A   15. Safety of principal with yields slightly higher than government bond fund

B   16. Seek investments in undervalued companies

Match the description to the type of fund.

    A. Principal-protected fund
    B. Blend/core fund
    C. Fund of funds
    D. Dual-purpose fund

C   17. Invests in other mutual funds

D   18. A closed-end investment company

B   19. May invest in growth stocks and value stocks

A   20. May have a 5- to 10-year lockup period

COMPARING MUTUAL FUNDS

When comparing mutual funds, investors should select funds that match their personal objectives. When comparing funds with similar objectives, the investor should review information regarding each fund's:

- performance;

- costs;

- taxation;

- portfolio turnover; and

- services offered.

Performance

Securities law requires that each fund disclose the average annual total returns for one-, five-, and 10-year periods, or since inception. Performance must reflect full sales loads with no discounts. The manager's track record in keeping with the fund's objectives in the prospectus is also important.

TEST TOPIC ALERT   Fund quotations of average annual return must be for one-, five-, and 10-year periods, or as long as the fund has operated.

Costs

Sales loads, management fees, and operating expenses reduce investor returns because they reduce the amount of money available for investment.

Sales Loads

Historically, mutual funds have charged front-end loads of up to 8.5% of the money invested. This percentage compensates a sales force. Many low-load funds charge between 2% and 5%. Other funds may charge a back-end load when funds are withdrawn. Some funds charge ongoing fees under Section 12b-1 of the Investment Company Act of 1940. These funds deduct annual fees to pay for marketing and distribution costs. Sales loads will be covered in detail later in this unit.

Expense Ratio

A fund's expense ratio relates the management fees and operating expenses to the fund's net assets. All mutual funds, load and no-load, have expense ratios. The expense ratio is calculated by dividing a fund's expenses by its average net assets. An expense ratio of 1% means that the fund charges $1 per year for every $100 invested. Typically, aggressive funds and international funds have higher expense ratios.

Stock funds generally have expense ratios between 1% and 1.5% of a fund's average net assets. For bond funds, the ratio is typically between .5% and 1%.

You may be asked about the factors included in calculating a mutual fund's expense ratio. The BOD stipend, investment adviser fee, custodian fee, and transfer agent fee are all included. The sales load is not. The formula for the computation of a mutual fund's expense ratio is:

Fund expenses ÷ average net assets = expense ratio

$$\frac{\$1 \text{ million expenses}}{\$100 \text{ million average net assets}} = 1\% \text{ expense ratio}$$

The **fund's expense ratio** is found in the prospectus and measures the efficiency of its management. The largest part of the expense ratio is the investment advisory fee.

Taxation

Mutual fund investors pay taxes on capital gains the fund distributes. These taxes are based on how long the fund owned the security it sold. Because tax rates for long-term gains are typically lower than for short-term gains, it is better for an investor in a high tax bracket to receive a long-term gain than a short-term gain.

Portfolio Turnover

The costs of buying and selling securities, including commissions or mark-ups and markdowns, are reflected in the **portfolio turnover ratio**. It is not uncommon for an aggressive growth fund to reflect an annual turnover rate of 100% or more. A 100% turnover rate means the fund replaces its portfolio annually. If the fund achieves superior returns, the strategy is working; if not, the strategy is subjecting investors to undue costs.

The portfolio turnover rate reflects a fund's holding period. If a fund has a turnover rate of 100%, it holds its securities, on average, for less than one year. Therefore, all gains are likely to be short-term and subject to the maximum tax rate; a portfolio with a turnover rate of 25% has an average holding period of four years and gains are likely taxed at the long-term rate.

Services Offered

The services mutual funds offer include:

■ retirement account custodianship;

■ investment plans;

■ check-writing privileges;

■ telephone transfers;

- conversion privileges;

- combination investment privileges; and

- withdrawal plans.

Investors should always weigh the cost of services provided against the value of the services to the investor.

Terms and Concepts Checklist

✓	✓	✓
☐ Mutual fund concept	☐ Stock fund	☐ Dual purpose fund
☐ Redeemable security	☐ Growth fund	☐ Balanced fund
☐ Undivided interest	☐ Blend/core fund	☐ Asset allocation fund
☐ Guaranteed marketability	☐ Value, or special situation fund	☐ Bond fund
☐ Assets, liabilities, net assets	☐ Income fund	☐ Corporate bond fund
☐ Shares outstanding	☐ Specialized, sector fund	☐ Municipal, tax-free bond fund
☐ NAV	☐ Stock income fund	☐ US government bond fund
☐ Sales charge	☐ Foreign, or international fund	☐ Fund of funds
☐ POP	☐ Global fund	☐ Fund of hedge funds
☐ Front end load	☐ Quantitative risk management	☐ Money market fund
☐ Back end load, CDSC	☐ Preservation of capital	☐ Performance factors
☐ Level load, 12b-1 fee	☐ Defensive strategy	☐ Sales load
☐ No-load	☐ Aggressive strategy	☐ Expense ratio
☐ Professional investment management	☐ Balanced strategy	☐ Taxation
☐ Fractional share		☐ Portfolio turnover
☐ Form 1099		☐ Services offered

MUTUAL FUND PURCHASE AND WITHDRAWAL PLANS

Mutual fund investors may select from several methods to purchase mutual fund shares or withdraw money from the mutual fund account.

TYPES OF MUTUAL FUND ACCOUNTS

When an investor opens an account with a mutual fund, he makes an initial deposit and specifies whether fund share distributions are to be made in cash or reinvested. If the customer elects to receive distributions in cash rather than reinvesting them, his proportionate interest in the fund is reduced each time a distribution is made. The customer may make additional investments in an open account at any time and in any dollar amount; that is, the law sets no minimum requirement, although each fund may set its own.

Accumulation Plans

Mutual funds have established several accumulation plans that allow investors to use the dollar cost averaging strategy.

Voluntary Accumulation Plan

A **voluntary accumulation plan** allows a customer to deposit regular periodic investments on a voluntary basis. The plan is designed to help the customer form regular investment habits while still offering some flexibility.

Voluntary accumulation plans may require a minimum initial purchase and minimum additional purchase amounts. Many funds offer automatic withdrawal from customer checking accounts to simplify contributions. If a customer misses a payment, the fund does not penalize him because the plan is voluntary. The customer may discontinue the plan at any time.

TAKE NOTE

In a voluntary accumulation plan, once the account has been opened, contribution and frequency are very flexible.

Dollar Cost Averaging. One method of purchasing mutual fund shares is called **dollar cost averaging**, where a person invests identical amounts at regular intervals. This form of investing allows the individual to purchase more shares when prices are low and fewer shares when prices are high. In a fluctuating market and over a period of time, the average cost per share is lower than the average price of the shares. However, dollar cost averaging does not guarantee profits in a declining market because prices may continue to decline for some time. In this case, the investor buys more shares of a sinking investment.

EXAMPLE

The following illustrates how average price and average cost may vary with dollar cost averaging:

Month	Amount Invested	Price per Share	No. of Shares
January	$600	$20	30
February	$600	$24	25
March	$600	$30	20
April	$600	$40	15
Total	**$2,400**	**$114**	**90**

The average cost per share equals $2,400 (the total investment) divided by 90 (the total number of shares purchased), or $26.67 per share, while the average price per share is $28.50 ($114 ÷ 4). The average cost is $1.83 less than the average price per share ($28.50 − $26.67 = $1.83).

Average price per share is found by dividing the total of all the prices paid per share by the number of investments made.

The exam may ask you to calculate the average cost per share, the average price per share, or the difference between the two. Review the calculation above as practice, but more importantly, understand the concept of dollar cost averaging. It involves investing a fixed amount of money every period, regardless of market price fluctuation. If the market price of shares is up, fewer shares are purchased; if the market price of shares is down, more shares are purchased. Over time, if the market fluctuates, dollar cost averaging is likely to achieve a lower average cost per share than average price per share.

Dollar cost averaging is effective if the average cost per share is less than the average price per share. This method historically outperforms attempts to time the market but can never be guaranteed.

Contractual Accumulation Plan

In a **contractual plan**, the investor signs an agreement to invest a specified dollar amount over a set period of time. Although called a contractual plan, the agreement is only binding on the company; the investor cannot be held to the contract.

Contractual Plans

A contractual plan, also called a **periodic payment plan**, enables a person to invest in a mutual fund on a periodic basis over a fixed period of time. The plan allows the individual to invest an amount that is typically less than the amount a mutual fund requires. An investor may begin a contractual plan for as little as $20 per month, with future payments of as little as $10 per month. The investor signs an agreement stating that he intends to invest a fixed number of dollars over a defined period of time. This agreement is not binding on the investor, but he may incur penalties if he terminates the plan before completion.

When a contractual plan is sold, two sales actually take place. First, the customer agrees to make periodic payments to a contractual plan company and is given a plan certificate issued by the company. Second, as the investor makes periodic payments, the plan company uses the money to buy shares in a mutual fund.

Contractual plan companies are organized as UITs. The customer's monthly payments buy units that are credited to the customer's plan account. The dollars represented by these units, in turn, are invested in shares the mutual fund issues. Thus, a double sale occurs—the sale of units in the plan account and the sale of shares in the fund, which means that two prospectuses are required.

Plan companies have their own plan custodians. Plan custodians have many of the same duties and functions as investment company transfer agents.

Insurance companies also offer plan completion insurance.

Front-End Load and Spread Load

Whether a plan company operates under the Investment Company Act of 1940 or the Investment Company Act Amendments of 1970, the maximum sales charge allowable is 9% over the life of the plan.

Front-End Load. The Investment Company Act of 1940 allows the plan company to collect sales charges of up to 50% of an investor's deposits in the first year. The Act of 1940 plans are known as **front-end load plans**.

Spread Load (27-H). The Investment Company Act Amendments of 1970, which amended paragraph 27-H of the 1940 Act, allow the plan company to charge up to 20% of an investor's deposit in any one year as long as the average charge over the first four years does not exceed 16% annually. This arrangement is known as a **spread-load plan** or **27-H plan**.

Terms	1940 Act (Front-End Load)	1970 Act (Spread-Load, 27-H)
Maximum sales charges (life)	9%	9%
Maximum sales charges in any one year	50% (first year only)	20%
Maximum sales charges over first four years	No limit set	16% average per year
45-day free-look letter	Refund of current NAV + any sales charges	Refund of current NAV + any sales charges
Termination within first 18 months	Refund of current NAV + any sales charges in excess of 15% of total payments	Refund of NAV only

---

TAKE NOTE   Although contractual plans are not frequently sold today, the exam may ask several questions about them.

Use the Rule of 90 as a device to remember the 9% sales load over the life of contractual plans and the maximum sales charge in the first year under a contractual plan.

Front-End Load Act		Spread-Load Act	
Investment Company Act of 1940	40	Investment Company Act of 1970	70
First year maximum sales charge	+ 50%	Maximum sales charge in any one year	+ 20%
	= 90		= 90
Under the Act of 1940, 40 + ? = 90. The maximum first year sales charge under the Act of 1940 is 50%.		Under the Act of 1970, 70 + ? = 90. The maximum sales charge in any one year under the Act of 1970 is 20%.	

Know the names Front-End Load Act and Spread-Load Act. An easy way to remember these acts is to think of "F" for the Act of 1940 (50%, front-end load) and "S" for the Act of 1970 (spread-load, 16% average).

Terminating a Plan

Under provisions of the Investment Company Act of 1940, front-end load and spread-load plans must let investors change their purchase decisions.

Right of Withdrawal (45-Day Free-Look Period). A fund's custodian must provide each investor with a written notice detailing the total sales charges that will apply over the life of the plan. The notice must be sent within 60 calendar days of the date a contractual plan certificate is issued to the customer.

The customer may surrender the certificate and terminate the plan within 45 days from the mailing date of the custodian's written notice. If the customer surrenders the certificate within that time, he is entitled to:

■ a 100% refund of all sales charges paid to date; plus

■ the investment's current value (NAV).

The value of the fund shares liquidated at NAV may result in a profit or loss on the investment, depending on the NAV at the time of purchase.

After the 45-day free-look period, the amount of refund depends on whether a plan company operates under the Act of 1940 or the Act of 1970.

Under the Act of 1940, the rules are:

■ termination after the 45-day free-look period but before the end of 18 months—investor receives the current NAV plus the amount of the sales charge in excess of 15% of the total amount of money invested; and

■ termination after 18 months—investor receives NAV only.

Under the Act of 1970, the rule is:

■ termination after the 45-day free-look period—investor receives NAV only.

TAKE NOTE

The contractual plan administrator has 60 days to send out the 45-day free-look letter. This letter offers a refund of 100% of sales charge plus the NAV of the account within the 45-day period starting with the mailing date of the letter. This does not ensure that an investor will get all of his money back; he may get more or less, depending on the NAV of the account.

After the 45-day free-look period, refund provisions under the plan differ. The Act of 1970 is easy: after the 45-day free-look period, the investor receives the NAV only.

The Act of 1940 is more complex. After the 45-day free-look period, but before the end of 18 months, the investor gets back NAV plus the amount of sales charge that exceeds 15% of the investment. After 18 months, the investor is returned only the NAV.

If you were asked to calculate the refund under the Act of 1940 in the 10th month, look for an answer choice that is more than the NAV only, but less than the NAV plus the sales charge paid. Thinking logically will help eliminate answers and save a tedious math computation.

EXAMPLE

A customer agrees to invest $100 a month into a front-end loaded contractual plan. After 10 months, the customer cancels. At the time, the NAV of his shares is $540. How much will the customer receive as a refund?

Answer: The customer will receive NAV plus all sales charges paid in excess of 15% of total payments. His payments total $1,000 (10 x $100). The sales charge taken out during this period was $500 (50% x $1,000). 15% of total payments is $150. Therefore, the customer will receive $350 ($500 – $150) plus NAV of $540 for a total of $890.

QUICK QUIZ 2.7

Match the following items to the appropriate descriptions below.

  A. Front-End Load Act
  B. 15
  C. 45
  D. 16

  C 1. Number of days in contractual plan free-look period

  D 2. Maximum average sales charge that can be withdrawn over the first four years of a spread-load act plan

  A 3. The act that allows a first-year sales charge of 50%

  B 4. Sales charges in excess of this percentage of the investment amount must be returned after 45 days but before the end of 18 months under an Act of 1940 contractual plan

Match the following numbers to the best descriptions below.

  A. 9
  B. 60
  C. 18
  D. 20

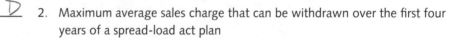

  B 5. Plan company must send the free-look letter within this number of days

  D 6. Maximum sales charge percent in the first year under Act of 1970 plan

  C 7. After this number of months the refund under an Act of 1940 plan is NAV only

  A 8. Maximum sales charge over the life an Act of 1940 or Act of 1970 contractual plan

Withdrawal Plans

In addition to lump-sum withdrawals where customers sell all of their shares, mutual funds offer systematic withdrawal plans (normally a free service). Most mutual funds require a customer's account to be worth a minimum amount of money before a withdrawal plan may begin. Additionally, most funds discourage continued investment once withdrawals start.

Not all mutual funds offer withdrawal plans, but those that do may offer plans that include the following.

Fixed-Dollar Plan

A customer may request the periodic withdrawal of a fixed-dollar amount. Thus, the fund liquidates enough shares each period to send that sum. The amount of money liquidated can be more or less than the account earnings during the period.

Fixed-Percentage or Fixed-Share Plan

Under a fixed-percentage or fixed-share withdrawal plan, either a fixed number of shares or a fixed percentage of the account is liquidated each period.

Fixed-Time Plan

Under a fixed-time withdrawal plan, customers liquidate their holdings over a fixed period of time.

Withdrawal Plan Disclosures

Withdrawal plans are not guaranteed. With fixed-dollar plans, only the dollar amount to be received each period is fixed. All other factors, including the number of shares liquidated and a plan's length, are variable. For a fixed-time plan, only the period of time is fixed; the amount of money the investor receives varies each period. Because withdrawal plans are not guaranteed, a registered representative must:

- never promise an investor a guaranteed rate of return;

- stress to the investor that it is possible to exhaust the account by overwithdrawing;

- state that during a down market, it is possible that the account will be exhausted if the investor withdraws even a small amount; and

- never use charts or tables unless the SEC specifically clears their use.

TAKE NOTE   Mutual fund withdrawal plans are not guaranteed in any way. Charts and tables regarding withdrawal plans must be cleared by the SEC before use.

1. Under which of the following circumstances will dollar cost averaging result in an average cost per share that is lower than the average price per share?

    I.   The price of the stock fluctuates over a period of time.
    II. A fixed number of shares is purchased regularly.
    III. A fixed dollar amount is invested regularly.
    IV. A constant dollar plan is maintained.

    A. I and II
    B. I and III
    C. II and III
    D. III and IV

2. All of the following statements regarding dollar cost averaging are true <u>EXCEPT</u>

    A. dollar cost averaging results in a lower average cost per share
    B. dollar cost averaging is not available to large investors
    C. more shares are purchased when prices are lower
    D. in sales literature, dollar cost averaging cannot be referred to as *averaging the dollar*

3. Which of the following is a risk of a withdrawal plan?

    A. The sales charge for the service is high.
    B. The cost basis of the shares is high.
    C. The plan is illegal in many states.
    D. The investor may outlive his income.

4. An investor has requested a withdrawal plan from his mutual fund and currently receives $600 per month. This is an example of what type of plan?

    A. Contractual
    B. Fixed-share periodic withdrawal
    C. Fixed-dollar periodic withdrawal
    D. Fixed-percentage withdrawal

Terms and Concepts Checklist

✓

- ☐ Accumulation plan
- ☐ Periodic payment plan
- ☐ Dollar cost averaging
- ☐ Withdrawal plan
- ☐ Fixed dollar plan
- ☐ Fixed time plan
- ☐ Fixed percentage, fixed share plan

✓

- ☐ Contractual plan
- ☐ Front-end load plan
- ☐ Spread load plan (27-H)
- ☐ 45-day free-look period
- ☐ 45-day free-look letter
- ☐ Terms of withdrawal
- ☐ Refund, partial refund, of sales charge

TRACKING INVESTMENT COMPANY SECURITIES

Investment company prices, like those for individual securities, are quoted daily in the financial press. However, because various methods are used to calculate sales charges, the financial press provides several footnotes to explain the type of sales charge a mutual fund issuer uses. A registered representative must understand the presentation and meaning of the footnotes associated with investment company quotes so that he can accurately describe the quotes to the investing public.

Most newspapers carry daily quotes of the NAVs and offer prices for major mutual funds. A mutual fund's NAV is its bid price. The offer price (also called the public offering price or POP) is the ask price; it is the NAV plus the maximum sales charge, if any. The "NAV Chg" column reflects the change in NAV from the previous day's quote.

EXAMPLE

In the figure, look at the family of funds called ArGood Mutual Funds. ArGood Growth Fund is a part of this group; its NAV, offering price, and the change in its NAV per share are listed. As stated previously, when a difference exists between the NAV and the offering price, the fund is a load fund. A no-load fund is usually identified by the letters "NL" in the "Offer Price" column.

Look at the Best Mutual funds, a family of no-load funds.

Mutual Fund Quotations

Tuesday, September 6, 2005

Price ranges for investment companies, as quoted by the National Association of Securities Dealers. NAV stands for net asset value per share. The offering price includes net asset value plus maximum sales charge, if any.

	NAV	Offer Price	NAV Chg		NAV	Offer Price	NAV Chg
ArGood Mutual Funds				**FastTrak Funds**			
CapApp	4.80	5.04	+ .02	App	13.79	14.44	− .01
Grwth	6.87	7.21	+ .02	CapAp	22.13	23.17	+ .15
HiYld	10.28	10.79	+ .01	Grwth	18.33	19.24	− .10
TaxEx	11.62	12.20	− .04	**Z Best Invest**			
Best Mutual				Grth p	14.81	15.59	− .03
Balan	12.32	NL	− .06	HiYld p	9.25	9.74	+ .03
Canada	10.59	NL	− .04	Inco p	7.95	8.37	− .04
US Gov	10.49	NL	− .02	MuniB p	8.11	8.54	− .03

e: Ex-distribution. **f:** Previous day's quote. **s:** Stock split or div. **x:** Ex-dividend. **NL:** No load.
p: Distribution costs apply, 12b-1 plan. **r:** Redemption charge may apply.

* This sample comprises formats, styles, and abbreviations from a variety of currently available sources and has been created for educational purposes.

The final column shows the change in a share's NAV since the last trading date. A plus (+) indicates an upward move and minus (−) indicates a downward turn. From this information, you can calculate any mutual fund's sales charge.

Find the FastTrak group of funds in the Mutual Fund Quotations. The first entry is App.

The sales charge formula:

$$\text{Public offering price} - \text{NAV} = \text{sales charge}$$

$$\$14.44 - \$13.79 = \$.65$$

Remember, to calculate the sales charge percentage, use the following formula:

Sales charge ÷ public offering price = sales charge percentage

$.65 ÷ $14.44 = 4.5%

You can also watch the movements of the fund's share value.

Stock guides such as Standard & Poor's include summaries of mutual funds for the year. The graphic on this page shows a portion of a table taken from a Standard & Poor's Stock Guide; you can use it to evaluate mutual funds.

To the right of the third fund listed on the table, Alliance Fund, the following information is listed:

- **Principal objective of the fund**: "G" means Alliance is a growth fund. Other objectives might be income, return on capital, and stability; they are listed in the footnotes below the table.

Standard & Poor's Mutual Fund Summary

FUND	Prin Obj	Type	Dec. 31, 2001 Total Net Assets (MILS)	Cash & Equiv (MILS)	Net Assets per Share % of Chg frm prev. Dec 31 at Dec 31			Min Unit	Max Sales Chg %	$10,000 Invested 12-31-91 Now Worth	Price Record 2001		NAV per Share as of 12-31-01	
					1999	2000	2001				High	Low	NAV per Shr.	Offer Price
Acorn	G	C	525.8	47.0	+ 3.9	+30.1	+15.4	$4,000	None	29,603	47.71	37.81	47.71	47.71
ALFA Securities	G	C	672.6	22.9	+33.5	+41.1	+21.6	$1,000	None	32,518	24.75	19.62	24.47	24.47
Alliance Fund	G	C	948.2	19.0	− 5.2	+29.5	+ 8.9	$250	5.5	24,661	9.67	6.96	9.45	10.00
Alliance Tech	G	C	200.8	10.0	−16.4	+26.1	+12.0	$250	5.5	...	36.47	23.44	34.24	36.23
Amer Balanced	IS	B	202.0	24.0	+ 7.7	+27.1	+15.8	$500	8.5	27,889	12.61	10.92	12.32	13.46
Amer Cap Corp Bond	IS	BD	136.0	16.0	+ 9.2	+24.6	+10.8	$500	8.5	23,457	7.51	7.12	7.12	7.48
Amer Cap Mun Bond	I	TF	187.0	7.0	+10.0	+22.0	+15.9	$500	4.75	22,897	21.74	18.53	19.14	20.09
Analytic Opt Equity	GI	C	85.7	11.7	+ 6.6	+15.5	+10.2	$5,000	None	20,662	15.59	13.88	15.45	15.45
Axe-Houghton Bond	SIR	B	204.5	4.0	+ 5.8	+31.6	+21.5	$1,000	None	27,766	12.16	10.26	11.93	11.93
Axe-Houghton Stock	G	C	93.4	2.0	−15.0	+31.1	+10.8	$1,000	None	28,394	11.46	11.13	11.13	11.13

Principal Objective: G-Growth; I-Income; R-Return on Capital; S-Stability; E-Objectives treated Equally; P-Preservation of Capital; Listed in order of importance. Type: B-Balanced; BD-Bond; C-Common; CV-Conv Bond and Prefd Stock; FL-Flexible; GB-Long-term Gov't; GL-Global; H-Hedge; L-Leverage; P-Preferred; PM-Precious Metals; O-Options; SP-Specialized; TF-Tax Free; ST-Short-term investments

- **Type of fund**: Alliance Fund is a "C" or common stock fund. Other types of funds are listed in the footnotes. They include the following:

B—balanced	FL—flexible
BD—bond	H—hedge
C—common	L—leverage
CN—Canadian	P—preferred
CV—convertible bond, preferred stock	SP—specialized
	TF—tax free

- **Total net assets** lists total net assets at market value (assets minus liabilities). Alliance Fund has total net assets of $948.2 million.

- **Cash and equivalents** includes cash and receivables, short-term government securities, and other money market instruments less current liabilities. Cash and equivalents are part of the total net assets.

- **Percentage change in net assets per share**: these columns show a fund's performance over a specific period—in this case, from the previous December 31. For instance, on December 31, 2000, Alliance Fund had a 29.5% increase in NAV per share since December 31, 1999.

- **Minimum unit** is the minimum initial purchase of shares (Alliance Fund = $250).

- **Maximum sales charge**: Alliance Fund charges 5.5%. If a fund is a no-load fund, it levies no sales charge.

- **Current worth of $10,000 invested December 31, 1991,** provides a gauge of a fund's performance over several years. In this case, $10,000 invested in Alliance Fund on December 31, 1991, would have more than doubled, growing to $24,661.

- **Price record**: from these columns, you can learn a share's percentage of appreciation from its low price of the year. To determine the percentage, subtract the low price from the latest NAV per share, then divide the difference by the low price. For instance, during 2001, Alliance Fund sold at a low of 6.96. If on June 30, 2001 (current date), its NAV per share was 9.67, the appreciation would be computed as follows:

$$
\begin{array}{lr}
\text{NAV} & 9.67 \\
\text{Low} & \underline{-\ 6.96} \\
 & 2.71
\end{array}
$$

$$2.71 \div 6.96 = 38.93\% \text{ Appreciation}$$

- **NAV per share** shows the current NAV per share and the current POP.

Terms and Concepts Checklist

✓   ✓

☐ Mutual fund quotations   ☐ Principal objective

☐ NAV = bid price   ☐ Fund type

☐ POP = offer price   ☐ Percentage of appreciation

☐ Maximum sales charge   ☐ Price record

☐ Minimum unit

ANNUITY PLANS

An **annuity** is an insurance product designed to provide retirement income. The term *annuity* refers to a stream of payments guaranteed for some period of time—the life of the annuitant, until the annuitant reaches a certain age, or a specific number of years. The actual amount to be paid out may or may not be guaranteed, but the stream of payments itself is, making this a unique securities product.

TYPES OF ANNUITY CONTRACTS

Life insurance companies offer fixed and variable annuities. With both, the annuitant makes lump-sum or periodic payments to the insurance company, which invests the money in an account. At retirement, the funds become available for withdrawal, either as a lump sum or as periodic payments to the annuitant, typically for life. Withdrawals before the age of 59½ result in a 10% penalty in addition to full income tax on anything over cost basis taken out of the account.

Fixed Annuities

In a **fixed annuity**, investors pay premiums to the insurance company that are invested in the company's general account. The insurance company is then obligated to pay a guaranteed amount of payout (typically monthly) to the annuitant based on how much was paid in.

Note that the insurer guarantees a rate of return and, therefore, bears the investment risk. Because the insurer is the one at risk, this product is not a security. An insurance license is required to sell fixed annuities, but a securities license is not.

Purchasing power risk is a significant risk associated with fixed annuities. The fixed payment that the annuitant receives loses buying power over time due to inflation.

An individual who bought a fixed annuity in 1960 began to receive monthly income of $375 in 1980. Years later, this amount, which seemed sufficient monthly income at the time, may no longer be enough to live on.

Equity-Indexed Annuities (EIAs) are currently popular among retirement investors. They are considered a type of fixed annuity, but there may be a question about them on the exam. Unlike a traditional fixed annuity, an EIA credits interest to the owner's account, using a formula based on the performance of a particular stock index such as the S&P 500. If the index does well, the annuitant is credited with a specified fraction of the growth of the index—typically 80% or 90% of the growth. This is known as the participation rate. If the index does poorly, the annuitant may receive the EIA's minimum guaranteed return—typically 3 or 4%.

Thus, consider an EIA with a participation rate of 80% and a minimum guarantee of 3%. If the index shows growth of 9% during the EIA's lifetime, the annuitant would be credited with 7.2% growth (80% of 9%). If the index performed at only 1%, the annuitant would receive the minimum guarantee of 3%.

There are several methods of charting the performance of the index, each with its advantages and disadvantages for the investor. The issuer also levies fees to offset its risk; they are known as **margin**, **spread**, or **administrative fees**. There is also a minimum time period that must elapse before the guarantee goes into effect. Early withdrawal can be expensive for the annuitant. In short, however these products are categorized, the customer must understand them thoroughly before investing.

Variable Annuities

Insurance companies introduced the **variable annuity** as an opportunity to keep pace with inflation. For this potential advantage, the investor assumes the investment risk rather than the insurance company. Because the investor takes on this risk, the product is considered a security. It must be sold with a prospectus by individuals who are both insurance licensed and securities licensed.

As with a fixed annuity, the purchaser makes payments to the insurer. However, the premium payments for variable annuities are invested in the **separate account** of the insurer. This account is separated from the general funds of the insurer because it is invested differently. Investments include common stock, bonds, and mutual funds with the objective of achieving growth that will match or exceed the rate of inflation.

Key Features of Fixed Annuities and Variable Annuities

	Fixed Annuity	Variable Annuity
Payments made with:	after-tax dollars	after-tax dollars
Payments invested in:	the general account	the separate account
Portfolio of:	fixed income securities and real estate	equity, debt, or mutual funds
Who assumes investment risk?	Insurer	Annuitant
Is it a security?	No	Yes
Rate of return:	guaranteed	depends on performance of separate account
Administrative expenses:	fixed	fixed
Income guaranteed:	for life	for life
Monthly payments:	never fall below guaranteed minimum	may fluctuate up or down
Purchasing power risk protection?	No	Typically provides some protection
Regulation?	Subject to insurance regulation	Subject to insurance and securities regulation

Although annuitants are guaranteed monthly income for life, the amount of monthly income received is dependent on the performance of the separate account. Monthly income either increases or decreases, as determined by the separate account's performance.

Investors may purchase a **combination annuity** to receive the advantages of both the fixed and variable annuities. In a combination annuity, the investor contributes to both the general and separate accounts, which provides for guaranteed payments as well as inflation protection.

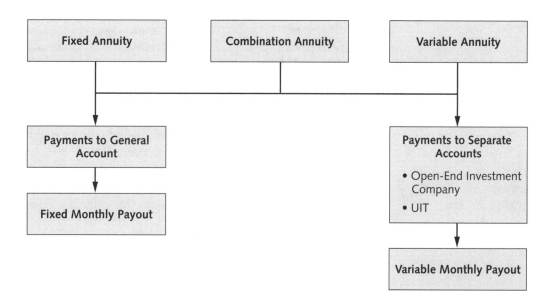

Investing Variable Annuity Premium Dollars

Fixed vs. Variable Annuity

COMPARISON OF MUTUAL FUNDS AND VARIABLE ANNUITIES

The separate account of the variable annuity consists of the purchasers' funds pooled together, which is invested in a diversified portfolio of stocks, bonds, and mutual funds. Investors each own a proportionate share of these securities and the value of their shares rises and falls based on the performance of the securities in the separate account. This is precisely how mutual funds perform; the separate account of a variable annuity is operated and regulated just like a mutual fund.

Mutual Funds vs. Variable Annuities

	Mutual Fund	Variable Annuity
Pricing	NAV calculated once per business day	Unit value calculated once per business day
Share value:	depends on performance of fund	depends on performance of separate account
Regulated by:	Act of 1933, Act of 1934, Investment Company Act of 1940, Investment Advisers Act of 1940	Act of 1933, Act of 1934, Investment Company Act of 1940, Investment Advisers Act of 1940
Fees paid to:	portfolio manager	separate account manager

If the investment manager of an insurance company is responsible for selecting the securities to be held in the separate account, the separate account is **directly managed** and must be registered under the Investment Company Act of 1940 as an open-end management investment company. However, if the investment manager of the insurance company passes the portfolio management responsibility to another party, the separate account is **indirectly managed** and must be registered as a unit investment trust under the Investment Company Act of 1940.

Although there are many similarities between mutual funds and variable annuities, there are two extremely significant features that differentiate the products: a variable annuity offers the advantage of guaranteed lifetime income (unlike mutual funds) and the earnings on dollars invested into a variable annuity accumulate tax deferred.

Mutual funds periodically distribute dividends and capital gains, and all of these distributions are typically taxable upon receipt. Such distributions are never paid directly to owners of annuities; instead, they increase the value of units in the separate account. Tax liability is postponed until withdrawals take place. This feature of tax-deferred growth has established the annuity as a popular product for retirement accumulation. As with other retirement products, if withdrawals are made before age 59½, a 10% penalty is applied to the earnings.

TAKE NOTE   Remember the unique tax feature of variable annuities: earnings accumulate tax deferred. Because of this feature, brokerage firms, banks, and insurance companies sell many annuities.

TEST TOPIC ALERT   Remember the similarity of annuities and mutual funds when you take the Series 6 exam. In fact, if an annuity question appears confusing, try substituting the term *mutual fund* for *variable annuity*.

QUICK QUIZ 2.9   1. Which of the following represent the rights of an investor who has purchased a variable annuity?

   I.   Right to vote on proposed changes in investment policy
   II.   Right to approve changes in the plan portfolio
   III. Right to vote for the investment adviser
   IV.   Right to make additional purchases at no sales charge

   A. I and III
   B. I and IV
   C. II and III
   D. II and IV

2. Which of the following are TRUE for both variable annuities and mutual funds?

    I.   They contain managed portfolios.
    II. An owner's account value typically passes to his estate at the time of his death.
    III. They are regulated by the Investment Company Act of 1940.
    IV. All investment income and realized capital gains are taxable to the owner in the year they are generated.

    A. I and III
    B. I and IV
    C. II and III
    D. II and IV

3. Which of the following most significantly affects the value of annuity units in a variable annuity?

    A. Changes in the Standard & Poor's Index
    B. Cost-of-living index
    C. Fluctuations in the securities held in the separate account
    D. The amount invested by the annuitant

4. Variable annuity salespeople must register with the

    I.   SEC
    II. state banking commission
    III. NASD
    IV. state insurance department

    A. I and II
    B. I and III
    C. I, III and IV
    D. II and IV

5. A variable annuity contract guarantees a

    I.   rate of return
    II. fixed mortality expense
    III. fixed administrative expense

    A. I and II
    B. I and III
    C. II and III
    D. I, II and III

6. Separate accounts are similar to mutual funds in that both

    I.   may have diversified portfolios of common stock
    II. are managed by full-time professionals
    III. give investors voting rights

    A. I and II
    B. I and III
    C. II and III
    D. I, II and III

7. Which of the following information must be included in a prospectus describing variable annuities to clients?

    I.   Summary explanation in nontechnical terms of the contract's principal features

    II.   Statement of the separate account's investment policy

    III.   Statement of the separate account's net investment return for the past 10 years or the life of the account, whichever is shorter

    IV.   Statement of the deductions and charges against the gross premium, including all commissions paid to agents for each policy year the commissions are to be paid

    A.   I and II

    B.   I and III

    C.   III and IV

    D.   I, II, III and IV

Purchasing Annuities

An investor is offered a number of options when purchasing an annuity. Payments to the insurance company can be made either with a single lump-sum payment or periodically on a monthly, quarterly, or annual basis.

A **single premium deferred annuity** is purchased with a lump sum, but payment of benefits is delayed until a later date selected by the annuitant.

A **periodic payment deferred annuity** allows investments over time. Benefit payments for this type of annuity are always deferred until a later date selected by the annuitant.

An **immediate annuity** is purchased with a lump sum, and the payout of benefits usually commences within 60 days.

Bonus Annuities

Direct financial benefits are sometimes offered with annuities, called **bonus annuities**. These benefits include enhancement of the buyer's premium, with the insurance company contributing an additional 3–5% to the premium payment. This comes with a cost, of course, in the form of higher fees and expenses, and in the form of an extension of the surrender period from a typical seven years to a typical eight to nine years. Bonus annuities also allow withdrawal of 10–15% of premiums, or all of earnings, whichever is greater, without a penalty from the insurance company (though there may be the federal 10% penalty and income tax to be paid). Recommendations to customers must include the additional costs as well as the benefits of the bonuses and enhancements.

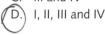

TEST TOPIC ALERT   There is no such thing as a periodic payment immediate annuity.

Accumulation Stage

The variable annuity has two distinct phases. The growth phase is its **accumulation phase**, while the payout phase is its **annuity phase**. A contract owner's interest in the separate account is known as either **accumulation units** or **annuity units** depending on the contract phase. Both accumulation units and annuity units vary in value based on the separate account's performance.

When the annuitant decides to begin receiving payments from the annuity, he may choose to **annuitize** his contract. At that point, the accumulation units he has purchased over time will be converted into annuity units, whose number becomes one of the factors used to calculate his payout each month of his retirement.

Annuitization

Accumulation phase	----------------->	Annuity phase
Accumulation units	----------------->	Annuity units

RECEIVING DISTRIBUTION FROM ANNUITIES

Annuity Payout Options

An annuity offers several payment options for money accumulated in the account. The investor can withdraw the funds randomly, in a lump sum, or annuitize the contract (receive monthly income).

If the investor chooses annuitization, the actuarial department of the insurance company determines the initial value for the annuity units and the amount of the first month's annuity payment. At this time, an **assumed interest rate (AIR)** is established. The AIR is a conservative projection of the performance of the separate account over the estimated life of the contract. It only applies if the investor annuitizes.

The value of an annuity unit and the annuitant's subsequent monthly income will vary, depending on separate account performance as compared to the AIR. To determine whether the monthly payment will increase, decrease, or stay the same as the previous month, the following rules apply.

■ If separate account performance is greater than the AIR, next month's payment is more than this month's.

■ If separate account performance is equal to the AIR, next month's payment stays the same as this month's.

■ If separate account performance is less than the AIR, next month's payment is less than this month's.

TAKE NOTE   Although the AIR formula sounds logical, it can be confusing.

EXAMPLE   Assume an AIR of 4% and that the actuaries have determined the first month's payment to be $1,000.

Month 1's payment, then, is $1,000. Month 1's separate account performance then proves to be 8%, which is well above the AIR of 4%.

Month 2's payment is therefore more than that of Month 1. Month 2's separate account performance now turns out to be 6%, lower than Month 1's, but still above AIR.

Month 3's payment is therefore more than that of Month 2. Month 3's separate account performance now turns out to be 4%, right at AIR.

Month 4's payment is therefore the same as Month 3's. Month 4's separate account performance now turns out to be 3%, which is below AIR.

Month 5's payment is therefore less than that of Month 4. Month 5's separate account performance now turns out to be 3% again, which although the same as month 4's, is still below AIR.

Month 6's payment is therefore less than that of Month 5. Month 6's separate account performance is not shown, but if it is above the AIR of 4%, Month's 7's payment will be more than $1,050; if it is below the AIR of 4%, Month 7's payment will be less than $1,050.

	Month 1	Month 2	Month 3	Month 4	Month 5	Month 6
Separate Account Return	8%	6%	4%	3%	3%	
Monthly Payment	$1,000	$1,100	$1,150	$1,150	$1,100	$1,050

Effect of Investment Return on Annuity Payments

Separate Account Return	Value of Annuity Unit	Next Month's Payment
Above AIR	Increases	More than this month's
Same as AIR	Stays the same	The same as this month's
Below AIR	Decreases	Less than this month's

TAKE NOTE

In an illustration, the maximum performance that may be used is 12%. If 12% is used, the illustration must also show a performance of 0% to demonstrate a worst-case scenario.

QUICK QUIZ 2.10

1. A customer invests in a variable annuity. At age 65, she chooses to annuitize. Under these circumstances, which of the following statements are TRUE?

    I.   She will receive the annuity's entire value in a lump-sum payment.
    II. She may choose to receive monthly payments for the rest of her life.
    III. The number and value of the accumulation units is used to calculate the total number of annuity units.
    IV. The accumulation unit's value is used to calculate the annuity unit's value.

    A. I and III
    B. I and IV
    C. II and III
    D. II and IV

2. An investor is in the annuity period of a variable annuity purchased 15 years ago. During the present month, the annuitant receives a check for an amount that is less than the previous month's payment. The payment is smaller because the account's performance was

    A. less than the previous month's performance
    B. greater than the previous month's performance
    C. less than the assumed interest rate
    D. greater than the assumed interest rate

3. An insurance company offering a variable annuity makes payments to annuitants on the 15th of each month. The contract has an AIR of 3%. In July of this year, the contract earned 4%. In August, the account earned 6%. If the contract earns 3% in September, the payments to annuitants in October will be

    A. greater than the payments in September
    B. less than the payments in September
    C. the same as the payments in September
    D. less than the payments in August

Annuity Payout Options

If the annuitant wishes, he can simply cash in his annuity without annuitizing it. In that case, he will be liable for income tax on the growth and accumulation (plus a 10% penalty if he is under the age of 59½).

If the annuitant dies during the accumulation period, the death benefit takes effect. The beneficiary is guaranteed either the total value of the annuity or the total amount invested, whichever is greater. The amount paid is includable in the decedent's estate for estate tax purposes, and the beneficiary pays income tax on the growth and accumulation portion.

If he elects to annuitize, he must select a payout option:

- life income;

- life with period certain;

- joint and last survivor; or

- unit refund.

Life Annuity/Straight Life. If an annuitant selects the life income option, the insurance company will pay the annuitant for life. When the annuitant dies, there are no continuing payments to a beneficiary. Money remaining in the account reverts to the insurer.

TAKE NOTE
The life annuity probably would not have been a good choice if the annuitant died after receiving only one month's payment. With the life income option, all money accumulated that was not paid out at the time of the annuitant's death would belong to the insurer.

The following options are a little less risky because they allow for payments to a beneficiary.

Life Annuity With Period Certain. To guarantee that a minimum number of payments are made even if the annuitant dies, the life with period certain option can be chosen. The contract will specifically allow the choice of a period of 10 or 20 years, for instance. The length of the period certain is a choice that is made when a payout option is selected. The annuitant is guaranteed monthly income for life with this option, but if death occurs within the period certain, a named beneficiary receives payments for the remainder of the period.

TAKE NOTE

To illustrate the life annuity with period certain option, assume a client selects a life annuity with a 10-year period certain. If the annuitant lives to be 150 years old, annuity payments are still made by the insurer. But, if the annuitant dies after receiving payments for two years, the beneficiary will receive payments for eight more years.

Joint Life With Last Survivor Annuity. The joint life with last survivor option guarantees payments over two lives. It is often used for spouses.

EXAMPLE

If the husband were to die first, the wife would continue to receive payments as long as she lives. If the wife were to die first, the husband would receive payments as long as he lives. Typically the payment amount is reduced for the survivor.

Unit Refund Option. If the annuitant chooses this option, a minimum number of payments are made upon retirement. If value remains in the account after the death of the annuitant, it is payable in a lump sum to the annuitant's beneficiary.

TEST TOPIC ALERT

There is a risk-reward trade-off with these payout options. The exam is likely to look at payout options in questions similar to the following.

Which of the following annuity options typically pays the largest monthly income?
A. Life only
B. Joint life with last survivor
C. Life with 10-year period certain
D. Contingent deferred option

Answer: A. Life only: there is no beneficiary with this option, so that payments cease with death and money remaining reverts to the insurer.

This question illustrates an important exam-taking principle. The term in D, *contingent deferred* is a distracter; it refers to sales charges for mutual funds.

TAKE NOTE

If a term is unfamiliar or out of place, it is almost certainly not the correct answer.

EXAMPLE

Which of the following annuity options is likely to provide the smallest monthly income?

A. Life only
B. Joint life with last survivor
C. Life with 10-year period certain
D. Life with 20-year period certain

Answer: B. Joint life with last survivor: there is a cost in the monthly income amount for the guarantee on two lives.

QUICK QUIZ 2.11

Match the following items to the appropriate description below.

A. Accumulation unit
B. Joint and last survivor annuity
C. Deferred annuity
D. Monthly payment

___C___ 1. Delays distributions until the owner elects to receive them

___A___ 2. Determines an annuitant's interest in the insurer's separate account during accumulation stage of an annuity

___D___ 3. Performance of a separate account determines value

___B___ 4. Annuity payments continue as long as one of the annuitants is alive

Match the following items to the appropriate description below.

A. Assumed interest rate
B. Immediate annuity
C. Life income with period certain
D. Separate account

___B___ 5. Contract starts to pay the annuitant immediately following its purchase

___A___ 6. Forms the basis for projected annuity payments but is not guaranteed

___D___ 7. Holds funds paid by variable annuity contract holders

___C___ 8. If the annuitant dies before a specified time expires, payments go to the annuitant's named beneficiary

Terms and Concepts Checklist

✔   ✔   ✔

☐ Annuity plan	☐ Accumulation unit	☐ General account
☐ Fixed annuity	☐ Annuity stage	☐ Separate account
☐ Equity-indexed annuity	☐ Annuity unit	☐ Direct management
	☐ AIR	☐ Indirect management
☐ Variable annuity	☐ Life only, straight life	☐ Single premium deferred annuity
☐ Combination annuity	☐ Life with period certain	
☐ Bonus annuity		☐ Periodic payment deferred annuity
☐ Payout options	☐ Joint with last survivor	
☐ Payout factors		☐ Voting rights
☐ Accumulation stage	☐ Unit refund	
	☐ Purchasing power risk	

LIFE INSURANCE

A life insurance policy is a contract between an insurance company and an individual that is designed to provide financial compensation to the policy owner's beneficiaries in the event of the policyowner's death.

Many types of life insurance contracts are available; each type serves a different need. We will focus on those contracts that use separate accounts to fund the death benefits and those that are considered securities, as defined by the Securities Act of 1933.

Whole Life Insurance (WLI)

Also known as permanent or cash value insurance, **whole life insurance (WLI)** provides protection for the whole of life. Coverage begins on the date of issue and continues to the date of the insured's death, provided the premiums are paid. The benefit payable is the face amount of the policy, which remains constant throughout the policy's life. The premium is set at the time of the policy's issue and it, too, remains level for the policy's life.

Cash Values

Unlike term insurance, which provides only a death benefit, whole life insurance combines a death benefit with an accumulation, or a savings element. This accumulation, commonly referred to as the policy's **cash value**, increases each year the policy is kept in force. In traditional whole life insurance, the insurer invests reserves in conservative investments (e.g., bonds, real estate, mortgage loans).

Because of the low risk of such investments, the insurer can guarantee the policy's cash value and the nonforfeiture options that are based on that cash value. Traditional life insurance reserves are held in the insurer's general accounts.

Variable Life Insurance

Variable life insurance differs from whole life insurance in that the premiums are invested not in the insurance company's general account, whose investments are determined by the insurance company, but in a separate account, in whose investments the insured has some choice—common stock, bonds, money market instruments, and so on. The purpose is to let the customer assume some investment risk in an attempt to get inflation protection for his death benefit.

Cash value in the policy fluctuates with the performance of the separate account and is not guaranteed. Variable life policies provide policy owners with a **minimum guaranteed death benefit**. The benefit may increase above this minimum amount depending on investment results but can never fall below.

TAKE NOTE

Because a variable life insurance policy has a minimum death benefit, the premiums necessary to fund this part of the death benefit are held in the insurer's general account. Any policy benefit that is guaranteed is invested in the insurer's general account.

Any premium above what is necessary to pay for the minimum death benefit is invested in the separate account. This portion of the premium is subject to investment risk. The death benefit will grow above the minimum guaranteed amount if the separate account performs positively. The death benefit will never be less than the minimum guarantee, even if the separate account performs poorly.

Universal variable life insurance (UVL) is a type of variable life insurance with flexible premiums (and thus flexible death benefit). If variable life insurance is analogous to a combination annuity, then UVL is analogous to a variable annuity. Premiums are invested only in a separate account, and there is only a variable death benefit (though some policies allow a small guaranteed death benefit to allow for funeral expenses). The insured has the option to increase or reduce his premium payments, though he must of course maintain a minimum cash value, and the death benefit is adjusted appropriately.

Comparison of Whole Life and Variable Life Policies

Whole Life	Variable Life (VLI)	Universal Variable Life (UVL)
Scheduled premium	Scheduled premium	Flexible premium
Fixed death benefit	Minimum guaranteed plus variable death benefit	Variable death benefit
Premiums to general account	Premiums to general and separate account	Premiums to separate account
Guaranteed cash value	No guaranteed cash value	No guaranteed cash vale

Scheduled Premiums

A **scheduled-premium** (or **fixed-premium**) **VLI contract** is issued with a minimum guaranteed death benefit. (The premiums for some variable life contracts are flexible; this is discussed later under *Universal Variable Life*.) A scheduled-premium VLI contract's death benefit is determined at issue, and evidence of insurability is required.

The premium is calculated according to the policyowner's age and sex and the policy's face amount (guaranteed amount) at issue. Once the premium has been determined and the expenses have been deducted, the net premium is invested in a separate account the policyowner selects.

Charges and Expenses

Charges and expenses are deducted either from the gross premium or from the separate account. The charges and expenses must be reasonable and as described in the VLI contract. When and how they are collected is important because it affects the amount of premium that may be invested in the separate account and the separate account's investment return.

Deductions from the Premium

Deductions from the gross premium normally reduce the amount of money invested in the separate account. The greater the deductions, the less money available for the investment base in the separate account. Charges deducted from the gross premium include:

■ the administrative fee;

■ the sales load; and

■ state premium taxes.

The administrative fee is normally a one-time charge to cover the cost of processing the application.

The allowable sales load on variable life insurance is the equivalent of an average of 9% of premium per year, computed over a 20-year period. The sales charge may be front-end loaded to 50% of the first year's premium, but must average out to 9% over a 20-year period.

Deductions from the Separate Account

Deductions from the separate account normally reduce the investment return payable to the policy owner. Charges deducted from the separate account include:

■ mortality risk fee (cost of insurance);

■ expense risk fee; and

■ investment management fee.

The **mortality risk fee** covers the risk that the policyowner may live for a period shorter than assumed. The **expense risk fee** covers the risk that the costs of administering and issuing the policy may be greater than assumed.

TAKE NOTE

The exam may ask you which charges are deducted from the gross premium and which are deducted from the separate account (the net premium). Remember the acronym **S-A-S** to make it simple. The charges deducted from the gross premium are:

■ **S**ales load;

■ **A**dministrative fee; and

■ **S**tate premium taxes.

Any other charges; such as cost of insurance, expense risk fees, and investment management fees, are deducted from the net premium, which is invested in the separate account.

Assumed Interest Rate and Variable Death Benefit

The death benefit payable under a variable life insurance policy consists of two parts: a guaranteed minimum provided by the portion of funds invested in the general account, and a variable death benefit provided by those invested in the separate account. The guaranteed minimum does not change, but the variable portion of the death benefit must be recalculated at least annually.

The effect that a change in earnings has on the contract's variable death benefit depends on a comparison of actual account performance and the performance assumed by the insurance company. If the separate account returns are greater than the AIR, additional funds are available to the policyowner. These extra earnings are reflected in an increase in death benefit and cash value. If the separate account returns equal the AIR, actual earnings meet estimated expenses, resulting in no change in benefit levels. Should the separate account returns be less than the AIR, the contract's death benefit may decrease; however, it may never fall below the amount guaranteed at issue.

TAKE NOTE

The variable death benefit is typically adjusted annually, while the cash value is computed monthly. If there have been several months of negative performance, therefore, they must be offset by equivalent positive performance before the variable death benefit can be adjusted upward.

Cash Value

The policyowner's cash values reflect the investments held in the separate account. The individual policy's cash value must be calculated at least monthly.

The cash value, like the death benefit, may increase or decrease depending on the separate account's performance. If performance has been negative, the cash value may decrease to zero, even if the contract has been in force for several years. The cash value cannot be negative, but the insurance company keeps track of negative performance. Therefore, like the death benefit, the cash value may not increase until prior negative performance has been offset.

TAKE NOTE   The AIR has no effect on cash value accumulation in a variable life policy. The cash value will grow whenever the separate account has positive performance. The AIR, however, does affect the death benefit. Just remember the rules for variable annuities. The rules for the death benefits are as follows.

- If the separate account performance is greater than the AIR, the death benefit will increase.

- If the separate account performance is equal to the AIR, the death benefit will stay the same.

- If the separate account performance is less than the AIR, the death benefit will decrease.

TEST TOPIC ALERT   You may see a question that asks about the frequency of certain calculations associated with variable life insurance policies. Know that:

- death benefits are calculated annually;

- cash value is calculated monthly; and

- unit values are calculated daily.

Loans

Like traditional WLI, a VLI contract allows the insured to borrow against the cash value that has accumulated in the contract. However, certain restrictions exist. Usually, the insured may only borrow a percentage of the cash value. The minimum percentage that must be made available is 75% after the policy has been in force for three years. If the death benefit becomes payable during the period that a loan is outstanding, the loan amount is deducted from the proceeds payable. The interest rate charged is stated in the policy.

If an extreme decline in account value occurs during the loan's term, the policyowner is liable for maintaining a positive net cash value in the account.

If an outstanding loan reduces apparent cash value to a negative amount, the insured has 31 days to deposit enough into his account to make it positive. If he fails to do so, the insurance company may terminate the contract. If this happens, the loan, of course, need not be repaid.

TEST TOPIC ALERT   Several testable facts about policy loans are as follows.

- 75% of the cash value must be available for policy loan after three years.

- The insurer is never required to loan 100% of the cash value. Full cash value is obtained by surrendering the policy to the insurer.

■ If, due to poor separate account performance, the loan exceeds the policy cash value, the policyowner must make payment to the insurer within 31 days.

■ If the insured dies with a loan outstanding, the death benefit is reduced by the amount of the loan.

■ If the insured surrenders his contract with a loan outstanding, cash value is reduced by the amount of the loan.

Contract Exchange

During the early stage of ownership, a policyowner has the right to exchange a VLI contract for a traditional fixed-benefit WLI contract. The length of time this exchange privilege is in effect varies from company to company, but under no circumstances can the period be less than 24 months (federal law).

The exchange is allowed without evidence of insurability. If a contract is exchanged, the new WLI policy has the same contract date and death benefit as the minimum guaranteed in the VLI contract. The premiums equal the amounts guaranteed in the new WLI contract (as if it were the original contract).

TEST TOPIC ALERT

Two testable facts about the contract exchange provision are as follows.

■ The contract exchange provision must be available for a minimum of two years.

■ No medical underwriting (evidence of insurability) is required for the exchange.

Sales Charges and Refunds

The separate accounts that fund VLI contracts are defined under the Investment Company Act of 1940 as periodic payment plans. They normally operate as either front-end load or spread-load plans.

Sales Charges

The sales charges on a fixed-premium VLI contract may not exceed 9% of the payments to be made over the life of the contract. The contract's **life** means the greater of 20 years or the insured's life expectancy.

Refund Provisions

The **refund provisions** under VLI contracts differ from the refund provisions of the Investment Company Act of 1940. The insurer must extend a free-look period to the policyowner for 45 days from the execution of the application or for 10 days from the time the owner receives the policy, whichever is longer. During the free-look period, the policyowner may terminate the policy and receive all payments made. Under other periodic payment plans, the sales charge and current net asset value are refunded, which may be more or less than the payments made.

The refund provisions extend for two years from issuance of the policy. If, within the two-year period, the policyowner terminates participation in the contract, the insurer must refund the contract's cash value (the value calculated after the insurer receives the redemption notice) plus all sales charges deducted in excess of 30% in the first year of the contract and 10% in the second year. After the two-year period has lapsed, only the cash value need be refunded; the insurer retains all sales charges.

TEST TOPIC ALERT

Several testable facts about sales charges and refunds are as follows.

- Because variable life is considered a contractual plan, the maximum sales charge over the life of the contract is 9%.

- A policyowner who wants a refund within 45 days receives all money paid.

- Refund provisions are for two years:

    — For the first year, the refund is sales charges in excess of 30% of the premiums paid plus the cash value.

    — For the second year, the refund is sales charges in excess of 10% of the premium paid plus the cash value.

    — Thereafter, the policyowner has access to the cash value only.

Voting Rights

Contract holders receive one vote per $100 of cash value funded by the separate account. As with other investment company securities, changes in investment objectives and other important matters can be accomplished only by a majority vote of the separate account's outstanding shares or by order of the state insurance commissioner. Contract holders must be given the right to vote on matters concerning separate account personnel at the first meeting of contract holders within one year of beginning operations.

TEST TOPIC ALERT

Do not confuse the voting rights of variable annuities and variable life. Variable annuities and mutual funds are the same: one vote per unit (share). Variable life is one vote per $100 of cash value.

QUICK QUIZ 2.12

Match each of the following numbers with the best description below.

A. 75
B. 24
C. 9
D. 10

 D   1. Sales charge percent of premium kept if cancellation is in the second year

A   2. Minimum percent of cash value that must be available for a policy loan after 3 years

_B_   3.   Number of months contract exchange provision must be in place

_C_   4.   Maximum sales charge allowed over life of variable life contract

---

QUICK QUIZ 2.13   Choose **W** for whole life, **V** for variable life, and **U** for universal variable life. More than one may apply to each choice.

W _✓_   1.   Features a stated premium   _W V_

WV U _✓_   2.   Always has some guaranteed death benefit   _WVU_

W _✓_   3.   Features a guaranteed cash value   _WV_

_✓U_   4.   Cash value not guaranteed

WVU   5.   Policy loans available

Terms and Concepts Checklist

✓		✓	
☐	Whole life	☐	Fixed death benefit
☐	Variable life (VLI)	☐	Minimum guaranteed death benefit
☐	Universal variable life (UVL)	☐	Variable death benefit
☐	Fixed premium, scheduled premium	☐	Cash value
☐	Flexible premium	☐	Deductions from premium
☐	Deductions from separate account	☐	Administrative fee
☐	Mortality risk fee, guarantee	☐	Sales load
☐	Expense risk fee, guarantee	☐	State premium taxes
☐	Investment management fee	☐	Adjustment of variable death benefit
☐	Policy loans	☐	Contract exchange
☐	Sales charges	☐	Refund provisions
☐	Voting rights		

HOTSHEETS

For your convenience, Unit HotSheets summarizing the key points are located at the end of the manual on perforated pages.

U N I T   T E S T

1. What is the cost basis for mutual fund shares that are transferred at the death of the owner?
   A. The original price of purchase
   B. The current market price if bought in the secondary market
   C. The net asset value of the shares at the time of death
   D. The net asset value of the shares at the end of tax year before the transfer

2. Who sets a mutual fund's ex-dividend date?
   A. The fund's board of directors
   B. The shareholders
   C. The NASD
   D. The exchange on which the mutual fund trades

3. Under NASD advertising rules, a money market mutual fund with a portfolio composed primarily of US government short-term obligations and NAV that has never varied from $1.00 per share may state which of the following?
   A. "The portfolio of the fund is principally invested in US government short-term debt instruments and an NAV of $1.00 will be maintained."
   B. "The fund has a portfolio invested primarily in short-term US government debt instruments for stability of principal and regular interest. The fund's NAV has, since the inception of the fund, never varied from $1. The fund will make every effort to maintain the NAV at $1; however, past performance is not an indicator of future results."
   C. "The portfolio of the fund is invested principally in US government short-term debt instruments. Because these investments are guaranteed by the full faith and credit of the US government, the fund provides guaranteed protection from default and loss of principal for its investors."
   D. "Money market mutual funds invested primarily in US Treasury bills will maintain a stability of NAV at $1 per share because T-bills are guaranteed to mature at face amount and are backed by the full faith and credit of the US government."

4. The Board of Directors of an open-end investment company may vote to determine a change in all of the following EXCEPT
   I. securities in the mutual fund portfolio
   II. sponsoring underwriter
   III. investment objective
   IV. custodian
   A. I and III
   B. I and IV
   C. II and III
   D. II and IV

5. According to the Investment Company Act of 1940, which of the following are required to start an open-end investment company?
   I. $100,000 of net assets
   II. $1,000,000 of net assets
   III. 100 investors
   IV. A clearly defined investment objective
   A. I and III
   B. I, III and IV
   C. II and IV
   D. III and IV only

6. Which of the following would cause an increase in NAV?
   I. The fund purchases $10 million in portfolio securities.
   II. Investment income is received by the fund.
   III. The securities in the portfolio appreciate.
   IV. Capital gains are distributed by the fund.
   A. I and II
   B. II and III
   C. II and IV
   D. III and IV

7. A mutual fund has $3 million in assets. What is the maximum amount it may borrow?
   A. $0
   B. $1 million
   C. $3 million
   D. $9 million

8. Assuming that expense ratios for the funds listed are identical, rank the funds below in order, from lowest to highest yield.

    I.   Municipal bond fund
    II. Government bond fund
    III. Corporate bond fund

    A. I, II, III
    B. I, III, II
    C. II, I, III
    D. III, II, I

9. How do closed-end investment companies differ from open-end investment companies?

    I.   Closed-end companies register their shares with the SEC; open-end companies do not.
    II. Closed-end company shares are sold with prospectus only in IPOs; open-end shares solicitations must always be accompanied by a prospectus.
    III. Closed-end companies issue a fixed number of shares; there is no limit on the number of shares issued by an open-end company.
    IV. Closed-end companies may only sell shares to institutional investors; open-end companies may sell to any investor.

    A. I and II
    B. I and III
    C. II and III
    D. III and IV

10. Mutual fund redemption fees are

    A. not charged by no-load funds
    B. used to defray fund distribution costs
    C. typically 1% or less of the redeemed value
    D. also known as 12b-1 fees

11. A unit investment trust can best be described as a

    I.   managed investment company
    II. nonmanaged investment company
    III. company that issues redeemable securities
    IV. company that issues securities that are actively traded in the secondary marketplace

    A. I and III
    B. I and IV
    C. II and III
    D. II and IV

12. A client invested in the XYZ Bond mutual fund 5 years ago. The client took dividend distributions in cash and reinvested capital gains distributions into more shares. Interest rates have declined over the past 5 years. Which of the following statements is TRUE?

    A. The client's proportionate interest in the fund has not changed.
    B. The reinvested capital gains have accumulated tax deferred.
    C. The NAV per share of the XYZ Bond mutual fund increased.
    D. The dividend distributions were subject to capital gains taxation.

13. Which of the following is an advantage to a customer who invests in a contractual plan?

    A. The customer may invest with a low load.
    B. The customer may invest with small deposits.
    C. Because of plan completion insurance, a beneficiary will receive an immediate cash benefit if the contract holder dies.
    D. The sales load is taken equally from each payment over the life of the plan.

14. The total return of a mutual fund is equal to

    A. the return attained by reinvestment of all dividend and capital gains distributions
    B. annualized fund dividends divided by the current POP
    C. all realized and unrealized capital appreciation
    D. the reinvestment of all unrealized dividend and capital gain income

15. All of the following charges are included in the computation of a mutual fund's expense ratio EXCEPT

    A. the fee paid to board members
    B. the sales load paid to the underwriters
    C. the investment adviser fee
    D. the transfer agent fee

16. Your customer feels she is overburdened with taxes and would like relief. You discuss the MNO Municipal Bond Fund with her and advise her of the tax treatment of the distributions. Which of the following statements would be the correct advice?

   A. "Dividends and capital gains are federally tax exempt and may even be state exempt if issues in the portfolio are issues in your state of residence."

   B. "Dividends and capital gains are federally tax exempt but only the dividends may qualify for state exemption."

   C. "Dividends are federally tax exempt and capital gains are subject to taxation."

   D. "Both dividends and capital gains are taxable at favorable capital gains rates."

17. ABC is a diversified, open-end investment company with assets of $20 million, of which $5 million is invested in real estate that it wishes to retain. The rest is invested in securities. ABC wishes to invest in Kramer Manufactures, Inc., a company whose outstanding stock is valued at $4 million. If ABC wishes to retain its diversified status, what is the most it may invest in Kramer Manufactures, Inc.?

   A. $2 million
   B. $1 million
   C. $750,000
   D. $400,000

18. Which of the following statements about mutual funds is NOT true?

   A. Mutual funds are also referred to as open-end investment companies.
   B. When investors sell mutual fund shares, the shares are redeemed at their net asset value.
   C. Mutual funds can continually issue new shares.
   D. The POP of a mutual fund is the net asset value minus any sales charges.

plus

19. Which of the following statements regarding dollar cost averaging is TRUE?

   A. It is effective if smaller dollar purchases are made when the market prices rise.
   B. When the market fluctuates, it will result in a lower average cost per share.
   C. It will protect investors from losses in a falling market.
   D. It is most effective when the market remains constant.

20. Your customer invests $200 monthly into a mutual fund. His daughter plans to enter college soon, and he would like to send her $100 monthly. Which of the following actions should you recommend to him?

   A. Invest $100 monthly into the mutual fund and send his daughter $100 monthly.
   B. Invest $200 monthly into the mutual fund and send all dividends to his daughter.
   C. Invest $200 monthly into the mutual fund and redeem shares when needed.
   D. Begin a systematic withdrawal program of $100 monthly.

21. An annuitant received payments until his death from a nonqualified variable annuity. At his death, his wife received a lump sum payment from the annuity. This example illustrates which type of annuity?

   A. Straight life
   B. Cash balance
   C. Joint and last survivor
   D. Unit refund

22. A customer has a variable life policy and has made 2 annual premium payments. From the first year's premium, $600 was deducted in sales charges. From the second year's premium, $400 was deducted. If the customer terminates the policy before the end of the second year, which of the following statements are TRUE?

   A. The customer is not entitled to a policy refund but may exchange the policy into a traditional whole life policy.
   B. The customer is refunded all premiums paid.
   C. The customer is refunded a portion of premiums paid.
   D. The customer receives the policy cash value only.

23. A customer is considering the purchase of either a variable annuity or variable life insurance. In discussing the merits of the respective contracts, a registered representative can state that all of the following characteristics are common to both contracts EXCEPT
    I. all gains are tax deferred
    II. the AIR is a factor in determining certain values
    III. fixed contributions are required
    IV. contract owners have the right to vote

    A. I and II
    B. II and III
    C. III only
    D. III and IV

24. Which of the following types of annuity contracts would your customer NOT be able to purchase?

    A. Periodic payment deferred annuity
    B. Periodic payment immediate life annuity
    C. Lump-sum payment immediate life annuity
    D. Lump-sum payment deferred annuity

25. Which of the following products need not register with the SEC?

    A. Equity Indexed Annuity
    B. Variable Annuity
    C. Universal Variable Life Insurance
    D. Combination Annuity

26. A 60-year-old male customer is interested in investing in a variable annuity. Which of the following would you consider to be the least important in the investment decision?

    A. The customer's investment objective
    B. The customer's gender
    C. The performance history of the variable annuity
    D. The investment choices available in the variable annuity

27. The AIR for your customer's variable annuity contract is 5%. In February, the separate account earned 7%. In March, the separate account earns 5%. The April annuity payment will be

    A. higher than the March payment
    B. lower than the March payment
    C. equal to the March payment
    D. equal to the original payment amount at the time of annuitization

28. A registered representative presenting a variable life insurance policy proposal to a prospect must disclose which of the following about the insured's rights of exchange of the VLI policy?

    A. The insurance company will allow the insured to exchange the VLI policy for a traditional whole life policy within 45 days from the date of the application or 10 days from policy delivery, whichever is longer.
    B. Federal law requires the insurance company to allow the insured to exchange the VLI policy for a traditional whole life policy issued by the same company for 2 years with no additional evidence of insurability.
    C. Within the first 18 months, the insured may exchange the VLI policy for either a whole life or universal variable policy issued by the same company with no additional evidence of insurability.
    D. The insured may request that the insurance company exchange the VLI policy for a traditional whole life policy issued by the same company within 2 years. The insurance company retains the right to have medical examinations for underwriting purposes.

29. Guaranteed cash value is a standard feature found in which of the policies listed below?

    A. Whole life
    B. Term life
    C. Variable life
    D. Whole life and variable life

30. Which of the following is typically the largest single expense of a mutual fund?

    A. Investment adviser's fee
    B. Custodial fee
    C. Transfer agent's expenses
    D. Underwriter's compensation

ANSWERS AND RATIONALES

1. **C.** The cost basis for shares transferred at death is the net asset value of the shares at the time of death, also called the fair market value.

2. **A.** A mutual fund's ex-dividend date is established by its board of directors. An NASD rule governs the ex-dividend date for stock and certain closed-end funds. Mutual funds do not trade on exchanges.

3. **B.** Even when fully invested in US government securities, money market mutual funds are specifically prohibited from implying a government guarantee or insurance on their portfolios. The principal value of these instruments is continually subject to market value fluctuation. Mutual funds may state their past performance history with the caveat that past performance is not an indicator of future results.

4. **A.** Changes in the mutual fund portfolio are determined by the investment adviser. A change in the fund's investment objective must be approved by a majority of outstanding shares. The board of directors may change the sponsoring underwriter and custodian.

5. **B.** To start an investment company, the Investment Company Act of 1940 requires $100,000 of net assets, 100 investors, and a clearly defined investment objective.

6. **B.** Dividends and interest received by the fund and appreciation of the portfolio cause an increase in NAV. The purchase of securities with cash results in no change of NAV because the outlay of cash is offset by the increased value of the portfolio. Any dividends or gains distributed by the fund would cause a decrease in NAV.

7. **B.** The Investment Company Act of 1940 mandates that a mutual fund must have $3 of assets for each $1 it borrows.

8. **A.** Corporate bonds have the greatest amount of credit risk and therefore the highest yield. Government bond funds yield more than municipal bond funds because interest paid on government bonds is federally taxable.

9. **C.** Closed-end companies issue a fixed number of shares, whereas open-end companies do not specify the number of shares to be issued. Both types of companies register issues with the SEC, and any investor may invest in either type of company.

10. **C.** Redemption fees are charged by some mutual funds when investors sell back shares to the fund. They are usually 1% or less of the redemption value of the redeemed fund shares. They may be charged by no-load funds, typically as a means of discouraging frequent switching of fund choices. 12b-1 fees are a separate charge against the net asset value for fund distribution costs.

11. **C.** A unit investment trust is a nonmanaged investment company that issues redeemable securities. There is no active investment manager, which means that once the securities for the trust have been selected they are held. UIT units do not trade in the secondary marketplace.

12. **C.** When interest rates decline, bond prices increase. The increased value of bonds in the portfolio causes an increase in the NAV. The client's ownership interest in the fund decreased as dividend distributions were received in cash. The dividend distributions were taxable each year as ordinary income. Reinvested capital gains or dividends are currently taxable. Earnings in mutual fund portfolios do not accumulate tax deferred.

13. **B.** The opportunity to invest with small deposit amounts is an advantage of contractual plans. Contractual plans do not offer low loads; their average lifetime loads are higher than those of traditional mutual funds, with first-year loads as high as 50% under certain plans. Plan completion insurance operates to ensure that the plan is completed and thus provides no immediate cash benefit to a beneficiary.

14. **A.** The total return assumes reinvestment of all dividend distributions and capital gains distributions.

15. **B.** The expense ratio of a mutual fund is calculated by dividing the expenses of the fund by the fund's average net assets. Fund expenses include the fee paid to board members, the investment adviser's fee, the custodian's fee, the transfer agent's fee, and related expenses. The sales load paid to the underwriters is not an expense of the fund.

16. **C.** Dividends from municipal bond funds are tax exempt because they represent tax-exempt interest paid to the portfolio. Capital gains distributions are taxable.

17. **D.** ABC must comply with the 75-5-10 rule. It wishes to retain its real estate investments, which comprise 25% of its portfolio, or $5 million. Of the remaining $15 million, Kramer Manufactures may not comprise more than 5% of ABC's assets, and ABC may not own more than 10% of Kramer. The latter figure—$400,000—is the smaller figure, so that is what ABC must limit its investment to.

18. **D.** Each share's public offering price (POP) is based on the net asset value of the share plus sales charges.

19. **B.** Dollar cost averaging is effective when the market price of securities is fluctuating and investors continue to invest a fixed amount of money every period. Under these circumstances, the average cost per share will be lower than the average price that would have been paid for shares over the same period. Dollar cost averaging offers no advantage in a constant market and does not protect investors from loss in a falling market.

20. **A.** There is some cost to investing money and immediately withdrawing it. Any time that funds are deposited into a mutual fund, a sales charge of some sort would apply (unless it is a money market fund). For this reason, your customer should reduce his investment in the mutual fund and send the extra money to his daughter.

21. **D.** When the unit refund option is chosen, the insurer pays the annuitant a minimum number of payments, and at death, the survivor receives the balance of the account in a lump-sum payment. In a joint and last survivor annuity, payments continue as long as either spouse is alive. A straight life annuity pays only to the annuitant; at death, the account balance reverts to the insurer. There is no such thing as a cash balance annuity.

22. **C.** The variable life refund provision allows for a return of a portion of the premiums paid within the first two policy years.

23. **C.** The AIR affects the death benefit in variable life insurance and the payout in a variable annuity. All gains are deferred until withdrawn. Only variable life requires a fixed contribution (scheduled premiums). Both contracts have voting privileges.

24. **B.** Periodic payment annuities can only be purchased on a deferred basis. Annuitization and regular payments into an annuity cannot occur simultaneously.

25. **A.** Equity Indexed Annuities need not register with the SEC at this time, and the Series 6 license is not needed to sell these products.

26. **B.** Because payouts for males and females are actuarially equal, gender is not a significant consideration in the purchase of a variable annuity. The customer's investment objective, past performance of the variable annuity, and available fund choices are critical considerations.

27. **C.** When the separate account return is equal to the AIR, the monthly payment amount does not change. The April payment will be equal to the March payment. The payment increases if the separate account is greater than the AIR and decreases if the separate account performance is less than the AIR.

28. **B.** Federal law requires that issuers of variable life insurance policies allow exchange of these policies for traditional whole life policies issued by the same company for a period of no less than 2 years. The exchange must be made without additional evidence of insurability.

29. **A.** Traditional whole life policies offer guaranteed cash values and death benefits. The insurer assumes the investment risk by promising a fixed rate of policy return, regardless of investment performance. Term insurance is pure insurance protection and builds no cash value. Variable life cash value is not guaranteed; cash value may be available depending on the performance of investments in the separate account.

30. **A.** The investment adviser is paid as a fraction of assets under management and is typically the largest single fee among a mutual fund's expenses. The underwriter is compensated from sales charge and may not be an expense to the fund.

QUICK QUIZ ANSWERS

Quick Quiz 2.1

1. **C.**
2. **O.**
3. **C.**
4. **C.**
5. **C.**
6. **O.**
7. **O.**
8. **C.**
9. **O.**
10. **O.**

Quick Quiz 2.2

1. **D.** All are covered under the Act of 1940. Unit investment trusts, face-amount, and management companies are all mentioned in this act. Open-end and closed-end management companies are subclassifications of management investment companies.

2. **B.** The closed-end company does not redeem the shares it issues. The closed-end company has a fixed capitalization and, as with other corporations, outstanding shares trade on the open market.

3. **C.** A diversified investment company must have at least 75% of its assets invested in cash and securities; have no more than 5% of its total assets invested in one company; and may own no more than 10% of the voting stock of any one company.

4. **C.** Unlike unit investment trusts (which issue redeemable securities), face-amount certificate companies issue installment certificates with guaranteed principal and interest. A unit investment trust has a diversified portfolio that, once established, does not change. Therefore, it cannot be called a management company. A closed-end investment company is a type of management company.

5. **C.** Open-end (but not closed-end) investment companies can make continuous offerings of shares, redeem their shares, and issue only common stock.

Quick Quiz 2.3

1. **F.** Mutual funds may use covered option strategies but typically not naked or uncovered options.

2. **F.** A change in the investment objectives of the fund requires a majority vote of the outstanding shares, not shareholders.

3. **F.** Mutual funds may be used as collateral in margin accounts but may not be purchased on margin.

4. **T.** Open-end companies must have 100 shareholders and $100,000 of assets before they can operate as an investment company.

5. **T.** Mutual funds are required to file registration statements with the SEC before shares are sold to the public.

6. **F.** Mutual funds make continuous primary or new offerings of securities and must be sold by prospectus.

7. **F.** The debt-to-asset ratio of a mutual fund cannot exceed 1:3, or 33%.

8. **F.** Open-end companies are called mutual funds.

Quick Quiz 2.4

1. **B.** The main functions of the custodian, usually a commercial bank, are to hold the fund's cash and assets for safekeeping and to perform related clerical duties.

2. **C.** Investment company financial statements must be sent to shareholders at least semiannually: one audited annual report, and one unaudited semiannual report.

3. **C.** The underwriter markets the fund's shares. Choice A is a responsibility of the custodian, B is a responsibility of the board of directors, and D is a responsibility of the fund manager.

4. **B.** The transfer agent (also known as the customer services or shareholder services agent) is responsible for keeping records related to the fund's shareholders.

5. **C.** Typically, the largest single expense for a mutual fund is the management fee, the fee paid to the management company for buying and selling securities and managing the portfolio. A typical annual fee is ½ of 1% (or .5%) of the portfolio's asset value.

Quick Quiz 2.5

1. **F.** Mutual fund shareholders own an undivided interest in the fund's portfolio.

2. **T.**

3. **T.**

4. **F.** The custodian holds the fund's assets for safekeeping.

5. **T.**

6. **F.** The reinstatement provision allows for reinvestment of funds withdrawn within 30 days at no load.

7. **T.**

8. **F.** Like common shareholders, mutual fund shareholders do not vote on matters involving dividends.

Quick Quiz 2.6

1. **D.**
2. **B.**
3. **A.**
4. **C.**
5. **D.**
6. **A.**
7. **B.**
8. **C.**
9. **C.**
10. **D.**
11. **B.**
12. **A.**
13. **C.**
14. **D.**
15. **A.**
16. **B.**
17. **C.**
18. **D.**
19. **B.**
20. **A.**

Quick Quiz 2.7

1. **C.**
2. **D.**
3. **A.**
4. **B.**
5. **B.**
6. **D.**
7. **C.**
8. **A.**

Quick Quiz 2.8

1. **B.** Dollar cost averaging benefits the investor if the same amount is invested on a regular basis over a substantial period of time, during which the price of the stock fluctuates. A constant dollar plan (Choice IV) is one in which the investor maintains a constant dollar value of securities in the investment portfolio.

2. **B.** Dollar cost averaging is available to both small and large investors.

3. **D.** Mutual fund withdrawal plans are not guaranteed. Because principal values fluctuate, investors may not have sufficient income for their entire lives.

4. **C.** If the investor receives $600 a month, the dollar amount of the withdrawal is fixed; therefore, this must be a fixed-dollar plan.

Quick Quiz 2.9

1. **A.** Owners of variable annuities, like owners of mutual fund shares, have the right to vote on changes in investment policy and the right to vote for an investment adviser.

2. **A.** The Act of 1940 regulates both mutual funds and variable annuities. Mutual funds owned in a single name typically pass to the owner's estate at death. Variable annuity proceeds, however, usually pass directly to the owner's designated beneficiary at death, like a typical insurance policy. Investment income and realized capital gains generate current income to the owner of mutual funds, but in variable annuities, income is deferred until withdrawal begins.

3. **C.** Annuity unit price changes are based on changes of value of securities held in the separate account. This price change is a risk that is passed on to the investor in a variable annuity.

4. **C.** Variable annuity salespeople must be registered with the NASD and the state insurance commission. Registration with the NASD is de facto registration with the SEC. No registration is required by the state banking commission.

5. **C.** A variable annuity does not guarantee an earnings rate. However, it does guarantee payments for life, though the payment amount may fluctuate, and normally guarantees that expenses will not increase above a specified level.

6. **D.** Separate accounts as well as mutual funds may contain diversified portfolios of securities and be managed by professional investment advisers. Voting rights for policy and management elections are available.

7. **D.** All of the information listed must be presented in the prospectus distributed to clients.

Quick Quiz 2.10

1. **C.** When a variable contract is annuitized, the number and value of the accumulation units determine the number of annuity units in the annuitant's account, which does not change. This number is used with other factors to compute the annuitant's first monthly payment. Thereafter, the performance of the separate account compared to AIR determines the monthly payment.

2. **C.** In the annuity period of a variable annuity, the amount received depends on the account performance compared to the assumed interest rate. If actual performance is less than the AIR, the payout's value declines.

3. **C.** The contract earned 3% in September. The AIR for the contract is 3%. Payment size in October will not change from that of September.

Quick Quiz 2.11

1. **C.**
2. **A.**
3. **D.**
4. **B.**
5. **B.**
6. **A.**
7. **D.**
8. **C.**

Quick Quiz 2.12

1. **D.**
2. **A.**
3. **B.**
4. **C.**

Quick Quiz 2.13

1. **W, V.**
2. **W, V, U.**
3. **W.**
4. **V, U.**
5. **W, V, U.**

3

Securities and Tax Regulations

Since the Great Depression, the securities industry has been closely monitored in the interest of protecting the small investor. The processes of issuing securities and trading them once issued are carefully regulated. It is recognized that investing money is inherently risky, so laws cannot require that risk be eliminated; rather, the laws require that the investor receive enough information to be able to assess the risk accurately and make sound investment decisions.

Since tax law and securities law are, for the present, indissolubly connected, the registered representative must also be able to inform his customer of the tax consequences of his investment decisions, whether they involve individual securities, investment company securities, or the contracts governing variable annuities or variable life insurance, which are funded by securities.

The Series 6 exam will include 23 questions on the topics covered in this Unit. ■

When you have completed this Unit, you should be able to:

■ **describe** the process of issuing a new security and how new issues are regulated;

■ **list** the four secondary securities markets and how they operate;

■ **explain** the tax treatment of distributions from mutual funds, variable annuities, and variable life insurance;

■ **differentiate** the features of traditional whole life, variable life, and universal variable life insurance;

■ **discuss** the provisions governing Section 1035 exchanges;

■ **identify** the differences between qualified, nonqualified, and individual retirement plans;

■ **distinguish** among retirement plans as to their specific characteristics and who may own or offer each type;

■ **identify** penalties that affect retirement plan investors;

■ **specify** ERISA guidelines for the operation of qualified retirement plans;

■ **describe** the important provisions of the Securities Investor Protection Act and the Insider Trading and Securities Fraud Enforcement Act of 1988;

■ **describe** the purposes of the NASD and how it operates; and

■ **discuss** NASD's requirements for continuing education and compliance review.

ISSUING SECURITIES

In general, securities are bought either as new issues from a corporation, municipality, or federal government or in the secondary market as trades between investors. This section introduces the market for newly issued securities and the role an investment banker plays in various types of offerings.

INVESTMENT BANKING

A business or municipal government that plans to issue securities usually works with an **investment bank** (a securities broker/dealer that specializes in underwriting new issues). An investment bank's functions may include:

- advising corporations on the best ways to raise long-term capital;

- raising capital for issuers by distributing new securities;

- buying securities from issuers and reselling them to the public;

- distributing large blocks of stock to the public and to institutions; and

- helping issuers comply with securities laws.

TAKE NOTE

Investment bankers help issuers raise money through the sale of securities. They do not loan money. They are sometimes also called underwriters. All underwriters of corporate securities must be NASD member firms.

Participants in a Corporate New Issue

The main participants in a new issue are the company selling the securities and the broker/dealer acting as the underwriter.

The Issuer

The **issuer**, or the party selling the securities to raise money, must do the following:

- File an S-1 Registration Statement with the SEC. This document requires that the issuer supply sufficient information about the security and the corporation and its officers to allow an investor to make a sound investment decision. When the SEC reviews this document, during what is known as the 20-day cooling-off period, they look for sufficiency of investment information rather than accuracy, though upon completion of the review, they do not guarantee adequacy of the prospectus.

- File a registration statement with the states in which it intends to sell securities (also known as **blue-skying** the issue).

- Negotiate the securities' price and the amount of the spread with the underwriter.

The Underwriter

The **underwriter** assists with the registration and distribution of the new security and may advise the corporate issuer on the best way to raise capital.

Underwriting Compensation, also known as the Spread. The price at which underwriters buy stock from issuers always differs from the price at which they offer the shares to the public. The price the issuer receives is known as the underwriting proceeds, and the price investors pay is the public offering price. The underwriting spread, the difference between the two prices, consists of the:

- manager's fee, for negotiating the deal and managing the underwriting and distribution process;

- underwriting fee, for assuming the risk of buying securities from the issuer without assurance that the securities can be resold; and

- selling concession, for placing the securities with investors.

TAKE NOTE

The largest part of the underwriting spread is the selling concession.

Types of Offerings

A new stock offering is identified by who is selling the securities as well as by whether the company is already publicly traded.

Primary Offering

In a primary offering, the underwriting proceeds go to the issuing corporation. The corporation increases its capitalization by selling stocks or bonds, in either new or additional issues.

- New issues—The new issue market is comprised of companies that are raising capital from the public for the first time in an **initial public offering (IPO)**.

- Additional issues—The additional issue market is made up of new securities being offered to the public by companies that are currently publicly traded.

Secondary Offering and Split Offering

In a secondary offering, one or more major stockholders sells control stock to the public for the first time, and the proceeds of the offering belong to the stockholder, not the issuer.

A split offering, or combined distribution, is a public offering where the proceeds are split and distributed to the issuer (primary offering) and major stockholders (secondary offering).

Such transactions, like any other first-time offering, must be done by prospectus.

TYPES OF UNDERWRITING COMMITMENTS

Different types of underwriting agreements require different levels of commitment from underwriters—and different levels of risk. Before the sale can begin, the issuer and underwriter must hold a due diligence meeting.

Firm Commitment

The **firm commitment** is the most commonly used type of underwriting contract. Under its terms the underwriters (investment bankers) commit to buy the securities from the issuer and resell them to the public. The underwriters assume the financial risk of incurring losses in the event they are unable to distribute all the shares to the public.

A firm commitment underwriting can be either a **negotiated underwriting contract** or a **competitive bid arrangement**. Negotiated underwriting contracts are used in most corporate issues. The issuer selects an underwriter and they negotiate the conditions of the underwriting contract. A competitive bid arrangement is the standard for new issue offering in the municipal securities market. The underwriting contract is awarded to the underwriter who presents the most competitive bid, or lowest interest cost, to the issuer. Sales begin on the effective date of the offering.

TAKE NOTE

In a firm commitment underwriting, the managing underwriter takes on the financial risk because he purchases the securities from the issuer. Because he purchases and resells the shares, he is acting in a principal capacity.

The managing underwriter may share the risk with other broker/dealers by forming a syndicate. He may also hire saleswork from skilled broker/dealers, who form a selling group.

A **standby underwriting** is also considered a firm commitment type of underwriting. The standby underwriter unconditionally agrees to buy all shares that remain unsold in an additional issue. The underwriter assumes the financial risk in the event that existing shareholders fail to exercise their preemptive rights and there are unsold shares in the offering.

Best Efforts

In a **best efforts arrangement**, the underwriter acts as agent for the issuing corporation. The deal is contingent on the underwriter's ability to sell shares to the public. In a best efforts underwriting, the underwriter sells as much as possible, without financial liability for what remains unsold. The underwriter is acting in an **agency capacity** with no financial risk.

QUICK QUIZ 3.1   Match the following items to the appropriate description below.
A. Best efforts
B. Investment banker
C. Standby
D. Firm commitment
E. Spread

__B__   1. Assists an issuer in determining what securities to issue

__A__   2. Underwriter acts as an agent for the issuer and attempts to sell as many
            shares as possible

__E__   3. Compensation paid to underwriters in a new issue

__D__   4. Underwriter acts as principal and takes liability for unsold shares

__C__   5. A firm commitment offering involving rights

Quick Quiz answers can be found at the end of the Unit.

Terms and Concepts Checklist

✓

□ Issuer

□ Investment banker

□ Underwriter

□ Primary offering, IPO

□ Secondary offering

□ Split offering

□ Sale by prospectus

✓

□ Negotiated contract

□ Competitive bid

□ Firm commitment

□ Principal capacity

□ Best efforts

□ Agency capacity

□ Standby underwriting

THE REGULATION OF NEW ISSUES

After the devastating market crash of 1929, Congress examined the cause and passed laws to prevent its recurrence. The Securities Act of 1933 was the first of the regulations enacted in response to the crash.

THE SECURITIES ACT OF 1933

Investigation of the conditions that led to the 1929 market crash determined that investors had little protection from fraud in the sale of new issues of securities and that rumors, exaggerations, and unsubstantiated claims led to excessive speculation in newly issued stock. Congress passed the Securities Act of 1933 to require issuers of new securities to file registration statements with the SEC in order to provide investors with complete and accurate information. New securities that are subject to the act's requirements are called **nonexempt issues**. **Exempt securities** are not subject to these requirements.

TAKE NOTE

- *Nonexempt* means "must register with the SEC under the Act of 1933." Think of corporate issues as nonexempt.

- *Exempt* means "not required to register with the SEC." Think of government securities and municipals as exempt.

Listed below are the most important provisions of the Act of 1933.

- Issuers of nonexempt securities must file registration statements with the SEC.

- Prospectuses must be provided to all purchasers of new, nonexempt issues for full and fair disclosure.

- Fraudulent activity in connection with underwriting and issuing of all securities is prohibited.

- Criminal penalties are assessed for fraud in the underwriting and sale of new issues.

TAKE NOTE

If a question on the exam discusses the new issue market or primary market, or any activity associated with the sale of new issues, the regulation involved is the Act of 1933.

The Act of 1933 is associated with:

- new issues;
- underwriting;
- registration statement;
- prospectuses; and
- primary market.

REGISTRATION OF SECURITIES

The Securities Act of 1933 requires new issues of corporate securities to be registered with the SEC. The corporate issuer does so by filing a registration statement. Most of the registration statement becomes the prospectus.

TAKE NOTE

Think of the Act of 1933 as the **Paper Act** because of the registration statement and prospectus. It will remind you of the paperwork requirements for full and fair disclosure.

State Registration

State securities laws, also called **blue-sky laws**, require state registration of securities, broker/dealers, and registered representatives. An issuer or investment banker may blue-sky an issue by one of the following methods.

- **Qualification**—The issuer files with the state, independent of federal registration, and must meet all state requirements.

- **Coordination**—The issuer registers simultaneously with the state and the SEC. Both registrations become effective on the same date.

- **Notice Filing**—Securities listed on the major exchanges and on the Nasdaq National Market as well as investment companies registered under the Investment Company Act of 1940 are known as federal covered securities. State registration is not required, but most states require the filing of a notice that the issuer intends to offer its securities for sale in that state and the state may assess a filing fee.

Exempt Issuers and Securities

The Act of 1933 provides specific exemptions from its registration provisions. Among the exemptions are the following issuers:

- The US government

- US municipalities and territories

- Nonprofit religious, educational, and charitable organizations

- Public utilities and common carries whose activities are regulated by the Public Utilities Holding Company Act of 1935.

The following securities are exempt from the Act of 1933:

- Commercial paper—maturity less than 270 days

- Bankers' acceptances—maturity less than 270 days

- Securities acquired in private placements—restricted stock

Private Placements

In addition to the above exemptions, Regulation D under the Securities Act of 1933 allows the offer and sale of securities to accredited investors (and to no more than 35 nonaccredited investors) without registration under the act. These transactions are called **private placements**.

TAKE NOTE   An accredited investor can be (1) an insider at the issuer, (2) a professional, sophisticated, or institutional investor, or (3) an individual who meets one of two criteria: at least $1 million net worth or at least $200,000 in income for the last two years with good prospects of reaching that level in the current year ($300,000 if the investor is a married couple).

You may see a question similar to the following:

The Securities Act of 1933 regulates all of the following activities EXCEPT
A. delivery of prospectuses for full and fair disclosure
B. registration of securities at the state level
C. underwriting of new issues
D. securities fraud in the primary market

Answer: B. The Securities Act of 1933 regulates federal registration of new issues with the SEC. The Uniform Securities Act regulates the registration of securities at the state level. Registering at the state level is called **blue-skying the issue**.

The Prospectus

After an issuer files a registration statement with the SEC, a 20-day **cooling-off period** begins. During the cooling-off period, the SEC reviews the security's registration statement and can issue a stop order if the statement does not contain all of the required information.

The Three Phases of an Underwriting

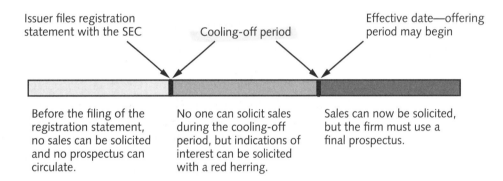

Issuer files registration statement with the SEC	Cooling-off period	Effective date—offering period may begin
Before the filing of the registration statement, no sales can be solicited and no prospectus can circulate.	No one can solicit sales during the cooling-off period, but indications of interest can be solicited with a red herring.	Sales can now be solicited, but the firm must use a final prospectus.

Red Herring. The **red herring (preliminary prospectus)** is used to gauge investor reactions and gather **indications of interest**. A registered representative may discuss the issue with prospects during the cooling-off period and provide them with preliminary information through the red herring. It must carry a legend, printed in red, that declares that a registration statement has been filed with the SEC but is not yet effective. The final offering price and underwriting spread are not included in the red herring.

Allowable Activity During the Cooling-off Period

Can:	Cannot:
distribute red herrings	offer securities for sale
publish tombstone advertisements	distribute final prospectuses
gather indications of interest	disseminate advertising material
	disseminate sales literature
	take orders
	accept postdated checks

SEC rules prohibit the sale of public offering securities without a prospectus, which means that no sales are allowed until the final prospectus is available.

Tombstone Advertisements. During the cooling-off period, sales of the security and related activities are prohibited. Nonbinding indications of interest may be gathered with the preliminary prospectus. Although the use of advertising and sales literature is generally prohibited, an exception is made for **tombstone advertisements**. These announcements, typically published in financial periodicals, offer information to investors; they do not offer the securities for sale. Issuers are not required to publish tombstones but may do so to announce an upcoming issue of securities.

QUICK QUIZ 3.2

Answer **Y** if an activity is allowed during the cooling-off period and **N** if not.

_Y_ 1. Indications of interest are gathered.

_Y_ 2. Tombstone advertisements are published.

_N_ 3. Sales literature is sent to future clients.

_N_ 4. Postdated checks are accepted.

_Y_ 5. Red herrings are provided to potential customers.

_N_ 6. Orders are taken.

The Final Prospectus (Effective Prospectus). When the registration statement becomes effective, the issuer amends the preliminary prospectus and adds information, including the final offering price and the underwriting spread for the final prospectus. Registered representatives may then take orders from those customers who indicated interest in buying during the cooling-off period.

A copy of the final prospectus must precede or accompany all sales confirmations. The prospectus should include:

- a description of the offering;
- the offering price;
- selling discounts;
- the offering date;
- use of the proceeds;
- a description of the underwriting, but not the actual contract;
- a statement of the possibility that the issue's price may be stabilized;
- a history of the business;
- risks to the purchasers;
- a description of management;
- material financial information;
- a legal opinion concerning the formation of the corporation;

- an SEC disclaimer; and

- an SEC review.

SEC Disclaimer. The SEC reviews the prospectus to ensure that it contains the necessary material facts, but it does not guarantee the disclosure's accuracy. Furthermore, the SEC does not approve the issue but simply clears it for distribution. Implying that the SEC has approved the issue violates federal law. Finally, the SEC does not pass judgment on the issue's investment merit.

The front of every prospectus must contain a clearly printed SEC disclaimer specifying the limits of the SEC's review procedures. A typical SEC disclaimer clause reads as follows:

> These securities have not been approved or disapproved by the Securities and Exchange Commission or by any State Securities Commission nor has the Securities and Exchange Commission or any State Securities Commission passed upon the accuracy or adequacy of this prospectus. Any representation to the contrary is a criminal offense.

The information supplied to the SEC becomes public once a registration statement is filed.

TAKE NOTE

Anything that says the SEC approves or disapproves an issue of securities is wrong. The SEC does not approve or disapprove—it clears or releases issues of securities for sale. When the SEC has completed its review, the registration becomes effective.

QUICK QUIZ 3.3

1. ABC, Inc., will be offering $8 million of its common stock in its home state and in three other states. For the offering to be cleared for sale by the SEC, ABC must file
   A. an offering circular
   B. a standard registration statement
   C. a letter of notification
   D. nothing

2. Which of the following is not required in a preliminary prospectus?
   A. Written statement in red that the prospectus may be subject to change and amendment and that a final prospectus will be issued
   B. Purpose for which the funds being raised will be used
   C. Final offering price
   D. Financial status and history of the company

3. All of the following statements about a red herring are true EXCEPT
   A. a red herring is used to obtain indications of interest from investors
   B. the final offering price does not appear in a red herring
   C. additional information may be added to a red herring at a later date
   D. registered representatives may send a copy of the company's research report with it

4. Registered representatives can use a preliminary prospectus to
    A. obtain indications of interest from investors
    B. solicit orders from investors for the purchase of a new issue
    C. solicit an approval of the offering from the SEC
    D. obtain the NASD's authorization to sell the issue

5. If the SEC has cleared an issue, which of the following statements is TRUE?
    A. The SEC has guaranteed the issue.
    B. The underwriter has filed a standard registration statement.
    C. The SEC has endorsed the issue.
    D. The SEC has guaranteed the accuracy of the information in the prospectus.

Civil Liabilities Under the Act of 1933

The seller of any security being sold by prospectus is liable to purchasers if the registration statement or prospectus contains false statements, misstatements, or omissions of material facts. Any person acquiring the security may sue:

- those who signed the registration statement;

- directors and partners of the issuer;

- anyone named in the registration statement as being or about to become a director or partner of the company;

- accountants, appraisers, and other professionals who contributed to the registration statement; and/or

- the underwriters.

NASD RULE 2790

It is vital that you recognize and understand NASD Rule 2790. The rule applies to IPOs of common stock and is not affected by whether the stock trades at an immediate premium in the secondary market. Rule 2790 prohibits member firms from selling a new common stock issue to any account where restricted persons have a beneficial interest. Restricted persons are:

- any NASD member broker/dealer;

- any officer, director, general partner, associated person, or employee of a member;

- any other broker/dealer (other than a limited business broker/dealer such as one limited to investment companies/variable contracts);

- their immediate family;

- finders and fiduciaries acting on behalf of the managing underwriter (e.g., attorneys and accountants);

- portfolio managers; and

- any person owning 10% or more of a member firm.

The definition of immediate family means a person's parents, mother-in-law or father-in-law, spouse, brother or sister, brother-in-law or sister-in-law, son-in-law or daughter-in-law, and children, and any other individual to whom the person provides material support.

Under this rule, before selling a new common stock issue to an account, firms are required to obtain a written representation from the account owner that the account is eligible to purchase the new issue, in other words, that the purchaser is not a restricted person. All representations must be obtained within the 12-month period before the sale of the new issue.

The rule does not apply to sales to and purchases by the following accounts or persons, whether directly or through accounts in which such persons have a beneficial interest:

- an investment company registered under the Investment Company Act of 1940 (but the rule does apply to the portfolio manager);

- an insurance company general, separate, or investment account, provided that the account is funded by premiums from 1,000 or more policyholders, or, if a general account, the insurance company has 1,000 or more policyholders (but the rule does apply to the portfolio manager); and

- a publicly traded entity (other than a broker/dealer or an affiliate of a broker/dealer) that:

  — is listed on a national securities exchange;

  — is traded on the Nasdaq National Market; or

  — is a foreign issuer whose securities meet the quantitative designation criteria for listing on a national securities exchange or trading on the Nasdaq National Market.

EXAMPLE

According to NASD Rule 2790, who of the following would not be required to be treated as a restricted person?

A.   The manager of a New York Stock Exchange member firm
B.   A trust officer at a large commercial bank
C.   A registered representative employed by a limited securities broker/dealer whose sales are confined to mutual funds
D.   The portfolio manager for the GHI Special Situations Fund

Answer: C. Rule 2790 deals with the sale of initial public offerings (IPOs). Under the rule, most individuals and firms in the securities business are considered restricted persons. Those individuals with the power to control portfolio investments are generally placed into that category as well. Specifically excluded are those firms and their employees whose only securities activity consists of the sale of investment company products and variable contracts of insurance companies.

Terms and Concepts Checklist

✓   ✓

☐ Securities Act of 1933   ☐ SEC disclaimer

☐ Registration with the SEC   ☐ NASD Rule 2790

☐ Exempt and nonexempt securities   ☐ Restricted person

☐ Private placement   ☐ Exemptions from Rule 2790

☐ 20-day cooling-off period   ☐ Blue-sky laws

☐ Tombstone ad   ☐ Coordination

☐ Red herring, preliminary prospectus ☐ Notice filing

☐ Prospectus, final prospectus   ☐ Qualification

TRADING SECURITIES

Stock and bond trades take place on exchanges and through a nationwide network of broker/dealers known as the over-the-counter market. The terminology of trading securities is discussed below.

SECURITIES MARKETS

A **market** is the exchange on which securities are traded. The market in which securities are bought and sold is also known as the **secondary market,** as opposed to the primary market for new issues. All securities transactions take place in one of four trading markets.

Exchange Market (First Market)

The **exchange market** consists of the national exchanges—the New York Stock Exchange (NYSE) and the American Exchange (AMEX)—and the various regional exchanges such as the Boston, Chicago, and Cincinnati Exchanges, the Pacific Exchange, and the Philadelphia Stock Exchange. The regional exchanges list stocks and bonds of local interest in their areas. The national exchanges list securities of national trading interest, and on a typical day, may see hundreds of millions of shares change hands on their floors.

Over-the-Counter Market (Second Market)

The **OTC market** is an interdealer market in which unlisted securities (securities not listed on any exchange) trade.

In the OTC market, securities dealers across the country are connected by computer and telephone. Tens of thousands of securities are traded OTC, including stocks, bonds, and all municipal and US government securities.

Third Market (OTC-Listed)

The **third market** is a trading market in which exchange-listed securities are traded in the OTC market. Broker/dealers registered as OTC **market makers** in listed securities arrange third-market transactions. All securities listed on the NYSE and AMEX and most securities listed on the regional exchanges are eligible for OTC trading.

Fourth Market

The **fourth market** is a market for institutional investors in which large blocks of stock, both listed and unlisted, trade in privately negotiated transactions unassisted by broker/dealers. The networks used for these transactions are called **Electronic Communications Networks (ECNs)**. INSTINET and Island are examples of ECNs.

Exchange Markets

Each stock exchange requires companies to meet certain criteria before it will allow their stock to be listed for trading on an exchange.

Location

Exchange markets, such as the NYSE or AMEX, have central marketplaces and trading floor facilities.

Pricing System

Exchange markets operate as **double-auction markets**. Floor brokers compete among themselves to execute trades at prices most favorable to the public.

Price Dynamics

When a floor broker representing a buyer executes a trade by taking stock at a current offer price higher than the last sale, a **plus tick** occurs (market up); when a selling broker accepts a current bid price below the last sale price, a **minus tick** occurs (market down).

The Specialist: Major Force in the Market

The **specialist** maintains an orderly market and provides price continuity. Specialists fill limit and market orders for the public and trade for their own accounts to either stabilize or facilitate trading when imbalances in supply and demand occur. Each stock will have several specialists assigned to it who are not employees, but members of the exchange. The specialist may not execute an order for his own account if there is a competing unfilled customer order.

OTC Markets

Historically, the criteria a company needed to meet to have its stock traded in the OTC market were rather loose. In recent years, however, the quality of companies that trade OTC has improved substantially.

Location

No central marketplace facilitates OTC trading. Trading occurs over the phone and computer networks and in trading rooms across the country.

Pricing System

The OTC market works through an interdealer network. Registered market makers compete among themselves to post the best bid and ask prices. The OTC market is a **negotiated market**.

Price Dynamics

When a market maker raises its bid price to attract sellers, the stock price rises; when a market maker lowers its ask price to attract buyers, the stock price declines.

Market Makers—Major Force in the Market

Market makers post the current bid and ask prices. The best price at which the public can buy (best ask) and the best price at which the public can sell (best bid) is called the inside market.

TEST TOPIC ALERT

Know the following basic terminology of the securities marketplace:

Exchange = listed securities = prices determined by auction
OTC = unlisted securities = prices determined by negotiation

Government and municipal bonds and unlisted corporate stocks and bonds trade in the OTC market.

ROLE OF THE BROKER/DEALER

Firms engaged in buying and selling securities for the public must register as broker/dealers. Most firms act both as brokers and dealers, but not in the same transaction.

Brokers

Brokers are agents that arrange trades for clients and charge commissions. Brokers do not buy shares but simply arrange trades between buyers and sellers.

Dealers

Dealers, or **principals**, buy and sell securities for their own accounts, often called **position trading**. When selling from their inventories, dealers charge their clients markups rather than commissions. A markup is the difference between the current interdealer offering price and the actual price charged the client. When a price to a client includes a dealer's markup, it is called the **net price**.

TAKE NOTE

If you're uncertain about the role of dealers in the securities market place, try thinking of them as car dealers. If you were a car dealer, you would maintain an inventory of cars. If someone bought a car from you, you wouldn't sell it at the wholesale price, but would mark up the price for profit. If someone wanted to sell you their used car, you wouldn't offer top dollar. Instead, you would mark down the price so you could later make a profit. Securities dealers hold inventories of securities and buy and sell from inventory. They profit on transactions by charging markups and markdowns.

Filling an Order

A broker/dealer may fill a customer's order to buy securities in any of the following ways.

- The **broker** may act as the client's agent by finding a seller of the securities and arranging a trade.

- The **dealer** may buy the securities from a market maker, mark up the price and resell them to the client.

- If it has the securities in its own inventory, the **dealer** may sell the shares to the client, with a markup, from that inventory.

Broker/Dealer Role in Transactions

A firm cannot act as both a broker and a dealer in the same transaction.

Broker	Dealer
Acts as an agent in transacting orders on the client's behalf	Acts as a principal, dealing in securities for its own account and at its own risk
Charges a commission	Charges a markup or markdown
Is not a market maker	Makes markets and takes positions (long or short) in securities
Must disclose its role to the client and the amount of its commission	Must disclose its role to the client, but not necessarily the amount or source of the markup or markdown (except for Nasdaq trades)

All firms can act in one of two capacities in a customer transaction. If the firm acts as agent, it is the broker between the buying and selling parties. Agents receive commissions for transactions they perform, and commissions must be disclosed on confirmations.

If the firm acts as a dealer and transacts business for/from its inventory, it acts in a principal capacity and is compensated by a markup or markdown.

Confirmations do not disclose markups or markdowns (except for Nasdaq trades).

A firm is never allowed to act as both agent and principal in a single transaction.

An easy way to remember the roles of broker/dealers is to memorize the letters ABC and DPP.

> ABC = Agents are brokers and are paid commissions
> DPP = Dealers act as principals for profit

BROKERAGE OFFICE PROCEDURES

Transactions and Trade Settlement

A representative who accepts a buy or sell order from a customer by filling out an order ticket must be assured that the customer can pay for or deliver the securities. If the customer claims the securities are being held **in street name** at another firm, the representative must verify this before executing a sale for the customer.

When the trade is completed, an execution report is filled out.

Trade Confirmations

A confirmation is a printed document that confirms a trade, its settlement date, and the money due from or owed to the customer. For each transaction, a customer must be sent or given a written confirmation of the trade at or before the completion of the transaction, the **settlement date**.

Exceptions are made for wire order purchases of mutual funds (for which selling agents may send confirmations as late as the day after the settlement date). A registered representative receives a copy of a customer's confirmation and checks its accuracy against the order ticket.

When must a customer receive a confirmation?

Answer: Confirmations must be sent to customers no later than the settlement date of a transaction.

Customer Confirmation

Confirmation of your order:

Order	No.	Description	Price	Amount	Inter. or Tax	Reg. Fee	Commission
BOT	100	G. Heileman	28.90	2890.00	.00	.10	85.00

						Odd-lot Diff.
Trade Date 5/16/05		**Account No.**	**AE No.**	**AE Name**		00.00
						Net Amount
Settlement 5/19/05		453-01243-1	27	Walker		2975.10

Customer Name/Address:

Ms. Jaxson Poll
5047 W. Kenneth Ave.
Chicago, IL 60699-3287

PLEASE NOTE: On odd-lot orders (orders for other than 100-share lots) on all exchanges, purchases are executed at the round-lot price plus a premium (odd-lot differential). Sales are executed at the round-lot price less a discount.

Payment for securities bought and delivery of securities sold are due promptly and in any event on or before the end of payment period in order to comply with federal Regulation T and to avoid interest or premium charges.

| **ALFA Financial Services, Inc.** | **Please keep a copy of this confirmation for your records.** |

Transaction Settlement Dates and Terms

Settlement date is the date on which ownership changes between buyer and seller. It is the date on which broker/dealers are required to exchange the securities and funds involved in a transaction and the date on which customers are requested to pay for securities bought and deliver securities sold. The **Uniform Practice Code (UPC)** standardizes the dates and times for each type of settlement.

Regular Way Settlement. Regular way settlement for most securities transactions is the third business day following the trade date (T+3).

EXAMPLE

If a trade occurs on a Tuesday (trade date), it settles regular way on Friday. If the trade is on a Thursday, it settles the following Tuesday.

If the seller delivers before the settlement date, the buyer may either accept the security or refuse it without prejudice.

US government note and bond transactions settle regular way the next business day. Money market securities transactions settle the same day.

Cash Settlement. Cash settlement, or same day settlement, requires delivery of securities from the seller and payment from the buyer on the same day a trade is executed. Stock or bonds sold for cash settlement must be available on the spot for delivery to the buyer.

Cash trade settlement occurs no later than 2:30 pm ET if the trade is executed before 2:00 pm. If the trade occurs after 2:00 pm, settlement is due within 30 minutes.

Regulation T Payment. Regulation T specifies the date customers are required to pay for purchase transactions. Under Regulation T, payment is due two business days after regular way settlement. Customer payment is due one calendar week after the trade date.

TAKE NOTE Under regular way settlement, payment is due three business days after the trade. Under Regulation T, payment is due five business days after the trade.

Extensions. If a buyer cannot pay for a trade within five business days from the trade date, the broker/dealer may request an extension from its **designated examining authority (DEA)** before the fifth business day. DEAs include the NASD and the NYSE.

If the customer cannot pay by the end of the extension, the broker/dealer sells the securities in a **close-out transaction**. After the closeout, the account is frozen for 90 days. A frozen account must have sufficient cash before a buy transaction may be executed.

The broker/dealer has the option of ignoring amounts of less than $1,000 without violating Regulation T requirements.

Frozen Accounts. If a customer buys securities and sells them before paying for the buy side, the account is frozen. It is unfrozen if the customer's check arrives before the end of the fifth business day.

Summary of Contracts and Settlement Dates

Delivery Contracts	Delivery Time	
	Corporate and Municipal Securities	Government Securities
Cash	By 2:30 pm on the same day as the trade	By 2:30 pm on the same day as the trade
Regular way	On the third business day after the trade date	On the first business day after the trade date

---

TAKE NOTE Consider the relationship between regular way and Regulation T settlement this way: brokerage firms request customers to settle trades within three business days because Regulation T requires final settlement within five business days. If customer settlement does not take place as planned, the firm has two days to correct the problem before it is out of compliance with Regulation T.

TEST TOPIC ALERT Assume the question is asking about the normal customer settlement terms, regular way, unless the question specifically mentions Regulation T.

Match the following items to the appropriate description below.

A. $1,000
B. Third business day after the trade
C. T+5
D. 90 days

___B___ 1. Regular way settlement for corporate securities

___A___ 2. Amount that can be ignored by a broker/dealer without violating Regulation T settlement

___D___ 3. The length of time for which frozen account status is imposed

___C___ 4. Regulation T settlement

Dividend Department

The **dividend department** collects and distributes cash dividends for stocks held in street name. In addition to processing cash dividends, the department handles registered bond interest payments, stock dividends, stock splits, rights offerings, warrants, and any special distributions to a corporation's stockholders or bondholders.

Transfer Agent

Dividends are actually disbursed, on the payable date, by a party known as the transfer agent. The corporation itself may have the transfer agent on its payroll, or the transfer agent may be a bank or trust company that keeps track of the stockholders and disburses dividends when declared.

Dividend Disbursing Process

Declaration Date. When a company's board of directors approves a dividend payment, it also designates the payment date and the dividend record date. The SEC requires any corporation that intends to pay cash dividends or make other distributions to notify the NASD or the appropriate exchange at least 10 business days before the record date. This enables the NASD or exchange to establish the ex-date.

Ex-Dividend Date. Based on the dividend record date, the NASD Uniform Practice Committee, or the exchange if the stock is listed, posts an **ex-date**. The ex-date is two business days before the record date. Because most trades settle regular way—three business days after the trade date—a customer must purchase the stock three business days before the record date to qualify for the dividend.

TAKE NOTE

For dividend purposes, an investor does not own the stock until settlement date, three business days after the trade date.

On the ex-date, the stock's opening price drops to compensate for the fact that customers who buy the stock that day or later do not qualify for the dividend. Trades executed regular way on or after the ex-date do not settle until after the record date.

A customer who buys the stock before the ex-date receives the dividend but pays a higher price for the stock. The customer who buys the stock on or after the ex-date does not receive the dividend but pays a lower price for the stock.

Dividend Record Date. The stockholders of record, as of the record date receive the dividend distribution.

Payable Date. Two or three weeks after the record date, the dividend disbursing agent sends dividend checks to all stockholders whose names appeared on the books as of the record date.

TAKE NOTE

The acronym **DERP** will help you remember the order in which the dates involving dividend distributions occur.

The **D**eclaration takes place first; the **P**ayment of the dividend is actually the last step in the process. The dividend is paid to owners on the date of **R**ecord. The corporation's board of directors determines the declaration, record and payable dates. The **ex**-date is determined by NASD rules.

TAKE NOTE

The calendar shown here assumes a record date of June 21:

June						
Sun	Mon	Tue	Wed	Thu	Fri	Sat
				1	2	3
4	5	6	7	8	9	10
11	12	13	14	15	16	17
18	19	20	21	22	23	24
25	26	27	28	29	30	

Record Date → 21

Will an investor who purchases stock on Friday, June 16, receive the dividend?

The investor would receive the dividend because regular way settlement takes place three business days after the trade. Monday, Tuesday, and Wednesday are the three business days that must be counted. The investor settles on Wednesday, June 21, which means he owns the stock on the record date and is entitled to the dividend, which is paid on the payable date.

What if the transaction had taken place on Monday, June 19?

Counting the three business days required, regular way settlement would take place on Thursday, June 22. The investor would own the stock on the business day after the record date—too late to receive the dividend.

This example illustrates that June 19 is the first day the investor buys the stock without the dividend (the ex-date) when the record date is June 21. An investor must buy the stock before the ex-date to get the dividend. The seller receives the dividend if the transaction takes place on or after the ex-date.

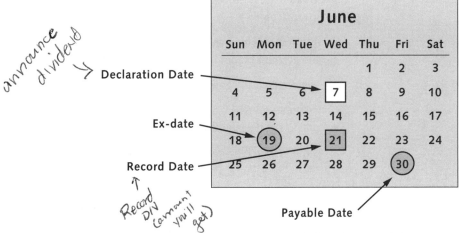

The ex-date is two business days before the record date in transactions executed with regular way settlement.

Consider an investor who purchases the stock on Wednesday, June 21, in a cash settlement transaction. Because the settlement takes place the same day, the investor receives the dividend and owns the stock on the record date of June 21.

As you will learn in the next Unit, mutual fund ex-dates are typically the business day after the record date.

Event	Definition	Duration/Expiration
Trade date	Date on which the transaction occurs	Initiation date for all types of payment contracts; due date for cash settlements
Settlement date	Date on which payment must be received under NASD, NYSE, or MSRB rules	The investor must have settled the transaction to be considered the stockholder of record on the record date
Record date	Determines who is eligible to receive dividends or rights distributions; fixed by the issuing corporation	The investor must have settled the transaction to be considered the stockholder of record on the record date
Ex-date (ex-dividend date)	Set by the Uniform Practice Committee after being informed of the distribution declaration by the issuer; stock is sold without (ex) the right to receive the dividend	One-day period dictated by the record date for distributions; normally two business days before the record date; stock trades with out (ex) rights or dividends
Payable date	Date on which dividend is paid	Date appears on dividend checks

QUICK QUIZ 3.5

Match the following items to the appropriate description below.

A. Trade date
B. Settlement date
C. Ex-date
D. Frozen account

_D_ 1. Account requiring cash in advance before a buy order is executed because the account holder has violated Regulation T

_A_ 2. The day that obligates the parties to the terms of the trade

_C_ 3. First date on which a security trades without entitling the buyer to receive a previously declared distribution

_B_ 4. Date on which ownership changes between buyer and seller

True or False?

_F_ 5. To receive a dividend, a shareholder must own the stock on the ex-date.

_F_ 6. The ex-date is 2 business days following the record date.

_F_ 7. The buyer gets the dividend if a trade takes place on the ex-date.

_F_ 8. The payable date is usually before the record date.

Rules of Good Delivery

A security must be in good delivery form before it can be delivered to a buyer.

Good delivery describes the physical condition of, signatures on, attachments to, and denomination of the certificates involved in a securities transaction. Good delivery is normally a back-office consideration between buying and selling brokers. In any broker-to-broker transaction, the delivered securities must be accompanied by a properly executed uniform delivery ticket. The transfer agent is the final arbiter of whether a security meets the requirements of good delivery.

Terms and Concepts Checklist

✓	✓	✓
☐ Exchanges, first market	☐ Auction market	☐ Markup, markdown
☐ Specialist	☐ Negotiated market	☐ Broker/dealer
☐ OTC, second market	☐ Broker, agent	☐ Position trading
☐ Market maker	☐ Commission	☐ Regulation T payment
☐ Third market	☐ Transfer agent	☐ Regular way settlement
☐ Fourth market	☐ Declaration date	☐ Cash settlement
☐ Trade date	☐ Ex-dividend date	☐ Extension
☐ Customer confirmation	☐ Record date	☐ Frozen account
☐ Dividend payment	☐ Payable date	☐ Rules of good delivery
	☐ Dealer, principal	

THE REGULATION OF TRADING

As the Securities Act of 1933 regulates primary issues of securities, the Securities Exchange Act of 1934 regulates secondary trading.

TAKE NOTE

Like the Act of 1933, key words help identify the Act of 1934.

Consider the Act of 1934 as the **People and Places Act:** it regulates all persons involved in trading securities on behalf of customers and the markets, (exchanges), where that trading takes place.

Although certain securities are exempt from the registration requirements of the Act of 1933, no security is exempt from the antifraud provisions of the Act of 1934.

This statement means that certain securities are exempt from registration and prospectus requirements, but you cannot use fraud in the trading of any security, exempt or nonexempt.

THE SECURITIES EXCHANGE ACT OF 1934

The **Securities Exchange Act of 1934 (Exchange Act)** formed the SEC and gave it the authority to regulate the securities exchanges and the OTC markets to maintain a fair and orderly market for the investing public. The act addresses the:

■ creation of the SEC;

■ regulation of exchanges;

■ regulation of credit by the Federal Reserve Board (FRB);

■ registration of broker/dealers;

■ regulation of insider transactions, short sales, and proxies;

■ regulation of trading activities;

■ regulation of client accounts;

■ customer protection rules;

■ regulation of the OTC market;

■ net capital rule and financial responsibility for broker/dealers; and

■ know your customer rule.

The Securities Exchange Act of 1934 requires exchange members, broker/dealers that trade securities OTC and on exchanges, and individuals who make securities trades for the public to be registered with the SEC.

QUICK QUIZ 3.6

Determine whether each phrase below describes the Act of 1933 or 1934.

_33_ 1. Prohibits fraud in the primary markets

_34_ 2. Requires registration of broker/dealers

_34_ 3. Created the SEC

_33_ 4. Requires nonexempt issuers to file registration statements

_34_ 5. Prohibits fraudulent trading practices

_33_ 6. The Paper Act

_33_ 7. Regulates underwriting activity

_34_ 8. Regulates extension of credit by brokerage firms

_34_ 9. Regulates client accounts

_34_ 10. The People and Places Act

The Securities and Exchange Commission (SEC)

The SEC enforces the 1934 Act by regulating the securities markets and behavior of market participants.

Registration of Exchanges and Firms

The 1934 Act requires national securities exchanges to file registration statements with the SEC. By registering, exchanges agree to comply with and help enforce the rules of this act. Each exchange gives the SEC copies of its bylaws, constitution, and articles of incorporation. An exchange must disclose to the SEC any amendment to exchange rules as soon as it is adopted.

The act of 1934 also requires companies that list their securities on the exchanges and certain firms traded OTC to file with the SEC. An SEC-registered company must file annual audited reports informing the SEC of its financial status and providing other information.

Regulation of Broker/Dealers. Broker/dealers must comply with SEC rules and regulations when conducting business. A broker/dealer that does not comply is subject to:

- censure;

- limits on activities, functions, or operations;

- suspension of its registration (or one of its associated person's license to do business);

- revocation of registration; or

- a fine.

Although a broker/dealer must register with the SEC, the broker/dealer may not claim that this registration in any way implies that the Commission has passed upon or approved the broker/dealer's financial standing, business, or conduct. Any such claim or statement is a misrepresentation.

The Maloney Act. An amendment to the act of 1934, the **Maloney Act of 1938**, created the NASD. The Maloney Act allows the NASD to act as the self-regulatory organization (SRO) for the over-the-counter market.

SROs, such as the NASD, the NYSE, the MSRB (Municipal Securities Rulemaking Board), and others must be registered with the SEC. Although permitted to make rules for their member firms, all SROs are subject to regulation by the SEC.

Fingerprinting. Registered broker/dealers must have fingerprint records made for all of their employees, directors, officers, and partners and must submit those fingerprint cards to the US attorney general for identification and processing. Broker/dealer employees (typically clerical) are exempt from the fingerprinting requirement if they:

- are not involved in securities sales;

- do not handle or have access to cash or securities or to the books and records of original entry relating to money and securities; and

- do not supervise other employees engaged in these activities.

An additional exemption applies to broker/dealers and their employees involved exclusively in the sales of mutual fund shares, unit investment trusts, and variable contracts, as certificates for these securities are not ordinarily issued.

Regulation of Credit

The act of 1934 authorized the **Federal Reserve Board (FRB)** to regulate margin accounts, the credit extended for the purchase of securities. Within FRB jurisdiction are:

- **Regulation T**, which regulates the extension of credit to customers by broker/dealers; and

- **Regulation U**, which regulates the extension of credit to customers for the purpose of purchasing securities by banks and other lenders.

The 1934 Act prohibits the extension of credit based on new issue securities as collateral for 30 days. Mutual funds, even though continuously offered as new securities, may be used as collateral as long as they have been held for 30 days. Although mutual fund shares can be used as collateral in a margin account, they can never be purchased on margin.

TAKE NOTE   Regulation U regulates the extension of credit from banks to their customers.
Regulation T regulates the extension of credit from broker/dealers to their customers.

THE INVESTMENT ADVISERS ACT OF 1940

The Investment Advisers Act of 1940 was passed to regulate the activities of persons giving customers advice about securities. An **investment adviser** is one who, for compensation, provides advice about investing in securities.

Exclusions

The definition of investment adviser does not include:

- banks and bank holding companies;

- publishers of any bona fide newspaper, newsmagazine, or business or financial publication of general and regular circulation (such as *The Wall Street Journal* or *Business Week*);

- brokers or dealers (or their associated persons and registered representatives) whose investment advice is incidental to the conduct of the broker/dealer's business and who receive no special compensation for the advice;

- persons who advise solely on US government securities; or

- persons whose giving of investment advice is incidental to their professions (e.g., lawyers, accountants, teachers, engineers).

TAKE NOTE   This last exclusion can be remembered using the acronym LATE.

TAKE NOTE   The exception granted to broker/dealers only applies if the firm does not charge specifically for giving advice. If a member firm were to set up a financial planning operation and charge separately for this service, the firm would be considered an investment adviser.

Registration of Investment Advisers

Any person, unless exempt, who falls within the federal definition of an investment adviser must register with the SEC under the Investment Advisers Act of 1940. SEC-registered investment advisers are known as **federal covered investment advisers**. That term originated with the **National Securities Markets Improvement Act of 1996**, generally referred to as **NSMIA**. NSMIA split the responsibility of regulation of investment advisers between the states and the SEC based upon the amount of money the adviser had under management. An investment adviser that is not subject to federal registration requirements must register with the state in which it conducts business.

EXAMPLE   An investment adviser managing less than $25 million in assets must register with the state(s).

TAKE NOTE Under SEC regulations, advisers managing between $25 and $30 million have the option to register with either the state(s) or the SEC.

Federal registered investment advisers are exempt from state registration. While exempt from state registration, these investment advisers are still required to pay state filing fees and give notice.

State Administrators are responsible for overseeing the business activities of all investment advisers that conduct business within the state and for enforcing the antifraud provisions under state law.

Investment Adviser Representative

In the same manner that registered representatives are associated persons of broker/dealers, **investment adviser representatives** are associated persons of investment advisers. The term applies to any partner, officer, or director of an investment adviser (or any person performing similar functions), or any person directly or indirectly controlling or controlled by the investment adviser, including any employee of that investment adviser, except that persons associated with an investment adviser whose functions are clerical or ministerial are not included in the meaning of the term.

TAKE NOTE Persons who must register under the Investment Advisers Act of 1940 include financial planners, pension consultants, investment counselors, and investment advisory services. Anyone who receives a fee for investment advising must register.

Terms and Concepts Checklist

✓

- ☐ The Securities Exchange Act of 1934
- ☐ SEC
- ☐ Registration
- ☐ The Investment Advisers Act of 1940
- ☐ Investment adviser
- ☐ Investment adviser representative
- ☐ Exemptions and exclusions under the Investment Advisers Act

✓

- ☐ The Maloney Act of 1938
- ☐ Fingerprint rule
- ☐ FRB
- ☐ Regulation T
- ☐ Regulation U
- ☐ Federal registered adviser
- ☐ State administrator

MUTUAL FUND DISTRIBUTIONS AND TAXATION

Distributions from mutual funds are derived from income received from portfolio securities or gains from the sale of portfolio securities. Whether taken in cash or reinvested, distributions are taxable.

DISTRIBUTIONS FROM MUTUAL FUNDS

Mutual fund distributions are taxed according to the **conduit theory** (also known as the **pipeline theory**).

The Conduit Theory

Because an investment company is organized as a corporation or trust, you might assume its earnings are subject to tax. Consider, however, how an additional level of taxation shrinks a dividend distribution's value.

EXAMPLE   GEM Fund owns shares of Mountain Brewing Co. First, Mountain Brewing is taxed on its earnings before it pays a dividend. Then, GEM Fund pays tax on the amount of the dividend it receives. Finally, the investor pays income tax on the distribution from the fund.

Triple taxation of investment income may be avoided if the mutual fund qualifies under Subchapter M of the Internal Revenue Code (IRC). If a mutual fund acts as a conduit (pipeline) for the distribution of net investment income, the fund may qualify as a regulated investment company subject to tax only on the amount of investment income the fund retains. The investment income distributed to shareholders escapes taxation at the mutual fund level.

To avoid taxation under Subchapter M, a fund must distribute at least 90% of its net investment income to shareholders. The fund then pays taxes only on the undistributed amount.

EXAMPLE   If a fund distributes 89%, it must pay taxes on 100% of net investment income.

EXAMPLE   What are the tax consequences to a fund that distributes 98% of its net investment income? In this situation, the fund does not pay taxes on the 98% that is distributed; it pays taxes only on the 2% of retained earnings.

Dividend Distributions

A mutual fund may pay dividends to each shareholder in the same way corporations pay dividends to stockholders. Dividends are paid from the mutual fund's net investment income.

Net investment income includes gross investment income—dividend and interest income from securities held in the portfolio—minus operating expenses. Advertising and sales expenses are not included in a fund's operating expenses when calculating net investment income. Dividends from net investment income are taxed as ordinary income to shareholders.

Net investment income = dividends + interest − expenses of the fund

TEST TOPIC ALERT
You may see a question on the exam that asks for this calculation and gives a list of items to exclude or include in the calculation. Remember **D + I – E** and it will be easy to remember which items to include.

Net investment income is distributed to shareholders as dividends. Dividends paid to shareholders may be reinvested or taken in cash. The shareholder pays ordinary income taxes on the dividends in either case.

Capital Gains Distributions

The appreciation or depreciation of portfolio securities is unrealized capital gain or loss if the fund does not sell the securities. Therefore, shareholders experience no tax consequences. When the fund sells the securities, the gain or loss is realized. A **realized gain** is an actual profit made.

Capital gains distributions are derived from realized gains. If the fund has held the securities for more than one year, the gain is a long-term capital gain, taxed at the long-term capital gains rate. The mutual fund may retain the gain or distribute it to shareholders. A long-term capital gains distribution may not be made more often than once per year.

TAKE NOTE
Capital gains distributions may be made no more than once per year.

Any gains distribution from a mutual fund is long term. A short-term gain is identified, distributed, and taxed as a dividend distribution.

TAKE NOTE
The terms *realized gains* and *unrealized gains* can be confusing. Think of an **unrealized gain** as a paper profit and **realized gain** as actual profit made.

EXAMPLE
If you had purchased a house for $150,000 and its value had appreciated to $200,000, you would experience an unrealized gain of $50,000. You would have no taxes to pay on these paper profits. If you had sold the house, the $50,000 would be taxable to you as a capital gain. The gain resulting from a sale is known as a realized gain. Unrealized profits are not taxable; realized profits are taxable as capital gains.

A mutual fund portfolio that has increased in value has unrealized profits; these are not taxable to investors. But, when the fund sells appreciated portfolio securities, it has realized profits. These profits are distributed as capital gains to shareholders. Shareholders can take these capital gain distributions in cash or reinvest them to purchase additional shares. In either case, these distributions are taxable as capital gains to shareholders.

Reinvestment of Distributions

Dividends and capital gains are distributed in cash. However, a shareholder may elect to reinvest distributions in additional mutual fund shares. The automatic reinvestment of distributions is similar to compounding interest. The reinvested distributions purchase additional shares, which may earn dividends or gains distributions.

TAKE NOTE

Frequently, mutual funds allowed reinvestment of dividend and capital gains distributions at the NAV. Now all newly formed funds offer this feature. This means that investors are able to buy new shares without a sales load—a significant advantage that results in faster growth to the investor.

Typically, customers may systematically reinvest dividends and capital gains at less than the POP and use them to purchase full and fractional shares provided that:

- shareholders who are not already participants in the reinvestment plan are given a separate opportunity to reinvest each dividend;

- the plan is described in the prospectus;

- the securities issuer bears no additional costs beyond those that it would have incurred in the normal payout of dividends; and

- shareholders are notified of the availability of the dividend reinvestment plan at least once every year.

A mutual fund may apply a reasonable charge against each dividend reinvestment. If a company wishes to establish a plan through which investors can reinvest their capital gains distributions (as opposed to their dividends) at a discount to the POP, the following rules apply.

- The plan must be described in the prospectus.

- All participants must be given a separate opportunity to reinvest capital gains at each distribution.

- All participants must be notified at least once every year of the availability of the distribution reinvestment plan.

TAKE NOTE

Ordinary income is income that is received from dividends from stock and interest from bonds. **Capital gains** are from the sale of securities at a profit; when securities are bought low and sold for a higher price, capital gains are realized.

Taxation of Reinvested Distributions

Distributions are taxable to shareholders whether the distributions are received in cash or reinvested. The fund must disclose whether each distribution is from income or capital gains. **Form 1099**, which is sent to shareholders after the close of the year, details tax information related to distributions for the year.

TAKE NOTE

Just as with dividend distributions, whether capital gains are taken in cash or reinvested, they are currently taxable to the shareholder. Dividends must be reported as ordinary income; long-term capital gains distributions must be reported on the investor's capital gains schedule.

TAKE NOTE

It is the shareholder's responsibility to report all dividends and capital gains distributions to the IRS and state tax agency.

QUICK QUIZ 3.7

True or False?

___F___ 1. A portfolio's unrealized gains are taxable to mutual fund shareholders.

___F___ 2. Capital gains distributions are typically paid quarterly.

___F___ 3. Mutual fund capital gains distributions are taxable to shareholders as short-term capital gains.

___T___ 4. Mutual funds pay dividends to shareholders from net investment income.

___T___ 5. IRC Subchapter M requires a fund to distribute a minimum of 90% of its net investment income to avoid taxation as a corporation on what it distributes.

___F___ 6. Funds that comply with IRC Subchapter M are considered registered investment companies.

___F___ 7. Reinvested dividend distributions are not currently taxable to shareholders.

___T___ 8. Form 1099 classifies mutual fund distributions to shareholders.

Calculating Fund Yield

To calculate fund yield, divide the yearly dividend paid from net investment income by the current offering price. Yield quotations must disclose:

- the general direction of the stock market for the period in question;

- the fund's NAV at the beginning and the end of the period; and

- the percentage change in the fund's price during the period.

Current yield calculations may only be based on dividend distributions for the preceding 12 months. Gains distributions may not be included in yield calculations. **Total return** is the return that would be achieved if dividends and capital gains distributions were reinvested.

Most mutual funds with income objectives distribute dividends quarterly. A mutual fund must disclose the source of a dividend payment if it is from other than retained or current income.

EXAMPLE

ABC mutual fund distributed dividends of $1 and capital gains of $1 in the past year. The current NAV of ABC shares is $19.50 and the POP is $20. What is the current yield of ABC shares? The correct answer is 5%.

Mutual fund yield is found exactly like the current yield on common stock:

$$\frac{\text{Annual dividend}}{\text{POP}}$$

The annual dividends of $1 divided by the POP of $20 equals current yield of 5%. Never include capital gains in the calculation of current yield.

The calculation of total return assumes the reinvestment of both dividends and capital gains.

Ex-Dividend Date

Unlike the ex-dividend date for other corporate securities, the ex-dividend date for mutual funds is set by the board of directors. Normally, the ex-dividend date for mutual funds is the day after the record date.

TAKE NOTE

Remember that the ex-date for mutual funds is determined by the BOD, but it is normally the next business day after the record date.

Selling Dividends

If an investor buys fund shares just before the ex-dividend date, the investor will receive the dividend, pay tax on the distribution, and see his share price reduced by the amount of the dividend. A registered representative may not encourage investors to purchase fund shares before a distribution because of this tax liability. Doing so is **selling dividends,** a violation of NASD rules.

TAKE NOTE

Selling dividends is a prohibited practice because the investor is immediately taxed on distributions received and the value of shares is reduced by the dividend distributed—so not only are investors subject to taxation, they have also experienced an immediate depreciation in the value of their shares.

Fund Share Liquidations to the Investor

An investor who sells mutual fund shares must establish the **cost base (basis)** in the shares to calculate the tax liability. A simple definition of cost base is the amount of money invested on which taxes have been paid. Upon liquidation, cost base represents a return of capital and is not taxed again.

Valuing Fund Shares

The cost base of mutual fund shares includes the shares' total cost, including sales charges, plus any reinvested income and capital gains. For tax purposes, the investor compares cost base to the amount of money received from selling the shares. If the amount received is greater than the cost base, the investor reports a taxable gain. If the amount received is less than the cost base, the investor reports a loss. Calculate the gain or loss on mutual fund shares as illustrated below.

Total value of fund shares – cost base = taxable gain or loss

The investor does not receive a separate tax form from the mutual fund identifying the cost base of the shares sold. Recordkeeping for purchases and sales is the shareholder's responsibility.

TAKE NOTE

To find the cost basis of mutual fund shares, add the price paid and all reinvested distributions. These distributions become part of the cost basis because they have already been taxed.

EXAMPLE

An investor bought shares for $10 and redeemed them for $15. The investor had reinvested dividend distributions of $1 per share and capital gains of $.50. What was the investor's cost basis and capital gain?

The cost basis is found by adding the initial share cost and the reinvested distributions ($10 + 1 + .50 = $11.50 cost basis). The capital gain is found by subtracting the cost basis from the sales proceeds ($15 – cost basis of $11.50 = capital gain of $3.50 per share).

If the shares had been sold for $11.00 instead, the investor would have experienced a capital loss of $.50 because the cost basis of $11.50 was $.50 greater than the sales proceeds of $11.00.

Calculating Net Gains and Losses

To calculate tax liability, taxpayers must first add all capital gains for the year. Then, they separately add all capital losses. Finally, they offset the totals to determine the net capital gain or loss for the year. Net capital losses are deductible against earned income up to a maximum of $3,000 per year. Any capital losses not deducted in a year may be carried forward indefinitely to be used in future years.

EXAMPLE

An investor's capital gains schedule reports the following:

Capital Gains	Capital Losses
$20,000	$30,000

The investor experiences a net capital loss of $10,000. Of this loss, $3,000 can be used to reduce the investor's ordinary income in the current tax year. The remaining $7,000 net capital loss may be carried forward indefinitely, and $3,000 per year can be used as a deduction until the full amount is used up.

Accounting Methods

An investor who decides to liquidate shares determines the cost base by electing one of three accounting methods: **first in, first out (FIFO)**; share identification; or average basis. If the investor fails to choose, the IRS assumes the investor liquidates shares on a FIFO basis.

First In, First Out (FIFO)

When FIFO shares are sold, the cost of the shares held the longest is used to calculate the gain or loss. In a rising market, this method normally creates adverse tax consequences.

Share Identification

When using the **share identification accounting method**, the investor keeps track of the cost of each share purchased and uses this information when deciding which shares to liquidate. He then liquidates the shares that provide the desired tax benefits.

Average Basis

The shareholder may elect to use an **average cost basis** when redeeming fund shares. The shareholder calculates average basis by dividing the total cost of all shares owned by the total number of shares. The shareholder may not change his decision to use the average basis method without IRS permission.

EXAMPLE

An investor has purchased shares as follows:

1990: Cost basis $10.00

1995: Cost basis $20.00

If the investor wants to redeem shares this year at the current NAV of $25.00, which shares would result in the least capital gains taxation?

Redemption of the shares with the highest cost basis results in the least tax. Redemption of the 1995 shares would result in a gain of $5.00 per share ($25.00 – $20.00 = $5.00). However, if the investor redeems the 1990 shares, the capital gain is $15.00 per share ($25.00 – $10.00 = $15.00).

Investors are entitled to choose which shares they wish to redeem first under the share identification method. If they do not choose, the IRS assumes FIFO. FIFO generally results in the largest taxation because the shares acquired earliest typically have the lowest basis.

Other Mutual Fund Tax Considerations

Mutual fund investors must consider many tax factors when buying and selling mutual fund shares.

Withholding Tax

If an investor neglects or fails to include their tax ID number (Social Security number) when purchasing mutual fund shares, the fund must withhold 31% of the distributions to the investor as a withholding tax.

Cost Basis of Shares Inherited

The cost basis of inherited property is either stepped up or stepped down to its fair market value (FMV) at the date of the decedent's death.

Dividend Exclusions

Corporations that invest in other companies' stock may deduct 70% of dividends received from taxable income. No similar exclusion exists for individual investors.

Taxation of Investment Returns

The taxation of investment returns can be summarized as follows:

Income distributions:	taxed as ordinary income
Capital gains distributions:	taxed at investor's capital gains tax rate
Profit or loss on sale:	short- or long-term gain or loss depending on length of holding period and cost basis

Exchanges Within a Family of Funds

Even though an exchange within a fund family incurs no sales charge, the IRS considers a sale to have taken place, and if a gain occurs, the customer is taxed. This tax liability can be significant, and shareholders should be aware of this potential conversion cost.

Wash Sales

Capital losses may not be used to offset gains or income if the investor sells a security at a loss and purchases the same or a substantially identical security within 30 days before or after the trade date. The sale at a loss and the repurchase within this period is a **wash sale.**

The rule disallows the loss or tax benefit from selling a security and repurchasing the security or one substantially identical to it in this manner. The term *substantially identical* refers to any other security with the same investment performance likelihood as the one being sold. Examples are:

- securities convertible into the one being sold;

- warrants to purchase the security being sold;

- rights to purchase the security being sold; and

- call options to purchase the security being sold.

31st		SELL		31st
DAY <-----------------------------------		@	----------------------------->DAY	
OK	30 Days	LOSS	30 Days	OK

TAKE NOTE   The wash sale rule covers 30 days before and after the trade date. Including the trade date, this is a total time period of 61 days.

TEST TOPIC ALERT

- Funds that comply with Subchapter M (conduit theory) are known as **regulated investment companies**.

- Mutual fund yield is calculated by dividing the annual dividend by the POP. Capital gains distributions are not included.

- If asked the ex-date of a mutual fund, the best answer is as determined by the BOD; otherwise, choose the business day after the record date.

- Dividends and capital gains are taxable whether reinvested or taken in cash.

- An investor's cost basis in mutual fund shares is what was paid to buy the share plus reinvested dividends and capital gains distributions.

- The IRS always assigns FIFO for share liquidation unless the investor chooses a different method.

- $3,000 of net capital loss may be used as a deduction against ordinary income each tax year. Unused capital loss may be carried forward indefinitely.

- There is no tax exclusion available on dividends paid to individuals, but corporations may exclude 70% of dividends received from taxation.

- Although an exchange from one fund to another within the same family is not subject to a sales charge, it is a taxable event. Any gain or loss on the shares sold is reportable at the time of the exchange.

- When a shareholder dies, his shares are assigned a cost basis equal to the value of the shares on the date of death.

QUICK QUIZ 3.8

1. Which of the following decides when a mutual fund goes ex-dividend?
    A. NASD
    B. NYSE
    C. SEC
    D. Board of directors of the fund

2. The conduit theory
    A. is described in the Investment Company Act of 1940
    B. refers to a favorable tax treatment available to investment companies
    C. was developed by the NASD
    D. is stated in the SEC statement of policy

3. Your client owns shares in an open-end investment company. The shares are currently quoted at $10 bid and $10.80 ask. Within the past 12 months, the investment company has distributed capital gains of $1.20 per share and dividends of $.60 per share. What is the current yield on your client's shares?
    A. 1.8%
    B. 5.0%
    C. 5.6%
    D. 6.0%

    $$\frac{.60}{10.80} = 5.60\%$$

Terms and Concepts Checklist

✓

- ☐ Conduit, pipeline theory
- ☐ Regulated investment company
- ☐ Dividend distributions
- ☐ Capital gains distributions
- ☐ Reinvestment of distributions
- ☐ Tax on distributions
- ☐ Taxable gain or loss
- ☐ Realized, unrealized gain
- ☐ Cost base
- ☐ FIFO
- ☐ LIFO
- ☐ Share identification
- ☐ Average basis

✓

- ☐ Net investment income
- ☐ Expenses
- ☐ Ordinary income
- ☐ Short-term, long-term capital gains
- ☐ Yield and yield disclosures
- ☐ Total return
- ☐ Mutual fund ex-date
- ☐ Selling dividends
- ☐ Wash sales
- ☐ Inherited shares
- ☐ Corporate dividend exclusion
- ☐ Exchanges within a family of funds

TAXATION OF VARIABLE CONTRACT PRODUCTS

TAXATION OF ANNUITIES

Individual annuities, not being tax qualified, are purchased with after-tax dollars. Payments into the account therefore comprise the annuitant's cost basis and are not taxed or penalized when withdrawn. Accumulation and earnings are taxed as ordinary income (plus a 10% penalty if the annuitant is not yet 59½) and must be withdrawn first if the account has not been annuitized.

It is also important to remember that if funds are withdrawn from an annuity very early, the issuing insurance company will levy its own penalty over and above the federal penalty. The longer the annuitant leaves his money in the account, the lower the penalty upon withdrawal, until the insurance company's penalty reaches zero, typically after seven years. This is known as an annuity's **contingent-deferred sales charge** because the penalty is considered a form of sales charge. The sales charge paid at the time of purchase of the annuity, or at the time of each periodic payment, is known as the annuity's **level sales charge.** Note the differences between these charges and contingent-deferred and level sales charges with mutual funds.

TEST TOPIC ALERT   Assume an annuity is nonqualified unless the question specifically states otherwise.

EXAMPLE   An investor has contributed $100,000 to a variable annuity. The annuity is now worth $150,000. What is the investor's cost basis and what amount is taxable upon withdrawal?

Assume the $100,000 in contributions were made with after-tax dollars. Cost basis is equal to the contributions, so $100,000 is the investor's cost basis. The taxable amount at withdrawal will be the earnings of $50,000.

A good way to understand taxation of annuity withdrawals is to remember that with random withdrawals, growth and accumulation must be taken out first, whether the annuitant is over the age of 59½ or not. Until the annuitant dies or reaches his life expectancy, annuitized withdrawals, on the other hand, are part cost base (not taxable) and part growth and accumulation (taxable). The relationship between the two is known as the **exclusion ratio**. With the mortality guarantee, if the annuitant outlives his life expectancy, he will have used up his cost base, and 100% of withdrawals become taxable. The amount of each payment considered a return of cost basis is determined by dividing the annuity owner's cost basis by his life expectancy.

EXAMPLE   For example, payments to an annuitant with an actuarial life expectancy of 20 years and a cost basis of $100,000 would have a yearly cost basis of $5,000 ($100,000 ÷ 20).

TEST TOPIC ALERT

You will not be asked to calculate the amount of each annuity payment that is taxable or nontaxable; however, you may be asked a question similar to the following.

The amount of each month's annuity payment that is considered by the IRS as a return of cost basis is determined by which of the following calculations?

A.   LIFO

B.   FIFO

C.   Cost basis divided by life expectancy

D.   Income averaging

Answer: C. The calculation that is made to identify the portion of each month's income that is a return of the after-tax dollars invested (the investor's cost basis) is:

Annuity owner's cost basis ÷ annuitant's life expectancy

For lump-sum or random withdrawals from annuities, growth and accumulation must be withdrawn and taxed (and possibly penalized) first—LIFO, last in, first out. Once all earnings have been withdrawn, cost basis can be withdrawn with neither tax nor penalty.

EXAMPLE

Assume $100,000 after-tax contributions (cost basis):

$50,000   earnings

$150,000   total account value

If the investor makes a random withdrawal of $60,000, what are the tax consequences?

Remember that LIFO applies—the IRS wants tax revenue as early as possible. Those earnings that accumulated tax deferred are now fully taxable. The investor must pay ordinary income taxes on the first $50,000 withdrawn because that is the amount of earnings. And, if the investor is under age 59½, an extra 10% early withdrawal tax applies. The remaining $10,000 is a return of the cost basis and is not taxed or penalized.

TEST TOPIC ALERT

Any answer choice that mentions capital gains taxation on annuities or retirement plans is wrong. There is only ordinary income tax on distributions from annuities and retirement plans.

QUICK QUIZ 3.9

1.   A customer buys a nonqualified variable annuity at age 60. Before the contract is annuitized, she withdraws some of her funds. What are the consequences?

A.   10% penalty plus payment of ordinary income on all funds withdrawn

B.   10% penalty plus payment of ordinary income on all funds withdrawn in excess of basis

C.   Capital gains tax on earnings in excess of basis

D.   Ordinary income tax on earnings in excess of basis

2. Distributions from both an IRA and a variable annuity are subject to which of the following forms of taxation?
   A. Short-term capital gains
   B. Long-term capital gains
   C. Ordinary income
   D. No tax due

3. Joe, who is 42, is investing in a nonqualified variable annuity. This year, the securities in his separate account experience capital gains of $4,000. What tax must he pay on the gains this year?
   A. 0%
   B. 10%
   C. 25%
   D. 50%

TEST TOPIC ALERT Be prepared for a question about taxation of early withdrawals or surrender of the contract before annuitization similar to the following.

1. An annuity contract owner, age 45, surrenders his annuity to buy a home. Which of the following statements best describes the tax consequences of this action?
   A. Ordinary income taxes and a 10% early withdrawal penalty will apply to all money withdrawn.
   B. Capital gains tax will apply to the amount of the withdrawal that represents earnings; there will be no tax on the cost basis.
   C. Ordinary income taxes and a 10% early withdrawal penalty will apply to the amount of the withdrawal that represents earnings; there will be no tax on the cost basis.
   D. Ordinary income taxes apply to the amount of the withdrawal that represents earnings; the 10% early withdrawal penalty does not apply to surrenders.

   Answer: C. Interest earnings are always withdrawn first and are taxable as ordinary income. They are also subject to the 10% early withdrawal penalty when withdrawn prior to age 59½. Note that this tax treatment is no different than random or lump-sum withdrawal tax treatment.

2. After the death of the annuitant, beneficiaries under a life and 15-year period certain option are subject to
   A. capital gains taxation on the total amount of payments received
   B. ordinary income taxation on the total amount of payments received, plus a 10% withdrawal penalty if the annuitant was under the age of 59½
   C. ordinary income taxation on the amount of the payment that exceeds the cost basis
   D. tax-free payout of all remaining annuity benefits

   Answer: C. Payments from the annuity to the beneficiary through a period certain option are taxed in the same way as all other annuity payments: benefits over the amount of the cost basis are taxable as ordinary income. However, no 10% penalty applies in this situation.

TAXATION OF LIFE INSURANCE

Tax Treatment to the Policyholder

During the life of the policy, net investment income (from dividends and interest paid to the separate account) and capital gains (both realized and unrealized) are not taxable to the policyholder. There is also no tax liability when a loan is taken against the cash value.

If the policy is surrendered, policy proceeds equal to the amount of premiums paid are tax free. The premiums paid are considered the cost basis of the policy. Any earnings over the cost basis are treated as income to the policyholder.

A death benefit that is paid to the beneficiary of a life insurance policy is exempt from federal taxation as income. However, the full amount of the policy's death benefit can be included in the estate of the deceased policyowner for federal estate tax purposes.

1035 Exchange Provision

The IRS allows variable annuity and variable life policyholders to exchange their policies without tax liability. For example, if a variable life policyholder wanted to exchange his policy to that of another company, he could transfer all values from the old policy into the new policy without recognizing any tax consequences. This **1035 exchange provision** applies to transfers from fixed policies to variable policies and vice versa. It also applies to transfers of life insurance to annuities; however, it cannot be used for transfers from an annuity to a life insurance policy.

TAKE NOTE   The 1035 provisions apply only to taxation. The insurance company itself may impose penalties if a contract or policy is exchanged under the 1035 provisions.

QUICK QUIZ 3.10

True or False?

_F_   1. Policy death benefits are taxable as income to beneficiaries.

_F_   2. Policy death benefits are excluded from the estate of the deceased policyowner.

_T_   3. The cost basis of an insurance policy is equal to the premiums paid.

_F_   4. A 1035 exchange from an insurance policy to an annuity is not permitted

_T_   5. A 1035 exchange can be made between fixed and variable policies

_F_   6. When a policy is surrendered, any earnings in excess of the cost basis are subject to taxation as capital gains.

_T_   7. The amount withdrawn for a policy loan is not taxable to the policyholder.

Terms and Concepts Checklist

✓	✓
☐ Contingent deferred sales charge	☐ Exclusion ratio
☐ Level sales charge	☐ 1035 Exchange
☐ Random withdrawal	☐ Life expectancy

RETIREMENT PLANNING

An important goal for many investors is to provide themselves with retirement income. Many individuals accomplish this through corporate retirement plans, others set up their own plans, and some have both individual and corporate retirement plans.

There are two types of retirement plans in the United States, qualified and nonqualified. The basic difference between the two is that qualified plans allow pretax contributions to be made, while nonqualified plans may be contributed to only with after-tax money. Both, however, allow earnings to grow tax deferred until retirement.

Contribution limits for qualified retirement plans vary and are adjusted from year to year.

Qualified vs. Nonqualified Plans

Qualified Plans	Nonqualified Plans
Contributions currently tax deductible	Contributions not currently tax deductible
Plan approved by the IRS	Plan does not need IRS approval
Plan cannot discriminate	Plan can discriminate
All withdrawals taxed	Excess over cost base taxed
Plan is a trust	Plan is not a trust
Strict IRS and Labor Department reporting and disclosure	Limited reporting and disclosure
Plan must be in writing	Plan must be in writing
Tax on accumulation is deferred	Tax on accumulation is deferred

NONQUALIFIED RETIREMENT PLANS

Types of Plans

Deferred compensation and payroll deduction programs are two types of nonqualified retirement plans. Both plans may be used to favor certain employees (typically executives) because nondiscrimination rules are not applicable to nonqualified plans.

TAKE NOTE   When a plan is nondiscriminatory, all persons that meet certain criteria must be eligible to participate. In a discriminatory plan, the employer can choose to provide benefits to certain employees but exclude others.

A **nonqualified deferred compensation plan** is a contractual agreement between a company and an employee in which the employee agrees to defer receipt of current income in favor of payout at retirement. It is assumed that the employee will be in a lower tax bracket at retirement age. These plans are not available to company board members because they are not considered employees for retirement planning purposes.

Deferred compensation plans may be somewhat risky because the employee covered by the plan has no right to plan benefits if the business fails. In this situation, the employee becomes a general creditor of the firm. Covered employees may also forfeit benefits if they leave the firm before retirement. When the benefit is payable at the employee's retirement, it is taxable as ordinary income to the employee. The employer now deducts the benefits as a business expense.

Payroll deduction plans allow employees to authorize their employer to deduct a specified amount for retirement savings from their paychecks. The money is deducted after taxes are paid and may be invested in any number of retirement vehicles at the employee's option.

Section 457 plans are nonqualified retirement plans set up by state and local governments and tax-exempt employers for their employees. They function as deferred compensation plans in which earnings grow tax deferred and growth and accumulation are taxed only at the time of distribution. Employees may defer up to 100% of their compensation, up to an indexed contribution limit.

TEST TOPIC ALERT   For NASD exams, 401(k) plans are considered salary reduction plans, not payroll deduction plans. In any question, assume payroll deduction plans are nonqualified.

QUICK QUIZ 3.11

1. Each of the following is an example of a qualified retirement plan EXCEPT
    A. a deferred compensation plan
    B. a 401(k) plan
    C. a pension and profit-sharing plan
    D. a defined benefit plan

2. A corporate profit-sharing plan must be in the form of a(n)
    A. trust
    B. conservatorship
    C. administratorship
    D. beneficial ownership

3. Deferred compensation plans
    I.   are available to a limited number of select employees
    II. must be nondiscriminatory
    III. cannot include corporate officers
    IV. cannot include members of the board of directors
    A. I and II
    B. I and IV
    C. II and III
    D. III and IV

4. A customer invests in a tax-qualified variable annuity. What is the tax treatment of the distributions he receives?
    A. Partially tax free, partially ordinary income
    B. Partially tax free, partially capital gains
    C. All ordinary income
    D. All capital gains

INDIVIDUAL RETIREMENT ACCOUNTS (IRAs)

Individual retirement accounts (IRAs) were created to encourage people to save for retirement in addition to other retirement plans in which they participate. Anyone who has earned income is allowed to make an annual contribution of up to $4,000 or 100% of earned income, whichever is less. Earned income is defined as income from work (e.g., wages, salaries, bonuses, commissions, tips, alimony). Income from investments is not considered earned income. If the contribution limit is exceeded, a 6% excess contribution penalty applies to the amount over the allowable portion (unless corrected shortly thereafter as defined by IRS rules).

Individuals with nonworking spouses may contribute up to a total of $8,000 split between two accounts with no more than $4,000 per account. This benefit is known as the **spousal IRA contribution** and is only available to couples filing joint tax returns.

TAKE NOTE   Taxpayers age 50 and above may contribute an additional $1,000 to their IRAs. This applies to both traditional and Roth IRAs.

Contributions

Between January 1 and April 15, contributions and adjustments may be made to an IRA for both the current year and the previous year. Contributions of earned income may continue until age 70½.

Distributions

Distributions may begin without penalty after age 59½ and must begin by April 1 of the year after the individual turns 70½. Distributions before age 59½ are subject to a 10% penalty as well as regular income tax, except in the event of:

■ death;

■ disability;

■ purchase of a principal residence by a first-time homebuyer;

■ education expenses for the taxpayer, a spouse, child, or grandchild;

■ medical premiums for unemployed individuals; or

■ medical expenses in excess of defined AGI (adjusted gross income) limits.

If distributions do not begin by April 1 of the year after the individual turns 70½, a 50% insufficient distribution penalty applies. It is applicable to the amount that should have been withdrawn based on IRS life expectancy tables. Ordinary income taxes also apply to the full amount.

Contributions to IRAs may or may not be tax deductible. Contributions are fully deductible, regardless of income, if the investor is ineligible to participate in any qualified plan. If eligible to participate in other qualified plans, contributions are deductible if the taxpayer's AGI falls within established income guidelines.

TEST TOPIC ALERT

It is not necessary to memorize the tax-deductible IRA contribution limits. The exam will not ask about these specific limits because they are being phased in gradually. In general, the test focuses on the ability to contribute to rather than deduct IRA contributions. With any qualified plan question, unless otherwise specified, assume contributions have been made on a pretax basis.

Certain investments are not permitted for funding IRAs, including:

■ collectibles (e.g., antiques, gems, rare coins, works of art, stamps);

■ life insurance contracts; and

■ municipal bonds (which are considered inappropriate because the benefit of their tax-free interest is lost within a retirement plan).

Certain investment practices are also considered inappropriate. Those that are not permitted within IRAs or any other retirement plan include:

■ short sales of stock;

■ speculative option strategies; or

■ margin account trading.

Covered call writing is permissible because it does not increase risk.

Ineligible Investments:	Ineligible Investment Practices:
Collectibles	Short sales of stock
Life insurance	Speculative option strategies
Municipal bonds	Margin account trading

TAKE NOTE   Although life insurance is not allowed within IRAs, other life insurance company products, such as annuities, are. Annuities are frequently used as funding vehicles for IRAs. Following is a partial list of which investments are appropriate for IRAs:

- Stocks and bonds

- Mutual funds (other than municipal bond funds)

- Unit investment trusts (UITs)

- Government securities

- US government-issued gold and silver coins

- Annuities

Rollovers and Transfers

Individuals may move their investments from one IRA to another IRA or from a qualified plan to an IRA. These movements are known as rollovers or transfers. Assets may also be rolled over into an employer's retirement plan, provided the employer is willing to accept such deposits.

A **rollover** occurs when an IRA account owner takes temporary ownership of IRA account funds when moving the account to another custodian. Rollovers may take place once in a 12-month period and must be completed within 60 days; 100% of the funds withdrawn must be rolled into the new account or they will be subject to tax and a 10% early withdrawal penalty if applicable.

If a participant in an employer-sponsored qualified plan leaves his place of employment, he may move plan assets to a **conduit IRA**. If the employee takes possession of the funds, 20% of the distribution must be withheld. The employee may then apply for a refund of the 20% withheld on his next income tax return. The 20% withholding is avoided if the distribution is made payable directly to another custodian instead of the employee.

IRA assets may be directly transferred from an IRA or qualified plan. A **transfer** occurs when the account assets are sent directly from one custodian to another, and the account owner never takes possession of the funds. There is no limit on the number of transfers that may be made during a 12-month period.

An employee leaves work and the company must distribute the balance of his 401(k) plan. If the proceeds are made payable to the employee, a 20% withholding applies. If the proceeds are sent to another plan trustee, there is no withholding. By contrast, if an individual chooses to transfer proceeds from one IRA to another, there is no 20% withholding, even if the proceeds are made payable to the participant. Withholding only applies if paid from an employer's qualified plan.

Roth IRAs

Created in 1997, **Roth IRAs** allow after-tax (nondeductible) contributions of up to $4,000 per individual and $8,000 per couple, split between two accounts. Earnings accumulate tax deferred as in typical IRA accounts. The advantage of these IRAs is that distributions that satisfy holding period requirements are not taxable.

Withdrawals from a Roth IRA, which need not begin at age 70½, are tax free, provided two conditions are met: the owner must be at least 59½, and the money withdrawn must have been in the account for at least five years. Penalty-free withdrawals may be made for death of owner, a first-time home purchase, or for total disability.

Coverdell Education Savings Accounts (CESAs)

Coverdell Education Savings Accounts, like Roth IRAs, were created in 1997. These IRAs allow after-tax contributions of up to $2,000 per student per year for children younger than 18.

Contributions may be made by any adult, provided the total contribution per child does not exceed $2,000 in one year. Distributions are tax free as long as the funds are used for education.

TAKE NOTE

CESAs are also known as Education IRAs.

TEST TOPIC ALERT

Assume questions are about traditional IRAs unless they specifically state *Roth* or *Education*. Some key points to remember about these newer IRAs follow:

Roth IRA

- Maximum contribution of $4,000 per year per individual.

- $4,500 after age 50.

- Contributions are not tax deductible.

- Distributions are tax free if taken after age 59½ and money has been in the account for at least five years.

- Distributions are not required to begin at age 70½.

- No 10% early distribution penalty for death, disability, and first-time home purchase.

Coverdell Education Savings Accounts (CESAs)

■ Contribution limit is $2,000 per year per child under age 18.

■ Contributions can be made by adults other than parents; total for one child is still $2,000.

■ Contributions must cease at age 18.

■ Contributions are not tax deductible.

■ Distributions are tax free if taken before age 30 and used for education expenses.

Section 529 Plans

There are two basic types of 529 plans: **prepaid tuition plans** and **college savings plans**. Prepaid tuition plans allow donors to lock in current tuition rates by paying now for future education costs. However, the more popular option is a college savings plan.

Any adult can open a 529 plan for a future college student and the donor does not have to be related to the student. With a 529 plan, the donor can invest a lump sum or make periodic payments. When the student is ready for college, the donor withdraws the amount needed to pay for qualified education expenses (e.g., tuition, room and board, books).

Contributions are made with after-tax dollars. Withdrawals taken for college tuition and expenses are reduced by tax-free scholarships, fellowships, and certain other financial assistance. If the remaining expenses are less than the qualified distributions, part of the earnings will be taxable, so that a withdrawal for qualified expenses is not necessarily tax free. Also, most, but not all, states allow qualified withdrawals that are free from state tax.

Other points to note include the following.

■ College savings plans (but not prepaid tuition plans) may be set up in more than one state, though the allowable contribution amount varies from state to state.

■ There are no income limitations on making contributions to a 529 plan.

■ Contributions may be made in the form of periodic payments, but contributions follow the tax rules for gifts. They are thus limited to $11,000 per year per donor, though the donor may contribute $55,000 in one year (or, a married couple may contribute $110,000 in one year) but then may make no more contributions for five years.

■ There are few restrictions on who may be the first beneficiary of a 529 plan. However, if the beneficiary is redesignated, the new beneficiary must be a close family member of the first.

■ The assets in the account remain the property of the donor, even after the beneficiary reaches legal age. However, if the account is not used for higher education, and the IRS concludes that the plan was not established in good faith, it may impose fines and other sanctions.

■ Plan assets remain outside the owner's estate for estate tax purposes.

Money-purchase plans are the simplest of the qualified defined contribution plans. Any employer that meets funding requirements can offer such a plan. The employer simply contributes a specified fraction of the employee's compensation—up to 25% or $42,000, whichever is less, for the year 2005—to the retirement account.

A **simplified employee pension (SEP) plan** is a qualified plan that offers ease of administration to small-business owners. Employees open IRAs and the employer makes contributions on their behalf. Employee contributions may be made into the same IRA accounts.

An employer is allowed to contribute up to 25% of an employee's salary, up to a maximum of $42,000 (in 2005), each year. Any employee that is at least 21 years of age, has worked for the employer for three of the past five years, and has received at least $450 of compensation in the current year is eligible to participate.

Savings incentive match plans for employees (SIMPLEs) are retirement plans for businesses with fewer than 100 employees that have no other retirement plan in place. The employee makes pretax contributions into a SIMPLE up to the contribution limit ($10,000 in 2005). The employer makes matching contributions, with no upper limit as to the percentage matched, as long as the total contributed does not exceed the limit.

QUICK QUIZ 3.12

1. An individual who is less than age 70½ may contribute to an IRA
   A. if he has earned income
   B. provided he is not covered by a pension plan through an employer
   C. provided he does not own a Keogh plan
   D. provided his income is between $40,000 and $50,000 if married and $25,000 and $35,000 if single

2. A 50-year-old individual wants to withdraw funds from her IRA. The withdrawal will be taxed as
   A. ordinary income
   B. ordinary income plus a 10% penalty
   C. capital gains
   D. capital gains plus a 10% penalty

3. Premature distribution from an IRA is subject to a
   A. 5% penalty plus tax
   B. 6% penalty plus tax
   C. 10% penalty plus tax
   D. 50% penalty plus tax

4. Who of the following will NOT incur a penalty on an IRA withdrawal?
   A. A man who has just become totally disabled
   B. A woman who turned 59 a month before the withdrawal
   C. A woman, age 50, who decides on early retirement
   D. A man in his early 40s who uses the money to buy a second home

5. All of the following statements regarding IRAs are true EXCEPT
    A. IRA rollovers must be completed within 60 days of receipt of the distribution to avoid penalty
    B. cash-value life insurance is a permissible IRA investment, but term insurance is not
    C. the investor must be younger than 70½ to open and contribute to an IRA
    D. distributions may begin at age 59½ and must begin by the year after the year in which the investor turns 70½

6. SEP IRAs
    A. are used primarily by large corporations
    B. are used primarily by small businesses
    C. are nonqualified IRAs
    D. cannot be set up by self-employed persons

7. Which of the following is TRUE of both traditional IRAs and Roth IRAs?
    A. Contributions are deductible.
    B. Withdrawals at retirement are tax free.
    C. Earnings on investments are not taxed immediately.
    D. To avoid penalty, distributions must begin the year after the year the owner reaches age 70½.

8. What is the maximum amount that may be invested in an Education IRA in one year?
    A. $500 per parent
    B. $500 per child
    C. $2,000 per couple
    D. $2,000 per child

KEOGH (HR-10) AND SELF-EMPLOYED 401(k) PLANS

Keogh plans, also called **HR-10 plans**, are qualified plans intended for self-employed persons and owner-employees of unincorporated businesses or professional practices who file Schedule C, such as doctors or lawyers.

Owner-employees of businesses or professional practices must show a gross profit to qualify for a tax-deductible contribution to a Keogh plan. If a business does not profit, no contribution is allowed.

Contributions

The maximum contribution to a Keogh plan is 100% of postcontribution income, up to an indexed maximum. As with IRAs, a person may make contributions to a Keogh until age 70½. In addition, employers must make contributions into the plans of their eligible employees in an amount equal to their own postcontribution percentage. This requires some alertness during the test. If a self-employed proprietor of a plumbing shop earns a gross compensation of $100,000, of which he contributes $20,000 to his retirement and keeps $80,000 as net compensation, his contribution computes to be 25% ($20,000/$80,000). If one of his plumbers makes $60,000 that year, the business would have to contribute 25%, or $15,000, to his retirement.

Eligible employees must be allowed to participate in Keogh plans. ERISA eligibility rules apply. Employees are eligible if they:

- have worked at least 1,000 hours in the year;

- have completed one or more years of continuous employment; and

- are at least 21 years of age.

Differences Between Keogh Plans and IRAs

Characteristic	Keogh Plans	IRAs
Source of contributions	Employer; employee may also make nondeductible contributions	Employee
Permissible investments	Most equity and debt securities, US government-minted precious metal coins, annuities, and cash-value life insurance	Most equity and debt securities, US government-minted precious metal coins, and annuities
Nonpermissible investments	Term insurance and collectibles	Term insurance, collectibles, and cash-value life insurance
Change of employer	Lump-sum distribution can be rolled over into an IRA within 60 days	N/A
Penalty for excess contribution	10% penalty	6% penalty
Taxation of distributions	Taxed as ordinary income	Taxed as ordinary income
Penalty for early distribution	10% if before age 59½	10% if before age 59½

A **self-employed 401(k) plan** can be set up by a business with no full-time employees—only the owner(s), spouse(s), and part-time employees. Such plans offer higher contribution limits than other plans, greater flexibility as to when and how often contributions will be made, and penalty-free loans from the plan's funding, provided the load is paid back on time. The business can be a sole proprietorship, a partnership, or a C Corporation, S Corporation, or limited liability corporation.

QUICK QUIZ 3.13

1. Who among the following may participate in a Keogh plan?
   I. Self-employed doctor
   II. Analyst who makes extra money giving speeches outside regular work
   III. Individual with a full-time job who has income from freelancing
   IV. Corporate executive who receives $5,000 in stock options from his corporation

   A. I and II
   B. I and III
   C. I, II and III
   D. III and IV

2. Which of the following are characteristics of a Keogh plan?
    I.   Dividends, interest, and capital gains are tax deferred.
    II.   Distributions after age 70½ are tax free.
    III. Contributions are allowed for a nonworking spouse.
    IV.   Lump-sum distributions are allowed.

    A. I and II
    B. I and III
    C. I and IV
    D. II and III

3. Which of the following disqualify a person from a Keogh plan?
    A. Having only a corporate salaried position
    B. Having a salaried position in addition to self-employment
    C. A spouse who has company-sponsored retirement benefits
    D. Owning an IRA

403(b) PLANS

403(b) plans are a form of **tax-sheltered annuity (TSA)** available to employees of the following organizations:

- public educational institutions (403(b) institutions);

- tax-exempt organizations (501(c)(3) organizations); and

- religious organizations.

In general, the clergy and employees of charitable institutions, private hospitals, colleges and universities, elementary and secondary schools, and zoos and museums are eligible to participate if they are at least 21 and have completed one year of service. The 403(b) plans are sometimes referred to as **tax-sheltered annuities (TSAs)** or **tax-qualified annuities**.

The 403(b) plans are funded by elective employee deferrals. The employee may contribute up to an indexed maximum. The deferred amount is excluded from the employee's gross income and earnings accumulate tax free until distribution. A written salary reduction agreement must be executed between the employer and the employee.

Employer contributions may also be made. As with other qualified plans, a 10% penalty is applied to distributions before age 59½.

TEST TOPIC ALERT   A student cannot be a participant in a 403(b) because the plan is only available to employees.

CORPORATE RETIREMENT PLANS

Corporate pension plans fall into two categories: defined benefit or defined contribution. A **defined benefit plan** promises a specific benefit at retirement that is determined by a formula involving typical retirement age, years of service, and compensation. The amount of the contribution is determined by actuarial calculations because it involves complex assumptions about investment returns, future interest rates, and other matters. This type of plan may be used by firms that wish to favor older key employees because a much greater amount can be contributed for those with only a short time until retirement.

Defined contribution plans are much easier to administer. The current contribution amount is specified by the plan; however, the benefit that will be paid at retirement is unknown. A typical defined contribution formula might be 5% of salary. The maximum employee contribution in 2005 was $14,000.

Profit-sharing plans are a popular form of defined contribution plan. These plans do not require a fixed contribution formula and allow contributions to be skipped in years of low profits. Their flexibility and ease of administration have made them a popular retirement plan option for employers.

TAKE NOTE   All defined benefit and defined contribution plans, other than profit-sharing plans, require an annual contribution. Employers may skip contributions to profit-sharing plans in unprofitable years.

The most popular form of retirement plan, **401(k) plans**, are a type of defined contribution plan that allows the employee to elect to contribute a specific percentage of salary to a retirement account. Contributions are excluded from the employee's gross income and accumulate tax deferred. Employers may make matching contributions up to a specified percentage of the employee's contributions. Additionally, 401(k) plans permit certain hardship withdrawals.

Roth 401(k) plans were passed by Congress in 2001 to become available as a plan option on January 1, 2006. A Roth 401(k), like a Roth IRA, requires after-tax contributions but allows tax-free withdrawals, provided the plan owner is at least 59½—though unlike a Roth IRA, there are no income limitations on who may have such a plan, and there is no five-year requirement for tax-free withdrawals. Like a 401(k), it allows the employer to make matching contributions, but the employer's contributions must be made into a traditional 401(k) account. The employee, who would thus have two 401(k) accounts, may make contributions into either, but may not transfer money from one to the other once it has been deposited. Unlike with a Roth IRA, the account owner must begin withdrawals by the age of 70½.

Corporate Retirement Plans

	Defined Benefit	Defined Contribution
Benefit amount:	fixed	varies
Contribution:	amount varies	amount fixed
Assumes investment risk:	sponsor	participant
Plan favors:	older key employees	younger employees (more time to accumulate funds)

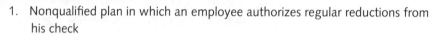

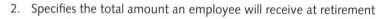

QUICK QUIZ 3.14

Match the following terms with the appropriate description below.
A. Defined benefit plan
B. Keogh plan
C. Spousal IRA contributions
D. Payroll deduction plan

___D___ 1. Nonqualified plan in which an employee authorizes regular reductions from his check

___A___ 2. Specifies the total amount an employee will receive at retirement

___B___ 3. Qualified retirement plan for self-employed individuals and unincorporated businesses

___C___ 4. IRA contributions made for a nonworking husband or wife

Match each of the following terms with the appropriate description.
A. Profit-sharing plan
B. Qualified plan
C. Deferred compensation plan
D. Rollover
E. Defined contribution plan

___E___ 5. A qualified plan that specifies an employer's annual funding

___A___ 6. Employees receive for retirement purposes a portion of profits from a business

___D___ 7. Movement of funds from one retirement plan to another, generally within a specified period of time

___C___ 8. Nonqualified retirement plan in which an employee delays receipt of current compensation, generally until retirement

___B___ 9. Plan meeting standards set by ERISA

EMPLOYEE RETIREMENT INCOME SECURITY ACT OF 1974 (ERISA)

The **Employee Retirement Income Security Act (ERISA)** of 1974 was established to prevent abuse and misuse of pension funds. ERISA guidelines apply to private sector (corporate) retirement plans and certain union plans—not public plans like those for government workers. Significant ERISA provisions include the following.

Participation

This identifies eligibility rules for employees. All employees must be covered if they are 21 years or older and have performed one year of full-time service, which ERISA defines as 1,000 hours or more.

Funding

Funds contributed to the plan must be segregated from other corporate assets. Plan trustees must administer and invest the assets prudently and in the best interest of all participants. IRS contribution limits must be observed.

Vesting

Employees are entitled to their entire retirement benefit within a certain number of years of service, even if they leave the company.

Communication

The plan document must be in writing, and employees must be given annual statements of account and updates of plan benefits.

Nondiscrimination

All eligible employees must be treated impartially through a uniformly applied formula.

Beneficiaries

Beneficiaries must be named to receive an employee's benefits at death.

TEST TOPIC ALERT

You may see a question that asks for the type of plans that ERISA regulates. ERISA applies to private sector plans (corporate) only. It does not apply to plans for federal or state government workers (public sector plans).

QUICK QUIZ 3.15

1. Regulations regarding how contributions are made to tax-qualified plans relate to which of the following ERISA requirements?
   A. Vesting
   B. Funding
   C. Nondiscrimination
   D. Reporting and disclosure

2. Which of the following determines the amount paid into a defined contribution plan?
   A. ERISA-defined contribution requirements
   B. Trust agreement
   C. Employee's age
   D. Employee's retirement age

3. A customer works as a nurse in a public school. He wants to know more about participating in the school's TSA plan. Which of the following statements are TRUE?
    I.   Contributions are made with before-tax dollars.
    II. He is not eligible to participate.
    III. Distributions before age 59½ are normally subject to penalty tax.
    IV. Mutual funds and CDs are available investment vehicles.

    A. I and II
    B. I and III
    C. I, III and IV
    D. III and IV

4. Which of the following statements regarding a defined benefit plan is TRUE?
    A. All employees receive the same benefits at retirement.
    B. All participating employees are immediately vested.
    C. High-income employees near retirement may receive much larger contributions than younger employees with the same salary.
    D. Contributions must be defined for each eligible employee.

5. The requirements of the Employee Retirement Income Security Act apply to pension plans established by
    A. US government workers
    B. only public entities, such as the city of New York
    C. only private organizations, such as Exxon
    D. both public and private organizations

Terms and Concepts Checklist

✓

- ☐ Nonqualified plan
- ☐ Individual plan
- ☐ Qualified plan
- ☐ Contribution limit
- ☐ SEP
- ☐ SIMPLE
- ☐ Keogh plan
- ☐ TSA, 403(b), 501(c)(3)
- ☐ 401(k) plan
- ☐ Self-employed 401(k)
- ☐ Roth 401(k)
- ☐ Defined benefit plan
- ☐ Defined contribution plan
- ☐ Profit-sharing plan
- ☐ Eligibility, participation rule
- ☐ Funding rule

✓

- ☐ Vesting
- ☐ Beneficiary
- ☐ Payroll deduction plan
- ☐ Deferred compensation plan
- ☐ Discrimination rule
- ☐ Nondiscrimination
- ☐ Section 457 plan
- ☐ IRA
- ☐ Roth IRA
- ☐ Spousal contribution
- ☐ Coverdell Educational Savings Account (CESA)
- ☐ Eligible investments
- ☐ Rollover, transfer
- ☐ Section 529 plan
- ☐ ERISA

SECURITIES INVESTOR PROTECTION CORPORATION (SIPC)

After many brokerage firm defaults in the 1960s, the Securities Investor Protection Act was passed in 1970 to protect customers from broker/dealer failure or insolvency. This act intensified broker/dealer financial requirements and created the **Securities Investor Protection Corporation (SIPC).**

SIPC is an independent nonprofit corporation that collects annual assessments from broker/dealers. These assessments create a general insurance fund for customer claims from broker/dealer failure. All broker/dealers that are registered with the SEC must be SIPC members except for:

- broker/dealers handling only mutual funds or unit trusts;

- broker/dealers handling only variable annuities or insurance; and

- investment advisers.

Firms that fail to pay their SIPC assessments cannot engage in the brokerage business.

TAKE NOTE   SIPC protects customers from the risk of broker/dealer bankruptcy only. It does not protect them from market risk or unwise investments.

PROTECTION OF CUSTOMERS

If SIPC believes that a firm is insolvent, it will petition a court to appoint a liquidating trustee, and the firm ceases doing business. When a liquidation proceeding takes place, the order of events is as follows.

- Securities held in customer name are delivered to the registered owners.

- Cash and street name securities are distributed on a pro rata basis.

- SIPC funds are distributed to meet remaining claims up to the maximum allowed per customer.

- Customers with excess claims become general creditors of the broker/dealer.

- The valuation date for customer securities claims is generally the day that the court appoints a trustee to oversee the liquidation.

Customer Account Coverage

Under SIPC, customer accounts are covered to a maximum of $500,000, with cash claims not to exceed $100,000 of that total. Each separate customer may enter a claim up to the $500,000 limit for all accounts in the customer's name. Commodities or futures contracts are not covered by SIPC because they are not considered securities.

Sample SIPC Customer Coverage Limit

Mr. Jones (2 accounts)	– cash account – margin account	1 customer = $500,000 coverage
Mr. and Mrs. Jones (1 account)	– joint account	1 customer = $500,000 coverage
Mr. Jones as custodian for Baby Jones (1 account)		1 customer = $500,000 coverage

The firm itself, its investment accounts, and its officers are not covered under the Act. Also, anything that is not cash or a security (e.g., commodities or futures contracts) is not covered.

TAKE NOTE   SIPC coverage is per customer, not per account. Cash and margin accounts are combined for SIPC coverage purposes.

Advertising SIPC Membership

Broker/dealers must include their SIPC membership on all advertising but may not imply that SIPC coverage is more than it actually is, nor that its benefits are unique to only that firm. The term *SIPC* may not appear larger than the firm's own name. All member firms must post a sign indicating SIPC membership.

Fidelity Bonds

Firms required to join SIPC must also purchase a blanket **fidelity bond**. The bond is to protect against employee loss or theft of customer securities. Minimum coverage is $25,000, but firms may require additional coverage based on their scope of operations. A firm must review the sufficiency of its fidelity bond coverage once per year.

TEST TOPIC ALERT   Expect at least one question similar to the following:

SIPC provides coverage up to $500,000

A.   with no more than $50,000 in cash
B.   with no more than $100,000 in cash
C.   with no more than $150,000 in cash
D.   in cash or securities

Answer: B. SIPC coverage is $500,000 per separate customer account, with coverage of cash and cash equivalents not to exceed $100,000.

Terms and Concepts Checklist

✓

- [ ] Securities Investor Protection Corporation
- [ ] Coverage limits, cash and securities

✓

- [ ] Advertising SIPC membership
- [ ] Fidelity bond
- [ ] Persons and accounts not covered

INSIDER TRADING AND SECURITIES FRAUD ENFORCEMENT ACT OF 1988

Although the Securities Act of 1934 prohibited the use of insider information in making trades, the act of 1988 specifies penalties for insider trading and securities fraud. An **insider** is any person who has access to nonpublic information about a company. Inside information is any information that has not been disseminated to, or is not readily available to, the general public.

The act prohibits insiders trading on or communicating nonpublic information. Both **tippers** (the person who gives a tip) and **tippees** (the person who receives a tip) are liable, as is anyone who trades on information that he knows or should know is not public, or has control over the misuse of this information. No trade need be made for a violation to occur; even a personal benefit of a nonfinancial nature could lead to liability under the rules.

The key elements of liability under insider trading rules follow.

- Does the tipper owe a fiduciary duty to a company/its stockholders? Has he breached it?

- Does the tipper meet the personal benefits test (even something as simple as enhancing a friendship or reputation)?

- Does the tippee know or should the tippee have known that the information was inside or confidential?

- Is the information material and nonpublic?

TAKE NOTE

Even a slip of the tongue by a corporate insider could create liability under these rules. The SEC has a greatly broadened scope of authority for investigating and prosecuting the abuse of inside information.

Written Supervisory Procedures

All broker/dealers must establish **written supervisory procedures** specifically prohibiting the misuse of inside information. Additionally, they must establish policies that restrict the passing of potentially material, nonpublic information between a firm's departments. This barrier against the free flow of sensitive information is known as a **Chinese wall** or **firewall**.

Penalties

The SEC can investigate any person suspected of violating any of the provisions of the Insider Trading Act. If the SEC determines that a violation has occurred, civil penalties of up to the greater of $1 million or 300% of profits made or losses avoided may be levied. Violators may also face criminal penalties of up to 10 years in jail.

The trader also has potential liability to other traders—called contemporaneous traders—who may have suffered loss because of his insider trading.

QUICK QUIZ 3.16

1. If a claim is not covered by SIPC in a broker/dealer bankruptcy, then the client
   A. becomes a secured creditor
   B. becomes a general creditor ●
   C. becomes a preferred creditor
   D. loses his investment

2. A client has a special cash account with stock valued at $460,000 and $40,000 in cash. The same client also has a joint account with a spouse with a market value of $320,000 and $180,000 in cash. What is SIPC coverage?
   A. $460,000 for the special cash account, $320,000 for the joint account
   B. $500,000 for the special cash account, $420,000 for the joint account
   C. $500,000 for the special cash account, $500,000 for the joint account ●
   D. Total of $1 million for both accounts

3. SIPC uses which of the following to determine the value of customer claims when a broker/dealer becomes insolvent?
   A. Market value on the date the broker/dealer becomes insolvent
   B. Market value on the date a federal court is petitioned to appoint a trustee
   C. Market value on the date the trustee pays the customers their balances
   D. Average market value from the time a trustee is appointed to the payment date

4. Regarding the civil penalties that may be imposed for insider trading violations under the Securities Exchange Act of 1934, which of the following statements is NOT true?
   A. A civil penalty may be imposed only on a person who is registered under a securities act.
   B. The violation for which a penalty may be imposed is defined as buying or selling securities while in possession of material, nonpublic information.
   C. The SEC may ask a court to impose a penalty of up to 3 times the loss avoided or profit gained on an illegal transaction.
   D. Improper supervision may cause a broker/dealer firm to be liable to pay a penalty if one of its representatives commits an insider trading violation.

5. For purposes of insider trading, who of the following are insiders?
    I.   Attorney who writes an offering circular for a company
    II. Bookkeeper in a company's accounting department
    III. Wife of a company's president
    IV. Brother of a company's president

    A. I and II
    B. I and III
    C. III and IV
    D. I, II, III and IV

Terms and Concepts Checklist

✓   ✓

- ☐ Insider Trading and Securities Fraud Enforcement Act of 1988
- ☐ Insider trading
- ☐ Tipper and tippee
- ☐ Insider information

- ☐ Written supervisory procedures
- ☐ Chinese wall, firewall
- ☐ Criminal penalties
- ☐ Civil penalties
- ☐ Contemporaneous traders

Stopped Reading

REGULATION S-P

Regulation S-P, adopted by the SEC, emanates from the privacy rules under the Gramm-Leach-Bliley Act where Congress stated that each financial institution has a responsibility "to protect the privacy of its customers' nonpublic personal information." Regulation S-P requires firms to maintain adequate safeguards to protect customer information from unauthorized access or use.

Disclosures

Disclosure of a firm's policies and procedures regarding customer privacy must be made no later than when the customer relationship is established, generally at the time a new customer opens an account. The customer must receive an updated notice containing the same information at least annually. These notices must be clear and conspicuous, meaning they should be reasonably understandable and designed to call attention to their significance.

Right to Opt Out

Federal law requires that each customer be given the opportunity to opt out of the sharing of nonpublic personal information. The opt-out notice must identify the products or services it is applicable to. In addition, the notice must clearly explain how to exercise one's right to opt out.

TAKE NOTE   Methods to opt out must be simple. Having a customer return a postage-paid reply card would be compliant with this regulation but requiring a customer to write a letter would not.

Terms and Concepts Checklist

✓   ✓

☐ Regulation S-P   ☐ Right to opt out

☐ Disclosures   ☐ Simple opt-out method

THE NATIONAL ASSOCIATION OF SECURITIES DEALERS (NASD)

The **National Association of Securities Dealers (NASD)** is the OTC industry's self-regulatory organization (SRO). It was founded under the Maloney Act of 1938 and was formed to help regulate the securities industry, specifically the over-the-counter marketplace, under the supervision of the SEC. The NASD is a membership corporation—that is, the NASD does not issue capital stock. The NASD's purposes and objectives are to:

■ promote the investment banking and securities business, standardize principles and practices, promote high standards of commercial honor, and encourage the observance of federal and state securities laws;

■ provide a medium for communication among its members and between its members, the government, and other agencies;

■ adopt, administer, and enforce the NASD's Conduct Rules and rules designed to prevent fraudulent and manipulative practices, as well as to promote just and equitable principles of trade;

■ promote self-discipline among members; and

■ investigate and adjust grievances between the public and members, as well as between members.

Districts

The NASD divides the United States into districts to facilitate its operation. Each district elects a district committee to administer NASD rules. Within each district, the **Department of Enforcement (Enforcement)** handles trade practice complaints. The NASD executive committee, made up of members of the board of governors, manages NASD national affairs.

NASD Dues, Assessments, and Other Charges

The NASD is funded by assessments of member firms' registered representatives and applicants and by annual fees. The annual fee includes:

■ the basic membership fee;

- an assessment based on gross income;

- a fee for each principal and registered representative; and

- a charge for each branch office.

Failure to pay dues can result in suspension or revocation of membership.

Use of the NASD's Corporate Name

NASD members cannot use the NASD name in any manner that suggests that the NASD has endorsed a member firm. Members may use the phrase *Member of the NASD* as long as the firm places no undue emphasis on it.

TAKE NOTE   Neither the NASD nor the SEC will approve the way a representative or firm conducts business. To suggest otherwise is prohibited.

EXAMPLE   What is wrong with this business card?

> **John H. Doe**
> **(555) 234-5678**
>
> ## NASD Registered Representative
>
> **ABC Securities**

Note that the large, bold print used to identify the NASD affiliation could mislead the recipient of this business card into thinking that John Doe is actually associated with the NASD. The NASD cannot be more prominent than the name of the representative's firm. Someone might mistakenly be led to believe that the NASD approves of or endorses this representative.

NASD Manual

NASD policies are specified in the **NASD Manual**. The manual describes four sets of rules and codes by which the OTC market is regulated.

- **Conduct Rules**—Set out fair and ethical trade practices that member firms and their representatives must follow when dealing with the public.

- **Uniform Practice Code**—Established the Uniform Trade Practices, including settlement, good delivery, ex-dates, confirmations, and other guidelines for broker/dealers when they do business with other member broker/dealer firms.

- **Code of Procedure**—Describes how the NASD hears and handles member violations of the Conduct Rules.

- **Code of Arbitration Procedure**—Governs the resolution of disagreements and claims between members, registered representatives, and the public; it addresses monetary claims.

NASD MEMBERSHIP AND REGISTRATION

The NASD's board of governors establishes rules, regulations, and membership eligibility standards. At present, the following membership standards and registration requirements are in place.

Broker/Dealer Registration

Any broker/dealer registered with the SEC may apply for membership in the NASD. Any person who effects transactions in securities as a broker, a dealer, or an investment banker also may register with the NASD, as may municipal bond firms. Application for NASD membership, done on Form BD, carries the applying firm's specific agreement to:

- comply with the association's rules and regulations;

- comply with federal securities laws; and

- pay dues, assessments, and other charges in the manner and amounts fixed by the association.

A membership application is made to the NASD office in the district in which the applying firm has its home office. If a district committee passes on the firm's qualifications, the firm can be accepted into NASD membership.

Office Registration

Each location where business is done (**branch office**) or supervised (**Office of Supervisory Jurisdiction [OSJ]**) must be registered with the NASD. A branch office is any location identified to the public where the member firm conducts investment banking or securities business. Some branch offices supervise other branches but need not be given OSJ status unless they perform certain specific supervisory functions such as maintaining custody of customer funds or securities, structuring securities offerings, and the like. If an office does not perform those specific supervisory functions but does provide supervision of another branch office or nonbranch location, it is always considered a branch office. On the other hand, if the public communication that identifies an office also identifies the location from which supervision is done for that office, the office itself may be considered a nonbranch location.

Associated Person Registration

Any person associated with an NASD member firm who intends to engage in the investment banking or securities business must be registered with the NASD as an associated person. Anyone applying for registration with the

NASD as an associated person must be sponsored by a member firm. A principal must verify the applicant's employment for the prior three years and attest to the character and reputation of the applicant.

Form U-4. To register an associated person with the NASD, the member files Form U-4. The information required on Form U-4 is extensive and includes:

■ name, address, and any aliases used;

■ five-year residency history;

■ 10-year employment history (verify the past three years); and

■ information on any charges, arrests, or convictions relating to the investment business. A *yes* answer to any of these questions requires a detailed explanation on a DRP (disclosure reporting form).

TAKE NOTE   Information on marital status and educational background is not required on Form U-4.

Any changes to this information require filing an amended form with the CRD (central registration depository) no later than 30 days after the member becomes aware of these changes. If the amendment involves a statutory disqualification, an amended form must be filed within 10 business days. In addition, if a person is suspended by a member or is subject to in-house disciplinary action involving the withholding of commissions or a fine in excess of $2,500, the NASD must be notified within 10 business days.

Qualifications Investigated. Before submitting an application to enroll a person with the NASD as a registered representative, a member firm must certify that it has investigated the person's business reputation, character, education, qualifications, and experience, and that the candidate's credentials are in order.

If, during its routine review of the U-4, the NASD discovers that any portion of the U-4 information submitted, especially relating to personal history and past disciplinary or law enforcement encounters, is misleading or omits material information, disciplinary action may be taken resulting in a bar to the individual. In addition, the principal signing on the application may be liable as well.

Rule 17f-2, the Fingerprint Rule, requires that every person who deals with securities certificates, records, or money must have their fingerprints taken and filed.

Failure to Register Personnel. A member firm's failure to register an employee who performs any of the functions of a registered representative will lead to disciplinary action by the NASD.

Member firms are generally in violation when unregistered sales assistants accept orders from customers.

Postregistration Rules and Regulations

Registered Persons Changing Firms

NASD registration of an associate is nontransferable. A registered person who leaves one member firm to join another must terminate registration at the first firm on a U-5 form and reapply for registration with the new member firm on a U-4 form.

Form U-5. Should an associated person registered with a member resign or be terminated, the member must file Form U-5 with the CRD within 30 days of termination date. The member must also provide a copy of the form to their former employee within the same time frame. Failure to do so within 30 days results in a late filing fee assessed against the member. The form requires the member to indicate the reason for termination and provide an explanation.

A member who learns of facts or circumstances that cause the information filed to be inaccurate must file an amended Form U-5 within 30 days of discovery and send a copy of the amended filing to the former employee.

If a registered person leaves one member firm to join another, the new employer must file a Form U-4 for the new employee and get a copy of the Form U-5 filed by the former member.

The former employer is not required to provide a copy to the new employing member firm. The new firm must get a copy from either the NASD or from its new employee. Under NASD rules, the new employee, if asked, must provide a copy within two business days of the request.

An individual cannot transact business as a registered representative unless associated with a broker/dealer. A representative's license is no longer effective upon leaving the firm.

Continuing Commissions

An individual must be registered to sell securities. A registered representative who leaves a member firm—upon retirement, for instance—may continue to receive commissions on business placed while employed. The most common example of business where commissions continue to come in after the departure of the registered representative is ongoing investment in mutual funds or variable annuities. However, the representative must have a contract to this effect before leaving the firm. If a contract exists, the deceased representative's heirs may receive continuing commissions on business the representative placed.

Notification of Disciplinary Action

A member firm must notify the NASD if any associated person in the firm's employment is subjected to disciplinary action by a:

- national securities exchange or association;

- clearing corporation;

- commodity futures market regulatory agency; or

- federal or state regulatory commission.

TAKE NOTE   Notification must include the individual's name and the nature of the action.

The rules also require the reporting of any case where an associated person is indicted, or convicted of, or pleads guilty to, or pleads no contest to, any felony; or any misdemeanor that involves the purchase or sale of any security, the taking of a false oath, the making of a false report, bribery, perjury, burglary, larceny, theft, robbery, extortion, forgery, counterfeiting, fraudulent concealment, embezzlement, fraudulent conversion, or misappropriation of funds, or securities, or a conspiracy to commit any of these offenses, or substantially equivalent activity in a domestic, military, or foreign court. A member firm also must notify the NASD of significant disciplinary action the firm itself has taken against an associated person. In particular, any action that involves a suspension, termination, withholding of commissions, or a fine in excess of $2,500 would have to be reported.

Terminations

Once an associated person voluntarily ends employment with a member, NASD registration ceases 30 calendar days from the date the NASD receives written notice from the employing member firm. If any registered person's employment is terminated, the member firm must notify the NASD and the NYSE in writing within 30 calendar days. If a firm or any of its associated persons terminates their membership, they are subject to complaints filed against it for a period of two years.

Terminating Representatives Under Investigation. If a registered representative or another associated person is under investigation for federal securities law violations or has disciplinary action pending against him from the NASD or any other SRO, a member firm may not terminate its business relationship with the person until the investigation or disciplinary action is resolved.

INVESTOR PROTECTION AND EDUCATION

Each member firm that holds customer funds or securities must, at least once every calendar year, provide in writing to each of its customers the following information:

■ the National Association of Securities Dealers Regulation (NASDR) Public Disclosure Program Hotline number;

■ the NASDR Website address; and

■ a statement as to the availability of an investor brochure that includes information describing the Public Disclosure Program.

The **central registration depository (CRD)** maintains information on all persons registered with the NASD, including information on customer complaints and disciplinary history. Public customers have access to some of this information via an 800 number maintained by the NASD or via the Association's Website.

Exemptions

Certain people are not required to register with the NASD as associated persons or are exempt from having to pass a qualification exam.

Foreign Associates

Foreign associates, noncitizens who conduct business outside the United States, must be registered with the NASD but are exempt from having to pass a qualification exam.

Clerical Personnel and Corporate Officers

A member firm's clerical employees need not register with the NASD. Corporate officers who are not involved with the member's investment banking business also are exempt from registration.

Employees in Other Specific Functions

Employees registered with an exchange as floor members who work or trade only on the floor or who transact business only in exempted securities or commodities are exempt from registration.

State Registration

In addition to registering with the NASD, registered representatives and broker/dealers must register with the state securities Administrator in each state in which they intend to do business.

QUICK QUIZ 3.17

True or False?

_F_   1. The wife of a deceased representative may continue to receive commissions based on a verbal agreement with the former employer.

_F_   2. A foreign representative of a foreign broker/dealer is not required to register with the NASD if it engages in business with a US citizen.

_T_   3. A member firm is required to investigate the background and character of any person it may hire.

_T_   4. A firm that terminates a registered representative must file a U-5 form.

_F_   5. If a representative is registered with the NASD, state registration is not necessary.

_F_   6. A member firm's clerical staff must register with the NASD.

_F_   7. Broker/dealers may not use the phrase *member of the NASD* on any sales literature they prepare.

Terms and Concepts Checklist

✓	✓
☐ NASD	☐ Conduct Rules
☐ District	☐ Code of Procedure
☐ Firm registration	☐ Code of arbitration procedure
☐ Form BD	☐ Uniform Practice Code
☐ Dues	☐ OSJ
☐ Assessments, fees, charges	☐ Supervisory, nonsupervisory branch
☐ Associated persons	☐ 17f-2, the fingerprint rule
☐ Individual registration	☐ Disciplinary action
☐ Form U-4	☐ Continuing commissions
☐ Exemptions from registration	☐ CRD
☐ Terminations	☐ Foreign associates
☐ Form U-5	☐ State registration

QUALIFICATION EXAMINATIONS

To become a registered representative or principal, an individual must pass the appropriate licensing examination(s).

REGISTERED REPRESENTATIVES

All associated persons engaged in the investment banking and securities business, whether licensed as principals or as registered representatives, are technically referred to as registered representatives, including:

- an assistant officer who does not function as a principal;

- individuals who supervise, solicit, or conduct business in securities; and

- individuals who train people to supervise, solicit, or conduct business in securities.

Limited Securities Representative License (Series 6)

The **Series 6** Investment Company/Variable Contracts Limited Representative license allows a representative to sell open-end investment companies, new issues of closed-end investment companies, and variable products. Series 6 can serve as a prerequisite for the Series 26 principal exam.

TAKE NOTE

Individuals who hold Series 6 licenses are permitted to sell investment company products, which include unit investment trusts, face-amount certificates, open-end company shares, and primary offerings of closed-end company shares.

Units in REITs (real estate investment trusts), limited partnerships, direct participation programs, and closed-end investment companies in secondary market transactions cannot be sold by Series 6-licensed individuals.

General Securities Representative License (Series 7)

A **Series 7** General Securities license allows a registered representative to sell almost all types of securities products. A general securities representative cannot sell commodities futures unless he has a Series 3 license.

Uniform Investment Adviser (Series 65)

The Uniform Investment Adviser Law exam, developed by the North American Securities Administrators Association, Inc. (NASAA), is designed to qualify candidates as investment adviser representatives (**Series 65**) and entitles the successful candidate to sell securities and give investment advice in states that require Series 65 registration.

The exam covers the principles of state securities regulation reflected in the Uniform Securities Act (also known as blue-sky laws) and federal securities laws and regulations.

EXAMPLE

A Series 6 registered representative may sell all of the following EXCEPT

A. face-amount certificates
B. aggressive growth mutual fund shares
C. closed-end company shares in the secondary market
D. unit investment trusts

Answer: C. Series 6 registered representatives may sell closed-end company shares in their primary offering stage (with prospectus), but once they begin trading in the secondary market, they must be sold by a Series 7 registered representative. Series 7 registration is required to transact business in the secondary market.

TAKE NOTE

A Series 6 representative cannot transact business in REITs (real estate investment trust units), limited partnerships, or DPPs (direct participation programs).

REGISTERED PRINCIPALS

Anyone who manages or supervises any part of a member's investment banking or securities business must be registered as a **principal** with the NASD. This includes people involved solely in training associated persons. Principals must review every customer order, all customer correspondence, and the handling of all customer complaints. Unless the member firm is a sole proprietorship, it must employ at least two registered principals.

Investment Company Principal License (Series 26)

The **Series 26** Investment Company Products/Variable Contracts Limited Principal license entitles a principal to supervise the solicitation, purchase, or sale of mutual funds and variable annuities. The Series 6 is a prerequisite for the Series 26 principal examination.

TEST TOPIC ALERT

A general rule to remember is that anyone who manages, trains, or supervises representatives must register as a principal. Each firm must have a minimum of two registered principals. Officers and partners must register as principals.

INELIGIBILITY AND DISQUALIFICATIONS

Individuals may not act as a registered representative or principal unless they meet NASD eligibility standards regarding training, experience, and competence.

Statutory Disqualification

Disciplinary sanctions by the SEC, another SRO, a foreign financial regulator, or a foreign equivalent of an SRO can be cause for statutory disqualification of NASD membership. Individuals applying for registration as an associated person will be rejected if they:

■ have been or are expelled or suspended from membership or participation in any other SRO or from the foreign equivalent of an SRO;

■ are under an SEC order or an order of a foreign financial regulator denying, suspending, or revoking registration, or barring them from association with a broker/dealer; or

■ have been found to be the cause of another broker/dealer or associated person being expelled or suspended by another SRO, the SEC, or a foreign equivalent of an SRO.

The following also can automatically disqualify an applicant for registration:

■ misstatements willfully made in an application for membership or registration as an associated person;

■ any felony conviction, either domestic or foreign, or a misdemeanor conviction involving securities or money within the past 10 years; and

■ court injunctions prohibiting the individual from acting as an investment adviser, an underwriter, or a broker/dealer or in other capacities aligned with the securities and financial services industry.

Continuing Education

All registered representatives are subject to NASD continuing education requirements and must periodically complete a **regulatory element** and a **firm element**.

Regulatory Element

The regulatory element of the continuing education requirement must be completed within 120 days of a person's second registration anniversary and every three years thereafter. It requires participation in an exercise involving industry regulation and ethics in dealing with customers. Registered representatives who fail to complete the required regulatory element have their registrations become inactive and cannot conduct business activities. Registrations that remain inactive for two years are terminated.

Firm Element

Any registered representative who has direct contact with customers in the sale of securities, and their principals, are subject to the firm element requirement on an annual basis. Member firms must design a written training program that is interactive and covers the following topics:

- Regulatory requirements that apply to business performed by the representative

- Suitability and ethical sales practices

- Overall investment features and related risk factors

Annual Compliance Review

The purpose of this meeting is to discuss compliance issues. All registered representatives and principals are required to attend. This is apart from, and should not be confused with, continuing education requirements. The venue for this meeting must be interactive.

QUICK QUIZ 3.18

Match the following numbers with the appropriate description below.

A.   30
B.   26
C.   10
D.   2

D   1.   The minimum number of principals a firm must have.

B   2.   A securities firm limiting its sales to mutual funds or variable contracts of insurance companies must have at least one person holding this series to manage and supervise.

A   3.   The number of days a broker/dealer has to notify the NASD of a representative's termination.

C   4.   A felony conviction within this number of years can disqualify an individual from registration.

Terms and Concepts Checklist

✓	✓
☐ Qualification examination	☐ Series 7
☐ Series 6	☐ General securities representative
☐ Limited securities representative	☐ Series 65
☐ Series 26	☐ Uniform investment adviser
☐ Investment company principal	☐ Continuing education
☐ Statutory disqualification	☐ Firm element
☐ Annual compliance review	☐ Regulatory element

HOTSHEETS

For your convenience, Unit HotSheets summarizing the key points are located at the end of the manual on perforated pages.

UNIT TEST

1. Regulation T addresses the extension of credit from
   - A. broker/dealers to customers
   - B. banks to broker/dealers
   - C. banks to customers
   - D. both banks and broker/dealers to customers

2. A shareholder has redeemed some mutual fund shares that were purchased over a period of 10 years. If the shareholder has not indicated on his tax return the specific dates of purchase and cost of the shares that were redeemed, the IRS will follow which of the following methods in determining the cost basis of shares redeemed?
   - A. Average cost of purchase
   - B. FIFO
   - C. LIFO
   - D. Step-up in basis

3. Which of the following statements regarding taxable investment company distributions to investors is TRUE?
   - A. Dividend distributions are reported on IRS Form 1099-DIV.
   - B. Dividends are distributed quarterly and capital gains are distributed semiannually.
   - C. Capital gains are generated from an investment company's net investment income.
   - D. Capital gains are generated when portfolio assets are sold at a profit but not when investor shares are redeemed at a profit.

4. All of the following are true regarding capital gains taxation EXCEPT
   - A. a mutual fund sells a security at a profit and reinvests the proceeds, including capital gains; this is a realized capital gain and is a reportable tax event to the shareholder
   - B. a mutual fund holds a security after it has appreciated; although it is not sold, the security's appreciation is a taxable event to the shareholder
   - C. if the fund has realized long-term capital gains, they are typically distributed at year end and taxed as long-term capital gains to the shareholder
   - D. realized profits on securities held for more than 12 months are taxed as long-term capital gains to the shareholder

5. An investor owns a variable life insurance policy on his wife. The policy names their daughter as the beneficiary. Presuming his wife dies, which of the following statements correctly describes the tax consequence associated with this policy?
   - A. The death benefit will be taxable to the wife's estate upon distribution.
   - B. The death benefit will not be taxable to the daughter upon distribution.
   - C. The policy owner can deduct premiums paid into the policy in the year they are paid.
   - D. There will be no federal income tax on any distribution if the variable life insurance separate account included only municipal bonds.

6. Your customer, a self-employed, <u>incorporated</u> small business owner, wishes to establish a Keogh plan for herself and her 2 employees. According to IRS rules, which of the following is TRUE?

   A. She may contribute a maximum of 50% of gross earnings for herself and must contribute the same percentage for her eligible employees.
   B. Her Keogh plan must be established as a defined benefit plan.
   C. Her Keogh plan is not subject to IRS approval.
   D. She and her employees are not eligible for a Keogh plan.

7. Tax-free distributions from a Roth IRA can be taken

   A. when the money has been in an account for 5 taxable years, and the owner is at least 59½
   B. when the owner buys rental property after holding the money in an account for 3 taxable years
   C. when an immediate family member becomes disabled
   D. only for medical emergencies

8. All the statements below regarding the exchange of a cash value life insurance policy for an annuity under Internal Revenue Code Section 1035 are true EXCEPT

   A. an annuity acquired under a Section 1035 exchange can be designed to provide income over one or more lifetimes
   B. permanent life insurance can be exchanged for an annuity contract without generating the adverse tax consequences generally associated with surrendering a life insurance policy
   C. the exchange of a life insurance policy for an annuity may appeal to taxpayers who feel they have too much life insurance and too little retirement income
   D. under Section 1035, a tax-free exchange may only occur if the original contract is exchanged for a contract issued by the same insurance company

9. Which of the following IRAs are funded only with after-tax contributions and provide tax-free distributions?

   I. Traditional IRAs
   II. Roth IRAs
   III. Coverdell Education Savings Accounts
   IV. SEP IRAs

   A. I and III
   B. I and IV
   C. II and III
   D. III and IV

10. While cold-calling, a registered representative encounters an individual interested in buying open-ended investment company shares. The representative and the client meet to discuss alternative investment choices. The individual then writes a check for the purchase of open-ended investment company shares without receiving a prospectus. The registered representative is in violation of the act of

    A. 1933
    B. 1934
    C. 1940
    D. 1970

11. Which of the following statements regarding dividend distributions are TRUE?

    I. Purchasing shares of a mutual fund immediately before its ex-dividend date is in the customer's interest because the dividend will be received.
    II. Purchasing shares of a mutual fund immediately before its ex-dividend date is not in the customer's best interest because the dividend is typically taxable to the customer.
    III. Selling dividends is permissible with mutual funds but not with common stock.
    IV. Selling dividends is a violation of NASD rules.

    A. I and II
    B. I and III
    C. II and IV
    D. III and IV

12. Which of the following changes to a Form U-4 must be communicated to the registered representative's broker/dealer and the NASD?

    A. Marital status
    B. Bankruptcy
    C. Birth of a child
    D. Purchase of property

13. An individual who holds a Series 6 license may sell all of the following EXCEPT

    A. unit investment trusts
    B. REITs
    C. open-end company shares
    D. face-amount certificates

14. According to NASD rules, which of the following brokerage firm employees is NOT required to be fingerprinted?

    A. Registered principal
    B. Telemarketing clerk
    C. Administrative assistant who handles customer funds
    D. Registered representative

15. What should be done when a registered representative is aware of a client trading on inside information?

    A. The registered representative should confront the client directly.
    B. The principal should be informed immediately.
    C. The NASD Department of Market Regulation should receive written notification.
    D. The issuer of the security should be contacted.

16. A company intends to issue 1 million shares of common stock. A tombstone advertisement for the company's stock

    A. is considered advertising and must be filed with the NASD
    B. can be published during the cooling-off period
    C. is considered an offer to sell securities by the SEC
    D. may be used instead of a prospectus to provide disclosure to potential investors

17. When a member firm terminates a registered representative, the terminating firm must

    A. destroy the original Form U-4
    B. submit a Form U-5
    C. notify the SEC immediately
    D. publish a notice in the local newspaper

18. Which of the following is a corporate qualified retirement plan?

    A. Keogh plan
    B. Section 529 plan
    C. 401(k) plan
    D. Deferred compensation plan

19. The NASD will deny a person's registration in all of the following situations EXCEPT

    A. when the applicant is not qualified because of lack of experience
    B. when the applicant was suspended by another SRO
    C. when the applicant was convicted of a securities misdemeanor within the past 10 years
    D. when the applicant provided false information when filing the Form U-4

20. Which of the following securities documents are NOT prepared by a broker/dealer?

    I. A research report on a new company
    II. A prospectus
    III. An ad for a company's stock
    IV. A preliminary prospectus

    A. I and III
    B. I and IV
    C. II and III
    D. II and IV

21. Your customer neglected to supply his tax ID number when purchasing some mutual fund shares. Of his next distribution, the fund will have to keep back how much as withholding tax?

    A. 5%
    B. 10%
    C. 20%
    D. 31%

22. The concept of a mutual fund passing distributions through to shareholders without first paying a tax is known as

    A. the pass-through theory
    B. the conduit theory
    C. tax-free passage
    D. free distribution

23. Your firm must make it known that it is a member of the Securities Investor Protection Corporation (SIPC). What limitations apply to how your firm may communicate its membership?

    I. It may not post a sign indicating its membership.
    II. It must post a sign indicating its membership.
    III. It may choose whether or not to post a sign.
    IV. SIPC logos on advertising may be no larger than the firm's name.

    A. I and IV
    B. II and IV
    C. III only
    D. III and IV

24. Which of the following is protected by the Securities Investor Protection Corporation (SIPC)?

    A. Broker/dealer failure
    B. Fraudulent transaction
    C. Issuer default
    D. Market risk

25. An employee involved in the management of an NASD member's business, particularly in the supervision of business solicitation or in training, would have to be registered as a

    A. broker
    B. dealer
    C. partner
    D. principal

ANSWERS AND RATIONALES

1. **A.** Regulation T deals with the extension of credit from broker/dealers. Regulation U covers the extension of credit from banks to broker/dealers.

2. **B.** If another method is not indicated on an investor's tax return, the IRS will assume the FIFO (first in, first out) method of accounting in determining the cost basis of the shares redeemed. Investors may choose to identify shares redeemed only if the cost of the shares and the date of purchase is recorded on the tax return. The average cost method is an alternative that a taxpayer can use continuously for a given investment.

3. **A.** Investment company distributions are reported to shareholders on IRS Form 1099-DIV. Dividends are paid as declared by the board of directors; capital gains are paid annually. Dividends, not capital gains, are paid from the company's net investment income. Capital gains are generated when an investor redeems appreciated shares of the investment company and when portfolio securities are sold.

4. **B.** An unrealized capital gain results in an increase in NAV but is not taxable to the shareholder until it is realized by the fund or the investor's shares are sold.

5. **B.** Death benefits under variable (and other) life insurance policies are generally not taxable to a beneficiary. Premiums are not deductible to the owner of the policy (payor). Presuming the insured is not the owner of the policy, the policy's death benefits are not included in the estate at death. Because of the tax-free buildup of life insurance cash values, variable life insurance products do not offer lower-yielding municipal bond subaccounts among their separate account choices.

6. **D.** Keogh plans are only available to self-employed, nonincorporated businesses. This customer and her employees cannot participate in a Keogh plan because the business is incorporated.

7. **A.** Tax-free distributions from a Roth IRA can begin after the money has been in an account for 5 taxable years and the owner reaches age 59½, dies, becomes disabled, or purchases a home for the first time.

8. **D.** Under Internal Revenue Code Section 1035, to accomplish a tax-free exchange of a life insurance contract for an annuity (or for another life insurance contract), no requirement exists that both contracts are issued by the same insurance company.

9. **C.** Roth IRAs and Coverdell Education Savings Accounts (Education IRAs) are funded entirely with after-tax contributions, and distributions are tax free. SEP IRAs are funded with pretax dollars and have taxable distributions. Traditional IRAs are funded with pretax or after-tax dollars (depending on the income level), and distributions that exceed after-tax contributions are taxable.

10. **A.** A registered representative must sell primary offerings of nonexempt issues with a prospectus under the 1933 Act. The 1934 Act regulates secondary market trading (mutual fund shares do not trade on the secondary market). Under the 1940 Act, the mutual fund issuer must register as an investment company.

11. **C.** Encouraging a customer to buy a stock or a mutual fund immediately before the ex-dividend date is not in the customer's best interest because the dividend received is usually taxable. Because the share price will drop by approximately the amount of the dividend, the customer who waits until after the ex-dividend date buys the shares cheaper and avoids a taxable distribution. Selling dividends violates NASD conduct rules.

12. **B.** The broker/dealer and the NASD must be notified if a registered representative files for bankruptcy. The other occurrences listed do not require NASD notification.

13. **B.** Individuals who hold Series 6 licenses are permitted to sell investment company products, which include unit investment trusts, face-amount certificates, open-end company shares, and primary offerings of closed-end company shares. Units in REITs (real estate investment trusts) can only be sold by Series 7-licensed individuals.

14. **B.** All registered persons and firm employees who handle customer funds and securities must be fingerprinted. A telemarketing clerk would not be handling certificates or money, and so would not need to be fingerprinted.

15. **B.** When inside information is suspected in any trade, registered representatives must immediately contact their principal. All broker/dealers are required to have written supervisory procedures in place to address this situation.

16. **B.** A tombstone advertisement may be published by an issuer of common stock during the cooling-off period. A tombstone for an equity issue is not considered advertising by the SEC and is not subject to NASD filing requirements. A tombstone offers information by telling investors where they can acquire a prospectus about the issue; it does not replace a prospectus and is not an offer to sell securities.

17. **B.** Whenever a registered representative leaves a member firm, a Form U-5 must be submitted to the NASD. There is no requirement that the Form U-4 on file with the NASD be destroyed, or that the SEC be notified, or that a public notice in the local newspaper be published.

18. **C.** A Keogh, or HR-10 plan, is for self-employed persons, not corporations. A Section 529 plan is not a retirement plan at all, and a deferred compensation plan is not a qualified plan.

19. **A.** The NASD will prohibit registration of individuals who have lied on their application forms, who have been suspended or expelled by another self-regulatory organization, or who were convicted of a felony or securities misdemeanor within the past 10 years. Lack of experience is not reason for denial of registration by the NASD.

20. **D.** The prospectus and the preliminary prospectus are prepared by the issuer of a new security, not the broker/dealer who will sell it.

21. **D.** In the absence of a tax ID number for a customer, funds must withhold 31% of distributions.

22. **B.** If a mutual fund distributes at least 90% of its net investment income to shareholders, it need not pay a tax on what it distributes. This saves the shareholder an extra tax loss and is known as the conduit theory.

23. **B.** Broker/dealers must indicate SIPC membership on all advertising and must post a sign indicating their membership. The SIPC logo may never be larger than the firm's own name.

24. **A.** SIPC was founded to protect investors in case their broker/dealer experienced financial failure.

25. **D.** Supervision or training of those who deal with the public on behalf of an NASD member firm requires registration as a principal.

Q U I C K   Q U I Z   A N S W E R S

Quick Quiz 3.1

1. **B.**

2. **A.**

3. **E.**

4. **D.**

5. **C.**

Quick Quiz 3.2

1. **Y.**

2. **Y.**

3. **N.**

4. **N.**

5. **Y.**

6. **N.**

Quick Quiz 3.3

1. **B.** Because ABC is a corporate issue that will be sold in different states, the issuer must file a standard registration statement with the SEC.

2. **C.** A preliminary prospectus is issued before the price is established, and it does not include the eventual offering date or the spread.

3. **D.** A registered representative is prohibited from sending a research report with either a preliminary or a final prospectus.

4. **A.** A preliminary prospectus is used to obtain indications of interest from investors.

5. **B.** The SEC does not approve, endorse, or guarantee the accuracy of a registration.

Quick Quiz 3.4

1. **B.**

2. **A.**

3. **D.**

4. **C.**

Quick Quiz 3.5

1. **D.**

2. **A.**

3. **C.**

4. **B.**

5. **F.** A shareholder must own the stock on the record date to receive the dividend.

6. **F.** The ex-date is 2 business days before the record date.

7. **F.** The buyer gets the dividend only if the stock is purchased before the ex-date. The seller gets the dividend if the transaction is on or after the ex-date.

8. **F.** The payable date is usually 3 to 4 weeks after the record date.

Quick Quiz 3.6

1. **1933**

2. **1934**

3. **1934**

4. **1933**

5. **1934**

6. **1933**

7. **1933**

8. **1934**

9. **1934**

10. **1934**

Quick Quiz 3.7

1. **F.** Unrealized gains, or paper profits, are not taxable to investors.

2. **F.** Capital gains distributions may not be made more than once a year.

3. **F.** Mutual fund gains distributions are all long-term. Mutual fund short-term gains are distributed as income.

4. **T.**

5. **T.**

6. **F.** Funds that comply with IRC Subchapter M are considered regulated investment companies.

7. **F.** Dividend distributions, whether taken in cash or reinvested, are taxable as ordinary income to shareholders.

8. **T.**

Quick Quiz 3.8

1. **D.** The ex-date for a mutual fund is set by its board of directors.

2. **B.** Regulated companies under Subchapter M of the IRS Code are allowed to pass through income to beneficial owners without a tax at the fund level on the distributed income (known as conduit or flow-through of income and taxation).

3. **C.** In open-end investment companies, current yield is calculated as follows: Annual dividends divided by asked price equals yield. The client would find the yield of the open-end investment company as follows: $.60 ÷ $10.80 = 0.0555 = 5.55% (5.6% rounded).

Quick Quiz 3.9

1. **D.** Income tax, not capital gains, is paid on annuity earnings. Since the annuitant is over 59½, there will be no 10% penalty.

2. **C.** All retirement account distributions exceeding cost basis are taxed at the owner's then-current ordinary income tax rate. The advantage of most retirement accounts is that withdrawals usually begin after an account owner is in a lower tax bracket (i.e., upon retirement).

3. **A.** Gains in a separate account are tax deferred. The annuitant pays ordinary income tax on the distribution only upon withdrawal.

Quick Quiz 3.10

1. **F.**

2. **F.**

3. **T.**

4. **F.**

5. **T.**

6. **F.**

7. **T.**

Quick Quiz 3.11

1. **A.** A deferred compensation plan is considered nonqualified because there are no tax benefits associated with contributions. An executive, in effect, simply agrees to a lower level of compensation in exchange for a promise of retirement benefits.

2. **A.** All corporate pension and profit-sharing plans must be set up under a trust agreement. A plan's trustee has fiduciary responsibility for the plan.

3. **B.** Deferred compensation plans can be offered to select employees. However, board members are not considered employees.

4. **C.** Because the annuitant has no cost basis, all payments are considered ordinary income. In a nonqualified annuity, contributions are

made with after-tax dollars, which establish the annuitant's basis. Annuity payments from a nonqualified annuity are treated as ordinary income to the extent that they exceed the cost basis.

Quick Quiz 3.12

1. **A.** Any individual with earned income who is under the age of 70½ may contribute to an IRA. The deductibility of those contributions will be determined by that person's coverage under other qualified plans and by level of income.

2. **B.** All withdrawals from IRAs are taxed at the individual's ordinary income tax rate at the time of withdrawal. Distributions taken before age 59½ will incur an additional 10% penalty.

3. **C.** The penalty for premature withdrawals from an IRA or a Keogh account is 10% plus normal income tax. Excess contribution penalty is 6%, while the 50% penalty applies after age 70½ to insufficient distributions.

4. **A.** Early withdrawals, without penalty, are permitted only in certain situations such as death or qualifying disability.

5. **B.** Cash-value life insurance, term insurance, and collectibles are not permissible investments in an IRA.

6. **B.** Small businesses and self-employed persons typically establish SEP IRAs because they are much easier and less expensive than other plans for an employer to set up and administer.

7. **C.** The common factor for both traditional and Roth IRAs is that investment earnings are not taxed when earned. Traditional IRAs offer tax-deductible contributions, but withdrawals are generally taxed. Roth IRAs do not offer tax-deductible contributions, but qualified withdrawals are tax free. Traditional IRAs require distributions to begin in the year after the year an owner reaches age 70½, but this is not true for Roth IRAs.

8. **D.** Only $2,000 may be invested in each child's education IRA every year. If a couple has three children, they may contribute $6,000 in total, or $2,000 for each child.

Quick Quiz 3.13

1. **C.** A person with self-employment income may allocate contributions to a Keogh plan. Keogh plans are not available to corporations or their employees.

2. **C.** All interest, dividends, and capital gains accumulated in a Keogh are tax deferred until their withdrawal (which must begin between age 59½ and the year after the year in which the account owner turns 70½). The account owner may choose to take distributions in the form of regular income payments or as a single lump sum.

3. **A.** Keogh plans are available only to nonincorporated businesses.

Quick Quiz 3.14

1. **D.**

2. **A.**

3. **B.**

4. **C.**

5. **E.**

6. **A.**

7. **D.**

8. **C.**

9. **B.**

Quick Quiz 3.15

1. **B.** Funding covers how an employer contributes to or funds a plan. Vesting describes how quickly rights to a retirement account turn over to the employee. Nondiscrimination refers to broad employee coverage by a plan. All retirement plans must meet ERISA's reporting and disclosure requirements.

2. **B.** The retirement plan's trust agreement contains a section explaining the formula(s) used to determine the contributions to a defined contribution plan.

3. **C.** Because he is employed by a public school system, your customer is eligible to participate in the tax-sheltered annuity plan. Employee contributions to a TSA plan are excluded from gross income in the year in which they are made. As in other retirement plans, a penalty tax is assessed on distributions received before age 59½. Mutual funds, CDs, and annuity contracts are among the investment choices available for TSA plans.

4. **C.** The rules regarding the maximum amount of contributions differ for defined contribution plans and defined benefit plans. Defined benefit plans set the amount of retirement benefits that a retiree receives as a percentage of the previous several years' salaries. For the highly paid individual nearing retirement, the defined benefit plan allows a larger contribution in a shorter period of time. Choice D describes a defined contribution plan rather than a defined benefit plan.

5. **C.** ERISA was established to protect the retirement funds of employees working in the private sector only. It does not apply to municipal or federal retirement plans.

Quick Quiz 3.16

1. **B.** Any customer claims that SIPC does not cover result in the customer becoming a general (unsecured) creditor of the company.

2. **B.** SIPC coverage is $500,000 per separate customer account, with cash not to exceed $100,000. Thus, in the single-name account, SIPC provides full coverage, while in the joint account, SIPC covers the full value of the securities but only $100,000 of the $180,000 in cash. The remaining $80,000 becomes a general debt of the bankrupt broker/dealer.

3. **B.** Under SIPC rules, customer claims are valued on the day customer protection proceedings commence; this is the day a federal court is petitioned to appoint a trustee.

4. **A.** The penalty may be imposed on anyone who trades on inside information, not just persons registered under the act. The other statements are correct: Choice B defines insider trading; the penalty is up to three times the profit gained or loss avoided (Choice C); and an advisory firm may face a penalty for the actions of its representatives (Choice D).

5. **D.** While the act of 1934 defines an insider as an officer, a director, or a 10% stockholder of a company, the courts have broadened the definition to include anyone who has inside information.

Quick Quiz 3.17

1. **F.** An agreement for continuing commissions must be a bona fide, written contract.

2. **F.** Foreign representatives are required to register if they attempt to transact business with US citizens.

3. **T.**

4. **T.**

5. **F.** Representatives and firms must be registered with the NASD and all states in which they conduct business.

6. **F.** Clerical staff is exempt from NASD registration.

7. **F.** The phrase *member of the NASD* is permissible—provided there is no undue emphasis on it.

Quick Quiz 3.18

1. **D.**

2. **B.**

3. **A.**

4. **C.**

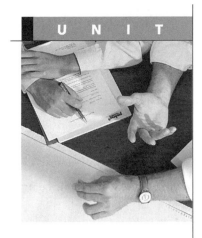

4

Marketing, Prospecting, and Sales Presentations

I n placing investment, retirement, and insurance securities in the hands of investors, the registered representative and his firm must inevitably approach the public. The NASD and other regulatory organizations formulate and enforce strict ethical rules regarding what is said to customers, who may in fact know very few of the details regarding how their investments work. Everything stated to a prospective customer must be strictly true, and no material fact may be omitted.

The Series 6 exam will include 18 questions on the topics covered in this Unit. ∎

When you have completed this Unit, you should be able to:

- **describe** the role of the NASD and SEC in regulating sales practices and communications;

- **distinguish** among the various forms of communications with the public, including advertising and sales literature;

- **describe** applicable disclosure and filing rules for sales material;

- **list** and describe at least 10 prohibited sales practices;

- **explain** the rules regarding the use of performance data;

- **discuss** the rules regarding telephone communications with the public;

- **assess** the different methods for valuing mutual fund shares and collecting (and reducing) sales charges;

- **describe** the advertising and sales literature rules as they apply to variable life insurance and variable annuities; and

- **distinguish** among the various mutual fund share classes and how they affect sales recommendations.

COMMUNICATIONS WITH THE PUBLIC

The NASD, as a self-regulatory organization, has taken the federal requirements on communications with the public and expanded upon them in their Conduct Rules. These rules require that all members observe high standards of commercial honor and just and equitable principles of trade. It is strictly prohibited to make use of any manipulative, deceptive, or other fraudulent devices or contrivances when conducting business with the public.

Broker/dealers and their associated persons use various forms of communication with their customers and the public. Examples include newspaper or television advertisements, Websites, newsletters, research reports, letters, and email. NASD and SEC rules deal with advertising, sales literature, and correspondence concerning a member's investment banking or securities business. You must be familiar with the standards for content, supervisory review and approval, and recordkeeping for such material.

NASD Rule 2210, Communications with the Public, provides definitions and categories that differentiate the various types of communications for which the principal is responsible.

It is also unlawful, under the Securities Act of 1933, to attempt to sell a security through interstate commerce for which no registration statement has been filed or for which no prospectus has been provided. There are some exceptions to this rule, but the necessity of giving full and fair disclosure of all material information to the investor must be observed without exception, both in the documentation provided by the issuer (the prospectus and preliminary prospectus) and in the advertising and sales literature provided by the broker/dealer.

TAKE NOTE

A limited securities principal (Series 26) may only approve sales literature for investment company products.

The definition of communications with the public not only includes advertisements, sales literature, and correspondence, but also public appearances, institutional sales material, and independently prepared reprints. The application of the rule differs depending on the category of a particular communication.

ADVERTISING AND SALES LITERATURE

The most significant difference between advertising and sales literature is how the NASD member selects the audience. If the member cannot select the audience, it is advertising; if the member can select the audience, it is sales literature.

Advertising

Advertising means a form of communication with the public at large, where the member does not control who receives the communication. Advertising is material published or designed to be reproduced in:

- newspapers, magazines, or other periodicals;
- television or radio;
- telephone or tape recordings;
- videotape displays;
- signs or billboards;
- motion pictures;
- telephone directories (other than routine listings); and
- electronic or other public media (including Websites).

Sales Literature

Sales literature is a form of communication intended to be directed to more than one person where the member has the ability to target who receives the material. Sales literature is generally written or electronic communication distributed or made generally available to customers or the public that does not meet the definition of advertising. Examples of sales literature include:

- circulars;
- research reports and market letters;
- performance reports or summaries;
- form letters, other than those considered correspondence;
- telemarketing scripts and seminar texts;
- reprints (that are not independently prepared reprints); or
- excerpts of any other advertisement, sales literature or published article, and press releases concerning a member's products or services.

Correspondence

Correspondence consists of any written letter or email message distributed by a member to:

- one or more of its existing retail customers; and
- fewer than 25 prospective retail customers within any 30 calendar-day period.

Public Appearance

Public appearance means participation in a seminar, forum (including an interactive electronic forum), radio or television interview, or other public appearance or public speaking activity.

Institutional Sales Material

Institutional sales material consists of any communication that is distributed or made available only to institutional investors. However, no member may treat a communication as having been distributed to an institutional investor if the member has reason to believe that the communication or any excerpt thereof will be forwarded or made available to any person other than an institutional investor.

Independently Prepared Reprint

An **independently prepared reprint** consists of any article reprint that meets certain standards that are designed to ensure that the reprint was issued by an independent publisher and was not materially altered by the member. A member may alter the contents of an independently prepared reprint in a manner necessary to make it consistent with applicable regulatory standards or to correct factual errors.

An article reprint qualifies as an independently prepared reprint under the rules only if, among other things, its publisher is not an affiliate of the member using the reprint or any underwriter or issuer of the security mentioned in the reprint. Also, neither the member using the reprint or excerpt nor any underwriter or issuer of a security mentioned in the reprint or excerpt has commissioned the reprinted or excerpted article.

TEST TOPIC ALERT

Be careful of questions that ask you to differentiate between advertising and sales literature according to the NASD definition.

■ Advertising is nontargeted: there is no control over who will read, see, or hear it.

■ Sales literature is targeted material: it is given or mailed to a specific group of recipients.

Whether a communication is classified as advertising or sales literature, it must still be approved by a principal before use and kept on file for three years from the date of first use.

QUICK QUIZ 4.1

Choose **A** (advertising), **SL** (sales literature), **PA** (public appearance), or **C** (correspondence) for the following public communications.

_A_ 1. Billboard

_PA_ 2. Seminar

_A_ 3. Radio broadcast

_C_ 4. Form letter to existing clients

_SL_ 5. Research report

_A_ 6. Recruitment advertisement

_SL_ 7. Circular

_PA_ 8. Television interview

_SL_ 9. Telemarketing script

_A_ 10. Telephone directory

Quick Quiz answers can be found at the end of the Unit.

TEST TOPIC ALERT

NASD rules on advertising specifically apply to which of the following?
A. Yellow Pages telephone listing
B. Market research reports
C. Telemarketing scripts
D. All of the above

Answer: A. The question asks about advertising, not sales literature. Of the choices offered, only a Yellow Pages listing is defined by the NASD as advertising.

Generic Advertising (Rule 135a)

Generic advertising promotes securities as an investment medium but does not refer to any specific security. Generic advertising often includes information about:

■ the securities investments that companies offer;

■ the nature of investment companies;

■ services offered in connection with the described securities;

■ explanations of the various types of investment companies;

■ descriptions of exchange and reinvestment privileges; and

■ where the public can write or call for further information.

All generic advertisements must contain the name and address of the sponsor of the advertisement. A generic advertisement can be placed only by a firm that offers the type of security or service described.

TAKE NOTE

A brokerage firm is not permitted to advertise no-load mutual funds if it does not sell them; firms must have available for sale the type of security or service they advertise.

Omitting Prospectus—Rule 482

There is a specific SEC rule permitting registered investment companies to use what is known as an **omitting prospectus**. SEC Rule 482 describes mutual fund tombstone advertisements. Even though tombstone advertisements are used to advertise, since the rule technically considers this a prospectus, the advertisements are subject to the same liabilities as any other prospectus as well as the antifraud provisions of the federal securities laws.

To comply with this rule, an omitting prospectus must meet the following criteria.

- The advertisement must state conspicuously from whom a prospectus may be obtained.

- The advertisement must urge investors to read the prospectus carefully before investing.

- Any past performance data, such as yields or return, that is quoted in the advertisements must be accompanied by appropriate disclaimer and disclosures of load, if any.

- The advertisement cannot be used to purchase the shares (purchase may be made only via an application found in the prospectus).

- If the advertisement shows performance, it must show (other than a money market fund) average annual total returns (after taxes on distributions) and average annual total returns (after taxes on distributions and redemptions) for one-, five- and 10-year periods.

- The advertisement may include information, the substance of which is not included in the statutory prospectus.

Funds may describe investment policies and objectives, services, principal officers, year of incorporation, and aggregate net asset value if the advertisement includes the following legend:

> *For more complete information about (fund's name), including charges and expenses, send for a prospectus from (name and address). Read it carefully before you invest or send money.*

TAKE NOTE   Although tombstone advertisements and generic advertising are both general in nature, the differences between the two are as follows.

- Generic advertisements may name only the principal underwriter, but tombstone advertisements name the specific investment company and the principal underwriter.

- Generic advertisements do not refer to a specific security, but tombstones identify the specific securities being advertised.

APPROVAL AND FILING REQUIREMENTS

The review requirements differ for the different categories of advertising and sales literature and correspondence.

Advertising and Sales Literature

NASD rules require that each item of advertising and sales literature must be approved in writing (signature or initial) by a registered principal of the member before use or filing with the NASD.

Correspondence

The NASD's supervision rule requires each member to have written procedures for the review and endorsement of outgoing written and electronic correspondence with the public by registered representatives and associated persons related to the member's investment banking and securities business. The supervisory procedures governing this review must be appropriate to the member's business, size, structure, and customers.

Incoming Written Correspondence Rule Amendment. The rule states that all member firms must create written policies to ensure a proper review of incoming correspondence by a specifically designated person who will make sure that customer complaints are addressed and funds are not misappropriated.

In offices organized to allow a review of all correspondence, a supervisor should be designated to identify all customer complaints and funds by opening and reviewing all correspondence.

Review of Opened Correspondence. Where it is not feasible for a designated person to oversee all incoming correspondence, alternative procedures include a frequent forwarding of opened correspondence for review.

RECORDKEEPING REQUIREMENTS

A separate file containing all advertising, sales literature, and independently prepared reprints (IPR), including the names of the persons preparing and approving their use, must be maintained for three years from the date of each use.

The NASD supervision rule also establishes recordkeeping requirements for correspondence. Each member must retain copies of its registered representatives' correspondence according to the NASD recordkeeping rules and SEC recordkeeping rules. A file of such material showing the names of the persons who prepared and approved the correspondence must be kept for at least three years.

TAKE NOTE   Outgoing electronic securities business correspondence is subject to the three-year requirement as well. One way to accomplish this is to require a copy of all email to go to a central mailbox for review and recordkeeping.

NASD Filing Requirements and Review Procedures

Advertising, sales literature, and IPR relating to investment companies must be filed with the NASD within 10 days of first use (**postfiling**).

Member Filing for First Year

New NASD members and other members who have not filed advertising previously must file all advertisements—but not sales literature or independently prepared reprints—with the NASD Advertising/Investment Companies Regulation Department for a period of one year. A filing must be made at least 10 days before use and must include the actual or anticipated date of first use of each such advertisement (prefiling).

TAKE NOTE   If the NASD believes a member's advertising or sales literature has departed from acceptable standards, it can mandate prefiling of any communications with the public.

Spot Checks

Each member's advertisements and sales literature are subject to routine spot checks. Members must comply with written requests for such material by the NASD Advertising/Investment Companies Regulation Department. Material filed previously with the NASD under this rule need not be resubmitted.

Exemptions from NASD Filing and Spot Check Requirements

Certain types of communications are excluded from the filing and spot check requirements described above. These exemptions include:

- material solely related to changes in a member's name, personnel, location, business structure, officers or partners, phone or teletype numbers, or concerning a merger with, or acquisition by, another member;

- material that only identifies the Nasdaq symbol of the member, a security in which the member is a Nasdaq market maker, or both;

- material that does no more than identify the member, offer a specific security at a stated price, or both;

- material sent to branch offices or other internal locations and not distributed to the public; and

- prospectuses, preliminary prospectuses, offering circulars, and similar documents used in connection with an offering of securities registered or filed with the SEC.

QUICK QUIZ 4.2   True or False?

 1. An established member firm's investment company advertising material must be submitted to the NASD advertising department before it is used.

F 2. A principal of the firm must approve all sales literature within 10 days of first use.

F 3. New firms are required to file all advertising material and sales literature with the NASD advertising department 10 days before use.

4. Member firm investment company advertising and sales literature is not subject to NASD spot checks.

5. Memos stamped *For Internal Use Only* must be approved by a principal before distribution.

NASD RULES CONCERNING PUBLIC COMMUNICATIONS

Securities rules and regulations protect the general public from unscrupulous investment professionals.

The two main problems that the NASD's code of professionalism addresses in advertising and sales literature are **omissions** and **distortions of material facts**. In general, all communications from a member to the public must be based on principles of fair dealing and good faith. A communication should provide a sound basis for evaluating the facts in regard to the product, service, or industry promoted. Exaggerated, unwarranted, or misleading statements are strictly prohibited.

Identification of Source

In general, sales literature, including market letters and research reports, must identify the member firm's name, the person or firm that prepared the material if any copy was prepared outside the member firm, and the date the material was first used.

Customer Recommendations

A member should have reasonable grounds for believing that a security is a suitable investment for a customer before recommending purchase. Investment recommendations must be consistent with customer needs, financial capability, and objectives. Investment recommendations should be in a customer's best interest, not the registered representative's. Each investment should be explained fully, especially its risks.

At no time should customers own investments that could put them at risk beyond their financial capacity.

Disclosure Requirements

Proposals and written presentations that include specific recommendations must have reasonable basis to support the recommendations. The member must offer to provide, upon request, investment information that supports the recommendation. The price of the security at the time the recommendation is made must be disclosed.

A recommendation may be supported by performance of past recommendations if it includes:

■ the price or price range of the recommended security at the date and time that the recommendation is made;

- the market's general direction;

- the availability of information supporting the recommendation;

- recommendations made of similar securities within the past 12 months, including the nature of the recommendations (buy, sell, hold);

- whether the firm intends to buy or sell any of the recommended security for its own account;

- whether the firm is a market maker in the recommended security;

- whether the firm or its officers or partners own options, rights, or warrants to buy the recommended security;

- whether the firm managed or co-managed a public offering of the recommended security or any other of the same issuer's securities during the past three years; and

- all recommendations (gainers and losers) the firm made over the period of time in question.

The time span covered in the list of recommendations must run through consecutive periods, without skipping periods in an attempt to hide particular recommendations or negative price performance data.

Knowledgeable investors use this type of information to determine if recommendations are appropriate for their situation. In addition to meeting these information requirements, the firm making the recommendation must not:

- imply that any guarantees accompany the recommendation;

- compare the recommended security to dissimilar products;

- make fraudulent or misleading statements about the recommended security; or

- make any predictions about the recommended security's future performance or potential.

TAKE NOTE   Be sure to make only suitable recommendations; unsuitable recommendations are prohibited by the NASD. Also, any statement of past performance must remind the reader or listener that past performance does not guarantee future results.

Communication Prohibitions

Claims and Opinions Couched as Facts and Conclusions

It violates regulations to pass off opinions, projections, and forecasts as guarantees of performance.

Testimonials. Testimonials and endorsements related to specific recommendations or investment results by celebrities and those who can influence public opinion must not mislead or suggest that past performance indicates future performance. If a member firm pays a fee or other compensation to a person for a testimonial or an endorsement, it must disclose this fact.

If a broker/dealer assembles a sales piece about a particular investment company that includes testimonials by one or more customers, the sales piece must state that:

- past performance does not indicate future performance;

- the company compensated the person who made the testimonial, if this is true; and

- the person making the testimonial has the qualifications to do so (these qualifications must be listed) if the testimonial implies that the statement is based on the customer's special experience or knowledge.

TAKE NOTE   A member could not include a testimonial by someone named Dr. Henderson about the investment potential of its new medical technology fund if the doctor's degree is in history.

Offers of Free Service. It is unprofessional to use offers of free service if the respondent must assume obligations of one sort or another. Reports, analyses, or other services offered to the public must be furnished entirely free and without condition or obligation.

Other Rules

The following are some additional rules regarding unprofessional practices.

- A communication must not state or imply that research facilities are more extensive than they actually are.

- Hedge clauses, caveats, and disclaimers must not be used if they are misleading or inconsistent with the material's content.

- Ambiguous references to the NASD or other SROs must not be made with the aim of leading people to believe that a broker/dealer acts with the endorsement and approval of the Association or one of the other SROs. If the NASD's name or logo is used in a member's sales literature, it must not appear in a typeface larger or more prominent than the one used for the member's own name.

TAKE NOTE   The name of the NASD should never appear larger than the name of the member. The size of the type and the bold print may mislead the public into thinking that the representative is in some way endorsed by the NASD.

Use of Member Names

General Standards

No material fact may be omitted if the omission causes the advertisement or sales literature to be misleading. All advertisements and sales literature must:

- clearly and prominently disclose the NASD member's name;

- clearly describe the relationship between the NASD member and the named entities and products when multiple entities and products are being offered;

- clearly disclose the relationship of an individual and an NASD member when an individual is named in the communication;

- not use or refer to nonexistent degrees or designations; and

- not use degrees or designations in a misleading manner.

Fictional Names

A fictional name or DBA (doing business as) designation is permitted if the name is filed with the NASD and the SEC.

Other Designations

A member may designate a portion of its business using a phrase such as *division of, service of,* or *securities offered through* only if a bona fide division exists. The member name must be clearly designated and the division be clearly identified as a division of the member.

Recruitment Advertising

Companies that advertise to attract new registered representatives are regulated by the same Conduct Rules that cover companies advertising investment products. The advertisements must be truthful, informative, and fair in representing the opportunities in the industry and must not contain exaggerated or unwarranted claims.

The advertisements may not emphasize the salaries of top-paid salespeople without revealing that they are not representative, and the advertisements may not contain any other statements that may be misleading or fraudulent.

Broker/dealers are permitted, in this one instance, to run blind advertisements—that is, advertisements that do not list a company's name.

TAKE NOTE   Recruitment advertisements are the only form of advertising not required to disclose the identity of the member firm. Such an advertisement may request someone to "send a resume to PO Box 54321" without stating the name of the firm.

Interviews

Once a company starts interviewing potential employees, it is the principal's responsibility to see that both the industry and the job opportunity are represented honestly. Any discussions of the business must present both the upside and the downside of the position and should not misrepresent the average employee's compensation.

QUICK QUIZ 4.3

True or False?

T ~~F~~   1.   It is permissible to omit facts in advertising and sales literature.

F   2.   Testimonials in investment company advertising are prohibited.

F   3.   Firms are not allowed to offer free services.

 T ~~F~~   4.   The price of the recommended security must always be disclosed at the time the recommendation is made.

F   5.   A recommendation showing past performance must include all recommendations made of similar securities within the past (six) months.

12

SPECIFIC RULES FOR INVESTMENT COMPANY SALES LITERATURE

SEC Rule 156 establishes additional guidelines for mutual fund sales literature. Any investment company sales literature that omits material facts, contains untrue statements, or is misleading is illegal. Sales literature may be considered misleading because of:

- inaccurate reports of investment performance;

- predictions made of future income or capital gains based on past performance;

- unsubstantiated claims about the skills of the investment company's management;

- exaggeration of the backgrounds of officers and directors;

- omissions of the shortcomings of investment performance;

- information reported out of context;

- distorted or incomplete performance comparisons to other investments or indices;

- presenting potential benefits without providing equal prominence to possible risks; and

- omission of information about general economic and financial conditions.

These restrictions apply to any form of communication where an offer to sell is made. Even spoken words are considered part of the company's sales literature. Registered representatives must tell the complete truth in presentations and not imply investment performance or guarantees that do not exist.

TAKE NOTE   In sales presentations, the downside of an investment opportunity must be as highly emphasized as its upside.

If in a sales presentation a representative draws additional charts or graphs to depict performance, the representative is in violation of Rule 156. All charts and graphs must be approved before use.

TAKE NOTE   Representatives are prohibited from marking or highlighting information on prospectuses distributed to prospective buyers by this rule.

Advertising Performance Data

Investment companies frequently choose to advertise measures of performance, such as return on investment or total return. When mutual funds, variable annuities, and unit investment trusts advertise such performance data, additional requirements apply under SEC Rule 482.

Performance data must be current. The rule assumes that data to the most recent calendar quarter is current.

Total Return

Total return is calculated by assuming the reinvestment of dividends and capital gains distributions. The computation of total return must be made in accordance with standardized procedures. If the average annual total return is included, the quotations must be for one-, five-, and 10-year periods, or since inception if the fund is new. The periods over which the computation has been made must be identified. Total return computation must be updated quarterly.

Advertising Fund Yield

If a fund chooses to disclose yield, current yield must be calculated according to standardized procedures. The base period of the calculation must be identified, and computation must reflect a 30-day period.

Past Performance

An advertisement containing performance data must clearly state that what is shown is past performance and that investment returns and principal values fluctuate. The advertisement must further state that an investor who redeems shares may receive more or less than the original cost. Money market funds are not required to state the risks of principal fluctuation.

Fees

Rule 482 also requires that the maximum amount of any sales load or non-recurring fee is disclosed in the advertisement. Funds may alternatively choose not to disclose such fees, but if they do, a disclosure statement must identify that the deduction of such fees is not reflected and that performance would be reduced if fees were deducted.

Omitting Prospectus

Advertising or sales literature under SEC Rule 482 is sometimes referred to as an **omitting prospectus**; that is, it omits certain information contained in the full prospectus. As a result, an omitting prospectus may never contain an application to invest. It must contain information on how to obtain a full prospectus.

Profile

The **profile rule** under SEC Rule 498 allows mutual funds to prepare a profile, which can include an application to invest. The profile must contain all of the information required by the SEC. Investors who purchase shares using a profile must receive the full prospectus with the confirmation of the sale. If a customer, after receiving the profile, requests additional information such as the SAI or the full prospectus, it must be provided within three business days.

Recommending Funds

When recommending mutual funds to clients as investments and when using advertisements or sales literature developed for those investments, a broker/dealer should:

- use charts or graphs showing a fund's performance over a period of time long enough to reflect variations in value under different market conditions, generally a period of at least 10 years;

- reveal the source of the graphics;

- separate dividends from capital gains when making statements about a fund's cash returns;

- not state that a mutual fund is similar to or safer than any other type of security;

- reveal a fund's highest sales charge, even if the client appears to qualify for a breakpoint; and

- not make a fraudulent or misleading statement or omit facts.

Periodic Payment Plans

Mutual fund plans that make periodic payments (frequently sold in this manner so investors receive the benefits of dollar cost averaging) cannot be described in advertisements or sales literature without the disclosure that:

- a profit is not assured;

- they do not provide protection from losses in a declining market;

- the plans involve continuous investments regardless of market fluctuations; and

- investors should consider their financial ability to continue purchases during periods of declining prices.

Review of NASD Regulations

The following summarizes the NASD regulations regarding communications with the public.

- A principal must approve all advertising, sales literature, and independently prepared reprints before use.

- All advertising, sales literature, independently prepared reprints, and institutional sales literature must be kept in a separate file for a minimum of three years.

- The member must provide for each filing with the NASD Advertising Department the actual or anticipated date of first use, the name and title of the registered principal who approved the advertisement or sales literature, and the date that the approval was given.

- The member must file most advertisements and sales literature concerning registered investment companies within 10 business days of first use.

- Each member that has not previously filed advertisements with the NASD (or with a registered securities exchange having standards comparable to those of the NASD) must file its initial advertisement with the NASD at least 10 business days before use and must continue to file its advertisements at least 10 business days before use for a period of one year.

- Correspondence and institutional sales literature are subject to review by a principal while independently prepared reprints require approval by a principal. These three items are never filed with the NASD Advertising Department.

TEST TOPIC ALERT

1. Which of the following is allowed in a mutual fund sales presentation?
   A. Highlighting charts or graphs in the fund prospectus
   B. Comparing capital gains distributions between a stock fund and a US government bond fund
   C. Creating a new chart on a separate sheet of paper to clarify a question raised by the customer
   D. Informing the customer of the tax status of dividend distributions

   Answer: D. It is appropriate for a representative to identify the tax status of dividend distributions in a mutual fund sales presentation. It is prohibited to make unfair comparisons, mark on the prospectus, or create new charts or graphs and use them without approval.

2.   All of the following must be disclosed in a mutual fund advertisement containing performance data EXCEPT

A.   the fact that investment returns fluctuate

B.   the SEC disclaimer stating that the securities have not been approved or disapproved by the SEC

C.   that investors who redeem shares may receive more or less than the original cost

D.   data represents past performance

Answer: B. The SEC disclaimer is not required in advertising material. The no-approval clause must be included in the prospectus.

3.   Which of the following about advertising mutual fund performance is TRUE?

A.   A comparison to any market index must be provided.

B.   The fund's total return must be included for a minimum period of one year.

C.   The advertisement must disclose the maximum amount of load or fee.

D.   All funds, including money markets, must make a disclosure about fluctuation of principal.

Answer: C. In performance advertisements, the maximum sales load or other non-recurring fee must be disclosed. Comparisons to market indexes are not required. Disclosure about fluctuation of principal is required for all funds except money market funds. The minimum period for total return is 10 years or since the fund's inception, whichever is shorter.

QUICK QUIZ 4.4

True or False?

___I___ 1.   All outgoing customer correspondence must be reviewed and endorsed by a principal.

___F___ 2.   Advertising, sales literature, and institutional sales literature must be ~~approved~~ reviewed by a principal before use.

___I___ 3.   A principal must approve all public communications.

___I___ 4.   Copies of advertising and sales literature must be retained for three years from last use.

Before or After? Identify whether the following advertising and sales literature must be filed 10 days before or within 10 days after first use.

A 5.   Advertising and sales literature related to investment companies.

B 6.   Any advertising filed by firms that have not previously filed any advertisements with the NASD.

B 7.   A testimonial used by a member firm must state which of the following?

A.   Qualifications of the person giving the testimonial if a specialized or experienced opinion is implied

B.   Fact that past performance does not indicate future performance and that other investors may not obtain comparable results

C.   If compensation was paid to the person giving the testimonial

D.   All of the above

8. Which of the following forms of written communication must be approved by a principal before its use?
   A. Letter to a customer confirming an annual account review appointment
   B. Letter sent to 30 prospective customers offering advice about a stock
   C. Interoffice memorandum
   D. Preliminary prospectus

VARIABLE LIFE AND VARIABLE ANNUITIES

The following standards apply to all communications related to variable life and variable annuities, in addition to the general NASD standards governing communications. These standards are applicable to advertisements and sales literature, as well as individualized communications such as personalized letters and computer-generated illustrations, whether printed or made available on-screen.

Product Communications

All communications must clearly describe the product as either variable life or a variable annuity, as applicable. Proprietary names may be used in addition to these descriptions. There can be no implication that the product being offered or its underlying account is a mutual fund.

Liquidity

Because variable life insurance and variable annuities frequently involve substantial charges and/or tax penalties for early withdrawal, there can be no representation or implication that these are short-term, liquid investments. Any statement about the ease of liquidation of these products must be accompanied by the negative impact of factors such as contingent deferred sales loads, tax penalties, and impact on cash value and death benefits.

Guarantees

Although insurance products contain a number of specific guarantees, the relative safety of the product from these guarantees cannot be overemphasized as it depends on the claims-paying ability of the insurance company. There can be no representation or implication that a guarantee applies to the investment return or principal value of the separate account. Also, it cannot be represented or implied that an insurance company's financial ratings apply to the separate account.

Fund Performance Predating Inclusion in a Variable Product

Illustrations are sometimes used to show how an existing fund would have performed as an investment option within a variable life or variable annuity policy. Performance that predates a fund's inclusion may be used only if no significant changes occurred to the fund at the time or after it became a part of the variable product.

Single Premium Variable Life

Communications regarding single premium variable life may only emphasize investment features of this product if an adequate explanation of the life insurance features is also provided. Tax law changes enacted in 1986 greatly reduced issuance of single premium life insurance.

Hypothetical Illustrations of Rates of Return in Variable Life Insurance

Hypothetical illustrations showing assumed rates of return may be used to demonstrate the performance of variable life policies. Rules that apply to the use of these illustrations include the following.

■ Hypothetical illustrations may not be used to project or predict investment results.

■ Illustrations may use any combination of assumed investment returns up to and including a gross rate of 12%, provided that one of the returns is a 0% gross rate. The maximum rate illustrated should be reasonable considering market conditions and the available investment options.

■ Illustrations must reflect the maximum mortality and expense charges associated with the policy for each assumed rate of return illustrated. Current charges may also be illustrated.

In general, variable life product performance may not be compared to other investment products. However, comparison of variable life to a term insurance product is permitted to demonstrate the concept of tax-deferred growth resulting from investment in the variable product.

Legal Recourse of Customers

The Securities Exchange Act of 1934 and the acts of 1933 and 1940 all contain sections prohibiting the use of any fraudulent or manipulative device in the selling of securities to the public. The rules make it unlawful for any person to use the mail or any facilities of interstate commerce to:

...employ, in connection with the purchase or sale of any security, any manipulative or deceptive device in contravention of such rules and regulations as the Commission may prescribe as necessary.

In essence, this passage states that an act is unlawful if the SEC says it is, and enforcement of the intent of the act is not to be limited by the letter of the law.

Statute of Limitations

Any client may sue for damages if he believes that a broker/dealer used any form of manipulative or deceptive practices in the sale of securities. The client must bring the lawsuit within three years of the manipulative act and within two years of discovery of the manipulation or deception.

TAKE NOTE   The statute of limitations stated above is applicable to the variable products being discussed here. This is different for federal law. Under the acts of 1933 and 1934, the statute of limitations is three years from the alleged violation and within one year of discovery.

TELEPHONE COMMUNICATIONS WITH THE PUBLIC

The **Telephone Consumer Protection Act of 1991 (TCPA)**, administered by the **Federal Communications Commission (FCC)**, was enacted to protect consumers from unwanted telephone solicitations. A telephone solicitation is defined as a telephone call initiated for the purpose of encouraging the purchase of or investment in property, goods, or services.

The act governs commercial calls, recorded solicitations from autodialers, and solicitations and advertisements to fax machines and modems.

The act requires an organization that performs telemarketing (cold calling, in particular) to:

- maintain a **Do Not Call list** of customers who do not want to be called and keep a customer's name on the list for 10 years from the time the request is made;

- institute a written policy on maintenance procedures for the Do-Not-Call list;

- train representatives on using the list;

- ensure that representatives acknowledge and immediately record the names and telephone numbers of customers who ask not to be called again;

- ensure that anyone making cold calls for the firm informs customers of the firm's name and telephone number or address;

- ensure that telemarketers do not call a customer within 10 years of a Do-Not-Call request; and

- ensure that a telephone solicitation occurs only between the hours of 8:00 am and 9:00 pm of the time zone in which the prospect is located.

The act exempts calls:

- made to parties with whom the caller has an established business relationship or where the caller has prior express permission or invitation;

- made on behalf of a tax-exempt nonprofit organization;

- not made for a commercial purpose; and

- made for legitimate debt collection purposes.

Under the TCPA of 1991, consumers, businesses, and state authorities may sue telemarketers who violate the act. Consumers may sue telemarketers in state court to prohibit further violations or to recover up to $500 in damages for each violation. The FCC can take appropriate actions against violators, which can include the issuance of warnings or fines up to $11,000 per violation.

TAKE NOTE   Fax communications are subject to the Telephone Consumer Protection Act, but Internet communications and email are not.

QUICK QUIZ 4.5

1. Which of the following parties is covered under the TCPA of 1991?
   A. University survey group
   B. Nonprofit organization
   C. Church group
   D. Registered representative

2. Which of the following must a representative do when making cold calls?
   I. Immediately record the names and telephone numbers of customers who ask not to be called again
   II. Inform customers of the firm's name and telephone number or address
   III. Limit calls to between the hours of 8:00 am and 9:00 pm of the time zone in which customers are located
   IV. Not call customers who make a Do-Not-Call request

   A. I and II
   B. I and IV
   C. II and III
   D. I, II, III and IV

Terms and Concepts Checklist

✓	✓
☐ NASD Rule 2210	☐ Public appearance
☐ Advertising	☐ Institutional sales material
☐ Sales literature	☐ Independently prepared reprint
☐ Correspondence	☐ Omitting prospectus
☐ Generic Advertising	☐ Approval requirements
☐ Written compliance procedures	☐ Recordkeeping requirements
☐ Designated principal	☐ New filer requirements
☐ Spot check requirements	☐ Established company requirements
☐ Disclosure requirements	☐ Communication prohibitions
☐ Member name use requirements	☐ Offer of free service
☐ Fictional names and designations	☐ Testimonial
☐ Past performance	☐ Recruitment advertising
☐ Predictions versus projections	☐ SEC Rule 482
☐ Performance data	☐ Profile
☐ Yield versus total return	☐ Variable contract requirements
☐ Telephone Consumer Protection Act of 1991	☐ Hypothetical illustrations
	☐ Do Not Call list

MUTUAL FUND MARKETING

Mutual fund shares may be marketed in several ways.

METHODS OF MARKETING MUTUAL FUND SHARES

A fund can use any number of methods to market its shares to the public. Following is a discussion of some of the various marketing methods firms use.

Fund to Underwriter to Dealer to Investor

An investor gives an order for fund shares to a dealer. The dealer then places the order with the underwriter. To fill the order, the fund sells shares to the underwriter at the current NAV. The underwriter sells the shares to the dealer at the NAV plus the underwriter's concession (the public offering price less the dealer's reallowance or discount). The dealer sells the shares to the investor at the full public offering price (POP).

TEST TOPIC ALERT   Fund underwriters (sponsors) must be NASD member firms. Only member firms can receive selling concessions.

Fund to Underwriter to Investor

The underwriter acts as dealer and uses its own sales force to sell shares to the public. An investor gives an order for fund shares to the underwriter. To fill the order, the fund sells shares to the underwriter at the current NAV. The underwriter then adds the sales charge and sells the shares to the investor at the POP. The sales charge is split among the various salespeople.

Fund to Investor

Some funds sell directly to the public without using an underwriter or a sales force and without assessing a sales charge. If an open-end investment company distributes shares to the public directly (without the services of a distributor) and the fund offers its shares with no sales charge and a 12b-1 fee of .25% or less, the fund is called a **no-load fund**. The fund pays all sales expenses.

Fund to Underwriter to Plan Company to Investor

Organizations that sell contractual plans for the periodic purchase of mutual fund shares are called **plan companies**. These companies purchase fund shares and hold them in trust for an individual purchasing the shares under a periodic payment plan.

Sales at the POP

Any sale of fund shares to a customer must be made at the POP. The NASD defines a **customer** as anyone who is not an NASD member. The route the sale takes is not important—the nonmember customer must be charged the POP. Only an NASD member acting as a dealer or an underwriter may buy the fund shares at a discount from the issuer.

TAKE NOTE   Remember that there are no discounts for the public or nonmember firms. Only member firms can receive a discount from the POP and only if they have a written sales agreement.

REDUCTIONS IN SALES CHARGES

If an investment company does not offer certain features, the maximum permitted sales charge is reduced. To qualify for the maximum 8.5% charge, investment companies must offer:

- breakpoints (a scale of declining sales charges based on the amount invested);

- rights of accumulation; and

- Automatic reinvestment of dividends and capital gains at NAV.

TEST TOPIC ALERT   Previously, automatic reinvestment of distributions at NAV was included as a feature investment companies had to offer in order to charge the maximum 8.5% sales charge. However, all newly formed investment companies are now required to offer this feature regardless of sales charge percentage.

Mutual Fund Share Classes

A single mutual fund may offer more than one class of its shares to investors, each having a different sales charge structure. Each class of shares represents a similar interest in the mutual fund's portfolio. The principal difference between the classes is the different costs associated with each class. The share class to recommend will always be the class that results in the lowest sales charge to the customer.

Class A Shares

Class A shares typically charge a **front-end sales charge**, also called a **front-end load**. Because the sales charge is deducted from the investor's funds, less than 100 cents of the investor's dollar is actually invested. Class A shares may also impose an asset-based sales charge, the 12b-1 fee, but it is generally less than the 12b-1 fee imposed by the other share classes.

EXAMPLE   The ABC Growth and Income Fund Class A shares have a 12b-1 fee of .30 (30 cents per $100). As such, a $10,000 investment in the fund would have an annual charge of $30 automatically deducted. If the value of the investor's account increases to $20,000, the 12b-1 fee would increase to $60 annually.

In addition, Class A shares typically allow sales charge discounts from the front-end load, called **breakpoints**.

Breakpoints

Breakpoints are available to any person. For a breakpoint qualification, **person** includes married couples, parents and their minor children, corporations, and certain other entities. Investment clubs or associations formed for the purpose of investing do not qualify for breakpoints.

The following are breakpoint considerations.

- Breakpoint rules vary across mutual fund families. There is no industry standardized breakpoint schedule.

- Mutual funds that offer breakpoints must disclose their breakpoint schedule in the prospectus and how an account is valued for breakpoint purposes.

- The SEC further encourages that breakpoint discount availability information be accessible through various means of communication including Websites.

- Discounts may be the result of a single large investment, a series of aggregated investments, or a promise to invest via a letter of intent (LOI).

- Purchases made by the same investor in various accounts can be aggregated to qualify for a breakpoint discount. Eligible accounts include traditional brokerage, accounts held directly with a fund company, 401(k), IRA, and 529 college savings.

- Shares purchased in the same fund family other than money market accounts are eligible to be aggregated together to qualify for a breakpoint discount, including those held at separate broker/dealers.

TEST TOPIC ALERT   You can expect a question on who is eligible for breakpoints. Married couples, parents with minor children, and corporations are eligible. Parents with adult children and investment clubs are not eligible.

The discounts of sales charges are spelled out in a mutual fund's prospectus, but the table below illustrates a typical example.

Purchase Amount	Sales Charge
$0 to $24,999	6.00%
$25,000 to $49,999	5.50%
$50,000 to $99,999	5.00%
$100,000 to $249,999	4.00%
$250,000 to $499,999	3.00%
$500,000 to $999,999	2.00%
$1,000,000 +	0.00%

Breakpoint Sales. The NASD prohibits registered representatives from making or seeking higher commissions by selling investment company shares in a dollar amount just below the point at which the sales charge is reduced. This violation is known as a **breakpoint sale**. The NASD considers this practice contrary to just and equitable principles of trade. It is the responsibility of all parties concerned, particularly the principal, to prevent deceptive practices.

TAKE NOTE   Breakpoints offer a significant advantage to mutual fund purchasers; however, breakpoint sales are prohibited.

Letter of Intent (LOI)

A person who plans to invest more money with the same mutual fund company may immediately decrease his overall sales charges by signing a **letter of intent**. In the LOI, the investor informs the investment company that he intends to invest the additional funds necessary to reach the breakpoint within 13 months.

The LOI is a one-sided contract binding on the fund only. However, the customer must complete the investment to qualify for the reduced sales charge. The fund holds the extra shares purchased from the reduced sales charge in escrow. If the customer deposits the money to complete the LOI, he receives the escrowed shares. Appreciation and reinvested dividends do not count toward the LOI.

EXAMPLE

Refer back to the sample breakpoint schedule. A customer investing $24,000 is just short of the $25,000 breakpoint. In this situation, the customer might sign a letter of intent promising an amount that will qualify for the breakpoint within 13 months from the date of the letter. Investing an additional $1,000 within 13 months qualifies the customer for the reduced sales charge. The customer is charged the appropriate reduced sales charge at the time of the initial purchase.

A customer who has not completed the investment within 13 months will be given the choice of sending a check for the difference in sales charges or cashing in escrowed shares to pay the difference.

Backdating the Letter. A fund often permits a customer to sign a letter of intent as late as the 90th day after an initial purchase. The LOI may be backdated by up to 90 days to include prior purchases but may not cover more than 13 months in total. A customer who signs the LOI 60 days after a purchase has 11 months to complete the letter.

EXAMPLE

Assume the following breakpoint schedule:

$1–$24,999	5.00%
$25,000–$49,999	4.25%
$50,000–$99,999	3.75%
$100,000 +	3.25%

If an investor wants to deposit $50,000 in a mutual fund over a 13-month period and puts in $25,000 when the account is opened, the investor is charged a sales charge of 3.75% on the initial and every subsequent investment if a LOI has been signed. If a letter was not signed, the sales charge on the initial amount of $25,000 would be 4.25%, based on this breakpoint schedule. The LOI allows for a discount on an installment plan purchase.

TEST TOPIC ALERT

■ Letters of intent are good for a maximum of 13 months and may be backdated 90 days.

■ If the letter of intent is not completed, the sales charge amount that applies is based on the total amount actually invested.

■ Share appreciation and income paid by the fund do not count toward completion of the letter.

Rights of Accumulation

Rights of accumulation, like breakpoints, allow an investor to qualify for reduced sales charges. The major differences are that rights of accumulation:

■ are available for subsequent investment and do not apply to initial transactions;

■ allow the investor to use prior share appreciation and reinvestment to qualify for breakpoints; and

■ do not impose time limits.

The customer may qualify for reduced charges when the total value of shares previously purchased and shares currently being purchased exceeds a certain dollar amount. For the purpose of qualifying customers for rights of accumulation, the mutual fund bases the quantity of securities owned on the higher of current NAV or the total of purchases made to date.

TAKE NOTE

Assume the following breakpoint schedule:

$1–$24,999	5.00%
$25,000–$49,999	4.25%
$50,000–$99,999	3.75%
$100,000 +	3.25%

An investor deposits $5,000 (paying a 5% sales charge) in a mutual fund but does not sign an LOI. The $5,000 grows to $10,000 over time and the investor decides to invest another $15,000. If rights of accumulation exist, the new $15,000 is charged a sales charge of 4.25%, which is based on the new money plus the accumulated value in the account ($15,000 + $10,000 = $25,000). If rights of accumulation do not exist, the sales charge would have been 5%.

Combination Privilege

A mutual fund company frequently offers more than one fund and refers to these multiple offerings as its **family of funds.** An investor seeking a reduced sales charge may be allowed to combine separate investments in two or more funds within the same family to reach a breakpoint.

Exchanges Within a Family of Funds

Many sponsors offer exchange or conversion privileges within their families of funds. Exchange privileges allow an investor to convert an investment in one fund for an equal investment in another fund in the same family, often without incurring an additional sales charge.

Mutual funds may be purchased at NAV under a no-load exchange privilege. The following rules apply.

- Purchase may not exceed the proceeds generated by the redemption of the other fund.

- The redemption may not involve a refund of sales charges.

- The sales personnel and dealers must receive no compensation of any kind from the reinvestment.

- Any gain or loss from the redemption of shares must be reported for tax purposes.

Class B Shares

Class B shares do not typically charge a front-end sales charge, but they do impose an asset-based 12b-1 fee greater than those imposed on Class A shares.

EXAMPLE

The ABC Growth and Income Fund Class B shares have a 12b-1 fee of .75 (75 cents per $100). As such, a $10,000 investment in the fund would have an annual charge of $75 automatically deducted. If the value of the investor's account increases to $20,000, the 12b-1 fee would increase to $150 annually.

Class B shares also normally impose a **contingent deferred sales charge (CDSC)**, also called a **back-end load**, which is paid when selling shares. Because of the back-end load and 12b-1 fee, Class B shares cannot be referred to as **no-load** shares. The CDSC normally declines and eventually is eliminated over time. Once the CDSC is eliminated, Class B shares often convert into Class A shares. When they convert, they will be charged the same (lower) asset-based 12b-1 fee as the Class A shares.

EXAMPLE

An investor buys $10,000 of the ABC Growth and Income Fund with the expectation of holding the investment for many years. However, 18 months after the initial purchase, the investor needs to sell the shares to meet unexpected financial needs. The shares have a CDSC of 4%. Therefore, if the value of the account is $10,000, the investor will be charged a 4% ($400) CDSC. If the value of the holding is $15,000, the investor will be charged a $600 CDSC.

Class B shares do not impose a sales charge at the time of purchase, so, unlike Class A share purchases, 100 cents of the invested dollar are invested.

The following table contains a typical CDSC Schedule for Class B Shares:

Year	CDSC
1–2	5%
2–3	4%
3–4	3%
4–5	2%
5–6	1%
6+	0%

Larger investments are usually more suited to Class A shares if they are eligible for sales charge discounts due to the lower ongoing 12b-1 fees.

TAKE NOTE

In determining whether Class A or B shares are an appropriate recommendation for a customer, determine which has the lowest sales charge.

Class C Shares

Like Class B shares, **Class C shares** do not usually impose a front-end sales charge on the purchase, so all of the customer's funds are invested. Often Class C shares impose a small charge, such as 1%, if shares are sold within a short time (usually within one year). Class C shares typically impose a 12b-1 asset-based fee comparable to Class B shares, that is, higher than Class A shares. Class C shares generally do not convert into Class A shares, so the asset-based sales charge will not be reduced over time.

Class C shares may be less expensive than Class A or B shares for investors with a short-term time horizon because there is little or no sales charge. However, the annual expenses could be higher than both Class A and B shares if shares are held for a long time.

Which Class to Recommend?

Identifying which class of shares is appropriate for a customer will be determined by each person's unique circumstances; however, some general principle may be used as guidelines.

■ For investors with substantial sums to invest ($50,000 or more), either in a lump sum or over a period of time, and with a long-term time horizon, Class A shares make the most sense because of the reduced sales charge and lower 12b-1 fees.

■ For investors with significantly less than $50,000 to invest (and who are unlikely to raise it within 13 months) and a long-term time horizon (five years or more), Class B shares are most suitable because of the greater amount of funds invested up front.

■ For investors with less than $50,000 to invest and a time horizon of less than five years, Class C shares make the most sense because of the low (or nonexistent) sales charge upon redemption.

Given below is a tabular summary of the characteristics of Class A, Class B, and Class C shares, with no-load shares added for comparison purposes.

Mutual Fund Share Class Table

	Class A	Class B	Class C	No-Load
Front-end load	Up to 8½%	No	No	No
Back-end Load (CDSC)	No	Yes	1%; drops to 0 after 1 year	Low or 0; short time
12b-1 Fee	0 to .25%	.75%; expires after 6–8 years	.75%; for life of account	0 to .25%
Expense Ratio	Low	High until conversion	Low	Low
Breakpoints LOI Rights of Accumulation	Yes	N/A	N/A	N/A
Conversion	No	Converts to Class A after 6–8 years	No	No
Investor	High amount Long time horizon	Low amount Long time horizon	Low amount Short time horizon	Amount neutral Time horizon neutral

REDEMPTION OF FUND SHARES

A mutual fund must redeem shares within seven days of receiving a written request for redemption. If the customer holds the fund certificates, the mutual fund must redeem shares within seven days of the date that the certificates and instructions to liquidate arrive at the custodian bank. The written request must be accompanied by a **signature guarantee**.

The price at which shares are redeemed is the NAV; it must be calculated at least once per business day. The redemption requirement may be suspended when:

- the NYSE is closed other than for a customary weekend or holiday closing;

- trading on the NYSE has been restricted;

- an emergency exists that would make disposal of securities owned by the company not reasonably practical; or

- the SEC has ordered the suspension of redemptions for the protection of the company's securities holders.

Otherwise, the fund must redeem shares upon request.

Cancellation of Fund Shares

Because an open-end mutual fund is a continuous initial public offering, after a mutual fund share has been redeemed, the share is destroyed. Unlike other corporate securities, mutual fund shares cannot be sold to other owners. An investor purchasing mutual fund shares receives new shares.

TEST TOPIC ALERT

- The maximum sales charge allowed by the NASD is 8.5% of the POP.

- An investor buys and redeems shares at the price next calculated (forward pricing).

- Only NASD member firms can buy below the POP—not the public or nonmembers (except foreign nonmembers).

- The NAV per share does not change when new shares are issued or when shares are redeemed.

- 12b-1 fees are charged quarterly but must be approved annually.

- Breakpoints are not allowed for investment clubs and a parent and child above the age of majority. They are allowed for corporations, husband and wife, or a parent and minor child.

- A fund can only charge an 8.5% sales load if it offers breakpoints, reinvestment at NAV, and rights of accumulation.

- Mutual fund shares that have been redeemed are cancelled; they are never reissued.

Redemption of Shares Within Seven Business Days of Purchase

If a customer redeems mutual fund shares within seven business days of purchase, any fees or concessions earned by the firm and the representative who sold the shares to the customer must be returned to the underwriter.

QUICK QUIZ 4.6

1. For an investment company to charge the maximum sales charge of 8.5%, it must offer all of the following EXCEPT
   I.   conversion privilege
   II. breakpoints
   III. letter of intent
   IV. rights of accumulation

   A. I and II
   B. I and III
   C. I and IV
   D. II and IV

2. A mutual fund is quoted at $16.56 NAV and $18.00 POP. The sales charge is
   A. 7.5%
   B. 7.75%
   C. 8%
   D. 8.5%

3. Redemption of a no-load fund may be made at the
    A.   NAV – the sales charge
    B.   POP
    C.   NAV + the sales charge
    D.   NAV

4. A customer purchased mutual fund shares with a net asset value of $7.82 and an 8% sales charge. She paid a sales charge of
    A. $.68
    B. $.74
    C. $.80
    D. $.87

5. Which of the following statements regarding an LOI and breakpoints are TRUE?
    I.   The letter of intent can be backdated a maximum of 30 days.
    II.   The letter of intent is valid for 13 months. ←
    III. The investor is legally bound to meet the terms of the agreement.
    IV.   The fund may hold shares in escrow.

    A.   I and II
    B.   II and III
    C.   II and IV
    D.   III and IV

6. Which of the following investors can take advantage of breakpoints?
    I.   Individual
    II.   Investment club
    III. Trust
    IV.   Corporation

    A.   I and II
    B.   I, III and IV
    C.   II and III
    D.   III and IV

7. Which of the following mutual fund purchases can generally be added together to help an investor reach a breakpoint?
    I.   Class A shares of ABC growth fund in his 401(k)
    II.   Shares of the ABC money market fund held directly with the fund company
    III. Class B shares of the ABC bond fund held in his brokerage account
    IV.   Shares of ABC technology fund held in his spouse's IRA

    A.   I and II
    B.   I, II and III
    C.   I, III and IV
    D.   III and IV

Terms and Concepts Checklist

✓		✓	
☐	Methods of marketing mutual fund shares	☐	Reductions in sales charges
		☐	Class A shares
☐	Fund to underwriter to dealer to investor	☐	Sales at the POP
		☐	Breakpoints
☐	Fund to underwriter to investor	☐	Letter of intent
☐	Fund to investor	☐	Automatic reinvestment at NAV
☐	Fund to underwriter to plan company to investor	☐	Class B shares
		☐	CDSC
☐	Rights of accumulation	☐	Class C shares
☐	Combination privilege	☐	12b-1 fee, level load
☐	Conversion and exchange privilege	☐	No load fund
☐	Redemption	☐	Return of sales charges

HOTSHEETS

For your convenience, Unit HotSheets summarizing the key points are located at the end of the manual on perforated pages.

U N I T   T E S T

1. From which of the following is the 12b-1 fee deducted?
   A. POP of a share
   B. Difference in POP and NAV
   C. Investment advisory fee
   D. Asset value of the fund

2. You are considering an investment in the ABC Fund. Because you desire long-term capital appreciation, which section of the prospectus would you consult to determine if this fund is appropriate?
   A. Investment Policies and Restrictions
   B. How the Funds are Managed
   C. Tax Treatment of Distributions
   D. The Investment Objectives

3. A registered representative has recommended a growth and income fund to her client because the fund pays relatively high income and maintains strong capital appreciation. The client wishes to use the fund as the foundation of a long-term strategy for eventual retirement. The representative's recommendations and disclosures should state that
   I. the client should reinvest any dividend and gain distributions to accelerate the growth process through a compounding effect
   II. the client should take any dividend and gain distributions in cash and invest them in a growth fund of another family for diversification
   III. all reinvested dividends and gains are currently taxable and become a part of the investor's cost basis in the fund upon redemption
   IV. if dividends are reinvested they are not currently taxable, which enhances growth within the fund

   A. I and II
   B. I and III
   C. I and IV
   D. II and IV

4. When a mutual fund does NOT assess a distribution charge, it is called a
   A. 12b-1 fund
   B. back-end load fund
   C. no-load fund
   D. level-load fund

5. Your customer, age 52, and his wife, age 56, have a large investment portfolio concentrated in stocks and stock mutual funds, including an international stock fund. They maintain their cash reserves in a money market account at their local bank. Your customer is employed as a consultant and earns a $400,000 salary. They are seeking a safe investment because they will need to liquidate a portion of their portfolio at retirement in about 5 years. They also recognize the need for additional diversification in their portfolio. Which of the following mutual funds is the most suitable for these customers?
   A. NavCo Tax-Free Municipal Bond Fund
   B. ATF Biotechnology Fund
   C. ATF Overseas Opportunities Fund
   D. ABC Stock Index Fund

6. The ABC Combination Fund has dual objectives of capital appreciation and current income. Last year, the fund paid quarterly dividends of $.25 per share and capital gains of $.10 per share. The annualized growth rate of the fund was 15%. The current net asset value (NAV) of the fund is $28.50 and the current public offering price (POP) is $30. Advertising and sales literature of the fund may report the current yield of the fund to be
   A. 27.2%
   B. 3.85%
   C. 3.33%
   D. 0.83%

7. An XYZ open-ended bond fund advertising its returns must show all of the following EXCEPT

   A. share prices based on the highest possible sales charge
   B. current yield based on annual dividends and capital gains divided by POP
   C. average annual total returns for 1-, 5-, and 10-year periods
   D. total returns quotations based on the most recent calendar quarter

8. A mutual fund investor wants to know how closely your firm adheres to the industry's standardized breakpoint schedule, and where he can find out more about breakpoints offered with the funds he is investing in. You tell him

   I. the NASD's standard breakpoint schedule is available only to professionals
   II. there is no industry standard breakpoint schedule
   III. the breakpoint schedule for a mutual fund is given in full only in the SAI
   IV. the breakpoint schedule for a fund is given in full in the prospectus

   A. I and III
   B. I and IV
   C. II and III
   D. II and IV

9. A tombstone advertisement may include all of the following EXCEPT

   A. the fund's investment adviser
   B. performance data
   C. the classification or subclassification of the investment company
   D. information on the fund's investment policies

10. All of the following communications require the review of a registered principal EXCEPT

   A. internal memos
   B. customer complaints
   C. form letters mailed to all customers
   D. a market letter

11. Under NASD filing requirements and review procedures, which of the following statements are TRUE?

   I. A new member firm must file advertising with NASD at least 10 days before use for the first 2 years.
   II. An established firm must file investment company advertising with NASD within 10 days of first use.
   III. Advertising and sales literature must be kept on file for 2 years.
   IV. Advertising and sales literature must be kept on file for 3 years.

   A. I and III
   B. I and IV
   C. II and III
   D. II and IV

12. A registered representative would most likely be accused of a prohibited practice if he encouraged a customer to switch her mutual fund when

   A. her investment objective changes
   B. her tax status changes significantly
   C. the fund's ranking changes in the latest magazine ranking
   D. her retirement plans dramatically change

13. A prospectus must accompany or precede which of the following?

   A. A sales presentation held in person at the representative's office
   B. A mutual fund seminar invitation mailed to the home of a prospective customer
   C. A general information brochure given to a customer to explain the basic features of mutual fund ownership
   D. A television advertisement explaining the benefits of investing in mutual funds to accumulate retirement savings

14. Which of the following is subject to the NASD rules on advertising?

   A. Research reports
   B. Market letters
   C. A Website
   D. A form letter to 200 prospective customers

15. Which of the following are included in the NASD rules on sales literature?

    I. A market research report
    II. A public appearance
    III. A letter sent out to 10 customers
    IV. A telemarketing script

    A. I and III
    B. I and IV
    C. II and III
    D. II and IV

16. Institutional sales material is defined as

    A. sales material received from a mutual fund or other institutional investor
    B. sales material sent only to an institutional investor
    C. sales material sent to both institutional investors and the general public
    D. sales material sent to an institutional investor for forwarding to its public clients

17. Which of the following might bring about a change in the NAV of a mutual fund?

    I. A large number of redemptions
    II. The fund pays a dividend
    III. The portfolio increases in market value
    IV. A large number of shares are purchased

    A. I and III
    B. I and IV
    C. II and III
    D. II and IV

18. Your established firm wishes to advertise a mutual fund it markets to the public. What approval and filing requirements apply to the advertisement?

    I. It must be filed with the NASD at least 10 days before first use.
    II. It must be filed with the NASD within 10 days of first use.
    III. It must be approved by an experienced registered representative.
    IV. It must be approved by a registered principal.

    A. I and III
    B. I and IV
    C. II and III
    D. II and IV

19. Under what circumstances could a testimonial be used in securities advertising?

    A. If compensation was paid for the testimonial, that fact must be disclosed.
    B. No specific securities product may be mentioned by name.
    C. Compensation may not be paid for a testimonial.
    D. Testimonials may not be used in securities advertising.

20. Investment recommendations must be fully explained, with special emphasis placed on

    A. the potential profit if the investment is successful
    B. the risks inherent in the investment
    C. the diversification the investment will bring to the customer's portfolio
    D. the liquidity of the investment, should it start to diminish in value

ANSWERS AND RATIONALES

1. **D.** A 12b-1 fee is charged against the assets of the fund and is based on a percentage of the average annual assets.

2. **D.** Of the prospectus sections listed, the Investment Objectives section defines the fund's goals for trading the portfolio.

3. **B.** Because the client's goal is to use the fund as part of a long-term strategy for retirement, reinvestment of distributions should be encouraged. The compounding effect of reinvestment increases the number of shares upon which distributions are based during each period. The fact that distributions are taxable whether taken in cash or reinvested must be disclosed to the client. Reinvested dividends increase the investor's total cost basis.

4. **C.** No-load funds do not assess a fee for sales or distribution of fund shares. Front-end loads are deducted when shares are purchased; back-end loads are charged when shares are redeemed. An annual asset-based percentage is deducted if the fund operates with a level load or 12b-1.

5. **A.** These customers are almost entirely invested in the stock market. As they approach retirement, they should shift some of their portfolio to bonds. Because they are in a high tax bracket, a municipal bond fund best meets their objectives of diversification and safety.

6. **C.** The current yield on mutual funds is calculated by dividing the annualized yield ($.25 × 4 = $1) by the POP. In this case, $1 ÷ $30 = .0333 × 100 = 3.33%. In calculating the current yield, capital gains and growth may not be included.

7. **B.** Current yield is calculated by dividing the annual dividends by the POP; capital gains are not included. Advertising must reflect the highest possible sales charge (no breakpoints), average annual total returns for 1-, 5-, and 10-year periods (or since inception if a new fund), and base total return quotations on the most recent calendar quarter returns.

8. **D.** The NASD does not have a standardized breakpoint schedule. Breakpoints vary from fund to fund, but must be described in full in the prospectus, together with how an account is assessed for breakpoint purposes.

9. **B.** Tombstones or tombstone-style advertising may include information about the fund's investment advisers, investment policies, objectives and services, and the fund's classification or subclassification. Tombstones are not permitted to include performance information.

10. **A.** Memos prepared for internal use only do not require review or approval of a registered principal before use. Registered principals must review and oversee the handling of customer complaints. They must also review and approve all forms of advertising and sales literature before use. Form letters and market letters are examples of sales literature and are subject to prior approval.

11. **D.** Investment company advertising must always be filed with NASD. New firms must file all advertising at least 10 days before use for the first year. Established firms must file investment company advertising within 10 days of first use. Advertising and sales literature must be kept on file for 3 years.

12. **C.** Significant changes in an investor's investment objective, tax status, or retirement planning may be justification for switching from one fund to another. Chasing the leader can result in continual tax exposures and possibly new sales loads. When a switch between funds occurs, the shareholder must recognize any capital gain or loss.

13. **A.** Any offer or advertisement of mutual fund shares must be accompanied by a prospectus. However, generic advertisements or purely informational material are excepted from this requirement. A prospectus must be given to all seminar attendees when they arrive, not when the invitations are mailed. The face-to-face meeting between the representative and the prospect is considered an offer and must be accompanied by a prospectus.

14. **C.** The Website is the only promotional material directed at an unknown audience. The other choices are promotional materials targeted to a specific audience and are considered sales literature.

15. **B.** The market research report and the telemarketing script are included in the definition of sales literature. The letter is correspondence, and the public appearance is not sales literature.

16. **B.** Institutional sales material is promotional material for institutional investors, not for consumption by the general public. A broker/dealer may not treat it as institutional sales material if he has reason to believe it has been or will be forwarded to public customers.

17. **C.** Purchases and redemptions cause a change in the net assets of the fund but are offset by a compensating change in the number of outstanding shares. Thus, the NAV remains constant. Changes in portfolio value and payment of a dividend, however, change the net assets without changing the number of outstanding shares.

18. **D.** If the firm were a new firm, it would have to file all advertising at least 10 days before first use. Your firm is well established; its advertising will be approved by a registered principal, and because it is for an investment company, the advertisement will be filed with the NASD within 10 days of first use.

19. **A.** Testimonials may be used in securities advertising. If payment was made, that fact must be disclosed. Furthermore, testimonials requiring expertise may be given only by qualified persons, whose credentials must be disclosed in the advertisement.

20. **B.** The attractive aspects of an investment may certainly be pointed out, but special emphasis must always be placed on the risks.

QUICK QUIZ ANSWERS

Quick Quiz 4.1

1. **A.**
2. **PA.**
3. **A.**
4. **C.**
5. **SL.**
6. **A.**
7. **SL.**
8. **PA.**
9. **SL.**
10. **A.**

Quick Quiz 4.2

1. **F.**   Established firms must file within 10 days of first use.
2. **F.**   Sales literature must be approved by a principal before use.
3. **F.**   Only advertising must be prefiled, not sales literature.
4. **F.**   All advertising and sales literature prepared by a member is subject to NASD spot checks.
5. **F.**   Documents for internal use only are exempt from filing and approval requirements.

Quick Quiz 4.3

1. **T.**   Only material facts must be disclosed.
2. **F.**   Testimonials are permitted with proper disclosure.
3. **F.**   Free services are allowed providing there are no strings attached.
4. **T.**   Recommendations must include the price at the time of the recommendation.
5. **F.**   All similar recommendations within the past 12 months must be included.

Quick Quiz 4.4

1. **T.**
2. **F.**   Institutional sales literature must be reviewed rather than approved.
3. **T.**
4. **T.**
5. **A.**   10 days after.
6. **B.**   10 days before, and prefiling must continue for a period of 1 year.
7. **D.**   Testimonials must state the giver's qualifications if a specialized or experienced opinion is implied, that the giver's experience may not indicate other investors' experiences, and if the testimonial giver was paid.
8. **B.**   Form letters sent to 25 or more prospective clients within a 30-day period fall into the category of sales literature and must be approved by a principal or manager before use.

Quick Quiz 4.5

1. **D.** The Telephone Consumer Protection Act of 1991 covers all registered representatives. Each firm must have a Do-Not-Call list that every registered representative is required to check before soliciting any person. The act applies to commercial solicitation and does not include a university survey group or nonprofit organization.

2. **D.** All of the choices are requirements of the TCPA of 1991.

Quick Quiz 4.6

1. **D.** The maximum sales load is 8½% only if the company offers breakpoints and rights of accumulation. Although common, LOI and conversion privileges are not required.

2. **C.** The formula is sales charge divided by public offering price. The sales charge is the difference between NAV and POP, or $1.44 per share. $1.44 ÷ $18 = 8%.

3. **D.** No-load funds are redeemed at net asset value. Mutual funds may also charge a redemption fee, which is subtracted from the NAV.

4. **A.** To find the dollar amount of the sales charge when the NAV and the sales charge percentage are provided, calculate the complement of the sales charge by subtracting the sales charge from 100% (100% − 8% = 92%). Then divide the NAV by the complement of the sales charge to find the offering price ($7.82 ÷ .92 = $8.50, the offering price). The dollar amount of the sales charge is the offering price minus the NAV ($8.50 − $7.82 = $.68, the sales charge).

5. **C.** Only Choices II and IV are true. Choice I is false because the LOI can be backdated 90 days. Choice III is false because the investor is not required by law to satisfy the letter of intent although, in the case of default, he will pay a higher sales charge.

6. **B.** Breakpoint advantages are available only to persons. An investment club is not considered a person; however, trusts and corporations are.

7. **C.** Shares of different funds and classes within the same fund family, except money market shares, are eligible for breakpoint discounts. This applies even if the shares are held in different types of accounts by spouses or parents and minor children.

5

Evaluation of Customers

An important part of a registered representative's work is to identify the customer, and understand his financial needs. Only with a thorough knowledge of the customer's financial and tax status can the representative make suitable investment recommendations and provide appropriate information for the customer to use in making investment decisions. The representative must also understand the various forms of investment risk and the relationship between risk and reward inherent in securities investment.

The Series 6 exam will include 13 questions on the topics covered in this Unit. ■

When you have completed this Unit, you should be able to:

■ **discuss** the concept of suitability in investment recommendations and transactions;

■ **state** the various items that make up a useful customer profile;

■ **enumerate** nonfinancial considerations that will affect customer investment decisions;

■ **explain** financial considerations that comprise your customer's financial status;

■ **state and explain** seven basic customer investment objectives;

■ **state and evaluate** 12 basic investment risks that customers face; and

■ **apply analysis skills** in matching customer needs with suitable investment recommendations.

KNOW YOUR CUSTOMER: SUITABILITY ISSUES

The more information a representative has about a customer's income, current investment portfolio, retirement plans, and net worth, as well as other aspects of his current financial situation, the better the recommendations will be. The more a customer knows about the risks and rewards of each type of investment, the better the customer's investment decisions will be.

CUSTOMER PROFILE

Before entering the first trade for a new customer, a representative must find out as much about that person's financial situation as possible.

Customer Balance Sheet

An individual, like a business, has a financial balance sheet—a snapshot of his financial condition at a point in time. A customer's net worth is determined by subtracting liabilities from assets (assets – liabilities = net worth). Representatives determine the status of a customer's personal balance sheet by asking questions similar to the following.

- What kinds of tangible assets do you own? Do you own your home? A car? Collectibles? A second home?

- What are your liabilities? Do you make mortgage payments on your home? Do you make car payments? Do you have any other outstanding loans or regular financial commitments?

- Do you own any marketable securities? What types of investments do you currently hold?

- Have you established long-term investment accounts? Do you have an IRA, Keogh, corporate pension, or profit-sharing plan? Are you contributing to annuities? What is the cash value of your life insurance?

- What is your net worth? How much of it is liquid?

Customer Income Statement

To make appropriate investment recommendations, representatives must know the customer's income situation. They gather information about the customer's marital status, financial responsibilities, projected inheritances, and pending job changes by asking the following questions.

- What is your total gross income? Total family income? How stable is this income? Do you anticipate major changes over the next few years?

- How much do you pay in monthly expenses? Is this a stable figure? Do you expect a change in this amount over the next few years?

- What is your net spendable income after expenses? How much of this is available for investment?

TAKE NOTE Before recommending any investment to a customer, a representative must, at a minimum, make a reasonable effort to obtain information concerning the customer's financial status, tax status, and investment objectives.

NONFINANCIAL INVESTMENT CONSIDERATIONS

Once representatives have an idea of the customer's financial status, they gather information on the nonfinancial status. Nonfinancial considerations often carry more weight than the financial information and include the following:

- Age
- Marital status
- Number and ages of dependents
- Employment
- Employment of family members
- Current and future family educational needs
- Current and future family health care needs
- Risk tolerance
- Attitude towards investing
- Tax status

No matter how much an analysis of a customer's financial status tells the representative about their ability to invest, it is the customer's emotional acceptance of investing and motivation to invest that mold the portfolio.

To understand a customer's aptitude for investment, the representative should ask questions similar to the following.

- What kind of risks can you afford to take?
- How liquid must your investments be?
- How important are tax considerations?
- Are you seeking long-term or short-term investments?
- What is your investment experience?
- What types of investments do you currently hold?
- How would you react to a loss of 5% of your principal? 10%? 50%?
- What level of return do you consider good? Poor? Excellent?
- What combination of risks and returns do you feel comfortable with?
- What is your investment temperament?

■ Do you get bored with stable investments?

■ Can you tolerate market fluctuations?

TAKE NOTE

A representative's job is to assist customers in meeting their financial objectives. Responsible reps must learn all about the customers' financial situations. Securities laws prohibit unsuitable recommendations.

CUSTOMER INVESTMENT OBJECTIVES

People have many reasons for investing. Most customers claim that they invest so that their money will grow. By careful questioning, however, representatives may learn that because of tax status, income, or other events, some growth investments are appropriate and others are not. Some basic financial objectives customers have are discussed in the following sections.

Preservation of Capital

For many people, the most important investment objective is to preserve their capital. In general, when clients speak of **safety**, they usually mean preservation of capital.

Current Income

Many investors, particularly those on fixed incomes, want to generate additional current income. Corporate bonds, municipal bonds, government and agency securities, income-oriented mutual funds, some stocks (including real estate investment trusts (REITs) and utilities), money market funds, and annuities are among the investments that can contribute current income through dividend or interest payments.

Capital Growth

Growth refers to an increase in an investment's value over time. This can come from increases in the security's value, the reinvestment of dividends and income, or both. The most common growth-oriented investments are common stock and stock mutual funds.

EXAMPLE

Cyclical stocks include durable goods (e.g., refrigerators, cars, and heavy equipment).

Tax Advantages

Investors often seek ways to reduce their taxes. Some products, like individual retirement accounts (IRAs) and annuities, allow interest to accumulate tax deferred (an investor pays no taxes until money is withdrawn from the account). Other products, like municipal bonds, offer tax-free interest income.

TAKE NOTE

Municipal bonds, which provide tax-free investment income, are not suitable for retirement accounts. Why buy tax-free interest income that will be fully taxable upon withdrawal?

Portfolio Diversification

Investors with portfolios concentrated in only one or a few securities or investments are exposed to much higher risks. For them, portfolio diversification can be an important objective. These customers are typically retirees with large profit-sharing distributions of one company's stock or investors with all of their money in CDs or US government bonds.

The Investment Pyramid: Categories Used in Portfolio Diversification

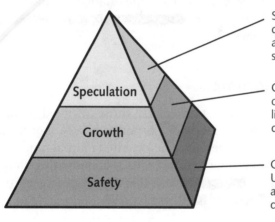

Speculative stocks and stock options, low-rated debt securities, precious metals, commodities and futures, speculative limited partnerships, speculative mutual funds

Growth and small-capitalization stocks, stock options, nonbank-grade bonds, growth-oriented limited partnerships, growth stock mutual funds, commodities funds, variable annuities

Cash, money market funds, certificates of deposit, US Treasury securities, bank-grade corporate and municipal bonds, blue-chip stocks, blue-chip stock and bond mutual funds

Speculation

Growth

Safety

Liquidity

Some people want immediate access to their money at all times. A product is **liquid** if a customer can sell it quickly at face amount (or very close to it) or at a fair market price without losing significant principal. Stock, for instance, has varying degrees of liquidity, while direct participation programs (DPPs), annuities, and bank CDs are considered illiquid. Real estate is a classic illiquid product because of the time and money it takes to convert it into cash.

Speculation

A customer may want to speculate—that is, try to earn much higher than average returns in exchange for higher than average risks. Investors who are interested in speculation may be interested in technology stocks, cyclical stocks, and growth stocks, which are expected to appreciate rapidly.

TEST TOPIC ALERT
A number of exam questions will require you to analyze a customer's situation and select an appropriate recommendation.

Investor Objective	Recommendations
Preservation of Capital/Safety	Government securities, Ginnie Maes
Growth	Common stock, common stock mutual funds
(Balanced/moderate growth)	Blue-chip stocks, defensive stocks
(Aggressive growth)	Technology stocks, sector funds cyclical stocks
Income	Bonds (but not zero coupons)
(Tax-free income)	Municipal bonds, muni bond funds
(High-yield income)	Corporate bonds, corporate bond funds
(From stock portfolio)	Preferred stock, utility stocks
Liquidity	Money market funds (DPPs, CDs, real estate, and annuities are not considered liquid)

QUICK QUIZ 5.1

1. Which of the following characteristics best define(s) the term *growth*?
    A. Increase in the value of an investment over time
    B. Increase in principal and accumulating interest and dividends over time
    C. Investments that appreciate tax deferred
    D. All of the above

2. Which of the following investments is least appropriate for a client who is primarily concerned with liquidity?
    A. Preferred stock
    B. Municipal bond mutual funds
    C. Bank savings accounts
    D. Penny stocks

3. Which of the following securities generates the greatest current income with moderate risk?
    A. Common stock of a new company
    B. Security convertible into the common stock of a company
    C. Fixed-income security
    D. Income bond

4. Which of the following investments is most suitable for an investor seeking monthly income?
    A. Zero-coupon bond
    B. Growth stock
    C. Mutual fund investing in small-cap issues
    D. GNMA mutual fund

Quick Quiz answers can be found at the end of the Unit.

Terms and Concepts Checklist

✓   ✓

☐ Customer profile   ☐ Customer balance sheet
☐ Financial investment considerations   ☐ Customer income statement
☐ Nonfinancial investment   ☐ Suitability of recommendations
   considerations

ANALYZING FINANCIAL RISKS AND REWARDS

Because all investments involve trade-offs, the representative's task is to select securities that will provide the right balance between investor objectives and investment characteristics.

New financial instruments, new classes of mutual funds, and new forms of variable contracts are also constantly being developed. The fact that something is the newest does not make it a good investment for a customer. Risk factors and suitability requirements apply to new investment instruments just as much to those that have been around for centuries.

SUITABILITY

Selecting suitable investments to meet investor needs is an art and a science, and negotiating the difference between what the representative considers suitable and what the customer wants is a legal, ethical, and personal dilemma.

If a customer asks a representative to enter a trade the representative feels is unsuitable, it is the representative's responsibility to explain why the trade might not be right for the customer. If the customer insists on entering the transaction, the representative should have the customer sign a statement acknowledging that the representative recommended against the trade, and the representative should mark the order ticket *unsolicited*.

Suitability issues can involve things like the source of the investor's funding. A customer may wish to liquify some of the additional equity available on his home in order to invest in a security. The customer must be made aware of the substantial risks inherent in such a step.

INVESTMENT RISKS

In general terms, the greater the risk the investor assumes, the greater the potential for reward. Representatives should consider all potential risks in determining the suitability of various types of investments. Following are the most common risks. Those that affect all investments are called systematic risks. Those that affect some and not others are nonsystematic.

Business Risk

Whether caused by bad management or unfortunate circumstances, some businesses will inevitably fail, even more so during economic recessions. Typically when a business fails, it liquidates (sells off its assets) in a bankruptcy, pays its creditors from the proceeds, and pays whatever is left, if anything, to its shareholders.

Inflation Risk

Also known as **purchasing power risk, inflation risk** is the effect of continually rising prices on investments. If a bond's yield is lower than the rate of inflation, a client's money will have less purchasing power as time goes on. A client who buys a bond or a fixed annuity may be able to purchase far less when the investment matures.

Capital Risk

Capital or **principal risk** is the potential for an investor to lose all his money (invested capital) under circumstances either related or unrelated to an issuer's financial strength.

Timing Risk

Even an investment in the soundest company with the most profit potential might do poorly simply because the investment was timed wrong. The risk to an investor of buying or selling at the wrong time and incurring losses or lower gains is known as **timing risk**.

Interest Rate Risk

Interest rate risk refers to the sensitivity of an investment's price or value to fluctuations in interest rates. The term is generally associated with bonds and preferred stocks because their prices change with shifts in interest rates.

Reinvestment Risk

When interest rates decline, it is difficult for bond investors to invest the proceeds from maturities and calls to maintain the same level of income without increasing their credit or market risks.

Market Risk

Both stocks and bonds involve some degree of **market risk**—the risk that investors may lose some of their principal due to price volatility in the overall market (also known as systematic risk).

An investor cannot diversify away market risk. If the entire market is in a tailspin, all of the investor's securities will likely decline. However, an investor can diversify away company-specific risk, known as **nonsystematic risk**. This is the risk that a particular investment will perform poorly. Having a diversified portfolio offsets this risk.

Bond prices fluctuate with changing interest rates. An inverse relationship between bond prices and bond yields exists: as bond yields go up, bond prices go down, and vice versa. The longer a bond's maturity, the more volatile it is in response to interest rate changes compared with similar short-term bonds. For bonds with short maturities, the opposite is true. Their prices remain fairly stable because investors generally will not sell them at deep discounts or buy them at high premiums. A client's income from short maturities, however, will be less than that from long-term maturities.

Credit Risk

Credit risk, also called **financial risk** or **default risk**, involves the danger of losing all or part of one's invested principal through an issuer's failure. Credit risk varies with the investment product.

Bonds backed by the federal government or municipalities tend to be very secure and have low credit risk. Long-term bonds involve more credit risk than short-term bonds because of the increased uncertainty that results from holding bonds for many years.

Preferred stocks generally are safer than common stocks, and mutual funds offer increased safety through diversification. On the other hand, penny stocks, nonbank-grade bonds, and some option positions can be risky, yet appropriate for some customers.

Bond investors concerned about credit risks should pay attention to the ratings. Two of the best known rating services that analyze the financial strength of thousands of corporate and municipal issuers are Moody's Investors Service and Standard & Poor's Corporation.

To a great extent, a bond's value depends on how much credit risk investors take. The higher the rating, the less likely the bond is to default and, therefore, the lower the coupon rate. Clients seeking the highest possible yields from bonds might want to buy bonds with lower ratings; higher yields reward investors for taking more credit risk.

There is also a variable price difference between speculative and investment grade debt, other things such as maturity date being equal. During times of confidence in the economy, the price of a AAA bond and that of a BB bond, for example, will be closer together than during periods of economic uncertainty. This reflects investors' reduced willingness to take risks during periods of uncertainty: speculative debt is discounted more than during periods of confidence.

Liquidity Risk

The risk that a client might not be able to sell an investment is known as **liquidity risk**. The marketability of the securities you recommend must be consistent with the client's liquidity needs.

EXAMPLE   Government bonds are sold easily, but thinly traded stocks are considered illiquid and difficult to sell. Municipal securities have regional rather than national interest and may be less marketable than more widely held securities.

Legislative Risk

Congress has the power to change laws affecting securities. The risk that a change in law might affect an investment adversely is known as **legislative risk** or **political risk**. When you recommend suitable investments, warn clients of any pending changes in the law that may affect those investments.

Call Risk

Related to reinvestment risk, **call risk** is rate that a bond might be called before maturity and investors cannot reinvest their principal at the same or a higher rate of return. When interest rates are falling, bonds with higher coupon rates are most likely to be called.

Investors concerned about call risk should look for call protection, a period of time during which a bond cannot be called. Corporate and municipal issuers generally provide some years of call protection.

Currency Risk

This is the risk that changes in the exchange risk will adversely affect an investment. As a rule of thumb, an investor who purchases a foreign security (e.g., a foreign bond fund) will lose if the US dollar appreciates against the foreign currency. The investor will profit if the US dollar weakens (depreciates) against the foreign currency.

TAKE NOTE   Between the various types of risks and suitability of recommendations, you may see between 10 and 15 questions on the exam.

QUICK QUIZ 5.2   Match the investment risk definitions with their descriptions below.
   A.   Market risk
   B.   Credit risk
   C.   Marketability risk
   D.   Purchasing power risk

   _C_   1.   Liquidity risk, or the risk that a security cannot be sold quickly at a fair market price

   _D_   2.   Inflation risk, or the risk of continually rising prices on investments

   _B_   3.   Default risk, or the risk that principal may be lost due to issuer failure

   _A_   4.   Systematic risk, or the risk that principal may be lost due to price volatility of the market

True or False?

___F___ 5. Interest rate risk is generally associated with equity investments.

___T___ 6. Default risk is the risk of losing invested principal due to the issuer's financial failure.

___F___ 7. Reinvestment risk is highest when interest rates are rising.

___F___ 8. Liquidity risk is also known as systematic risk.

___T___ 9. Bonds backed by the federal government tend to have low credit risk.

Terms and Concepts Checklist

✓

☐ Investment objectives
☐ Safety, capital preservation
☐ Income
☐ Growth
☐ Tax advantages
☐ Diversification
☐ Liquidity
☐ Speculation

✓

☐ Investment risks
☐ Business risk
☐ Inflation, purchasing power risk
☐ Capital risk
☐ Timing risk
☐ Interest rate risk

✓

☐ Reinvestment risk
☐ Market risk
☐ Credit, financial risk
☐ Liquidity, marketability risk
☐ Legislative risk
☐ Call risk
☐ Currency risk

MUTUAL FUND CUSTOMER SUITABILITY QUIZ

Joe Smith is a registered representative with ABC Investments, Inc. Last week, Joe opened accounts for 10 new customers. Each customer wants Joe to recommend the best mutual fund that he can find.

Joe knows that the best mutual fund for one customer is not necessarily the best choice for every customer. Before he makes a recommendation, he collects important information about the customer's needs, goals, and financial status. For example, Joe asks each customer:

■   What is your income?

■   How stable is your income?

■   What plans do you have for the money you invest?

■   What kinds of risks are you comfortable taking?

■   How liquid must your investments be?

■   How important are tax considerations?

■   Are you seeking long-term or short-term investments?

■   What is your investment experience?

After Joe has noted a customer's financial status and investment objectives, he can begin to search for the most appropriate mutual fund. Joe has prepared a brief description of each of his 10 new customers and a list of top-performing mutual funds in 10 categories.

Which mutual fund would you recommend to each of Joe's customers? After you have read the descriptions of the customers and the funds, match the customer to the fund by writing down the letter of the fund in the blank next to the customer description. Then you can compare your answers to the recommendations Joe made.

The Customers

_____ 1.   Andy Jones, 52, and Patty Jones, 56, have a large investment portfolio concentrated in stocks and stock mutual funds, including an international fund. They maintain their cash reserves in a money market account at their local bank. Andy is employed as a consultant, where he earns a $400,000/year salary. The Joneses are seeking a safe investment because they will need to liquidate a portion of their portfolio when Andy retires in about 5 years. They also recognize the need for additional diversification of their portfolio.

_____ 2.   Sarah Davis, 30, and Jim Davis, 32, have been married for 4 years. Both work and they have no children, so their disposable income is relatively high. They live in the suburbs and plan to buy a condominium downtown so they can enjoy some of their favorite activities on the weekends. They need a safe place to invest the amount they have saved for their down payment for about 6 months while they shop for the perfect unit.

_____ 3.   Adam Garcia is 26 and earns $45,000/year as an advertising executive. He already has accumulated $5,000 in a savings account and is seeking a secure place to invest the amount and begin a periodic investment plan. He knows his long-term time-frame means he should be willing to take some risk, but he is uncomfortable with the thought of losing money. Adam would prefer moderate overall returns rather than high returns accompanied by high volatility.

_____ 4.   Mark Blair is a retired widower, 72, seeking a moderate level of current income to supplement his Social Security benefits and his company pension plan. Mark is a Depression-era grandfather of 6 with a conservative attitude toward investments. An equally important goal for him is capital preservation.

_____ 5.   Helen Wong is 29 and is seeking a long-term growth investment. She is concerned about the loss of purchasing power as a result of inflation and often complains about high commissions and charges that reduce her investment returns. When she was in college, she took a few economics courses and firmly believes that securities analysts cannot consistently outperform the overall market.

_____ 6.   Gina and Peter Stout, both 42, have two children, ages 14 and 12. The Stouts have spent the past 10 years accumulating money to provide for their children's education. Their oldest child will enter college in 4 years and they are not willing to take risks with the money they worked hard to accumulate. They need a safe investment that provides regular income to help them meet tuition payments.

_____ 7. Pat Long, 60, and Sadie Long, 58, are married and have raised 3 children. Both have decided to retire this year and are looking forward to an active retirement. They have accumulated a nest egg of about $1 million, which they plan to use to travel the world, pursue their hobbies, and care for their health. Both are concerned about rising inflation and are comfortable with a reasonable level of risk.

_____ 8. Amy Cain, 50, and Eric Cain, 48, have a combined annual income of more than $200,000. Their portfolio consists of common stocks and bonds that offer a wide range of safety and return potential. The Cains are becoming even more concerned about the effects of rising inflation in the US economy. They are seeking to invest a small percentage of their portfolio in a fund that will provide additional diversification.

_____ 9. Mike and Mary Cole are both 34 and employed in their computer software business. They have one daughter, age 4. The Coles want to begin accumulating the money required to send their daughter to one of the nation's top universities in 14 years. In addition, they have not yet begun to accumulate money for their retirement.

_____ 10. Liz Scott, 45, is single and in search of maximum capital appreciation. She inherited a substantial amount of money a few years ago and has taken an active interest in managing her investments. Her portfolio is diversified among common stocks, tax-exempt bonds, international investments, and limited partnerships. She has a long-term time frame and is not averse to risk.

The Mutual Funds

A. Spencer Cash Reserve Fund.   The fund's objectives are to maintain a stable net asset value and to provide current income. The fund invests in high-quality short-term obligations, including US Treasury bills, commercial paper certificates of deposit, and repurchase agreements. Check-writing privileges are available.

B. XYZ Government Income Fund.   The fund seeks to maximize safety of invested principal while providing current income. By investing in a broad range of debt securities issued by the US Treasury as well as by government agencies such as the Government National Mortgage Association, the fund provides reduced risk. It aims for a current yield higher than the yield of short-term debt instruments and money market instruments.

C. Spencer Tax-Free Municipal Bond Fund.   The fund seeks to maximize tax-exempt current yield. It invests in a portfolio of high-quality municipal debt obligations. The portfolio is diversified among securities issued by many different state and municipal taxing authorities. Income distributions provided by the fund are exempt from federal income tax.

D. MacDonald Investment-Grade Bond Fund.   The fund seeks high current yield accompanied by reasonable risk. It invests most of its portfolio in corporate bonds having one of the top three ratings according to Moody's and Standard & Poor's. It seeks to reduce the risk associated with interest rate fluctuations by investing a portion of its assets in short-term corporate debt.

E. MacDonald Balanced Fund.   The fund seeks to preserve capital, to generate current income, and to provide long-term capital growth. Its strategy is to invest 60% of its portfolio in common stocks and 40% in bonds and fixed-income securities. Through diversification, the fund intends to provide protection against downturns in the market. In its endeavors to produce positive returns during market decline, the fund may not participate fully in rising stock markets.

F. Laramie Equity Income Fund.   The fund seeks primarily current income, with secondary objectives of capital growth and growth of income. Its portfolio is composed of common stock, preferred stock, and convertible securities of large, well-established companies with a history of paying high dividends. Its equity concentration can help protect against the loss of purchasing power owing to inflation.

G. MacDonald Stock Index Fund.   The fund seeks to duplicate the price and yield performance of Standard & Poor's Composite Index of 500 stocks. The fund invests in each of the index's 500 stocks in approximately the same composition as the index. The portfolio is not actively traded and therefore features a low turnover ratio.

H. ATF Capital Appreciation Fund.   The fund seeks to achieve maximum capital appreciation with little or no pursuit of current income. The fund invests in stocks of small and medium-size companies that demonstrate significant long-term growth potential. The fund's management believes that despite year-to-year fluctuations, the strategy of investing in companies that show strong earnings growth can result in superior investment returns.

I. **ATF Overseas Opportunities Fund.**   The fund seeks maximum capital appreciation by investing in common stocks of companies located outside the United States. The management selects well-established companies that are listed on their native stock exchanges and that have demonstrated high earnings potential. Although the fund may be affected by fluctuations in currency exchange rates, over the long term it may provide protection against downturns in US markets.

J. **ATF Biotechnology Fund.**   The fund seeks maximum capital appreciation through investment in stocks of companies providing innovative products in the biotechnology sector, including pharmaceutical developers and medical equipment suppliers. Fund management seeks to evaluate emerging economic and political trends and to select individual companies that may benefit from technological advances.

Choose the best fund of the selections offered for each of the 10 customer profiles.

Customer		Fund Choices
Profile #1	A	Spencer Cash Reserve Fund
	B	MacDonald Balanced Fund
	C	Spencer Tax-Free Municipal Bond Fund
	D	MacDonald Stock Index Fund
Profile #2	A	ATF Biotechnology Fund
	B	ATF Capital Appreciation Fund
	C	Spencer Cash Reserve Fund
	D	Laramie Equity Income Fund
Profile #3	A	Spencer Tax-Free Municipal Bond Fund
	B	MacDonald Balanced Fund
	C	XYZ Government Income Fund
	D	MacDonald Stock Index Fund
Profile #4	A	MacDonald Stock Index Fund
	B	Spencer Tax-Free Municipal Bond Fund
	C	XYZ Government Income Fund
	D	ATF Overseas Opportunities Fund
Profile #5	A	MacDonald Balanced Fund
	B	MacDonald Stock Index Fund
	C	Spencer Cash Reserve Fund
	D	ATF Biotechnology Fund
Profile #6	A	Laramie Equity Income Fund
	B	ATF Capital Appreciation Fund
	C	Spencer Cash Reserve Fund
	D	MacDonald Investment-Grade Bond Fund
Profile #7	A	Spencer Tax-Free Municipal Bond Fund
	B	XYZ Government Income Fund
	C	Laramie Equity Income Fund
	D	MacDonald Stock Index Fund
Profile #8	A	ATF Biotechnology Fund
	B	XYZ Government Income Fund
	C	MacDonald Stock Index Fund
	D	ATF Overseas Opportunities Fund
Profile #9	A	MacDonald Balanced Fund
	B	Laramie Equity Income Fund
	C	ATF Capital Appreciation Fund
	D	Spencer Tax-Free Municipal Bond Fund
Profile #10	A	Laramie Equity Income Fund
	B	ATF Capital Appreciation Fund
	C	MacDonald Balanced Fund
	D	ATF Biotechnology Fund

HOTSHEETS

For your convenience, Unit HotSheets summarizing the key points are located at the end of the manual on perforated pages.

UNIT TEST

1. A customer seeks additional steady income to supplement his other sources of retirement income and has a high-risk tolerance. Which of the following securities would be most suitable?
   A. Junk bonds
   B. Treasury receipts
   C. Municipal GOs
   D. Money market instruments

2. If a customer is concerned about interest rate risk, which of the following securities is <u>least</u> appropriate?
   A. Treasury bills
   B. 5-year corporate bonds
   C. 10-year corporate bonds
   D. 25-year municipal bonds

3. Rank the following in order of risk of loss of principal from lowest to highest.
   I.   US Treasury bond
   II. A rated debenture
   III. Common stock in a new company with strong prospects for growth
   IV. Money market mutual fund

   A. I, II, III, IV
   B. I, IV, II, III
   C. IV, I, II, III
   D. IV, I, III, II

4. A 27-year-old client is in a low tax bracket and wants an aggressive long-term investment. If his representative recommends a high-rated municipal general obligation bond, the representative has
   A. violated the suitability requirements of NASD and MSRB rules
   B. recommended a suitable investment because GOs are good long-term investments
   C. committed no violation because municipal bonds weather the ups and downs of the markets well
   D. committed no violation if the customer agrees to the transaction

5. An investor who desires minimal credit risk and monthly interest income should consider an investment in which of the following?
   A. Treasury bills
   B. Ginnie Maes
   C. STRIPS
   D. AAA corporate bonds

6. The risk of not being able to convert an investment into cash at a time when cash is needed is known as which of the following types of risk?
   A. Legislative
   B. Liquidity
   C. Market
   D. Reinvestment

7. A conservative customer is in the 28% federal income tax bracket. She notifies her representative that she has a high-grade corporate bond maturing in the near future and wishes to invest the proceeds in another bond as soon as possible to continue her income stream from the interest. After research, the representative discovers a municipal general obligation bond rated Moody's Baa, with a coupon rate of 5%. The representative has also researched a corporate bond paying a 6.5% coupon and carrying a rating of Standard & Poor's BBB. Considering the client's situation, which bond should the representative recommend?

   A. The corporate bond because it pays a higher interest rate and the investor wants regular income
   B. The municipal bond because it carries a higher rating from Moody's even though the income is lower
   C. The corporate bond because it provides the same income but has a higher rating
   D. The municipal bond because the tax-free equivalent yield is greater and its rating equals the corporate bond's

8. A couple in their early 30s has been married for 4 years. Both work and have no children, so their disposable income is relatively high. They live in the suburbs and are planning to buy a condominium downtown. They need a safe place to invest the amount they have saved for their down payment for about 6 months. Which of the following mutual funds is the most suitable for these customers?

   A. ATF Capital Appreciation Fund
   B. ABC Growth & Income Fund
   C. LMN Cash Reserves Money Market Fund
   D. XYZ Investment-Grade Bond Fund

9. Your customer is 26 years old and earns $45,000 a year as an advertising executive. He has already accumulated $5,000 in his savings account and is seeking a secure place to invest the amount and begin a periodic investment plan. He knows his long-term time frame means he should be willing to take some risk, but he is uncomfortable with the thought of losing money. He would prefer moderate overall returns rather than high returns accompanied by high volatility. Which of the following mutual funds is the most suitable for this customer?

   A. ATF Capital Appreciation Fund
   B. ATF Biotechnology Fund
   C. ABC Balanced Fund
   D. ATF Overseas Opportunities Fund

10. Your customer, age 29, makes $42,000 annually and has $10,000 to invest. Although he has never invested before, he wants to invest in something exciting. Which of the following should you suggest?

    A. An aggressive growth fund because the customer is young and has many investing years ahead
    B. A growth and income fund because the customer has never invested before
    C. A balanced fund because when the stock market is declining the bond market will perform well
    D. Your customer should provide more information before you can make a suitable recommendation

11. Your customer, age 45, is single and in search of maximum capital appreciation. She inherited a substantial amount of money a few years ago and has taken an active interest in managing her investments. Currently, her portfolio is diversified among common stocks, tax-exempt bonds, international investments, and limited partnerships. She has a long-term time frame and is not risk averse. Which of the following mutual funds is the most suitable for this customer?

    A. ABC Balanced Fund
    B. ATF Biotechnology Fund
    C. NavCo Cash Reserves Money Market Fund
    D. LMN Asset Allocation Fund

12. A retired individual seeking income has $200,000 to invest. Which of the following would be the least suitable portfolio?

   A. Small-cap stock fund, municipal bond fund, money market fund
   B. Municipal bond fund, US Treasury bond fund
   C. Small-cap stock fund, medium-cap stock fund
   D. Balanced fund, medium-cap stock fund

13. Your 45-year-old client is interested in obtaining the highest current income possible from his investment. He is willing to accept fluctuations in investment principal. Which of the following would best suit this client's investment objective?

   A. High yield bond fund
   B. Aggressive growth fund
   C. Tax-free money market fund
   D. Balanced fund

14. Your firm's market analyst believes the current bullish market in equities will continue. Which of the following mutual funds would be most suitable for a growth-oriented investor?

   A. Bond
   B. Blue-chip stock
   C. GNMA
   D. Preferred stock

15. Your customer is a 71-year-old retired widower. He is seeking a mutual fund to provide a moderate level of income in addition to his Social Security and pension. He is extremely conservative when investing and wishes to preserve capital. Which of the following funds is most suitable?

   A. Balanced fund
   B. Short-term US government bond fund
   C. Sector fund
   D. Gold fund

ANSWERS AND RATIONALES

1. **A.** Junk bonds have higher yields than investment-grade bonds. Since the client has a high-risk tolerance, these bonds are more appropriate than investment-grade bonds that yield less. Both, however, provide steady income. Treasury receipts are a type of zero-coupon bond and pay no current interest. Municipal GO bonds are usually high quality and lower yielding than higher-risk bonds. Money market securities are high-quality, short-term debt securities and therefore have low yields.

2. **D.** Interest rate risk is the danger that interest rates will rise and adversely affect a bond's price. This risk is greatest for long-term bonds. Short-term debt securities are affected the least if interest rates change.

3. **B.** US Treasury securities offer the lowest risk to investors because they are backed in full by the US government. Of the other choices, a money market mutual fund would be next lowest in risk because it is invested in a portfolio of short-term, high-grade debt securities. Debentures are unsecured corporate bonds and are the most risky corporate debt securities. Common stock is always considered more risky than debt securities.

4. **A.** In recommending a conservative, tax-exempt investment to this customer, the representative has failed to make a suitable recommendation given the client's objectives. Municipal bonds are better suited for individuals in high tax brackets. Further, these bonds offer little upside appreciation potential.

5. **B.** Because Government National Mortgage Association (GNMA) pass-through certificates are guaranteed by the US government, investors who purchase them face no credit risk. Income from GNMA is paid to the investor on a monthly basis; ownership certificates represent an interest in a pool of mortgages that homeowners pay on a monthly basis.

6. **B.** Liquidity risk is the measure of marketability (i.e., how quickly and easily a security can be converted to cash).

7. **D.** The municipal and corporate bonds have equal safety because Standard & Poor's BBB rating is equivalent to Moody's Baa. Both bonds are investment-grade bonds. The municipal bond has a higher tax-equivalent yield than the corporate bond. This is determined with the following formula: municipal yield ÷ (1 − tax bracket) = .05 ÷ .72 = 6.94%. A corporate bond, of equivalent quality, would have to pay 6.94% to be equivalent to the federally tax-free bond.

8. **C.** These customers are preparing to make a major purchase within the next few months. They require a highly liquid investment to keep their money safe for a short amount of time. The money market fund best matches this objective.

9. **C.** This customer is a young investor at the beginning of his earnings cycle. For other investors in his situation, an aggressive growth fund might help achieve maximum capital appreciation over a long-term time frame. However, he is risk averse and has not had any experience with investing in the securities markets. A balanced fund is a good place to begin investing for high total return and low volatility.

10. **D.** It is necessary to get more information about this customer and his definitions of an exciting investment opportunity before making any recommendations. A thorough suitability and risk tolerance analysis should be performed before a recommendation is made.

11. **B.** This customer has a high net worth and substantial investment experience. She is capable of assuming the higher risk and return potential of a speculative investment such as the biotechnology sector fund.

12. **C.** A retired individual who requires income should invest in bond or blue-chip stock funds, not growth.

13. **A.** Because this investor's objective is income, a bond fund is suitable. Investors who are willing to accept risk and who are interested in high income should invest in corporate bond funds with some risk of principal. These bond funds are known as high yield corporate bond funds.

14. **B.** A blue-chip stock fund would be a reasonable investment for a growth-oriented investor in a bullish economic environment. Bonds are not a growth-oriented investment vehicle. GNMAs provide monthly income, not the growth that the client seeks. Preferred stocks are appropriate for income-oriented investors.

15. **B.** A US government bond fund is the safest alternative and would preserve capital. Sector and gold funds are speculative. Balanced funds do not necessarily preserve capital because of stock within the portfolio.

QUICK QUIZ ANSWERS

Quick Quiz 5.1

1. **A.** Growth refers to an increase in the value of an investment over time. Growth can come from increases in the value of the security, the reinvestment of distributions, or both.

2. **D.** Penny stocks are often illiquid investments because there is a limited secondary market.

3. **C.** Of the answers offered, in order to generate the greatest returns, a fixed-income security (a bond) is most suitable. Common stock is not suitable; convertibles (bonds or preferred) generally pay out a lower income rate than nonconvertibles because the investors receive benefits from the conversion feature; income bonds pay interest only if the corporation meets targeted earnings levels.

4. **D.** The GNMA mutual fund is the most suitable investment for an investor seeking monthly income. The other securities offer higher long-term growth potential, but they are not designed to provide monthly income.

Quick Quiz 5.2

1. **C.**

2. **D.**

3. **B.**

4. **A.**

5. **F.** Bonds are most affected by interest rate risk.

6. **T.**

7. **F.** When interest rates are rising, there is little reinvestment risk for debt investors.

8. **F.** Market risk and systematic risk are synonymous terms that describe the risk of investors losing money due to market price volatility in the overall market.

9. **T.**

MUTUAL FUND CUSTOMER SUITABILITY QUIZ ANSWERS AND RATIONALES

1. **C.** **Spencer Tax-Free Municipal Bond Fund**   The Joneses are almost entirely invested in the stock market. As they approach retirement, they should shift some of their portfolio to bonds. Because they are in a high tax bracket, a municipal bond fund best meets their objectives of diversification and safety.

2. **C.** **Spencer Cash Reserve Fund**   Jim and Sarah Davis are preparing to make a major purchase within the next 6 months. They require a highly liquid investment to keep their money safe for a short time. The money market fund best matches this objective.

3. **B.** **MacDonald Balanced Fund**   Adam Garcia is a young investor who is at the beginning of his investment cycle. For other investors in his situation, an aggressive growth fund might help achieve maximum capital appreciation over a long-term timeframe. However, Adam is risk averse and has not had any experience investing in the securities markets. A balanced fund is a good place to begin investing for high total return and low volatility.

4. **C.** **XYZ Government Income Fund**   Mark Blair requires maximum safety and current income. While all fixed-income funds aim to provide current income, the US government bond fund offers the best combination of safety and a higher yield than a money market fund.

5. **B.** **MacDonald Stock Index Fund**   Helen Wong requires a mutual fund that offers the potential for long-term capital growth. She believes money managers cannot consistently outperform the overall market; this indicates that an index fund that attempts to match the performance of the stock market is the most appropriate investment for her.

6. **D.** **MacDonald Investment-Grade Bond Fund**   The Stouts' investment goal of providing for their children's education is about 4 years away. They cannot afford to take a risk that a downturn in the stock market will occur within that time. A safe alternative that also provides additional returns is the high-quality corporate bond fund.

7. **C.** **Laramie Equity Income Fund**   The Longs are preparing for retirement. They want to maintain a comfortable standard of living, which means staying ahead of inflation. A combined fund that offers both current income and growth potential is the best choice for this couple.

8. **D.** **ATF Overseas Opportunities Fund**   The Cains' substantial portfolio is diversified between equity and debt investments. However, to counteract the effects of the US economy on their portfolio returns, they should invest a portion of their assets in the international stock fund.

9. **C.** **ATF Capital Appreciation Fund**   The Coles require maximum capital appreciation. Their long-term timeframe enables them to ride out the fluctuations of the stock market. The best investment for them is the stock market fund that concentrates solely on achieving long-term growth rather than generating current income.

10. **D.** **ATF Biotechnology Fund**   Liz Scott has a high net worth and substantial investment experience. She is capable of assuming the higher risk and return potential of a speculative investment such as the biotechnology sector fund.

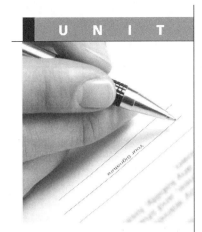
6

Opening and Servicing Customer Accounts

In dealing with customers and their accounts, the registered
representative must be both honest with the customer and thorough
with his documentation from the time the account is opened, through
all of his dealings with the customer. He must document all account activity
and confine himself to actions that are in the customer's interest. He will
be accountable to his firm, the NASD, and other regulatory bodies for strict
ethics and honesty in dealing with the investing public. He will also have
to demonstrate knowledge of a number of rules and laws that govern the
servicing of accounts.

The Series 6 exam will include 12 questions on the topics covered in
this Unit. ■

When you have completed this Unit, you should be able to:

- **explain** the steps required to open a new account;

- **enumerate** the various types of accounts and the rules governing them;

- **discuss** the various prohibited activities in the servicing of accounts;

- **explain** the rules governing lending arrangements between the registered representative and the customer;

- **describe** the criminal penalties associated with willfully violating federal securities regulations;

- **elucidate** the procedure by which violations of NASD rules are dealt with;

- **describe** the mediation process;

- **detail** the arbitration of disputes between broker/dealer firms, between firms and customers, and between firms and associated persons; and

- **discuss** the USA PATRIOT Act, anti-money laundering rules, and how they apply to securities and cash transactions.

OPENING ACCOUNTS

An account opened by a broker/dealer requires a completed new account form or new account card. A registered representative is required to fill out certain information on all new account forms including the following:

- Full name of each customer who will have access to the account

- Address and telephone number (business and residence)

- Social Security number if individual, or tax identification number if other legal entity

- Occupation, employer, and type of business

- Citizenship

- Whether the customer is of legal age (birth date is required)

- Estimated income and net worth

- Investment objectives

- Bank and brokerage references

- Whether the customer or their spouse is an employee of a member broker/dealer

- How the account was acquired

- Name and occupation of the person(s) with authority to make transactions in the account

- Signatures of the representative opening the account and a principal of the firm (the customer's signature is not required on the new account form)

In addition, US citizens must sign a W-9 form while non-US citizens must sign a W-8.

Customer Identification Program (CIP). A firm must take reasonable steps to establish the identity of a customer. A copy of the person's unexpired driver's license or a valid passport is sufficient for this purpose. After notifying the customer of its intent, the firm must also ask the Treasury Department if the person's name is on any list of known or suspected terrorists. The CIP must include procedures to follow if the firm cannot establish the customer's identity, which would normally be refusal to open an account.

TAKE NOTE   Remember, the customer's signature is not required on the new account form. The only signatures required to open an account are the representative's and the principal's.

Accounts may be opened by any legally competent person above the age of majority. Individuals who have been determined legally incompetent may not open accounts.

When opening an account, representatives should know all essential facts about a customer's current financial situation, present holdings, risk tolerance, needs, and objectives. Such information should be updated periodically as situations change.

If a customer refuses to provide all information requested, the account may still be opened if the firm believes the customer has the financial resources necessary to support the account. The registered representative can only make recommendations if sufficient information has been given to determine suitability.

TEST TOPIC ALERT   A partner or principal of the firm must approve every new account in writing on the new account form before—or promptly after—the completion of the first transaction in the account.

Account Ownership

Accounts can be opened with various types of ownership. The principal types of ownership are individual, joint, corporate, and partnership.

Trading Authorization

Accounts may be opened with someone other than the owner having the authority to buy and sell securities on behalf of the owner. This is known as **trading authorization** or **power of attorney**. The primary types of trading authorization are discretionary, custodial, and fiduciary.

- **Discretionary**—A registered representative (or some other person) has been given written authorization from a customer to make trading decisions for the customer.

- **Custodial**—An adult has been designated to act on behalf of a child, who is the beneficial owner of the account.

- **Fiduciary**—A third party has been legally appointed to prudently manage the account on behalf of another person or entity.

Payment Method

Customers may pay for securities with cash or on margin. In cash accounts, customers must pay the full purchase price of securities by the transaction settlement date. Margin accounts allow customers to borrow part of a security's purchase price from the broker/dealer.

Securities Traded

Customers must have special approval to make certain types of trades in their accounts, particularly options transactions. Normally, no special authorization is required to buy or sell stocks, bonds, or mutual funds.

DOCUMENTING NEW ACCOUNTS

Generally, any competent person of age may open an account. Any person declared legally incompetent may not. Fiduciary or custodial accounts may be opened for minors or legally incompetent individuals.

Approval and Acceptance

A partner or a principal of the firm must approve every new account in writing on the account form before or promptly after the completion of the first transaction in the account.

Documenting New Accounts

In addition to the new account form required for all accounts opened, other specific applications may be required, including:

- customer agreements;

- loan consent agreements;

- IRA contracts;

- Keogh forms;

- partnership agreements;

- corporate charters;

- simplified employee pension plan (SEP) applications;

- annuity contracts;

- trust documents;

- mutual fund applications; and

- full or limited powers of attorney.

Mailing Instructions

A customer gives specific mailing instructions when opening a new account. Statements and confirms may be sent to someone who holds power of attorney for the customer if the customer requests it in writing and if duplicate confirms are also sent to the customer. A member firm may hold a customer's mail for up to two months if the customer is traveling in the United States and for up to three months if the customer is abroad.

Retirement Accounts

Each type of personal and corporate retirement account has its own forms and applications. The most important are those that establish the firm's custodial relationship with the retirement account owner, necessary for IRS reporting purposes.

Business Accounts

When opening a business account of any type, the registered representative must establish:

■ the business's legal right to open an investment account;

■ an indication of any limitations that the owners, the stockholders, a court, or any other entity has placed on the securities in which the business can invest; and

■ who will represent the business in transactions involving the account.

A copy of the legal documents that established the business usually contains this information and must be kept on file with the other account forms.

Greenback Securities, Inc.

12654 Futurity Blvd.
Belmont, CA 99462

NEW ACCOUNT FORM

TAXPAYER ID NUMBER	□ SSN □ TAX ID	AGE	BRANCH#	RR#	ACCOUNT#	DATE

LEGAL NAME(S) AND MAILING ADDRESS	□ HOME □ BUS

ACCOUNT TYPE	□ CASH	□ OPTION
	□ MARGIN	□ COMMODITY

MARITAL STATUS	□ MARRIED	□ SINGLE
	□ DIVORCED	□ WIDOWED

ACCOUNT REGIS.	□ SINGLE	□ JTWROS
	□ JTIC	□ INV CLUB
	□ CORP	□ PARTNER
	□ RETIRE	□ OTHER

TELEPHONE NO.	□ HOME □ BUS	TELEPHONE NO.	□ HOME □ BUS	DIVIDENDS □ HOLD □ MAIL	U.S. CITIZEN?	□ YES □ NO ____

IS THE CUSTOMER OR SPOUSE EMPLOYED BY, OR RELATED □ YES   DUPLICATE □ YES   ATTACH SPECIAL INSTRUCTIONS
TO AN EMPLOYEE OF, ANY FINANCIAL INSTITUTION?   □ NO   CONFIRMS? □ NO

EMPLOYMENT

EMPLOYER'S NAME		YEARS EMPLOYED	DOCUMENTATION		OTHER (DESCRIBE)
			MARGIN AGR	□ PEND □ RCVD	____
ADDRESS			JOINT ACCT	□ PEND □ RCVD	____
			TRADING AUTH	□ PEND □ RCVD	____
			CORP/PART AGR	□ PEND □ RCVD	____
TYPE OF BUSINESS	CLIENT'S OCCUPATION		RETIRE ACCT	□ PEND □ RCVD	____
			SIG CARD	□ PEND □ RCVD	____

REFERENCE

BANK NAME AND ADDRESS	□ CHECKING	□ VERIFIED
	□ SAVINGS	□ NOT VERIFIED

DOES CLIENT HAVE AN ACCOUNT   □ YES   IF YES, WITH WHAT FIRM?
WITH ANOTHER BROKERAGE FIRM? □ NO

SPOUSE

NAME	OCCUPATION	AGE
EMPLOYER	ADDRESS	ANNUAL INCOME

INVESTMENT EXPERIENCE	DOES CLIENT OR SPOUSE HAVE ANOTHER ACCOUNT WITH US? □ YES □ NO IF YES, LIST: ____ ____ IS CLIENT NOW OR HAS CLIENT EVER BEEN A CORPORATE OFFICER OR OWNER OF 10% OF ANY CORPORATION'S SECURITIES? □ YES □ NO IF YES, NAME:	HOW WAS ACCOUNT ACQUIRED? □ WALK IN □ REFERRAL □ PHONE IN □ PROSPECT □ OTHER □ ACQUAINTANCE INITIAL TRANSACTION □ BUY DESCRIBE: □ SELL □ OTHER INITIAL DEPOSIT	OPTION TRADES ANTICIPATED □ BUY ONLY □ STRADDLES □ COV CALLS □ SPREADS □ COV PUTS □ COMBINS □ UNC OPTS □ OTHER IS CLIENT FAMILIAR WITH OPTIONS? □ YES □ NO HAS CLIENT RECEIVED OCC PROSPECTUS? □ YES DATE ____ HAS CLIENT PREVIOUSLY TRADED OPTIONS? □ YES □ NO ARE OPTIONS SUITABLE? □ YES □ NO
INVESTMENT OBJECTIVES □ GROWTH □ SPECULATION □ INCOME □ RETIREMENT □ GRO/INC □ TAX HOME □ OWN □ RENT NO. OF DEPENDENTS ____ ANNUAL INC ____ NET WORTH ____		DISCRETIONARY AUTHORIZATION □ FULL □ LIMITED □ NONE	

RR SIGNATURE	AGENT'S NAME AND ADDRESS
BRANCH MGR APPROVAL DATE	ROP SIGNATURE (OPTIONS APPROVAL)

Trading Authorization/Power of Attorney

A power of attorney or a discretionary power allows a party other than the account owner to make investment decisions for the account without consulting the account owner. When such authority has been established for an account, a signed copy of the document must be kept on file.

OPENING ACCOUNTS FOR EMPLOYEES OF OTHER BROKERS

The National Association of Securities Dealers (NASD), New York Stock Exchange (NYSE), and Municipal Securities Rulemaking Board (MSRB) require broker/dealers to give permission or written notification to other broker/dealers when establishing accounts for certain individuals, including employees of broker/dealers; and spouses or minor children of broker/dealer employees.

NASD Requirements

NASD rules do not require an employee of one NASD member firm to get the employer's permission to open an account with another NASD member, but they do require the firm opening the account to notify the customer's employer.

The employee is responsible for disclosing that he is an associated person of an NASD member when opening the account. Duplicate confirmations and statements must be sent to the employer broker/dealer if the employer requests them.

TEST TOPIC ALERT

When opening an account for an employee of another NASD firm, the following three steps must occur.

- The account holder must be advised that his employer will be notified of this account.

- The individual's employer must receive written notification that the account is being opened.

- The employer may request duplicate confirmations.

Note that the duplicate confirmations are not required to be sent, but they must be made available upon request by the employing firm. Also note that should an employee of another member firm wish to open an account at your firm and limit trading to redeemable investment company securities, no notification is required.

QUICK QUIZ 6.1

1. An employee of another NASD member broker/dealer wants to open an account with your firm. All of the following statements regarding the employee and the account are true EXCEPT

   A. the employer must receive duplicate copies of all transactions made in the account if requested
   B. the employer must be notified of the opening of the account
   C. the opening member must notify the employee in writing that the employer will be notified of the employee's intent to open the account
   D. the broker/dealer holding the account must approve each transaction made by the person before entry of the order

2. All of the following customer information is required on a new account form EXCEPT

A. name
B. customer signature
C. Social Security number
D. occupation

3. A registered representative may open all of the following customer accounts EXCEPT

A. an individual account opened by the individual's spouse
B. a minor's account opened by a custodian
C. a corporate account opened by the designated officer
D. a partnership account opened by the designated partner

4. Who of the following must sign a new account form?

I. Principal
II. Registered representative
III. Customer
IV. Spouse of the customer

A. I and II
B. I and III
C. II and III
D. III and IV

Quick Quiz answers can be found at the end of the Unit.

Terms and Concepts Checklist

✓

- ☐ Customer information
- ☐ Customer identification program (CIP)
- ☐ Account ownership
- ☐ Account approval
- ☐ Accounts for employees of other broker/dealers

✓

- ☐ Trading authorization
- ☐ Discretionary account
- ☐ Custodial account
- ☐ Fiduciary account

TYPES OF ACCOUNTS

When an account is opened, it is registered in the name(s) of one or more persons. They are the account owners and are the only individuals who are allowed access to and control of the investments in the account.

Individual Accounts

A **single (individual) account** has one beneficial owner. The account holder is the only person who can:

■ control the investments within the account;

■ request distributions of cash or securities from the account; and

■ A special type of individual account is a transfer on death (TOD) account. This allows the account holder to specify who is to receive the account on his death, and thus avoids probate. The account remains the holder's property during his lifetime and is not accessible to the creditors of the designee.

Joint Accounts

In a **joint account**, two or more adults are named on the account as co-owners, with each allowed some form of control over the account. In addition to the appropriate new account form, a joint account agreement must be signed, and the account must be designated as either tenants in common (TIC) or joint tenants with right of survivorship (JTWROS).

The account forms for joint accounts require the signatures of all owners. Both types of joint account agreements allow any or all tenants to transact business in the account. Checks must be made payable to the names in which the account is registered and must be endorsed for deposit by all tenants (although mail need be sent to only a single address). To be in good delivery form, securities sold from a joint account must be signed by all tenants.

Tenants in Common

Tenants in common (TIC) ownership provides that a deceased tenant's fractional interest in the account is retained by that tenant's estate and is not passed to the surviving tenant(s).

Joint Tenants with Right of Survivorship

Joint tenants with right of survivorship (JTWROS) ownership stipulates that a deceased tenant's interest in the account passes to the surviving tenant(s).

TEST TOPIC ALERT

JTWROS—all parties must have equal undivided interests
TIC—interest can be unequal

Parties in JTWROS and TIC have an undivided ownership interest. That means:

■ all parties own some of everything in the account;

■ any party can make a trade; and

■ checks or distributions must be made payable to all parties and endorsed by all parties.

Full Power of Attorney

A **full power of attorney** allows someone who is not the owner of an account to deposit or withdraw cash or securities and make investment decisions for the account owner. Custodians, trustees, guardians, and other people filling similar legal duties are often given full power of attorney.

Limited Power of Attorney

A **limited power of attorney** allows an individual to make only trading decisions.

A person with power of attorney over an account might be an investment adviser for an individual customer or a trustee in the case of a trust account. In either case, the broker/dealer firm must obtain a copy of the trust agreement or investment adviser contract as well as a signature from the designated person and the date on which the power of attorney was granted to him.

DISCRETIONARY ACCOUNTS

An account set up with preapproved authority for a registered representative to make transactions without having to ask for specific approval is a discretionary account. **Discretion** is defined as the authority to decide:

- which security;

- the number of shares or units; and

- whether to buy or sell.

Discretion does not apply to decisions regarding the timing of an investment or the price at which it is acquired.

EXAMPLE

An order from a customer worded "Buy 100 shares of ABC, Inc., for me whenever you think the price is right" is not a discretionary order.

Discretionary Authority

A customer can give discretionary power over an account only by filing a trading authorization or a limited power of attorney with the broker/dealer. No transactions of a discretionary nature can take place without this document on file.

Once authorization is given, the customer is legally bound to accept the registered representative's decisions, although the customer may continue to enter orders on his own.

The customer may give discretion for the account only to a specific individual. If the registered representative leaves the firm or in any way stops working with the account, discretionary authority ends immediately.

Regulation of Discretionary Accounts

In addition to requiring the proper documentation, discretionary accounts are subject to the following rules.

- Each discretionary order must be identified as such at the time it is entered for execution.

- A principal of the brokerage house must approve each order promptly and in writing, not necessarily before order entry.

- A record must be kept of all transactions.

- No excessive trading relative to the size of the account and the customer's investment objectives may occur in the account.

- To safeguard against churning, a designated supervisor or manager must review all trading activity frequently and systematically.

TAKE NOTE

An order is discretionary if any one of the three As are missing:

Activity (or **A**ction)
Amount
Asset

EXAMPLE

If a customer asks a representative to sell 1,000 shares of XYZ stock, the order is not discretionary even though the customer did not specifically say when or at what price.

Activity (or **A**ction) = sell (or buy)
Amount = 1,000 shares
Asset = XYZ stock

All three As were defined, so the order is not discretionary.

If a customer asks a representative to buy 1,000 shares of the best computer company stock available, the order is discretionary. *Asset* is missing because the company is not defined.

If a customer wants to buy 1,000 shares of XYZ whenever you think the price is best, the order is not discretionary. The *As* were all defined. Omitting the time or price does not make an order discretionary.

UNIFORM GIFTS TO MINORS ACT (UGMA) ACCOUNTS

Uniform Gifts to Minors Act (UGMA) and **Uniform Transfer to Minors Act (UTMA)** accounts require an adult or a trustee to act as custodian for a minor (the beneficial owner). Cash or securities and other forms of property (including variable but not fixed annuities) may be given to the account without limitation.

Donating to UGMA Accounts

When a person makes a gift to a minor under the UGMA laws, that person is the **donor**. A gift under UGMA conveys an indefeasible title; that is, the donor may not take back the gift, nor may a minor return the gift until they have reached the age of majority. Once a gift is donated, the donor gives up all rights to the property. When the minor reaches the specified age, the property in the account is transferred into the minor's (now an adult) name.

Custodian

Any assets given to a minor through an UGMA account are managed by a custodian until the minor reaches the age of majority. The custodian has full control over the minor's account and can:

- buy or sell securities;

- exercise rights or warrants; and

- liquidate, trade, or hold securities.

The custodian may also use the property in the account in any way he deems proper for the minor's support, education, maintenance, general use, or benefit. However, the account is not normally used to pay basic expenses associated with raising a child, such as food and clothing.

Registered representatives must know the following rules regarding UGMA custodial accounts.

- An account may have only one custodian and one minor or beneficial owner.

- A minor can be the beneficiary of more than one account and a person may serve as custodian for more than one UGMA provided each account benefits only one minor.

- The donor of securities can act as custodian or can appoint someone else to do so.

- Unless acting as custodians, parents have no legal control over an UGMA account or the securities in it.

The registered representative is not responsible for determining if an appointment is valid or whether a custodian's activities are appropriate.

Opening an UGMA Account

When opening an UGMA account, the representative must ensure that the account application contains the custodian's name, the minor's name and Social Security number, and the state in which the UGMA is registered.

Registration of UGMA Securities

Any securities in an UGMA account are registered in the custodian's name for the benefit of the minor; they cannot be registered in street name. Typically, the securities are registered to "Joan R. Smith as custodian for Brenda Lee Smith," for example, or a variation of this form. When the minor reaches the age of majority, all of the securities in the account will be registered in the minor's name (now an adult). The gift of securities is considered complete when this registration has been completed.

Fiduciary Responsibility

UGMA custodians are charged with fiduciary responsibilities in managing a minor's account. Certain restrictions are placed on what is considered proper handling of UGMA investments. This means that, since they are charged with investing or managing money for others, they must exercise special care in selecting investments. The most important limitations follow.

- UGMAs may be opened and managed as cash accounts only.

- A custodian may not purchase securities in an account on margin or pledge them as collateral for a loan.

- A custodian must reinvest all cash proceeds, dividends, and interest within a reasonable period of time. Cash proceeds from sales or dividends may be held in a noninterest-bearing custodial account for a reasonable period, but should not remain idle for long.

- Investment decisions must take into account a minor's age and the custodial relationship; commodities futures, naked options, and other high-risk securities are examples of inappropriate investments. To ensure appropriateness of investments, some states use a legal list, a list of investments compiled by a state agency such as the State Banking Commission, from which a fiduciary must select investments for the account he is managing. Other states use the prudent man rule: in determining liability for losses, investments are compared to what a prudent investor would have done under similar circumstances.

- Options may not be bought in a custodial account because no evidence of ownership is issued to an options buyer. Covered call writing is normally allowed.

- Stock subscription rights or warrants must be either exercised or sold.

- UGMA custodians may not grant trading authority to a third party.

- Custodians may loan money to an account but cannot borrow from it.

A custodian may be reimbursed for any reasonable expenses he incurs in managing the account unless the custodian is also the donor.

Taxation

The minor's Social Security number appears on an UGMA account, and the minor must file an annual income tax return and pay taxes on any income exceeding $1,500 produced by the UGMA at the parent's top marginal tax rate, regardless of the source of the gift, until the minor reaches the age of majority.

Until the minor reaches majority, the account will be taxed at the parents' tax rate. Although the minor is the account's beneficiary and is responsible for payment of taxes on the account, it is the custodian's responsibility to see that the taxes are actually paid.

Gift Tax Exemption

Individuals may give gifts of $12,000 per year to any number of individuals without incurring gift tax.

Death of the Minor or Custodian

If the beneficiary of an UGMA dies, the securities in the account pass to the minor's estate, not to the parents' or custodian's estate. In the event of the custodian's death or resignation, either a court of law or the donor must appoint a new custodian.

UTMAs

Although almost identical to UGMA accounts, UTMA accounts have one distinguishing feature: the age of transfer can be postponed until the child reaches age 25.

TEST TOPIC ALERT

You may see two or three questions about UGMA accounts on your exam. Know the following:

■ UGMA accounts must be one-to-one (one minor, one custodian).

■ Gifts under UGMA are irrevocable.

■ The gift can be of any size.

■ The donor (the giver of the gift) may be liable for gift tax on any gift of more than $11,000 in one year to one individual.

■ The child's Social Security number is on the account; the child is owner of the assets.

■ Speculative trading strategies are prohibited; no short selling, naked option, or margin accounts.

QUICK QUIZ 6.2

1. Which of the following persons are considered fiduciaries?

   I. Executor of an estate
   II. Administrator of a trust
   III. Custodian of an UGMA/UTMA account
   IV. Conservator for a legally incompetent person

   A. I and II
   B. I and III
   C. III and IV
   D. I, II, III and IV

2. A customer would like to open a custodial UGMA or UTMA account for his nephew, a minor. The uncle can

    A. open the account provided the proper trust arrangements are filed first
    B. open the account and name himself custodian
    C. only move ahead if he gets a legal document evidencing the nephew's parents' approval of the account
    D. be custodian for the account only if he is also the minor's legal guardian

3. An investor wishes to provide for his 3 nephews after his brother dies. Under the Uniform Gifts to Minors Act, which of the following actions may the investor take?

    A. Open 1 account for all 3 nephews
    B. Open 3 separate accounts and deposit cash and securities
    C. Open 3 separate accounts and deposit insurance policies
    D. Open 3 separate accounts and deposit fixed annuities

4. Securities owned by a donor and given to a minor under the Uniform Gifts to Minors Act become the property of the minor

    A. when the securities are paid for by the minor
    B. on the settlement date
    C. when the securities are registered in the custodian's name for the benefit of the minor
    D. when the donor decides to give the securities to the minor

Terms and Concepts Checklist

✔

- ☐ Individual account
- ☐ Joint account
- ☐ JTWROS
- ☐ TIC
- ☐ UGMA, UTMA accounts
- ☐ Taxation of custodial accounts

✔

- ☐ Full power of attorney
- ☐ Limited power of attorney
- ☐ Discretionary authority
- ☐ Discretionary orders
- ☐ Action, asset, amount

ETHICS IN THE SECURITIES INDUSTRY

ETHICAL BUSINESS PRACTICES

The securities industry is governed by a strict code of ethics. Unacceptable behavior is subject to sanctions ranging from fines and reprimands to expulsion from the industry. Business behavior and practices are measured against clear standards for fairness and equity.

Securities industry regulators work to prevent and detect unethical behavior. Investigators regularly examine activity at all levels—from large firms to investment advisers to registered representatives to individual investors. Even the most junior of broker/dealer employees is expected to adhere to high standards of business ethics and commercial honor in dealing with the public.

Under Rule 8210, member firms and their personnel are required to cooperate in any investigation conducted by the NASD, including giving information verbally or in writing or making records available in a timely fashion.

TAKE NOTE   NASD rules and other industry regulations basically remind representatives not to lie, cheat, or steal when dealing with customers. If you are uncertain about a question on prohibited practices or ethics, you are likely to be right if you choose the most conservative response.

PROHIBITED PRACTICES

The following practices in customer dealings are prohibited at all times.

Manipulative and Fraudulent Devices

NASD member firms are strictly prohibited from using manipulative, deceptive, or other fraudulent tactics or methods to induce a security's sale or purchase. The statute of limitations under the act of 1934 is three years from the alleged violation and within one year of its discovery. No dollar limit is placed on damages in lawsuits based on allegations of manipulation.

Private Securities Transactions

The NASD's Conduct Rules define a **private securities transaction** as any sale of securities outside an associated person's regular business and his employing member. Private securities transactions are known as **selling away**.

Notification

An associated person who wishes to enter into a private securities transaction must:

■ provide prior written notice to his employer;

■ describe in detail the proposed transaction;

■ describe in detail his proposed role in the transaction; and

■ disclose if he has or may receive compensation for the transaction.

If the associated person wishes to enter into the transaction or business activity for compensation, the employing member may approve or disapprove the associated person's participation. If the member approves the participation, it must treat the transaction as if it is being done on its own behalf by entering the transaction on its own books and supervising the associated person during the transaction. If the member disapproves the transaction, the associated person may not participate in it.

If the associated person has not or will not receive compensation for the private securities transaction, the employing member must acknowledge that it has received written notification and may require the associated person to adhere to specified conditions during his participation.

Transactions that the associated person enters into on behalf of immediate family members and for which the associated person receives no compensation are excluded from the definition of private securities transactions. Also excluded are personal transactions in investment company and variable annuity securities.

Outside Business Activities

Proper supervision involves knowing what registered representatives are doing even when they are not working for the member firm. The NASD has a rule dealing with business activity away from the firm. This rule states that no person associated with a member in any registered capacity may be employed by, or accept compensation from, any other person as a result of any business activity (other than as an investor) outside the scope of his relationship with his employer firm, unless he has provided prompt written notice to the employing member.

A **passive investment**, such as the purchase of a limited partnership unit, is not considered an outside employment or business activity, even if the purchaser receives money as a result of the investment. An associated person may make a passive investment for his own account without written notice to or receiving written approval from the employing broker/dealer.

VIOLATIONS OF FAIR DEALING

The NASD's Conduct Rules and the laws of most states require broker/dealers, registered representatives, and investment advisers to inquire into a customer's financial situation before making any recommendation to buy, sell, or exchange securities. This includes determining the client's other security holdings, income, expenses, and financial goals and objectives.

The following activities violate the fair dealing rules:

- Recommending any investment unsuitable for the customer's financial situation and risk tolerance

- Short-term trading of mutual funds

- Setting up fictitious accounts to transact business that otherwise would be prohibited

- Making unauthorized transactions or use of funds

- Recommending purchases that are inconsistent with the customer's ability to pay

- Committing fraudulent acts, such as forgery or the omission or misstatement of material facts

Excessive Trading

Excessive trading in a customer's account to generate commissions, rather than to help achieve the customer's stated investment objectives, is an abuse of fiduciary responsibility known as **churning**. Churning occurs because of either excessive frequency or excessive size of transactions.

To prevent such abuses, self-regulatory organizations require that a principal of the member firm frequently review all accounts, especially those in which a registered representative or an investment adviser has discretionary authority.

Influencing Employees of Other Firms

Broker/dealers cannot distribute business-related compensation, either cash or noncash gifts or gratuities, to the employees of other member firms. However, a broker/dealer may give other firms' employees some form of compensation without violating the rules if:

- the compensation is not conditional on sales or promises of sales;

- it has the employing member's prior approval; and

- the compensation's total value does not exceed the annual limit set by the NASD board of governors (currently $100 per year).

Employment Contracts

This rule does not apply to legitimate employment contracts in which an employee of one firm supplies or performs services for another firm. The leasing of another firm's employee is acceptable provided a written employment agreement specifies the employment duties and compensation and the person's employer, the temporary employer, and the employee give their written consent.

Selling Dividends

It is improper to recommend that an investor buy mutual fund shares just before a dividend distribution. The fund shares' market value will decrease by the distribution amount, and the customer will incur a tax liability on the distribution. A registered representative is forbidden to encourage an investor to purchase shares before a distribution because of this tax liability, and doing so is a violation known as **selling dividends**.

Breakpoint Sales

In a **breakpoint sale,** a customer unknowingly buys investment company shares in an amount just below an amount that would qualify the investment for a reduction in sales charges. As a result, the customer pays a higher dollar amount in sales charges, which reduces the number of shares purchased and increases the cost basis per share.

Encouraging a customer to purchase in such a manner, or remaining silent when a customer unknowingly requests such a transaction, is unethical and violates NASD Conduct Rules.

TAKE NOTE

A breakpoint is good—it allows the investor a volume discount when buying mutual fund shares. Breakpoint sales, however, are prohibited.

Suitability of Fee-Based Compensation

In accordance with the principles of dealing fairly with the public, members must not place a customer in an account where a fee-based structure can reasonably be expected to result in a greater cost than an alternative account that provides the same services, features, and general benefits to the client.

Before opening an account, the member must have reasonable grounds to believe a fee-based account is appropriate for a client. Obtaining information regarding the customer's profile, including but not limited to, financial status, investment objectives, and trading history, will assist the member in this process.

Borrowing and Lending

Firms that permit lending arrangements between representatives and customers must have written procedures in place to monitor such activity. Registered persons who wish to borrow from or lend money to customers are required to provide prior written notice of the proposed arrangement to the firm, and the firm must approve the arrangement in writing.

NASD rules permit five types of lending arrangements:

- there is an immediate family relationship between the representative and the customer, wherein, for purposes of loans, immediate family now includes grandparents, grandchildren, parents, children, spouse, siblings, nieces and nephews, uncles and aunts, and in-laws;

- the customer is in the business of lending money (e.g., a bank);

- the customer and the representative are both registered persons with the same firm;

- the customer and the representative have a personal relationship outside of the broker-customer relationship; and

- the customer and the representative have a business relationship outside of the broker-customer relationship.

Misrepresentations

Registered representatives and investment advisers may not misrepresent themselves or their services to clients or potential clients. Included in this prohibition are misrepresentations covering:

- qualifications, experience, and education;

- nature of services offered; and

- fees to be charged.

It is a misrepresentation to inaccurately state or fail to state a material fact regarding any of the above.

Research Reports

An investment adviser or a broker/dealer may not present to a client research reports, analyses, or recommendations prepared by other persons or firms without disclosing the fact that the adviser did not prepare them. An adviser or a broker/dealer may base a recommendation on reports or analyses prepared by others, as long as these reports are not represented as the adviser's or broker/dealer's own.

Conflicts of Interest

An investment adviser must disclose in writing to a client any areas in which the adviser's interests conflict or could potentially conflict with those of the client. Examples of such conflicts include:

- affiliations between an adviser and any product suppliers;

- compensation arrangements for advisory services to clients in addition to compensation from such clients for such services; and

- charging a client a fee for providing investment advice when the adviser or the adviser's employer will receive a commission for executing securities transactions based on that advice.

Directed Brokerage Arrangements

Another area of conflict that exists is between NASD members and investment companies, which has to do with **Investment Company Directed Brokerage Arrangements**. The rule governs the execution of investment company portfolio transactions.

It generally prohibits NASD members from favoring the sale of investment company shares based on commissions it has received, or expects to receive, for providing portfolio execution services for the investment company. This is known as the antireciprocal rule.

Guarantees and Sharing in Customer Accounts

Broker/dealers, investment advisers, and registered representatives cannot guarantee any customer against a loss or guarantee a gain. Members, advisers, and representatives are also prohibited from sharing in profits or losses in a customer's account. An exception is made if a joint account has received the member firm's prior written approval and the registered representative shares in the profits and losses only to the extent of his proportionate contribution to the joint account. The firm may share in a loss if the loss was due to an error by the firm.

If the member firm authorizes such a **shared account**, any such sharing must be directly proportionate to the financial contributions each party makes. If a member or an associated person shares an account with a member of that person's immediate family, directly proportionate sharing of profits and losses is not mandatory.

Immediate family members include parents, mother-in-law or father-in-law, husband or wife, children, and any relative to whom the officer or employee in question contributes financial support.

TAKE NOTE

An agent may share in an account with a customer if the agent has written consent from both the customer and the employing firm and shares in profits and losses proportionate to his contribution. In this situation, it is permissible to commingle agent and customer funds. A firm and a customer can never have a joint account.

Misuse of Nonpublic Information

Every investment adviser must establish, maintain, and enforce written policies and procedures to prevent the use of nonpublic inside information.

Fiduciary Information

During the course of business, employees of member firms will have access to proprietary information regarding individual customers and securities issuers. Such information must be treated with strict confidentiality.

Confidentiality of Customer Information

Broker/dealer and investment adviser employees may not divulge any personal information about customers without a customer's express permission. This includes security positions, personal and financial details, and trading intentions.

Confidentiality of Issuer Information

When a member broker/dealer serves an issuer as a paying agent, a transfer agent, or an underwriter or in another similar capacity, the member has established a fiduciary relationship with that issuer, and so may obtain confidential information. The member cannot use the information it obtains through its fiduciary role unless the securities issuer specifically asks and authorizes the member to do so.

Artificial Transactions

Transactions intended to portray an artificial market for a stock are strictly prohibited. These transactions are sometimes called **matching** or **matched buy-sell orders**.

TAKE NOTE

A summary of ethical behavior in the securities industry:

- Do not cheat or steal.

- Do not fabricate information or lie.

- Disclose any conflicts of interest.

- Know which investments are suitable for your customer's needs.

QUICK QUIZ 6.3

Match the following terms with the appropriate description below.

A. Selling away
B. Breakpoint sale
C. Selling dividends
D. Material facts
E. Excessive trading

___B___ 1. Encouraging a purchase below the amount that would qualify for a reduction in sales load

___D___ 2. Omitting these in a recommendation violates NASD rules

___C___ 3. Encouraging a customer purchase just before a distribution

___E___ 4. Also called churning

___A___ 5. A prohibited practice without the broker/dealer's knowledge and consent

CRIMINAL PENALTIES

A person who is convicted of willfully violating federal securities regulations, or of knowingly making false or misleading statements in a registration document, can be fined up to $1 million, sentenced to prison for up to 10 years, or both. The maximum fine is $2.5 million for other than a natural person (broker/dealers or other businesses).

Assistance to Foreign Authorities

The SEC is pledged to help foreign regulatory authorities investigate any person who has violated, is violating, or is about to violate any laws or rules relating to securities matters.

QUICK QUIZ 6.4

For the following business practices, write **U** for unlawful and **L** for lawful.

U 1. An agent explains to a mutual fund client that because the fund is invested in government securities, the client will not lose principal.

U 2. A customer calls his representative and instructs him to immediately buy 1,000 shares of a top Internet company. The representative enters an order for 1,000 shares of XYZ, which has been a market leader all week.

L 3. An agent receives a call from the wife of his client, advising him to sell his XYZ stock. The agent refuses the order.

U 4. A client writes a scathing letter to his agent regarding stocks that the agent had recommended that had subsequently performed very poorly. The agent calls the client and disposes of the letter after the client is calmed.

L 5. A representative borrows $10,000 from his client, First Federal Bank of Oconomowoc, Wisconsin.

U 6. An agent explains that because he is so convinced of the value of ABC Company stock, he will buy it back from the client if it is not up 10% in three months.

U 7. An agent contacts her client and suggests that she buy a total of 1,000 shares of ABC stock, but that she buy 100 shares on 10 different days to try and time the market.

Terms and Concepts Checklist

✓	✓

☐ Manipulative and fraudulent devices   ☐ Private securities transactions

☐ Excessive trading   ☐ Outside business activities

☐ Churning   ☐ Passive investment

☐ Selling dividends   ☐ Gifts and gratuities

☐ Breakpoint sales   ☐ Annual limit ($100)

☐ Misrepresentations, omissions   ☐ Fee-based compensation

☐ Research report rules   ☐ Borrowing and lending with customers

☐ Conflict of interest

☐ Guarantees   ☐ Directed brokerage arrangements

☐ Sharing in customer accounts   ☐ Misuse of nonpublic information

☐ Penalties for violating securities law   ☐ Artificial transactions

CODE OF PROCEDURE AND CODE OF ARBITRATION PROCEDURE

In connection with any investigation, complaint, or examination by the NASD, the Association can require a member firm or any person associated with a member to:

- provide information orally, in writing, or electronically;

- give testimony under oath; and

- provide access to or copies of any books, records, or accounts.

If a member or associated person fails to comply, the National Adjudicatory Council (NAC), after providing 20 days' written notice, has the right to suspend the member and revoke the registration of any associated person.

The NAC is responsible for the development of regulatory and enforcement policy and rule changes relating to the business and sales practices of member firms. It is also responsible for the oversight of the Department of Enforcement, which has the authority to file complaints against member firms and their associated persons.

CODE OF PROCEDURE

The **Code of Procedure** was created to deal with alleged violations of NASD rules and federal securities laws. If after an investigation or audit the NASD believes a member and/or its associated persons have violated a rule or laws, the Department of Enforcement will issue a formal complaint. With the filing of a complaint, the Department will name a Hearing Officer and appoint panelists to serve as a jury. All panelists in Code of Procedure hearings are from the industry.

The respondent (defendant) has 25 days after receiving the complaint to file an answer with the Hearing Officer. Answers must specifically admit, deny, or state that the respondent does not have sufficient information to admit or deny. If the respondent does not answer within 25 days, the Department will send a second notice requiring an answer within 14 days of receipt. This notice states that failure to reply allows the Hearing Officer to enter a default decision—in other words, guilty as charged.

Note that if a complaint is filed against a registered representative, it is not unusual for that person's designated supervisor (e.g., branch manager) to be charged for failure to supervise.

Offer of Settlement

A respondent has the option of proposing a settlement. An offer to settle must be in writing and must:

- describe the specific rule or law that the member or associated person is alleged to have violated;

- describe the acts or practices that the member or associated person is alleged to have engaged in or omitted;

- include a statement consenting to findings of fact and violations contained in the complaint; and

- propose sanctions consistent with the Association's sanction guidelines.

Uncontested Offer

By submitting an offer of settlement, the respondent waives the right to a hearing and the right to appeal. If the offer is accepted by the Department of Enforcement, it is then sent to the NAC for review. If uncontested by the NAC, the offer is accepted and final—case closed.

Contested Offer

If Enforcement opposes the offer, the offer is contested. At this point the offer and the Department's written opposition are submitted to the Hearing Officer. The Hearing Officer may order a settlement conference between the parties in an attempt to work out a compromise or may forward the offer and the Department's opposition to the NAC. If the NAC rejects the offer (or compromise offer), the hearings begin. If accepted by the NAC, the offer (or compromise offer) is final. The good news is that if an offer of settlement is ultimately rejected, it may not be introduced as evidence at the hearing.

Acceptance, Waiver, and Consent (AWC)

If the respondent does not dispute the allegations, the Department of Enforcement may prepare and request that the respondent sign a letter accepting a finding of violation, consenting to the imposition of sanctions, and waiving the right to a hearing and the right to appeal. If agreed to by the respondent, the letter is then sent to the NAC and, if approved, becomes final. If opposed by the NAC, the next stop is formal hearings.

TAKE NOTE   If the Department of Enforcement felt there was a chance of opposition from the NAC, it would not have offered AWC in the first place.

TAKE NOTE   An offer of settlement is a form of plea bargain initiated by the accused defendant while acceptance, waiver, and consent is a form of plea bargain initiated by the prosecution (the NASD).

Minor Rule Violation (MRV)

If the complaint involves a minor violation and the respondent does not dispute the allegation, the Department of Enforcement may prepare and request that the respondent sign an MRV letter, accepting a finding of violation. Minor rule violations include failure to:

- have advertising or sales literature approved by a principal before use;

- maintain a file for advertising and sales literature;

- file advertising and sales literature with the NASD within the required time frame;

- file timely reports on short positions;

- keep books and records in accordance with SEC rules;

- submit trading data if requested by the NASD; and

- timely submit amendments to the Form U-4 or Form U-5.

Once the respondent signs an MRV letter, the settlement is final. The NAC, as a sanction, may impose a fine up to exceed $2,500.

Prehearing Conference

Assuming the respondent does not make an offer of settlement or if an offer made is rejected and, assuming the Department of Enforcement doesn't offer either AWC or MRV as options, a prehearing conference is scheduled. Under Code of Procedure rules, it must be held within 21 days of receipt of the respondent's answer to the complaint, and attendance is mandatory.

Hearing

At the hearing, which resembles a courtroom proceeding, the prosecution (Department of Enforcement) goes first. Cross-examination of witnesses is permitted. At the conclusion, panelists convene and, within 60 days, render a written decision reflecting the majority view.

Sanctions

Sanctions against a member or associated person, if found guilty, are included with the written decision. Under the Code of Procedure, sanctions could include one or more of the following:

- censure;

- fine;

- suspension of NASD registration;

- expulsion of the member or revoking or cancelling the registration of an associated person;

- barring an associated person from association with any member; and/or

- imposition of any other fitting sanction.

If an associated person is suspended, that person cannot remain associated with the member in any capacity, including a clerical or administrative capacity (during the suspension period, that person cannot remain on the member's premises). Also, the member is prohibited from paying monies that the person might earn during the suspension period. Note that the suspended person could be paid monies earned before the suspension period.

However, it is possible for a principal to be suspended from acting as a principal and continue to function as a registered representative until the end of the suspension. During that period, no supervisory duties may be performed.

Appeals

If either side is displeased with the decision, an appeal can be made to the NAC. Any appeal must be made within 25 days of the decision date; otherwise, the decision is final. If no satisfaction is received from the NAC, the appealing party may take the case to the SEC. Again, if turned down, the appealing party has the right to continue the appeal process by taking its case to the federal court system. Appealing a decision stays the effective date of any sanctions, other than a bar or expulsion.

CODE OF ARBITRATION PROCEDURE

The **Code of Arbitration Procedure** offers participants a relatively easy method of settling disputes at a cost that is usually significantly lower than that of more formal procedures. Arbitration should not be confused with disciplinary proceedings under the Code of Procedure.

The Code of Arbitration of the NASD was originally established to mediate unresolved intraindustry disputes and was mandatory in controversies involving:

- a member against another member or registered clearing agency;

- a member against an associated person; and

- an associated person against another associated person.

Over time, customer complaints became subject to mandatory arbitration. In the absence of a signed arbitration agreement, a customer can still force a member to arbitration, but a member cannot force a customer to arbitration. Unresolved customer disputes must be settled under the Code of Arbitration Procedure.

Class action claims are not subject to arbitration, and claims alleging employment discrimination, including sexual harassment claims, are not required to be arbitrated unless the parties agree.

The advantages of arbitration versus suits in state or federal courts are time, money, and the fact that all decisions are final and binding—no appeals are allowed.

Predispute Arbitration Agreements

Customers must be advised about what they are agreeing to when they sign a predispute arbitration agreement. It is common practice that this agreement is contained within the new account form, though it can be a separate document. NASD Rule 3110 which governs this agreement, states the following.

- Language in the required disclosure must be easy to understand.

- Disclosure must be made that some arbitration forums, such as the NASD, may impose time limits for bringing claims via arbitration and that in some cases, though a claim may be ineligible for arbitration due to the time limit, it may still be brought in court.

- The delivery and customer acknowledgement of the agreement in writing must take place at the time of signing.

- Firms must supply a copy of the agreement clause that had been signed by a customer within 10 business days of receiving a request to do so.

TAKE NOTE

Customers can initiate arbitration against firms, but firms cannot initiate arbitration against customers unless the customer has given written consent.

Initiation of Proceedings

Any party to an unresolved dispute can initiate proceedings by filing a claim with the Director of Arbitration of the NASD. The statement of claim must describe the dispute, include documentation, and state the remedy being sought (in dollars). The Director will send a copy of the claim to the respondent.

The respondent then has 45 calendar days to respond to both the Director and the claimant. A respondent who fails to answer within 45 days may, in the sole discretion of the Director, be barred from presenting any matter, arguments, or defenses at the hearing. The claimant, after receiving the respondent's answer, must provide each party (the respondent and the Director) with a written reply within 10 calendar days. At this point, the initial discovery is over.

Mediation

If both parties agree, a process called **mediation** may take place, before any hearings convene, in which the two parties meet together to work out a settlement. The process is facilitated by a mediator, who may not render a binding decision. If mediation is not successful in producing a settlement, the matter goes to arbitration. In the case of unsuccessful mediation, the mediator may not sit on the arbitration panel.

Selection of Arbitrators

The NASD maintains a list of nonpublic and public arbitrators. A nonpublic arbitrator is one who is, or was, within the past three years, associated with a broker/dealer or registered under the Commodity Exchange Act. A public arbitrator is one who is not engaged directly or indirectly in the securities or commodities business. In disputes involving a customer, the majority of arbitrators will be public.

Simplified Arbitration

Any dispute involving a dollar amount of $25,000 or less is eligible for simplified arbitration, in which a single arbitrator reviews all of the evidence and renders a binding decision within 30 business days. If the dispute only involves persons in the industry, it is referred to as simplified industry arbitration. Note that both parties have to agree to this procedure, or a formal hearing is required.

Awards

All monetary awards must be paid within 30 days of decision date. Any award not paid within this time frame will begin to accrue interest as of the decision date. All awards and details on the underlying arbitration claim are made publicly available by the NASD.

Failure to Act

It is a violation of NASD rules for a member or an associated person to fail to:

- submit a dispute for arbitration;

- comply with any injunction order;

- appear or produce any document as directed;

- honor an award; or

- comply with an executed collective agreement obtained as the result of mediation.

Action by members requiring associated persons to waive the arbitration of disputes is also a rules violation.

Statute of Limitations

No claim is eligible for submission to arbitration if six years or more have elapsed from the time of the event giving rise to the claim.

■ Here's a tip to help distinguish between Code of Procedure and Code of Arbitration Procedure: the COP handles complaints.

■ If asked which section of the NASD rule manual addresses trade practice complaints, choose the Code of Procedure (COP).

■ If asked which section applies to settling disputes between members, or any problem between parties associated with the securities industry, choose the Code of Arbitration Procedure.

■ Arbitration is the industry choice over civil court because it is cheaper. There are no appeals, and decisions are binding on all parties.

■ Finally, the NASD has the authority to impose virtually any disciplinary action, other than a jail sentence, against a guilty representative or firm.

QUICK QUIZ 6.5

True or False?

_F_ 1. In the absence of a signed arbitration agreement, customers can still force member firms to arbitration, but member firms cannot force customers to arbitration.

_F_ 2. In customer simplified arbitration, a panel of three arbitrators reviews all the evidence and renders a binding decision.

_T_ 3. The statute of limitations for submission of a claim to arbitration is six years.

_T_ 4. Under the Code of Arbitration, a respondent to a statement of claim must respond to the Director of Arbitration of the NASD and the claimant within 45 days.

Match the following numbers with the appropriate description below. Choices can be used more than once.

    A. 25
    B. 45

_A_ 5. Number of days to begin an appeal of a DOE decision to the NAC

_A_ 6. Number of calendar days to respond to a DOE complaint notice

Terms and Concepts Checklist

✓	✓
☐ Code of Procedure	☐ Other fitting sanctions
☐ Department of Enforcement	☐ Appeals process
☐ Response times	☐ Code of Arbitration Procedure
☐ Offer of settlement	☐ Predispute arbitration agreement, Rule 3110
☐ Contested, uncontested offer	
☐ Minor rule violation (MRV)	☐ Initiation of proceedings
☐ Acceptance, waiver and consent	☐ Mediation
☐ Prehearing conference	☐ Public arbitrator
☐ Hearing	☐ Nonpublic arbitrator
☐ Sanctions	☐ Simplified arbitration
☐ Censure, fine	☐ Awards under arbitration
☐ Suspension, barring, expulsion	☐ Statute of limitations

USA PATRIOT ACT OF 2001

The **PATRIOT Act** establishes the US Treasury Department as the lead agency for developing regulations in connection with anti-money laundering programs and requires broker/dealers to establish internal compliance procedures to detect abuses.

Before September 11, 2001, money laundering rules were concerned with the origin of the cash. Under the PATRIOT Act, regulators are more concerned with where the funds are going. The idea is to prevent "clean" money from being used for "dirty" purposes (such as funding terrorist activities).

Currency Transaction Reports (CTRs)

Under the Bank Secrecy Act, currency transaction deposits or withdrawals of more than $10,000 must be reported to the Treasury Department's Financial Crimes Enforcement Network (FinCEN) on Form 104. This requirement applies to cash transactions used to pay off loans, the electronic transfer of funds, or the purchase of stocks, bonds, and mutual funds as well as other investments. Information must be supplied on both the transmitter and the recipient.

Structured transactions, or a series of small deposits, totaling more than $10,000 over a short period of time in an attempt to circumvent the reporting requirement, are also included for reporting purposes. Structured transactions may involve cash deposits, account transfers, wire transfers, or ATM or securities transactions. Additional care is required when monitoring clients with numerous accounts.

EXAMPLE   If a customer were to pay for a $60,000 mutual fund purchase with 120 $500 postal money orders, a Form 104 should be filed.

Suspicious Activity Reports (SARs)

Broker/dealers are required to file **suspicious activity reports (SARs)** involving transactions of $5,000 or more when financial behavior appears commercially illogical and serves no apparent purpose. Due diligence on the part of the firm is required before completing a transaction if it detects suspicious activity. While the detection of suspicious activity may be difficult, some examples where filing a SAR should occur are when:

- customers are not concerned about accounts or products losing value or alternates, which offer better potential returns or lower transaction costs;

- clients supply inadequate, false, or misleading information;

- clients decline to engage in a transaction when they know that a CTR will be filed, or they attempt to structure smaller transactions to avoid the filing of a CTR;

- funds are moved in and out of accounts in short periods of time;

- there are wire transfers to foreign countries or offshore accounts, particularly when coming from the proceeds of a loan; and

- customers with a known criminal background begin to conduct transactions substantial in number or size.

NASD ANTI-MONEY LAUNDERING RULES

Money laundering enables criminals to hide and legitimize proceeds derived from illegal sources. It involves disguising financial assets so that they may be utilized without detecting the illegal activity that produced them. Ultimately, the funds take on the appearance of having been generated in a legal fashion.

While techniques may vary, three basic stages of money laundering have been identified. They are placement, layering, and integration. It is important to remember that any or all of these stages can take place within financial institutions such as banks or broker/dealers or completely outside the realm of such institutions.

Placement

This first stage of laundering is when funds or assets are moved into the laundering system. This stage is recognized as the time when illegal funds are the most susceptible to detection.

Layering

The goal of money launderers during this stage is to conceal the source of the funds or assets. This is done through a series of layers of transactions that are generally numerous and can vary in form and complexity.

Integration

In the final stage, illegal funds are commingled with legitimate funds in what appear to be viable legitimate business concerns. This can be accomplished using front companies operating on a cash basis, import/export companies, as well as many other types of businesses.

As of April 24, 2002, under the NASD Anti-Money Laundering rules, all firms are required to, at a minimum:

■ establish and implement policies and procedures that can be reasonably expected to detect and cause reporting of suspicious transactions;

■ establish and implement policies, procedures, and internal controls reasonably designed to achieve compliance with anti-money laundering requirements;

■ provide for independent testing for compliance to be conducted by member personnel or by a qualified outside party;

■ designate an individual or individuals responsible for implementing and monitoring the day-to-day operations and internal controls of the program; and

■ provide ongoing training for appropriate personnel.

TAKE NOTE   Each firm's procedures must reflect their unique business model and customer base.

Office of Foreign Assets Control (OFAC)

The US Treasury's **Office of Foreign Assets Control** maintains a list of individuals and entities viewed as a threat to the United States. Those identified on the list of **Specially Designated Nationals (SDNs)** are subject to specific governmental sanctions.

Regulations require financial institutions to block or freeze assets of certain SDNs as they are identified and not to release those assets without the permission of OFAC. They may also require a financial institution to refuse to do business with certain SDNs. To assist financial institutions in determining which transactions to block, OFAC has created blocking profiles. Each blocked transaction must be reported to OFAC within 10 days of their occurrence.

Finally, OFAC requires financial institutions, including broker/dealers, to designate a compliance officer of the firm the responsibility of monitoring OFAC regulations and to oversee any blocked funds.

QUICK QUIZ 6.6   True or False?

___T___ 1. Filing a Currency Transaction Report (CTR) is required for any transaction over $10,000.

___F___ 2. Filing a Suspicious Activity Report (SAR) is required for any transaction of $10,000 or more.

___F___ 3. The US Treasury's Office of Foreign Assets Control (OFAC) can require a financial institution to block the transactions of certain individuals but may not prevent the financial institution from doing business with that person.

___T___ 4. The three stages of money laundering have been identified as placement, layering, and integration.

Terms and Concepts Checklist

✓

- ☐ USA PATRIOT Act of 2001
- ☐ CTRs
- ☐ SARs
- ☐ Office of Foreign Assets Control (OFAC)

✓

- ☐ Anti-money laundering rules
- ☐ Placement
- ☐ Layering
- ☐ Integration

HOTSHEETS

For your convenience, Unit HotSheets summarizing the key points are located at the end of the manual on perforated pages.

UNIT TEST

1. Which of the following statements regarding joint accounts is NOT true?

   A. Customers 1, 2, and 3 have a TIC account. Each deposits funds into the account. One of the 3 tenants must be designated to make trades for the account.

   B. Two customers have a TIC account. Customer 1 deposits $5,000 and Customer 2 deposits $10,000 into the account. If one joint owner dies, her assets will go to her estate. Both parties can place a trade.

   C. If an account has a joint registration, distributions must be made payable to all.

   D. Customers 1 and 2 have a JTWROS account. If Customer 1 were to die, his shares would be assumed by the survivor.

2. Which of the following statements concerning UGMA accounts is TRUE?

   A. UGMAs must have only 1 custodian and 1 minor.

   B. UGMAs may have several custodians but only 1 minor.

   C. UGMAs may have only 1 custodian but several minors.

   D. UGMAs may have several custodians and several minors.

3. Discretionary authority is required for a registered representative to determine

   I. which security to buy or sell
   II. the best time to enter the order
   III. the best price to execute the order
   IV. the number of shares

   A. I and IV
   B. II and III
   C. II and IV
   D. III and IV

4. Who is required to sign the new account form?

   A. Only the customer
   B. Only the registered representative
   C. Both the principal and the registered representative
   D. The customer, the registered representative, and the principal

5. After an NASD audit, the Department of Enforcement issues a formal complaint against a member firm for violations of the Conduct Rules. This complaint will be handled under the

   A. Uniform Practice Code
   B. Code of Procedure
   C. Code of Arbitration
   D. bylaws of the NASD

6. Under the NASD's Conduct Rules, which of the following are violations of the rules regarding fair and ethical treatment of customers?

   I. Encouraging customers to purchase mutual fund shares just before the ex-date to ensure that the customer receives the upcoming dividend

   II. Recommending that a customer regularly move his assets among several fund families with similar investment objectives to ensure diversification and top performance

   III. Recommending that a customer set up a scheduled investment program, depositing the same amount each period regardless of market value

   IV. Assuring a customer that because dollar cost averaging is one of the most effective means of investing for the long term, his account is unlikely to suffer any losses

   A. I and II
   B. I, II and IV
   C. II and III
   D. III and IV

7. All of the following actions are violations of the NASD Conduct Rules EXCEPT

   A. delivering a prospectus 48 hours after the sale of a mutual fund takes place

   B. opening a cash account for a customer without the customer's signature

   C. offering to trade mutual fund shares for a customer

   D. offering mutual fund shares to a customer at a discount from the POP

8. A customer sends a letter of complaint to a registered representative's home. What should the representative do with the letter?

   A. Call the customer and attempt to remedy the situation

   B. Take the letter to the representative's principal

   C. File the letter in the customer file the representative maintains

   D. Do nothing unless the customer contacts the representative again

9. When must a new account be approved by a principal?

   A. Before the account can be opened

   B. Before or promptly after completion of the first transaction

   C. Within 1 month of opening the account

   D. Does not need to be approved; the principal need only be informed of the account's opening

10. Under what circumstances could a third party open an account for a competent customer of legal age?

   A. None; competent persons of legal age must open their own accounts

   B. Only if the person opening the account was going to be given at least partial power of attorney over the account

   C. Only if the person opening the account was the spouse or another close family member of the account's owner

   D. Only if the person opening the account was going to be given full power of attorney over the account

11. Fiduciary and custodial accounts are similar in that, in both cases

   I. one party is acting on behalf of another party

   II. the account is being managed for the benefit of a minor

   III. the registered representative has trading authorization

   IV. the person managing the account must use prudence in his investment decisions

   A. I and III

   B. I and IV

   C. II and III

   D. II and IV

12. When opening a business account for a manufacturing firm, the registered representative must establish all of the following EXCEPT

   A. the business's legal right to open an investment account

   B. any limitations on the securities in which the firm can invest

   C. the business's market share within its industry

   D. who will represent the business in account transactions

13. You are about to open an account for someone who works for another NASD member firm. You must do all of the following EXCEPT

   I. obtain permission from the other firm to open the account

   II. notify the other firm that you are opening the account

   III. have an understanding with the customer that you will not order securities that he could order through his own firm

   IV. notify the customer that you intend to notify his firm of the opening of the account

   A. I and III

   B. I and IV

   C. II and III

   D. II and IV

14. Your customer has given power of attorney over his account to his investment adviser. You must

    A. obtain permission from the NASD before you can accept instructions from an investment adviser

    B. obtain the investment adviser's signature and the date on which he was given power of attorney

    C. explain to the customer that the account cannot be managed in this fashion

    D. assess the investment adviser's track record before agreeing to this arrangement.

15. Your customer has ordered $50,000 worth of shares of a particular mutual fund. The fund's ex-date is rapidly approaching, so you push the client to hurry up and send his check so that he can benefit from the distribution. This is known as

    A. churning

    B. front running

    C. a breakpoint sale

    D. selling dividends

ANSWERS AND RATIONALES

1. **A.** A joint account registration allows all tenants to place trades, regardless of their contributions. All owners, however, must endorse any certificates or checks. In a TIC account, the interest of a deceased tenant passes to the estate; in a JTWROS account, the interest of the deceased passes to the surviving tenant.

2. **A.** An UGMA account may have 1 custodian as a trustee for the account of 1 minor. Multiple custodians or minors are not permitted.

3. **A.** Discretionary authority allows the registered representative to choose which security, the number of shares, and whether to buy or sell. Deciding the best time and the best price are not discretionary actions.

4. **C.** Both the registered representative and the principal are required to sign the new account form (sometimes called the new account card). The representative signs to introduce the new account to the firm. The principal signs to accept the account on the firm's behalf. The customer is not required to sign the new account form.

5. **B.** Trade practice complaints, including violations of the Conduct Rules, and federal securities laws, are handled under the Code of Procedure of the NASD.

6. **B.** Choice I describes the prohibited practice of selling dividends, which subjects investors to adverse tax consequences. Choice II is the prohibited practice of switching funds, which may cause additional sales charges. Choice IV is prohibited because, although dollar cost averaging is a conservative method of investing, the representative can never guarantee a customer's account against loss. Choice III defines the practice of dollar cost averaging, which historically allows the customer to purchase shares at a lower average cost.

7. **B.** Cash accounts may be opened for customers without obtaining their signatures; margin accounts, however, require customer signature for account opening. A prospectus must be delivered to a mutual fund customer no later than the time of purchase. Mutual fund shares do not trade in the secondary market; they must be redeemed. Discounts from the POP are available to member firms only.

8. **B.** Complaint letters must be given to the representative's principal for disposition and must be filed in accordance with the NASD Conduct Rules.

9. **B.** Each account must be approved by a principal or partner of the firm, at latest promptly after the first transaction. Waiting a month would not be considered prompt.

10. **A.** Competent persons of legal age must open their own accounts. Later they may choose to give power of attorney to other persons, but they must open the account themselves.

11. **B.** Both fiduciary and custodial accounts put someone other than the account owner in charge of the account. This person is legally required to do his best to make only prudent investment decisions.

12. **C.** The registered representative must be aware of who he will be doing business with and any facts that might legally affect the account's transactions—not necessarily how the company is doing in its industry. Documentation must be obtained and kept on file with the other account forms.

13. **A.** The NASD does not require that firms give each other permission to open accounts for their employees, but it does require disclosure to the firm and to the prospective customer that disclosure will be given.

14. **B.** If power of attorney over an account is given to a third party, such as an investment adviser, the registered representative must obtain the person's signature and the date on which he was given power of attorney.

15. **D.** Urging or cajoling a customer to purchase a security early to receive a distribution is called selling dividends. It may close a deal faster and may generate a slightly higher commission, but it places the customer in an unwanted tax situation. He essentially receives some of his money back and must pay income tax on it. It is better to wait until the ex-date and pay a lower price for the shares.

QUICK QUIZ ANSWERS

Quick Quiz 6.1

1. **D.** The broker/dealer has no obligation to approve every transaction before entry.

2. **B.** The customer is not required to sign the new account form.

3. **A.** Representatives are not permitted to open an individual account in the name of another individual, even in the name of a spouse.

4. **A.** To open a cash account, only the signatures of the registered representative introducing the account and the principal accepting the account are required. For margin accounts, the signature of the customer is required on the margin agreement.

Quick Quiz 6.2

1. **D.** All of the persons listed have fiduciary responsibilities because they are entrusted with the authority to manage the money or property of others.

2. **B.** The donor may name himself the custodian of an UGMA or UTMA account. No documentation of custodial status is required to open an UGMA account. The custodian is not required to be the minor's legal guardian.

3. **B.** UGMA rules require that any UGMA account have only one beneficial owner and only one custodian. Cash and securities may be donated into the account, but insurance contracts and fixed annuities may not be donated; they are not securities.

4. **C.** Transfer of securities into the custodial account completes the gift. At that time, the minor becomes the owner of the securities.

Quick Quiz 6.3

1. **B.**

2. **D.**

3. **C.**

4. **E.**

5. **A.**

Quick Quiz 6.4

1. **U.** It is unlawful to guarantee performance of any security. Even government bond funds may lose principal value.

2. **U.** It is unlawful to enter a discretionary order without written authorization. This order is discretionary because the agent selected the company.

3. **L.** An agent must refuse to enter an order from someone, other than the customer, without proper written authorization.

4. **U.** All written customer complaints must be forwarded to the principal.

5. **L.** Agents may borrow money from customers that are recognized financial institutions.

6. **U.** This agent is guaranteeing protection against loss, and this activity is prohibited.

7. **U.** The agent is churning the account by making excessive transactions for the purpose of generating extra commission.

Quick Quiz 6.5

1. **T.**   Customers can force members into arbitration, but without an arbitration agreement, a member cannot force a customer to arbitration. However, virtually all new account forms contain a pre-dispute arbitration clause that must be signed by customers before opening an account; this way, unresolved customer complaints must be resolved under the Code of Arbitration.

2. **F.**   In customer simplified arbitration, a single arbitrator reviews the evidence and renders a binding decision within 30 days.

3. **T.**

4. **T.**

5. **A.**

6. **A.**

Quick Quiz 6.6

1. **T.**   CTRs are required for any transaction over $10,000.

2. **F.**   Filing an SAR is required for transactions of $5,000 or more.

3. **F.**   OFAC can require that a financial institution cease doing business with an individual or entity.

4. **T.**   The three stages of money laundering are placement, layering, and integration.

Common Abbreviations

ADR/ADS American depository receipt (share)

AIR assumed interest rate

BA banker's acceptance

BD broker/dealer

CD certificate of deposit

CMO collateralized mortgage obligation

CMV current market value

COP Code of Procedure

CPI Consumer Price Index

CY current yield

DJIA Dow Jones Industrial Average

EE Series EE savings bonds

EPS earnings per share

ERISA Employee Retirement Income Security Act of 1974

FAC face-amount certificate

FDIC Federal Deposit Insurance Corporation

FIFO first in, first out

FHLMC Federal Home Loan Mortgage Corporation

FNMA Federal National Mortgage Association

FOMC Federal Open Market Committee

FRB Federal Reserve Board

GDP gross domestic product

GNMA Government National Mortgage Association

GO general obligation bond

HH Series HH savings bond

IDR/IDB industrial development revenue bond

IPO initial public offering

IRA individual retirement account

IRC Internal Revenue Code

IRS Internal Revenue Service

JTIC joint tenants in common

JTWROS joint tenants with right of survivorship

LIFO last in, first out

LOI letter of intent

MSRB Municipal Securities Rulemaking Board

NASD National Association of Securities Dealers, Inc.

Nasdaq National Association of Securities Dealers Automated Quotation System

NAV net asset value

NL no load

NYSE New York Stock Exchange

OFAC Office of Financial Asset Control

OTC over the counter

POP public offering price

REIT real estate investment trust

REMIC real estate mortgage investment conduit

RR registered representative

SAI statement of additional information

SEC Securities and Exchange Commission

SEP simplified employee pension plan

SIPC Securities Investor Protection Corporation

SRO self-regulatory organization

STRIPS Separate Trading of Registered Interest and Principal of Securities

T+3 trade date plus three business days settlement

TCPA Telephone Consumer Protection Act

TSA tax-sheltered annuity

UGMA/UTMA Uniform Gifts (Transfers) to Minors Act

UIT unit investment trust

UPC Uniform Practice Code

VLI variable life insurance

YLD yield

YTM yield to maturity

ZR zero coupon

Calculations

To Calculate...	Use Formula...
Dividend Yield	$\dfrac{\text{Annual Dividend}}{\text{Current Market Price}}$
Current Yield	$\dfrac{\text{Annual Interest}}{\text{Current Market Price}}$
Number of Shares for Conversion	$\dfrac{\text{Par Value}}{\text{Conversion Price}}$
Parity	$\dfrac{\text{Bond Market Value}}{\text{Number of Shares}}$
Tax-Free or Municipal Equivalent Yield	Corporate Rate $\times$ (100% − Tax Bracket)
Taxable or Corporate Equivalent Yield	$\dfrac{\text{Municipal Rate}}{(100\% - \text{Tax Bracket})}$
NAV per share of a Mutual Fund	$\dfrac{\text{Fund Net Assets}}{\text{Number of Shares Outstanding}}$
Sales Charge Percentage	$\dfrac{\text{POP} - \text{NAV}}{\text{POP}}$
Public Offering Price (POP)	$\dfrac{\text{NAV per Share}}{(100\% - \text{Sales Charge Percentage})}$
Dollar Cost Average	$\dfrac{\text{Total Dollars Invested}}{\text{Number of Shares Purchased}}$
Average Market Price	$\dfrac{\text{Total of Share Prices}}{\text{Number of Investments}}$
Number of Outstanding Shares	Issued Shares − Treasury Shares
Shareholders' Equity	Assets − Liabilities

Glossary

A

account executive (AE) *See* registered representative.

accredited investor As defined in Rule 502 of Regulation D, any institution or individual meeting minimum net worth requirements for the purchase of securities qualifying under the Regulation D registration exemption. An accredited investor is generally accepted to be one who:

- has a net worth of $1 million or more; or
- has had an annual income of $200,000 or more in each of the two most recent years (or $300,000 jointly with a spouse), and who has a reasonable expectation of reaching the same income level in the current year.

accrued interest The interest that has accumulated since the last interest payment up to, but not including, the settlement date, and that is added to a bond transaction's contract price. There are two methods for calculating accrued interest: the 30-day-month (360-day-year) method for corporate and municipal bonds and the actual-calendar-days (365-day-year) method for government bonds. Income bonds, bonds in default, and zero-coupon bonds trade without accrued interest (flat).

accumulation stage The period during which contributions are made to an annuity account.

accumulation unit An accounting measure used to determine an annuitant's proportionate interest in the insurer's separate account during an annuity's accumulation (deposit) stage.

Act of 1933 *See* Securities Act of 1933.

Act of 1934 *See* Securities Exchange Act of 1934.

adjusted gross income (AGI) Earned income plus net passive income, portfolio income, and capital gains.

Administrator (1) A person authorized by a court of law to liquidate an intestate decedent's estate. (2) An official or agency that administers a state's securities laws.

ADR *See* American depositary receipt.

ADS *See* American depositary receipt.

advertisement Any promotional material designed for use by newspapers, magazines, billboards, radio, television, telephone recordings or other public media where the firm has little control over the type of individuals exposed to the material.

AE *See* registered representative.

affiliated person Anyone in a position to influence decisions made in a corporation, including officers, directors, principal stockholders, and members of their immediate families. Their shares are often referred to as control stock.

agency basis *See* agency transaction.

agency issue A debt security issued by an authorized agency of the federal government. Such an issue is backed by the issuing agency itself, not by the full faith and credit of the US government (except GNMA and Federal Import Export Bank issues). *See also* government security.

agency transaction A transaction in which a broker/dealer acts for the accounts of others by buying or selling securities on behalf of customers. *Syn.* agency basis.

agent (1) An individual or a firm that effects securities transactions for the accounts of others. (2) A person licensed by a state as a life insurance agent. (3) A securities salesperson who represents a broker/dealer or an issuer when selling or trying to sell securities to the investing public; this individual is considered an agent whether he actually receives or simply solicits orders.

aggressive investment strategy A method of portfolio allocation and management aimed at achieving maximum return. Aggressive investors place a high percentage of their investable assets in equity securities and a far lower percentage in safer debt securities and cash equivalents, and they pursue aggressive policies including margin trading, arbitrage, and option trading.

AGI *See* adjusted gross income.

AIR *See* assumed interest rate.

American depositary receipt (ADR) A negotiable certificate representing a given number of shares of stock in a foreign corporation. It is bought and sold in the American securities markets, just as stock is traded. *Syn.* American depositary share.

American Stock Exchange (AMEX) A private, not-for-profit corporation in New York that handles about one-fifth of all securities trades within the US.

AMEX *See* American Stock Exchange.

annual compliance review The annual meeting that all registered representatives and principals must attend, the purpose of which is to review compliance issues.

annual report A formal statement issued yearly by a corporation to its shareowners. It shows assets, liabilities, equity revenues, expenses, and so forth. It is a reflection of the corporation's condition at the close of the business year (balance sheet) and earnings performance (income statement).

annuitant Person who receives an annuity contract's distribution.

annuitize To change an annuity contract from the accumulation (pay-in) stage to the distribution (payout) stage.

annuity A contract between an insurance company and an individual, generally guaranteeing lifetime income to the individual on whose life the contract is based in return for either a lump-sum or a periodic payment to the insurance company. The contract holder's objective is usually retirement income.

annuity unit An accounting measure used to determine the amount of each payment during an annuity's distribution stage. The calculation takes into account the value of each accumulation unit and such other factors as assumed interest rate and mortality risk.

appreciation The increase in an asset's value.

approved plan *See* qualified retirement plan.

arbitration A process that allows industry disputes between members, member organizations, their employees, and customers to be heard and settled by either the NASD or a designated arbitration panel. Once the process is agreed to by both parties, there is no available appeal.

ask An indication of willingness by a trader or dealer to sell a security or a commodity; the price at which an investor can buy from a broker/dealer. *Syn.* offer.

asset (1) Anything that an individual or a corporation owns. (2) A balance sheet item expressing what a corporation owns.

asset allocation fund A mutual fund that splits its investment assets among stocks, bonds, and other vehicles in an attempt to provide a consistent return for the investor.

assignment (1) A document accompanying or part of a stock certificate that is signed by the person named on the certificate for the purpose of transferring the certificate's title to another person's name. (2) The act of identifying and notifying an account holder that the option owner has exercised an option held short in that account.

associated person of a member (AP) Any employee, manager, director, officer, or partner of a member broker/dealer or another entity (issuer, bank, etc.), or any person controlling, controlled by, or in common control with that member.

assumed interest rate (AIR) The net rate of investment return that must be credited to a variable life insurance policy to ensure that at all times the variable death benefit equals the amount of the death benefit. The AIR forms the basis for projecting payments, but it is not guaranteed.

auction market A market in which buyers enter competitive bids and sellers enter competitive offers simultaneously. The NYSE is an auction market. *Syn.* double auction market.

authorized stock The number of shares of stock that a corporation can issue. This number of shares is stipulated in the corporation's state-approved charter and may be changed by a vote of the corporation's stockholders.

automatic reinvestment An option available to mutual fund shareholders whereby fund dividends and capital gains distributions are automatically reinvested back into the fund.

average A price at a midpoint among a number of prices. Technical analysts often use averages as market indicators.

average price A step in determining a bond's yield to maturity. A bond's average price is calculated by adding its face value to the price paid for it and dividing the result by two.

B

back away The failure of an OTC market maker to honor a firm bid and asked price. Violates the NASD Conduct Rules.

back-end load A commission or sales fee that is charged when mutual fund shares or variable annuity contracts are redeemed. It declines annually, decreasing to zero over an extended holding period—up to eight years—as described in the prospectus. *Syn.* contingent-deferred sales load.

backdating The predating of a letter of intent (by as much as 90 days) to allow an investor to incorporate recent deposits for the purpose of qualifying for a sales load discount (breakpoint) on a purchase of open-end investment company shares.

balance sheet A report of a corporation's financial condition at a specific time.

balance sheet equation Formula stating that a corporation's assets equal the sum of its liabilities plus shareholders' equity.

balanced fund A mutual fund whose stated investment policy is to have at all times some portion of its investment assets in bonds and preferred stock as well as in common stock in an attempt to provide both growth and income.

balanced investment strategy Method of portfolio allocation and management aimed at balancing risk and return. A balanced portfolio may combine stocks, bonds, packaged products, and cash equivalents.

banker's acceptance (BA) A money market instrument used to finance international and domestic trade. A banker's acceptance is a check drawn on a bank by an importer or exporter of goods and represents the bank's conditional promise to pay the face amount of the note at maturity (normally less than three months).

basis point A measure of a bond's yield, equal to $1/100$ of 1% of yield. A bond whose yield increases from 5.0% to 5.5% is said to increase by 50 basis points.

BD *See* broker/dealer.

bear An investor who acts on the belief that a security or the market is falling or will fall.

bear market A market in which prices of a certain group of securities are falling or are expected to fall.

bearer bond *See* coupon bond.

best-efforts offering An offering of newly issued securities in which the investment banker acts as an agent of the corporation, promising only his best efforts in making the issue a success, but not guaranteeing the corporation that all shares will be sold or its money for an unsold shares.

beta coefficient A means of measuring the volatility of a security or a portfolio of securities in comparison with the market as a whole. A beta of 1 indicates that the security's price will move with the market. A beta greater than 1 indicates that the security's price will be more volatile than the market. A beta less than 1 means that it will be less volatile than the market.

bid An indication by an investor, a trader, or a dealer of a willingness to buy a security, the price at which an investor can sell to a broker/dealer.

blue-chip stock The equity issues of financially stable, well-established companies that have demonstrated their ability to pay dividends in both good and bad times.

blue-sky To register a securities offering in a particular state.

blue-sky laws Nickname for state regulations governing the securities industry. Coined in the early 1900s by a Kansas Supreme Court justice who wanted regulation to protect against "speculative schemes that have no more basis than so many feet of blue sky."

board of directors (1) Individuals elected by stockholders to establish corporate management policies. A board of directors decides, among other issues, if and when dividends will be paid to stockholders. (2) The body that governs the NYSE. It is composed of 20 members elected for a term of two years by the NYSE general membership.

board of governors The body that governs the NASD. It is composed of 27 members elected by both the NASD general membership and the board itself.

bona fide quote Offer from a broker/dealer to buy or sell securities; indicates willingness to execute a trade under terms and conditions accompanying the quote.

bond An issuing company's or government's legal obligation to repay the principal of a loan to bond investors at a specified future date. Usually issued with par or face values of $1,000, representing the amount of money borrowed. The issuer promises to pay a percentage of the par value as interest on the borrowed funds. The interest payment is stated on the face of the bond at issue.

bond fund A mutual fund whose investment objective is to provide stable income with minimal capital risk. It invests in income-producing instruments, which may include corporate, government, or municipal bonds.

bond quote One of a number of quotations listed in the financial press and most daily newspapers that provide representative bid prices from the previous day's bond market. Quotes for corporate and government bonds are percentages of the bonds' face values (usually $1,000). Corporate bonds are quoted in increments of $1/8$ where a quote of $99^1/_8$ represents 99.125% of par ($1,000), or $991.25. Government bonds are quoted in 32nds. Municipal bonds may be quoted on a dollar basis or on a yield-to-maturity basis.

bond rating An evaluation of the possibility of a bond issuer's default, based on an analysis of the issuer's financial condition and profit potential. Standard & Poor's, Moody's Investors Service, and Fitch Investors Service, among others, provide bond rating services.

bond yield The annual rate of return on a bond investment. Types of yield include nominal yield, current yield, yield to maturity, and yield to call. Their relationships vary according to whether the bond in question is at a discount, at a premium, or at par.

book-entry security A security sold without delivery of a certificate. Evidence of ownership is maintained on records kept by a central agency; for example, the Treasury keeps records of T-bill purchasers. Transfer of ownership is recorded by entering the change on the books or electronic files.

book value per share A measure of the net worth of each share of common stock. It is calculated by subtracting intangible assets and preferred stock from total net worth, then dividing the result by the number of shares of common outstanding. *Syn.* net tangible assets per share.

branch office Any location identified by any means to the public as a place where a registered broker/dealer conducts business.

breakeven point The point at which gains equal losses.

breakpoint The schedule of sales charge discounts a mutual fund offers for lump-sum or cumulative investments.

breakpoint sale The sale of mutual fund shares in an amount just below the level at which the purchaser would qualify for reduced sales charges. Violates the NASD Conduct Rules.

broad-based index An index designed to reflect the movement of the market as a whole. Examples include the S&P 100, the S&P 500, the AMEX Major Market Index, and the Value Line Composite Index.

broker (1) An individual or firm that charges a fee or commission for executing buy and sell orders submitted by another individual or firm. (2) The role of a firm when it acts as an agent for a customer and charges the customer a commission for its services.

broker/dealer (BD) Person or firm in the business of buying and selling securities. A firm may act as broker (agent) and dealer (principal), but not in the same transaction. Broker/dealers normally must register with the SEC, appropriate SROs, and any state in which they do business.

bull An investor who acts on the belief that a security or the market is rising or will rise.

bull market A market in which prices of a certain group of securities are rising or will rise.

business cycle A predictable long-term pattern of alternating periods of economic growth and decline. The cycle passes through four stages: expansion, peak, contraction, and trough.

business day A day on which financial markets are open for trading. Saturdays, Sundays, and legal holidays are not considered business days.

C

call (1) Option contract giving the owner the right to buy a specified amount of an underlying security at a specified price within a specified time. (2) The act of exercising a call option.

call buyer Investor who pays a premium for an option contract and receives, for a specified time, the right to buy the underlying security at a specified price.

call date The date, specified in the prospectus of every callable security, after which the security's issuer has the option to redeem the issue at par or at par plus a premium.

call feature *See* call provision.

call price Price, usually a premium over the issue's par value, at which preferred stocks or bonds can be redeemed before an issue's maturity.

call protection A provision in a bond indenture stating that the issue is noncallable for a certain period of time (5 years, 10 years, etc.) after the original issue date.

call provision The written agreement between an issuing corporation and its bondholders or preferred stockholders giving the corporation the option to redeem its senior securities at a specified price before maturity and under certain conditions. *Syn.* call feature.

call risk The potential for a bond to be called before maturity, leaving the investor without the bond's current income. As this is more likely during times of falling interest rates, the investor may not be able to reinvest his principal at a comparable rate of return.

call writer An investor who receives a premium and takes on, for a specified time, the obligation to sell the underlying security at a specified price at the call buyer's discretion.

callable bond A type of bond issued with a provision allowing the issuer to redeem the bond before maturity at a predetermined price.

callable preferred stock A type of preferred stock issued with a provision allowing the corporation to call in the stock at a certain price and retire it.

capital Accumulated money or goods available for use in producing more money or goods.

capital appreciation A rise in an asset's market price.

capital asset All tangible property, including securities, real estate, and other property, held for the long term.

capital gain Profit realized when a capital asset is sold for a higher price than the purchase price.

capital gains distributions Payments made to mutual fund shareholders of gains realized on the sale of the fund's portfolio securities. These amounts, if any, are paid once a year.

capital loss The loss incurred when a capital asset is sold for a lower price than the purchase price.

capital market The segment of the securities market that deals in instruments with more than one year to maturity—that is, long-term debt and equity securities.

capital risk Potential for an investor to lose all money invested due to circumstances unrelated to an issuer's financial strength (e.g., derivative instruments such as options carry risk independent of the underlying securities' changing value).

capital stock All of a corporation's outstanding preferred stock and common stock, listed at par value.

capital structure Composition of long-term funds (equity and debt) a corporation has as a source for financing.

capital surplus The money a corporation receives in excess of the stated value of stock at the time of first sale. *Syn.* paid-in capital; paid-in surplus.

capitalization The sum of a corporation's long-term debt, stock, and surpluses. *Syn.* invested capital.

cash account An account in which the customer is required by the SEC's Regulation T to pay in full for securities purchased no later than two days after the standard payment period set by the NASD's Uniform Practice Code. *Syn.* special cash account.

cash dividend Money paid to a corporation's stockholders out of the corporation's current earnings or accumulated profits. The board of directors must declare all dividends.

cash equivalent A security that can be readily converted into cash. Examples include Treasury bills, certificates of deposit, and money market instruments and funds.

cash transaction A settlement contract that calls for delivery and payment on the same day the trade is executed. Payment is due by 2:30 pm ET or within 30 minutes of the trade if it occurs after 2:00 pm ET. *Syn.* cash trade.

cashiering department The department within a brokerage firm that delivers securities and money to and receives securities and money from other firms and clients of the brokerage firm. *Syn.* security cage.

catastrophe call The redemption of a bond by an issuer owing to disaster (for example, a power plant that has been built with proceeds from an issue burns to the ground).

CD *See* negotiable certificate of deposit.

certificate A paper document used to evidence ownership of or creditorship in a corporation.

change (1) For an index or average, the difference between the current value and the previous day's market close. (2) For a stock or bond quote, the difference between the current price and the last trade of the previous day.

churning Excessive trading in a customer account by a registered representative who ignores customer interests and seeks only to increase commissions. Violates NASD Conduct Rules. *Syn.* overtrading.

Class A share A class of mutual fund share issued with a front-end sales load. A mutual fund offers different classes of shares to allow investors to choose the type of sales charge they will pay. *See also* Class B share; Class C share; Class D share; front-end load.

Class B share A class of mutual fund share issued with a back-end load. A mutual fund offers different classes of shares to allow investors to choose the type of sales charge they will pay. *See also* back-end load; Class A share; Class C share; Class D share.

Class C share A class of mutual fund share issued with a level load. A mutual fund offers different classes of shares to allow investors to choose the type of sales charge they will pay. *See also* Class A share; Class B share; Class D share.

Class D share A class of mutual fund share issued with both a level load and a back-end load. A mutual fund offers different classes of shares to allow investors to choose the type of sales charge they will pay. *See also* back-end load; Class A share; Class B share; Class C share.

close The price of the last transaction for a particular security on a particular day.

closed-end management company An investment company that issues a fixed number of shares in an actively managed portfolio of securities. The shares may be of several classes and are traded in the secondary marketplace, either on an exchange or over the counter. The shares' market price is determined by supply and demand, not by NAV. *Syn.* publicly traded fund.

CMV *See* current market value.

Code of Arbitration Procedure The NASD's formal method of handling securities-related disputes or clearing controversies between members, public customers, clearing corporations, or clearing banks. Such disputes involve violations of the Uniform Practice Code rather than the Conduct Rules. Any claim, dispute, or controversy between member firms or associated persons must be submitted to arbitration.

Code of Procedure (COP) NASD formal procedure for handling trade practice complaints involving violations of the Conduct Rules. The NASD Department of Enforcement is the first body to hear and judge complaints. The NASD board of governors handles appeals and review of Department of Enforcement decisions.

coincident indicator A measurable economic factor that varies directly and simultaneously with the business cycle, thus indicating the current state of the economy. Examples include nonagricultural employment, personal income, and industrial production.

collateralized mortgage obligation (CMO) A mortgage-backed corporate security. Unlike pass-through obligations issued by FNMA and GNMA, its yield is not guaranteed and it does not have the federal government's backing. These issues attempt to return interest and principal at a predetermined rate.

combination fund An equity mutual fund that attempts to combine the objectives of growth and current yield by dividing its portfolio between companies that show long-term growth potential and companies that pay high dividends.

combination privilege A benefit offered by a mutual fund whereby the investor may qualify for a sales charge breakpoint by combining separate investments in two or more mutual funds under the same management.

commercial paper An unsecured, short-term promissory note issued by a corporation for financing accounts receivable and inventories. It is usually issued at a discount reflecting prevailing market interest rates. Maturities range up to 270 days.

commission A service charge an agent assesses in return for arranging a security's purchase or sale. A commission must be fair and reasonable, considering all the relevant factors of the transaction. *Syn.* sales charge.

commissioner The state official with jurisdiction over insurance transactions.

Committee on Uniform Securities Identification Procedures (CUSIP) A committee that assigns identification numbers and codes to all securities, to be used when recording all buy and sell orders.

common stock A security that represents ownership in a corporation. Holders of common stock exercise control by electing a board of directors and voting on corporate policy.

common stock fund This is a mutual fund portfolio that consists primarily of common stocks. The emphasis of these portfolios is usually on growth.

completion of the transaction As defined by the NASD, the point at which a customer pays any part of the purchase price to the broker/dealer for a security he has purchased or delivers a security he has sold. If the customer pays the broker/dealer before payment is due, the transaction's completion occurs when the broker/dealer delivers the security.

compliance department The department within a brokerage firm that oversees the firm's trading and market-making activities. It ensures that the firm's employees and officers abide by the rules and regulations of the SEC, exchanges, and SROs.

concession The profit per bond or share that an underwriter allows the seller of new issue securities. The selling group broker/dealer purchases the securities from the syndicate member at the public offering price minus the concession. *Syn.* reallowance.

conduct rules A set of rules established and maintained by the NASD board of governors regulating the ethics employed by members in the conduct of their business.

conduit theory Means for an investment company to avoid taxation on net investment income distributed to shareholders. If a mutual fund acts as a conduit for the distribution of net investment income, it may qualify as a regulated investment company and be taxed only on the income it retains. *Syn.* pipeline theory.

confirmation Printed document that states the trade date, settlement date, and money due from or owed to a customer. It is sent or given to the customer on or before the settlement date.

Consolidated Tape (CT) A New York Stock Exchange service that delivers real-time reports of securities transactions to subscribers as they occur on the various exchanges. The Tape distributes reports to subscribers over two different networks that the subscribers can tap into through either the high-speed electronic lines or the low-speed ticker lines. Network A reports transactions in NYSE-listed securities. Network B reports AMEX-listed securities transactions, as well as reports of transactions in regional exchange issues that substantially meet AMEX listing requirements. *Syn.* Tape; Ticker Tape.

constant dollar plan A defensive investment strategy in which the total sum of money invested is kept constant, regardless of any price fluctuation in the portfolio. As a result, the investor sells when the market is high and buys when it is low.

constant ratio plan An investment strategy in which the investor maintains an appropriate ratio of debt to equity securities by making purchases and sales to maintain the desired balance.

constructive receipt Date on which the Internal Revenue Service considers that a taxpayer receives dividends or other income.

Consumer Price Index (CPI) Measure of price changes in consumer goods and services used to identify periods of inflation or deflation.

contingent-deferred sales load *See* back-end load.

contraction A period of general economic decline; one of the business cycle's four stages.

contractionary policy A monetary policy that decreases the money supply, usually with the intention of raising interest rates and combating inflation.

contractual plan A type of accumulation plan in which an individual agrees to invest a specific amount of money in the mutual fund during a specific time period. *Syn.* penalty plan; prepaid charge plan.

control (controlling, controlled by, under common control with) The power to direct or affect the direction of a company's management and policies, whether through the ownership of voting securities, by contract or otherwise. Control is presumed to exist if a person, directly or indirectly, owns, controls, holds with the power to vote, or holds proxies representing more than 10% of a company's voting securities.

control person (1) A director, officer, or another affiliate of an issuer. (2) A stockholder who owns at least 10% of any class of a corporation's outstanding securities.

control security Any security owned by a director, an officer, or another affiliate of the issuer or by a stockholder who owns at least 10% of any class of a corporation's outstanding securities. Who owns a security, not the security itself, determines whether it is a control security.

conversion parity Two securities, one of which can be converted into the other, of equal dollar value. A convertible security holder can calculate parity to help decide whether converting would lead to gain or loss.

conversion price The dollar amount of a convertible security's par value that is exchangeable for one share of common stock.

conversion privilege A feature the issuer adds to a security that allows the holder to change the security into shares of common stock. This makes the security attractive to investors and, therefore, more marketable.

conversion rate *See* conversion ratio.

conversion ratio The number of shares of common stock per par value amount that the holder would receive for converting a convertible bond or preferred share. *Syn.* conversion rate.

conversion value The total market value of common stock into which a senior security is convertible.

convertible bond A debt security, usually in the form of a debenture, that can be exchanged for equity securities of the issuing corporation at specified prices or rates.

convertible preferred stock An equity security that can be exchanged for common stock at specified prices or rates. Dividends may be cumulative or noncumulative.

cooling-off period The period (a minimum of 20 days) between a registration statement's filing date and the registration's effective date. In practice, the period varies in length.

coordination *See* registration by coordination.

corporate account An account held in a corporation's name. The corporate agreement, signed when the account is opened, specifies which officers may trade in the account. In addition to standard margin account documents, a corporation must provide a copy of its charter and bylaws authorizing a margin account.

corporate bond A debt security issued by a corporation. A corporate bond typically has a par value of $1,000, is taxable, has a term maturity, and is traded on a major exchange.

corporation The most common form of business organization, in which the organization's total worth is divided into shares of stock, each share representing a unit of ownership. A corporation is characterized by a continuous life span and its owners' limited liability.

cost basis The price paid for an asset, including any commissions or fees, used to calculate capital gains or losses when the asset is sold.

coupon bond A debt obligation with attached coupons representing semiannual interest payments. The holder submits the coupons to the trustee to receive the interest payments. The issuer keeps no record of the purchaser, and the purchaser's name is not printed on the certificate. *Syn.* bearer bond.

coupon yield *See* nominal yield.

covered call writer An investor who sells a call option while owning the underlying security or some other asset that guarantees the ability to deliver if the call is exercised.

CPI *See* Consumer Price Index.

credit risk The degree of probability that a bond's issuer will default in the payment of either principal or interest. *Syn.* default risk; financial risk.

cumulative preferred stock An equity security that offers the holder any unpaid dividends in arrears. These dividends accumulate and must be paid to the cumulative preferred stockholder before any dividends can be paid to the common stockholders.

cumulative voting A voting procedure that permits stockholders either to cast all of their votes for any one candidate or to cast their total number of votes in any proportion they choose. This results in greater representation for minority stockholders.

current assets Cash and other assets that are expected to be converted into cash within the next 12 months. Examples include such liquid items as cash and equivalents, accounts receivable, inventory, and prepaid expenses.

current liabilities A corporation's debt obligations due for payment within the next 12 months. Examples include accounts payable, accrued wages payable, and current long-term debt.

current market value (CMV) The worth of the securities in an account. The market value of listed securities is based on the closing prices on the previous business day. *Syn.* long market value.

current price *See* public offering price.

current yield The annual rate of return on a security, calculated by dividing the interest or dividends paid by the security's current market price.

CUSIP *See* Committee on Uniform Securities Identification Procedures.

custodial account Account in which a custodian enters trades on behalf of the beneficial owner, often a minor.

custodian An institution or a person responsible for making all investment, management, and distribution decisions in an account maintained in the best interests of another. Mutual funds have custodians responsible for safeguarding certificates and performing clerical duties.

customer Any person who opens a trading account with a broker/dealer. A customer may be classified in terms of account ownership, trading authorization, payment method, or types of securities traded.

customer statement A document showing a customer's trading activity, positions, and account balance. The SEC requires that customer statements be sent quarterly, but customers generally receive them monthly.

cyclical industry Fundamental analysis term for an industry that is sensitive to the business cycle and price changes. Most cyclical industries produce durable goods such as raw materials and heavy equipment.

D

dealer (1) An individual or a firm engaged in the business of buying and selling securities for its own account, either directly or through a broker. (2) The role of a firm when it acts as a principal and charges the customer a markup or markdown. *Syn.* principal.

death benefit provision This provision of an annuity allows for the payment to a beneficiary the greater of the value of the contributions or the value of the separate account at date of death. The provision is only effective during the accumulation period of the annuity, meaning if the annuitant dies before reaching the annuity (payout) phase.

debenture A debt obligation backed by the issuing corporation's general credit. *Syn.* unsecured bond.

debt financing Raising money for working capital or for capital expenditures by selling bonds, bills, or notes to individual or institutional investors. In return for the money lent, the investors become creditors and receive the issuer's promise to repay principal and interest on the debt.

debt security A security representing an investor's loan to an issuer such as a corporation, a municipality, the federal government, or a federal agency. In return for the loan, the issuer promises to repay the debt on a specified date and to pay interest.

declaration date The date on which a corporation announces an upcoming dividend's amount, payment date, and record date.

deduction An item or expenditure subtracted from adjusted gross income to reduce the amount of income subject to tax.

default Failure to pay interest or principal promptly when due.

default risk *See* credit risk.

defensive industry A fundamental analysis term for an industry that is relatively unaffected by the business cycle. Most defensive industries produce nondurable goods for which demand remains steady throughout the business cycle; examples include the food industry and utilities.

defensive investment strategy A method of portfolio allocation and management aimed at minimizing the risk of losing principal. Defensive investors place a high percentage of their investable assets in bonds, cash equivalents and stocks that are less volatile than average.

deferred annuity An annuity contract that delays payment of income, installments, or a lump sum until the investor elects to receive it.

deferred compensation plan A nonqualified retirement plan whereby the employee defers receiving current compensation in favor of a larger payout at retirement (or in the case of disability or death).

defined benefit plan A qualified retirement plan that specifies the total amount of money that the employee will receive at retirement.

defined contribution plan A qualified retirement plan that specifies the amount of money that the employer will contribute annually to the plan.

deflation A persistent and measurable fall in the general level of prices.

delivery The change in ownership or in control of a security in exchange for cash. Delivery takes place on the settlement date.

demand deposit A sum of money left with a bank (or borrowed from a bank and left on deposit) that the depositing customer has the right to withdraw immediately.

depression A prolonged period of general economic decline.

derivative An investment vehicle, the value of which is based on another security's value. Futures contracts, forward contracts, and options are among the most common types of derivatives. Institutional investors generally use derivatives to increase overall portfolio return or to hedge portfolio risk.

devaluation A substantial fall in a currency's value as compared to the value of gold or to the value of another country's currency.

dilution A reduction in earnings per share of common stock. Dilution occurs through the issuance of additional shares of common stock and the conversion of convertible securities.

discount The difference between the lower price paid for a security and the security's face amount at issue.

discount bond A bond that sells at a lower price than its face value.

discount rate The interest rate charged by the 12 Federal Reserve Banks for short-term loans made to member banks.

discretion The authority given to someone other than an account's beneficial owner to make investment decisions for the account concerning the security, the number of shares or units, and whether to buy or sell. The authority to decide only timing or price does not constitute discretion.

discretionary account An account in which the customer has given the registered representative authority to enter transactions at the representative's discretion.

discretionary order An order entered by a registered representative for a discretionary account allowing him to use his own judgment on the customer's behalf with respect to choice of security, quantity of security, and whether the transaction should be a purchase or sale.

disintermediation The flow of money from low-yielding accounts in traditional savings institutions to higher yielding investments. Typically, this occurs when the Fed tightens the money supply and interest rates rise.

disposable income (DI) The sum that people divide between spending and personal savings.

distribution Any cash or other property distributed to shareholders or general partners that arises from their interests in the business, investment company, or partnership.

distribution stage The period during which an individual receives distributions from an annuity account. *Syn.* payout stage.

diversification A risk management technique that mixes a wide variety of investments within a portfolio, thus minimizing the impact of any one security on overall portfolio performance.

diversified common stock fund A mutual fund that invests its assets in a wide range of common stocks. The fund's objectives may be growth, income, or a combination of both.

diversified management company As defined by the Investment Company Act of 1940, a management company that meets certain standards for the percentage of assets invested. These companies use diversification to manage risk.

dividend A distribution of a corporation's earnings. Dividends may be in the form of cash, stock, or property. The board of directors must declare all dividends. *Syn.* stock dividend.

dividend payout ratio A measure of a corporation's policy of paying cash dividends, calculated by dividing the dividends paid on common stock by the net income available for common stockholders. The ratio is the complement of the retained earnings ratio.

dividend yield Annual rate of return on a common or preferred stock investment. Yield is calculated by dividing the annual dividend by the stock's purchase price.

dividends per share The dollar amount of cash dividends paid on each common share during one year.

doctrine of mutual reciprocity The agreement that established the federal tax exemption for municipal bond interest. States and municipalities do not tax federal securities or properties, and the federal government reciprocates by exempting local government securities and properties from federal taxation. *Syn.* mutual exclusion doctrine; reciprocal immunity.

dollar cost averaging A system of buying mutual fund shares in fixed dollar amounts at regular fixed intervals, regardless of the share's price. The investor purchases more shares when prices are low and fewer shares when prices are high, thus lowering the average cost per share over time.

donor Person who makes a gift of money or securities to another. Once a gift is donated, the donor gives up all rights to it. Gifts of securities to minors under the Uniform Gifts to Minors Act provide tax advantages to the donor.

Dow Jones averages The most widely quoted and oldest measures of change in stock prices. Each of the four averages is based on the prices of a limited number of stocks in a particular category.

Dow Jones Industrial Average (DJIA) The most widely used market indicator, composed of 30 large, actively traded issues of industrial stocks.

dual-purpose fund A closed-end investment company that offers two classes of stock: income shares and capital shares. Income shares entitle the holder to share in the net dividends and interest paid to the fund. Capital shares entitle the holder to profit from the capital appreciation of all securities the fund holds.

duplicate confirmation A copy of a customer's confirmation that a brokerage firm sends to an agent or an attorney if the customer requests it in writing. In addition, if the customer is an employee of another broker/dealer, SRO regulations may require a duplicate confirmation to be sent to the employing broker/dealer.

E

earned income Income derived from active participation in a trade or business, including wages, salary, tips, commissions, and bonuses.

earnings per share (EPS) A corporation's net income available for common stock divided by its number of shares of common stock outstanding. *Syn.* primary earnings per share.

economic risk The potential for international developments and domestic events to trigger losses in securities investments.

Education IRA Education IRAs, which are also known as Coverdell Education Savings Accounts (ESAs), may be established for the purpose of paying qualified education expenses for the designated beneficiary of the account. Although contributions to Education IRAs are not tax deductible, the distributions are tax-free as long as the distributions are taken to pay for allowable educational expenses. The maximum annual contribution is $2,000 per beneficiary.

EE savings bond *See* Series EE bond.

effective date The date the registration of an issue of securities becomes effective, allowing the underwriters to sell the newly issued securities to the public and confirm sales to investors who have given indications of interest.

elasticity The responsiveness of consumers and producers to a change in prices. A large change in demand or production resulting from a small change in price for a good is considered an indication of elasticity.

Employee Retirement Income Security Act of 1974 (ERISA) The law that governs the operation of most corporate pension and benefit plans. The law eased pension eligibility rules, set up the Pension Benefit Guaranty Corporation, and established guidelines for the management of pension funds. Corporate retirement plans established under ERISA qualify for favorable tax treatment for employers and participants. *Syn.* Pension Reform Act.

endorsement The signature on the back of a stock or bond certificate by the person named on the certificate as the owner. An owner must endorse certificates when transferring them to another person.

EPS *See* earnings per share.

equity (EQ) Common and preferred stockholders' ownership interests in a corporation.

equity financing Raising money for working capital or for capital expenditures by selling common or preferred stock to individual or institutional investors. In return for the money paid, the investors receive ownership interests in the corporation.

equity option Security representing the right to buy or sell common stock at a specified price within a specified time.

equity security A security representing ownership in a corporation or another enterprise. Examples of equity securities include: common and preferred stock; interests in a limited partnership or joint venture; securities that carry the right to be traded for equity securities, such as convertible bonds, rights, and warrants; and put and call options on equity securities.

ERISA *See* Employee Retirement Income Security Act of 1974.

estate tax Tax imposed by a state or the federal government on the assets a person possesses at the time of death.

exchange Any organization, association, or group of persons that maintains or provides a marketplace in which securities can be bought and sold. An exchange need not be a physical place, and several strictly electronic exchanges do business around the world.

Exchange Act *See* Securities Exchange Act of 1934.

exchange-listed security A security that has met certain requirements and has been admitted to full trading privileges on an exchange. The NYSE, the AMEX, and regional exchanges set listing requirements for volume of shares outstanding, corporate earnings, and other characteristics. Exchange-listed securities can also be traded in the third market, the market for institutional investors.

exchange market All of the exchanges on which listed securities are traded.

exchange privilege A feature offered by a mutual fund allowing an individual to transfer an investment in one fund to another fund under the same sponsor without incurring an additional sales charge.

ex-date The first date on which a security is traded that the buyer is not entitled to receive distributions previously declared. *Syn.* ex-dividend date.

ex-dividend date *See* ex-date.

executor A person given fiduciary authorization to manage the affairs of a decedent's estate. An executor's authority is established by the decedent's last will.

exempt security A security exempt from the registration requirements (although not from the antifraud requirements) of the Securities Act of 1933. Examples include US government securities and municipal securities.

exercise To effect the transaction offered by an option, a right, or a warrant. For example, an equity call holder exercises a call by buying 100 shares of the underlying stock at the agreed-upon price within the agreed-upon time period.

exercise price Cost per share at which an option or a warrant holder may buy or sell the underlying security. *Syn.* strike price.

expansion A period of increased business activity throughout an economy; one of the four stages of the business cycle. *Syn.* recovery.

expansionary policy A monetary policy that increases the money supply, usually with the intention of lowering interest rates and combatting deflation.

expense ratio A ratio for comparing a mutual fund's efficiency by dividing the fund's expenses by its net assets.

F

face-amount certificate company (FAC) An investment company that issues certificates obligating it to pay an investor a stated amount of money (the face amount) on a specific future date. The investor pays into the certificate in periodic payments or in a lump sum.

face value See par.

Fannie Mae See Federal National Mortgage Association.

Farm Credit System (FCS) An organization of 37 privately owned banks that provide credit services to farmers and mortgages on farm property. Included in the system are the Federal Land Banks, Federal Intermediate Credit Banks, and Banks for Cooperatives.

FDIC See Federal Deposit Insurance Corporation.

Fed See Federal Reserve System.

Federal Deposit Insurance Corporation (FDIC) The government agency that provides deposit insurance for member banks and prevents bank and thrift failures.

federal funds These are immediately available funds representing noninterest-bearing deposits at Federal Reserve banks. Federal funds are the primary payment mode for government securities and are often used to pay for new issues of municipal securities and for secondary market transactions in certain types of securities.

Federal Home Loan Bank (FHLB) A government-regulated organization that operates a credit reserve system for the nation's savings and loan institutions.

Federal Home Loan Mortgage Corporation (FHLMC) A publicly traded corporation that promotes the nationwide secondary market in mortgages by issuing mortgage-backed pass-through debt certificates. Syn. Freddie Mac.

Federal Intermediate Credit Bank (FICB) One of 12 banks that provide short-term financing to farmers as part of the Farm Credit System.

Federal National Mortgage Association (FNMA) A publicly held corporation that buys conventional mortgages and mortgages from government agencies, including the Federal Housing Administration, Department of Veterans Affairs, and Farmers Home Administration. Syn. Fannie Mae.

Federal Open Market Committee (FOMC) A committee that makes decisions concerning the Fed's operations to control the money supply.

Federal Reserve Board (FRB) A seven-member group that directs the operations of the Federal Reserve System. The President appoints board members, subject to Congressional approval.

Federal Reserve System The central bank system of the United States. Its primary responsibility is to regulate the flow of money and credit. The system includes 12 regional banks, 24 branch banks, and hundreds of national and state banks. Syn. Fed.

FHLB See Federal Home Loan Bank.

FHLMC See Federal Home Loan Mortgage Corporation.

fictitious quotation A bid or an offer published before being identified by source and verified as legitimate. A fictitious quote may create the appearance of trading activity where none exists; violates NASD Conduct Rules.

fiduciary A person legally appointed and authorized to hold assets in trust for another person and manage those assets for that person's benefit.

filing date The day on which an issuer submits to the SEC the registration statement for a new securities issue.

final prospectus The legal document that states a new issue security's price, delivery date, and underwriting spread, as well as other material information. It must be given to every investor who purchases a new issue of registered securities. Syn. prospectus.

firm commitment underwriting An underwriting where the underwriter buys the entire issue from the issuer at an agreed upon price and then proceeds to sell the issue. The issuer has a firm commitment that all shares are sold because the entire issue is bought by the underwriter.

firm quote The actual price at which a trading unit of a security (such as 100 shares of stock or five bonds) may be bought or sold. All quotes are firm quotes unless otherwise indicated.

first in, first out (FIFO) An accounting method used to assess a company's inventory, in which it is assumed that the first goods acquired are the first to be sold. The same method is used by the IRS to determine cost basis for tax purposes. See also average basis; last in, first out; share identification.

fiscal policy The federal tax and spending policies set by Congress or the President. These policies affect tax rates, interest rates and government spending in an effort to control the economy.

5% markup policy The NASD's general guideline for the percentage markups, markdowns, and commissions on OTC securities transactions. The policy is intended to ensure fair and reasonable treatment of the investing public.

fixed annuity An insurance contract in which the insurance company makes fixed dollar payments to the annuitant for the term of the contract, usually until the annuitant dies. The insurance company guarantees both earnings and principal. Syn. fixed dollar annuity; guaranteed dollar annuity.

fixed dollar annuity *See* fixed annuity.

fixed unit investment trust An investment company that invests in a portfolio of securities in which no changes are permissible.

flat A term used to describe bonds traded without accrued interest. They are traded at the agreed-upon market price only.

flexible premium policy A variable or whole life insurance contract that permits the holder to adjust the premium payments and death benefit according to changing needs.

FNMA *See* Federal National Mortgage Association.

FOMC *See* Federal Open Market Committee.

foreign fund *See* sector fund.

45-day letter *See* free-look letter.

forward pricing The valuation process for mutual fund shares, whereby an order to purchase or redeem shares is executed at the price determined by the portfolio valuation calculated after the order is received. Portfolio valuations occur at least once per business day.

401(k) plan A tax-deferred defined contribution retirement plan offered by an employer.

403(b) plan A tax-deferred annuity retirement plan available to employees of public schools and certain nonprofit organizations.

fourth market The exchange where securities are traded directly from one institutional investor to another without a brokerage firm's services, primarily through the use of an ECN such as INSTINET.

fractional share A portion of a whole share of stock. Mutual fund shares are frequently issued in fractional amounts. Fractional shares used to be generated when corporations declared stock dividends, merged, or voted to split stock, but now it is more common for corporations to issue the cash equivalent of fractional shares.

fraud The deliberate concealment, misrepresentation, or omission of material information or the truth, so as to deceive or manipulate another party for unlawful or unfair gain.

FRB *See* Federal Reserve Board.

free credit balance The cash funds in customer accounts. Broker/dealers must notify customers of their free credit balances at least quarterly.

free-look letter A letter to mutual fund investors explaining a contractual plan's sales charge and operation. The letter must be sent within 60 days of a sale. During the free-look period, the investor may terminate the plan without paying a sales charge. *Syn.* 45-day letter.

freeriding Buying and immediately selling securities without making payment. This practice violates the SEC's Regulation T.

freeriding and withholding The failure of a member participating in the distribution of a hot issue to make a bona fide public offering at the public offering price. This practice violates the NASD Conduct Rules.

front-end load (1) Mutual fund commission or sales fee charged at the time shares are purchased. The load is added to the share's net asset value when calculating the POP. (2) System of sales charge for contractual plans permitting up to 50% of the first year's payments to be deducted as a sales charge. Investors have a right to withdraw from such a plan, but restrictions apply if this occurs.

frozen account An account requiring cash in advance before a buy order is executed and securities in hand before a sell order is executed. An account holder under such restrictions has violated the SEC's Regulation T.

Full Disclosure Act *See* Securities Act of 1933.

full power of attorney A written authorization for someone other than an account's beneficial owner to make deposits and withdrawals and to execute trades in the account.

full trading authorization An authorization, usually provided by a full power of attorney, for someone other than the customer to have full trading privileges in an account.

fully registered bond Debt issue that prints the bondholder's name on the certificate. The issuer's transfer agent maintains the records and sends principal and interest payments directly to the investor.

funded debt All long-term debt financing of a corporation or municipality (i.e., all outstanding bonds maturing in 5 years or more).

funding An ERISA guideline stipulating that retirement plan assets must be segregated from other corporate assets.

fund manager *See* portfolio manager.

fungible Interchangeable, owing to identical characteristics or value. A security is fungible if it can be substituted or exchanged for another security.

G

general account The account that holds all of an insurer's assets other than those in separate accounts. The general account holds the contributions paid for traditional life insurance contracts.

general obligation bond (GO) A municipal debt issue backed by the full faith, credit, and taxing power of the issuer for payment of interest and principal. *Syn.* full faith and credit bond. *See also* double-barreled bond; revenue bond.

General Securities Representative *See* Series 7.

generic advertising Communications with the public that promote securities as investments, but that do not refer to particular securities. *Syn.* institutional advertising.

GNMA *See* Government National Mortgage Association.

good delivery Proper delivery by a selling firm to the purchaser's office of certificates that are negotiable without additional documentation and that are in units acceptable under the Uniform Practice Code.

Government National Mortgage Association (GNMA) A wholly government-owned corporation that issues pass-through mortgage debt certificates backed by the full faith and credit of the US government. *Syn.* Ginnie Mae.

government security A debt obligation of the US government, backed by its full faith, credit, and taxing power, and regarded as having no risk of default. The government issues short-term Treasury bills, medium-term Treasury notes, and long-term Treasury bonds.

gross domestic product (GDP) Total value of goods and services produced in a country during one year; includes consumption, government purchase, investments, exports minus imports.

gross income All income of a taxpayer, from whatever source derived.

growth and income fund A mutual fund whose aim is to provide for a degree of both income and long-term growth.

growth fund A diversified common stock fund that has capital appreciation as its primary goal. It invests in companies that reinvest most of their earnings for expansion, research, or development.

growth industry An industry that is growing faster than the economy as a whole as a result of technological changes, new products, or changing consumer tastes.

growth stock A relatively speculative issue that is believed to offer significant potential for capital gains. It often pays low dividends and sells at a high price-earnings ratio.

guaranteed dollar annuity *See* fixed annuity.

guaranteed stock An equity security, generally a preferred stock, issued with a promise from a corporation other than the issuing corporation to maintain dividend payments. The stock still represents ownership in the issuing corporation, but it is considered a dual security.

guardian A fiduciary who manages the assets of a minor or an incompetent for that person's benefit.

H

hedge fund A mutual fund or investment company which, as a regular policy, hedges its market commitments. It does this by holding securities it believes are likely to increase in value and at the same time is short other securities it believes are likely to decrease in value. The sole objective is capital appreciation. This type of fund is highly aggressive, and is generally not available to ordinary investors.

HH savings bond *See* Series HH bond.

high The highest price a security or commodity reaches during a specified period of time.

hold in street name Securities transaction settlement and delivery procedure where customer securities are transferred into the broker/dealer's name and held by the broker/dealer. The broker/dealer is the nominal owner, but the customer is the beneficial owner.

holder The owner of a security.

holding company A company organized to invest in and manage other corporations.

holding period A time period signifying how long the owner possesses a security. It starts the day after a purchase and ends on the day of the sale.

HR-10 plan *See* Keogh plan.

I

identified security The particular security designated for sale by an investor holding identical securities with different acquisition dates and cost bases. Allows investors to control the amount of capital gain or loss incurred through the sale.

immediate annuity An insurance contract purchased for a single premium that starts to pay the annuitant immediately following its purchase.

immediate family A parent, mother-in-law or father-in-law, husband or wife, child, or another relative supported financially by a person associated with the securities industry.

incidental insurance benefit A payment received from a variable life insurance policy, other than the variable death benefit and the minimum death benefit, and including but not limited to any accidental death and dismemberment benefit, disability income benefit, guaranteed insurability option, family income benefit, or fixed-benefit term rider.

income bond A debt obligation that promises to repay principal in full at maturity. Interest is paid only if the corporation's earnings are sufficient to meet the interest payment and if the board of directors declares the interest payment. Income bonds are usually traded flat. *Syn.* adjustment bond.

income fund Mutual fund that seeks to provide stable current income by investing in securities that pay interest or dividends.

income statement The summary of a corporation's revenues and expenses for a specific fiscal period.

indefeasible title Ownership that cannot be declared null or void.

index A comparison of current prices to some baseline, such as prices on a particular date. Indexes are frequently used in technical analysis.

indication of interest (IOI) An investor's expression of conditional interest in buying an upcoming securities issue after the investor has reviewed a preliminary prospectus. An indication of interest is not a commitment to buy.

individual retirement account (IRA) Retirement investing tool for employed individuals that allows an annual contribution of 100% of earned income up to a maximum of $4,000 in 2005. Some or all of the contribution may be deductible from current taxes, depending on the individual's adjusted gross income and coverage by employer-sponsored qualified retirement plans.

industrial development (revenue) bond (IDB) In general, securities issued by a state, local government, or development agency to finance the construction or purchase of industrial, commercial, or manufacturing facilities to be purchased by or leased to a private user. IDBs are backed by the credit of the private user and generally are not considered liabilities of the governmental issuer (although in some jurisdictions they may also be backed by an issuer with taxing power).

industry fund *See* sector fund.

inflation A persistent and measurable rise in the general level of prices.

initial public offering (IPO) A corporation's first sale of common stock to the public.

inside information Material information that has not been disseminated to or is not readily available to the general public.

insider Any person who possesses or has access to material, nonpublic information about a corporation. Insiders include directors, officers, and stockholders who own more than 10% of any class of equity security of a corporation.

Insider Trading Act *See* Insider Trading and Securities Fraud Enforcement Act of 1988.

Insider Trading and Securities Fraud Enforcement Act of 1988 Legislation that defines what constitutes the illicit use of nonpublic information in making securities trades and the liabilities and penalties that apply. *Syn.* Insider Trading Act.

institutional account Account held for the benefit of others. Examples of institutional accounts include banks, trusts, pension and profit-sharing plans, mutual funds, and insurance companies.

institutional investor A person or an organization that trades securities in large enough share quantities or dollar amounts that it qualifies for preferential treatment and lower commissions. An institutional order can be of any size. Institutional investors are covered by fewer protective regulations since it is assumed they are more knowledgeable and more able to protect themselves.

interest The charge for the privilege of borrowing money, usually expressed as an annual percentage rate.

interest rate risk The risk associated with investments relating to the sensitivity of price or value to fluctuation in the current level of interest rates; also, the risk that involves the competitive cost of money. This term is generally associated with bond prices, but it applies to all investments. In bonds, prices carry interest risk because if bond prices rise, outstanding bonds will not remain competitive unless their yields and prices adjust to reflect the current market.

Internal Revenue Code (IRC) Legislation that defines tax liabilities and deductions for US taxpayers.

investment adviser (1) Person who makes investment recommendations in return for a flat fee or a percentage of assets managed. (2) For an investment company, the person who bears the day-to-day responsibility of investing the cash and securities held in the fund's portfolio in accordance with objectives stated in the fund's prospectus.

Investment Advisers Act of 1940 Legislation governing who must register with the SEC as an investment adviser.

investment banker An institution in the business of raising capital for corporations and municipalities. An investment banker may not accept deposits or make commercial loans. *Syn.* investment bank.

investment banking business A broker, dealer, or municipal or government securities dealer that underwrites or distributes new issues of securities as a dealer or that buys and sells securities for the accounts of others as a broker. *Syn.* investment securities business.

investment company A company engaged in the business of pooling investors' money and trading in securities for them. Examples include face amount certificate companies, unit investment trusts, and management companies.

Investment Company Act Amendments of 1970 Amendments to the Investment Company Act of 1940 requiring a registered investment company that issues contractual plans to offer all purchasers withdrawal rights and purchasers of front-end load plans surrender rights.

Investment Company Act of 1940 Congressional legislation regulating companies that invest and reinvest in securities. The act requires an investment company engaged in interstate commerce to register with the SEC.

Investment Company/Variable Contract Products Limited Principal *See* Series 26.

Investment Company/Variable Contract Products Limited Representative *See* Series 6.

investment grade The broad credit designation given to bonds which have a high probability of being paid and minor, if any, speculative features. Bonds rated BBB or higher by Standard and Poor's Corporation or Baa or higher by Moody's Investors Service, Inc., are deemed by those agencies to be investment grade.

investment grade security A security to which the rating services (Standard & Poor's, Moody's, etc.) have assigned a rating of BBB/Baa or above.

investment objective Any goal a client hopes to achieve through investing. Examples include current income, capital growth, and preservation of capital.

investment pyramid A portfolio strategy that allocates investable assets according to an investment's relative safety. The pyramid base is composed of low-risk investments, the mid portion is composed of growth investments, and the pyramid top is composed of speculative investments.

investor An individual who purchases an asset or a security with the intent of profiting from the transaction.

IPO *See* initial public offering.

IRA *See* individual retirement account.

IRA rollover The reinvestment of assets that an individual receives as a distribution from a qualified tax-deferred retirement plan into an individual retirement account within 60 days of receiving the distribution. The individual may reinvest the entire sum or a portion of the sum, but any portion not reinvested is taxed as ordinary income.

IRA transfer The direct reinvestment of retirement assets from one qualified tax-deferred retirement plan to an individual retirement account. The account owner never takes possession of the assets, but directs that they be transferred directly from the existing plan custodian to the new plan custodian.

irrevocable stock power *See* stock power.

issue Can be any of a company's class of securities or the act of distributing them.

issued stock Equity securities authorized by the issuer's registration statement and distributed to the public.

issuer The entity, such as a corporation or municipality, that offers or proposes to offer its securities for sale.

J

joint account An account in which two or more individuals possess some form of control over the account and may transact business in the account. The account must be designated as either tenants in common or joint tenants with right of survivorship.

joint life with last survivor An annuity payout option that covers two or more people, with annuity payments continuing as long as one of the annuitants remains alive.

joint tenants with right of survivorship (JTWROS) A form of joint ownership of an account whereby a deceased tenant's fractional interest in the account passes to the surviving tenant(s). It is used almost exclusively by husbands and wives.

K

Keogh plan A qualified tax-deferred retirement plan for persons who are self-employed and unincorporated or who earn extra income through personal services aside from their regular employment. *Syn.* HR-10 plan.

know your customer rule *See* Rule 405.

L

lagging indicator Measurable economic factor that changes after the economy has started to follow a particular pattern or trend. Lagging indicators are believed to confirm long-term trends (e.g., average duration of unemployment, corporate profits, labor cost per unit of output).

last in, first out (LIFO) An accounting method used to assess a corporation's inventory in which it is assumed that the last goods acquired are the first to be sold. The method is used to determine cost basis for tax purposes; the IRS designates last in, first out as the order in which sales or withdrawals from an investment are made. *See also* first in, first out; share identification.

leading indicator A measurable economic factor that changes before the economy starts to follow a particular pattern or trend. Leading indicators are believed to predict changes in the economy. Examples include new orders for durable goods, slowdowns in deliveries by vendors, and numbers of building permits issued.

legal list The selection of securities a state agency (usually a state banking or insurance commission) determines to be appropriate investments for fiduciary accounts such as mutual savings banks, pension funds, and insurance companies.

letter of intent (LOI) A signed agreement allowing an investor to buy mutual fund shares at a lower overall sales charge, based on the total dollar amount of the intended investment. An LOI is valid only if the investor completes the terms of the agreement within 13 months of signing the agreement. A letter of intent may be backdated 90 days. *Syn.* statement of intention.

leverage Using borrowed capital to increase investment return. *Syn.* trading on the equity.

liability A legal obligation to pay a debt owed. Current liabilities are debts payable within 12 months. Long-term liabilities are debts payable over a period of more than 12 months.

license *See* Series 6; Series 7; Series 26; Series 63; Series 65.

life annuity/straight life An annuity payout option that pays a monthly check over the annuitant's lifetime.

life annuity with period certain An annuity payout option that guarantees the annuitant a monthly check for a certain time period and thereafter until the annuitant's death. If the annuitant dies before the time period expires, the payments go to the annuitant's named beneficiary.

life contingency An annuity payout option that provides a death benefit during the accumulation stage. If the annuitant dies during this period, a full contribution is made to the account, which is paid to the annuitant's named beneficiary.

limited liability An investor's right to limit potential losses to no more than the amount invested. Equity shareholders, such as corporate stockholders and limited partners, have limited liability.

limited power of attorney A written authorization for someone other than an account's beneficial owner to make certain investment decisions regarding transactions in the account.

limited principal A person who has passed an examination attesting to the knowledge and qualifications necessary to supervise a broker/dealer's business in a limited area of expertise. A limited principal is not qualified in the general fields of expertise reserved for a general securities principal; these include supervision of underwriting and market making and approval of advertising.

limited representative A person who has passed an examination attesting to the knowledge and qualifications necessary to sell certain specified investment products.

limited trading authorization An authorization, usually provided by a limited power of attorney, for someone other than the customer to have trading privileges in an account. These privileges are limited to purchases and sales; withdrawal of assets is not authorized.

liquidity The ease with which an asset can be converted to cash in the marketplace. A large number of buyers and sellers and a high volume of trading activity provide high liquidity.

listed security A stock, bond, or security that satisfies certain minimum requirements and is traded on a regional or national securities exchange such as the NYSE.

LOI *See* letter of intent.

long Term used to describe the owning of a security, contract, or commodity (e.g., a common stock owner has a long position in the stock).

long-term gain Profit earned on the sale of a capital asset that has been owned for more than 12 months.

long-term loss Loss realized on the sale of a capital asset that has been owned for more than 12 months.

loss carryover A capital loss incurred in one tax year that is carried over to the next year or later years for use as a capital loss deduction.

low The lowest price a security or commodity reaches during a specified time period.

M

M1 A category of the money supply that includes all coins, currency and demand deposits—that is, checking accounts and NOW accounts.

M2 A category of the money supply that includes M1 in addition to all time deposits, savings deposits, and non-institutional money market funds.

M3 A category of the money supply that includes M2 in addition to all large time deposits, institutional money market funds, short-term repurchase agreements, and certain other large liquid assets.

Maloney Act An amendment enacted in 1938 to broaden Section 15 of the Securities Exchange Act of 1934. Named for its sponsor, the late Sen. Francis Maloney of Connecticut, the amendment provided for the creation of a self-regulatory organization for the specific purpose of supervising the over-the-counter securities market.

management company An investment company that trades various types of securities in a portfolio in accordance with specific objectives stated in the prospectus.

management fee Amount paid to the investment manager for its services in the supervision of the investment company's affairs. This fee is set as a percentage of the company's net assets.

margin The amount of equity contributed by a customer as a percentage of the current market value of the securities held in a margin account. *See also* equity; initial margin requirement; Regulation T.

market capitalization *See* capitalization.

market letter A publication that comments on securities, investing, the economy, or other related topics and is distributed to an organization's clients or to the public.

market maker A dealer willing to accept the risk of holding a particular security in its own account to facilitate trading in that security. *See also* make a market.

market order An order to be executed immediately at the best available price. A market order is the only order that guarantees execution. *Syn.* unrestricted order.

market risk The potential for an investor to experience losses owing to day-to-day fluctuations in the prices at which securities can be bought or sold.

market value Price at which investors buy or sell a share of common stock or a bond at a given time. Market value is determined by buyer and seller interaction.

marketability The ease with which a security can be bought or sold; having a readily available market for trading.

markup Difference between the lowest current offering price among dealers and the higher price a dealer charges a customer.

markup policy *See* 5% markup policy.

material information Any fact that could affect an investor's decision to trade a security.

maturity date Date on which a bond's principal is repaid to the investor and interest payments cease.

member (1) Of the New York Stock Exchange: one of the 1,366 individuals owning a seat on the Exchange. (2) Of the National Association of Securities Dealers: any broker or dealer admitted to membership in the Association.

member firm A broker/dealer in which at least one of the principal officers is a member of the New York Stock Exchange, another exchange, a self-regulatory organization, or a clearing corporation.

membership Members of the New York Stock Exchange, another exchange, an SRO, or a clearing corporation.

minimum death benefit The amount payable under a variable life insurance policy upon the policyowner's death, regardless of the separate account's investment performance. The insurance company guarantees the minimum amount.

monetary policy The Federal Reserve Board's actions that determine the size and rate of the money supply's growth, which in turn affect interest rates.

money market The securities market that deals in short-term debt. Money market instruments are very liquid forms of debt that mature in less than one year. Treasury bills make up the bulk of money market instruments.

money market fund A mutual fund that invests in short-term debt instruments. The fund's objective is to earn interest while maintaining a stable net asset value of $1 per share. Generally sold with no load, the fund may also offer draft-writing privileges and low opening investments.

money market instruments These are obligations that are commonly traded in the money market. These instruments are generally short-term and highly liquid. In addition to certain US government securities, such as T-bills, the following are commonly traded in the money market:

- bankers acceptance or BA
- certificate of deposit or CD
- commercial paper
- eurodollar deposit
- repurchase agreement or repo

money supply The total stock of bills, coins, loans, credit, and other liquid instruments in the economy. It is divided into four categories—L, M1, M2 and M3—according to the type of account in which the instrument is kept.

mortality guarantee All annuity contracts, fixed and variable, contain a mortality guarantee. This is the insurance company guarantee that the annuitant will receive payments as long as he lives. There is a charge made against the account as an operating expense to cover the cost of this guarantee. Mutual funds do NOT have a mortality guarantee.

MSRB *See* Municipal Securities Rulemaking Board.

multiplier effect The expansion of the money supply that results from a Federal Reserve System member bank's being able to lend more money than it takes in. A small increase in bank deposits generates a far larger increase in available credit.

municipal bond A debt security issued by a state, a municipality, or another subdivision (such as a school, park, sanitation or another local taxing district) to finance its capital expenditures. Such expenditures might include the construction of highways, public works or school buildings. *Syn.* municipal security.

municipal bond fund Mutual fund that invests in municipal bonds and operates either as a unit investment trust or an open-end fund. The fund's objective is to maximize federally tax-exempt income.

Municipal Securities Rulemaking Board (MSRB) A self-regulatory organization that regulates the issuance and trading of municipal securities. The Board functions under the Securities and Exchange Commission's supervision; it has no enforcement powers.

mutual fund An investment company that continuously offers new equity shares in an actively managed portfolio of securities. All shareholders participate in the fund's gains or losses. The shares are redeemable on any business day at the net asset value. Each mutual fund's portfolio is invested to match the objective stated in the prospectus. *Syn.* open-end investment company; open-end management company.

mutual fund custodian A national bank, stock exchange member firm, trust company, or another qualified institution that physically safeguards the securities a mutual fund holds. It does not manage the fund's investments; its function is solely clerical.

N

NASD *See* National Association of Securities Dealers, Inc.

NASD Bylaws The body of rules that describes how the NASD functions, defines its powers, and determines the qualifications and registration requirements for brokers.

NASD Conduct Rules Regulations designed to ensure that NASD member firms and their representatives follow fair and ethical trade practices when dealing with the public. The rules complement and broaden the Securities Act of 1933, the Securities Exchange Act of 1934, and the Investment Company Act of 1940.

NASD Department of Enforcement (Enforcement) A committee composed of up to 12 NASD members who each serves as Administrator for one of the 13 local NASD districts. The Department of Enforcement has original jurisdiction for hearing and judging complaints.

NASD Manual Publication that outlines NASD policies for regulating the OTC market. Included are the Conduct Rules, Uniform Practice Code, Code of Procedure, and Code of Arbitration Procedure.

Nasdaq *See* National Association of Securities Dealers Automated Quotation system.

National Association of Securities Dealers Automated Quotation system (Nasdaq) The nationwide electronic quotation system for up-to-the-minute bid and asked quotations on approximately 5,500 over-the-counter stocks.

National Association of Securities Dealers, Inc. (NASD) Organized under provisions of the 1938 Maloney Act; the NASD is the self-regulatory organization for the OTC market.

NAV *See* net asset value.

NAV of fund The net total of a mutual fund's assets and liabilities; used to calculate the price of new fund shares.

NAV per share Value of a mutual fund share, calculated by dividing the fund's total net asset value by the number of shares outstanding.

negotiability A characteristic of a security that permits the owner to assign, give, transfer, or sell it to another person without a third party's permission.

negotiable certificate of deposit (CD) An unsecured promissory note issued with a minimum face value of $100,000. It evidences a time deposit of funds with the issuing bank and is guaranteed by the bank.

negotiable order of withdrawal (NOW) account Bank account through which a customer can write drafts against money held on deposit; an interest-bearing checking account.

net asset value (NAV) A mutual fund share's value, calculated once a day, based on the closing market price for each security in the fund's portfolio. It is computed by deducting the fund's liabilities from the portfolio's total assets and dividing this amount by the number of shares outstanding.

net change The difference between a security's closing price on the trading day reported and the previous day's closing price. In over-the-counter transactions, the term refers to the difference between the closing bids.

net investment income The source of an investment company's dividend payments. It is calculated by subtracting the company's operating expenses from the total dividends and interest the company receives from the securities in its portfolio.

net investment return The rate of return from a variable life insurance separate account. The cumulative return for all years is applied to the benefit base when calculating the death benefit.

net worth Amount by which assets exceed liabilities. *Syn.* owners' equity; shareholders' equity; stockholders' equity.

new account form The form that must be filled out for each new account opened with a brokerage firm. The form specifies, at a minimum, the account owner, trading authorization, payment method, and types of securities appropriate for the customer.

new issue market The securities market for shares in privately owned businesses that are raising capital by selling common stock to the public for the first time. *Syn.* primary market.

New York Stock Exchange (NYSE) The largest stock exchange in the United States. It is a corporation, operated by a board of directors who is responsible for setting policy, supervising Exchange and member activities, listing securities, overseeing the transfer of members' seats on the Exchange, and judging whether an applicant is qualified to be a specialist.

no-load fund A mutual fund whose shares are sold without a commission or sales charge. The investment company distributes the shares directly.

nominal owner The person in whose name securities are registered if that person is other than the beneficial owner. This is a brokerage firm's role when customer securities are registered in street name.

nominal quote A quotation on an inactively traded security that does not represent an actual offer to buy or sell, but is given for informational purposes only.

nominal yield The interest rate stated on the face of a bond that represents the percentage of interest the issuer pays on the bond's face value. *Syn.* coupon rate; stated yield.

noncumulative preferred stock Equity security that does not have to pay any dividends in arrears to the holder.

nondiscrimination In a qualified retirement plan, a formula for calculating contributions and benefits that must be applied uniformly so as to ensure that all employees receive fair and equitable treatment.

nondiversification Portfolio management strategy that seeks to concentrate investments in a particular industry or geographic area in hopes of achieving higher returns.

nondiversified management company A management company that does not meet the diversification requirements of the Investment Company Act of 1940. Such a company is not restricted in the choice of securities or by the concentration of interest it has in those securities.

nonfixed unit investment trust An investment company that invests in a portfolio of securities and permits changes in the portfolio's makeup.

nonqualified retirement plan A corporate retirement plan that does not meet the standards set by the Employee Retirement Income Security Act of 1974.

nontax-qualified annuity An annuity that does not qualify for tax deductibility of contributions under IRS codes. It is funded with after-tax dollars, but the earnings in the account will accrue tax deferred. It is important to note that at payout of the annuity, all distributions in excess of the cost basis will be taxed as ordinary income.

note A short-term debt security, usually maturing in five years or less.

notification *See* registration by filing.

NOW account *See* negotiable order of withdrawal account.

numbered account Account titled with something other than a customer name. The title might be a number, symbol, or special title. A customer must sign a form designating account ownership.

NYSE *See* New York Stock Exchange.

O

odd lot An amount of a security that is less than the normal unit of trading for that security. Generally, an odd lot is fewer than 100 shares of stock or five bonds.

offer (1) *See* ask. (2) Under the Uniform Securities Act, any attempt to solicit a purchase or sale in a security for value.

open-end investment company *See* mutual fund.

option A security that represents the right to buy or sell a specified amount of an underlying security—a stock, bond, futures contract, etc.—at a specified price within a specified time. The purchaser acquires a right, and the seller assumes an obligation.

order memorandum Form completed by a registered representative that contains customer instructions regarding an order's placement. It contains such information as the customer's name and account number, a description of the security, the type of transaction (buy, sell, sell short, etc.) and any special instructions (such as time or price limits). *Syn.* order ticket.

ordinary income Earnings other than capital gain.

OTC *See* over-the-counter.

OTC market The security exchange system in which broker/dealers negotiate directly with one another rather than through an auction on an exchange floor. The trading takes place over computer and telephone networks that link brokers and dealers around the world. Both listed and OTC securities, as well as municipal and US government securities, trade in the OTC market.

outstanding stock Equity securities issued by a corporation and in the hands of the public; issued stock that the issuer has not reacquired.

over-the-counter (OTC) Term used to describe a security traded through the phone-linked and computer-connected OTC market rather than through an exchange.

P

par The dollar amount the issuer assigns to a security. For an equity security, par is usually a small dollar amount that bears no relationship to the security's market price. For a debt security, par is the amount repaid to the investor when the bond matures, usually $1,000. *Syn.* face value; principal; stated value.

parity In an exchange market, a situation in which all brokers bidding have equal standing and the winning bid is awarded by a random drawing. *See also* priority.

participating preferred stock Preferred stock that is entitled to its stated dividend and also to additional dividends as a specified percentage of dividends on common stock, if declared.

participation Provision of the Employee Retirement Income Security Act of 1974 requiring that all employees in a qualified retirement plan be covered within a reasonable time of their hire.

partnership A form of business organization in which two or more individuals manage the business and are equally and personally liable for its debts.

pass-through certificate Security representing an interest in a pool of conventional, VA, Farmers Home Administration, or other agency mortgages. The pool receives the principal and interest payments, which it passes through to each certificate holder. Payments may or may not be guaranteed.

payment date The day on which a declared dividend is paid to all stockholders owning shares on the record date.

payment period As defined by the Federal Reserve Board's Regulation T, the period of time corresponding to the regular way settlement period established by the NASD.

payout stage *See* distribution stage.

payroll deduction plan Retirement plan where an employee authorizes a deduction from his check on a regular basis. The plan may be qualified, such as a 401(k) plan, or nonqualified.

pension plan Contract between an individual and an employer, labor union, government entity, or another institution that provides for the distribution of pension benefits at retirement.

Pension Reform Act *See* Employee Retirement Income Security Act of 1974.

period certain annuity Settlement option that allows the annuitant to receive payments for as long as he lives, but also designates a minimum guaranteed period (i.e., 10 or 15 years) for which he will receive payments. If death occurs during this guaranteed period, then payments will continue for the remaining years of the period certain to a stated beneficiary.

periodic payment plan A mutual fund sales contract in which the customer commits to buying shares in the fund on a periodic basis over a long time period in exchange for a lower minimum investment.

person As defined in securities law, an individual, corporation, partnership, association, fund, joint stock company, unincorporated organization, trust, government, or political subdivision of a government.

personal income (PI) An individual's total earnings derived from wages, passive business enterprises, and investments.

pipeline theory *See* conduit theory.

point A measure of a bond's price; $10 or 1% of the par value of $1,000.

POP *See* public offering price.

portfolio income Earnings from interest, dividends, and all nonbusiness investments.

portfolio manager The entity responsible for investing a mutual fund's assets, implementing its investment strategy, and managing day-to-day portfolio trading. *Syn.* fund manager.

position The amount of a security either owned (a long position) or owed (a short position) by an individual or a dealer. Dealers take long positions in specific securities to maintain inventories and thereby facilitate trading.

possession of securities *See* control security.

power of substitution *See* stock power.

preemptive right A stockholder's legal right to maintain proportionate ownership by purchasing newly issued shares before the new stock is offered to the public.

preferred stock An equity security that represents ownership in a corporation. It is issued with a stated dividend, which must be paid before dividends are paid to common stock holders. It generally carries no voting rights.

preferred stock fund Mutual fund with investment objective of stable income and minimal capital risk; invests in income-producing instruments like preferred stock.

preliminary prospectus An abbreviated prospectus that is distributed while the SEC is reviewing an issuer's registration statement. It contains all of the essential facts about the forthcoming offering except the underwriting spread, final public offering price, and date on which the shares will be delivered. *Syn.* red herring.

premium The price of an option agreed upon by the buyer and seller through their representatives on the floor of an exchange. The premium is paid by a buyer to a seller.

primary offering The original sale of a security; all further trades are in the secondary market.

prime rate Interest rate commercial banks charge their prime or most creditworthy customers, generally large corporations.

principal (1) A person who trades for his own account in the primary or secondary market. (2) *See* dealer. (3) *See* par.

principal transaction A transaction in which a broker/dealer either buys securities from customers and takes them into its own inventory or sells securities to customers from its inventory.

private placement An offering of new issue securities that complies with Regulation D of the Securities Act of 1933. According to Regulation D, a security generally is not required to be registered with the SEC if it is offered to no more than 35 nonaccredited investors or to an unlimited number of accredited investors. *See also* Regulation D.

profit-sharing plan An employee benefit plan established and maintained by an employer whereby the employees receive a share of the business's profits. The money may be paid directly to the employees or deferred until retirement. A combination of both approaches is also possible.

progressive tax A tax that takes a larger percentage of the income of high-income earners than that of low-income earners (e.g., graduated income tax).

property dividend A distribution made by a corporation to its stockholders of securities it owns in other corporations or of its products.

prospectus *See* final prospectus.

proxy A limited power of attorney from a stockholder authorizing another person to vote on stockholder issues according to the first stockholder's instructions. To vote on corporate matters, a stockholder must attend the annual meeting or vote by proxy.

prudent investor rule A legal maxim that restricts discretion in a fiduciary account to only those investments that a reasonable and prudent person might make.

public offering The sale of an issue of common stock, either by a corporation going public or by an offering of additional shares.

public offering price (POP) (1) The price of new shares that is established in the issuing corporation's prospectus. (2) The price to investors for mutual fund shares, equal to the net asset value plus the sales charge.

put (1) Option contract giving the owner the right to sell a certain amount of an underlying security at a specified price within a specified time. (2) The act of exercising a put option.

put buyer Investor who pays a premium for an option contract and receives, for a specified time, the right to sell the underlying security at a specified price.

put writer Investor who receives a premium and takes on, for a specified time, the obligation to buy the underlying security at a specified price at the put buyer's discretion.

Q

qualification *See* registration by qualification.

qualified retirement plan A corporate retirement plan that meets the standards set by the Employee Retirement Income Security Act of 1974. Contributions to a qualified plan are tax deductible. *Syn.* approved plan.

quotation The price or bid a market maker or broker/dealer offers for a particular security. *Syn.* quote.

quote machine A computer that provides representatives and market makers with the information that appears on the Consolidated Tape. The information on the screen is condensed into symbols and numbers.

R

rating An evaluation of a corporate or municipal bond's relative safety, according to the issuer's ability to repay principal and make interest payments. Bonds are rated by various organizations, such as Standard & Poor's and Moody's. Ratings range from AAA or Aaa (the highest) to C or D (represents a company in default).

rating service A company, such as Moody's or Standard & Poor's, that rates various debt and preferred stock issues for safety of payment of principal, interest, or dividends. The issuing company or municipality pays a fee for the rating.

real estate investment trust (REIT) A corporation or trust that uses the pooled capital of many investors to invest in direct ownership of either income property or mortgage loans. These investments offer tax benefits in addition to interest and capital gains distributions.

realized gain Amount a taxpayer earns when he sells an asset.

recession General economic decline lasting from 6–18 months.

record date The date a corporation's board of directors establishes that determines which of its stockholders are entitled to receive dividends or rights distributions.

recovery *See* expansion.

red herring *See* preliminary prospectus.

redeemable security A security that the issuer redeems upon the holder's request. Examples include shares in an open-end investment company and Treasury notes.

redemption The return of an investor's principal in a security, such as a bond, preferred stock, or mutual fund shares. By law, redemption of mutual fund shares must occur within seven days of receiving the investor's request for redemption.

refunding Retiring an outstanding bond issue at maturity using money from the sale of a new offering. *See also* advance refunding.

regional exchange A stock exchange that serves the financial community in a particular region of the country. These exchanges tend to focus on securities issued within their regions, but also offer trading in NYSE- and AMEX-listed securities.

registered Term describing a security that prints the owner's name on the certificate. The owner's name is stored in records kept by the issuer or a transfer agent.

registered as to principal only The term describing a bond that prints the owner's name on the certificate, but that has unregistered coupons payable to the bearer. *Syn.* partially registered.

registered principal An associated person of a member firm who manages or supervises the firm's investment banking or securities business. This includes any individual who trains associated persons and who solicits business. Unless the member firm is a sole proprietorship, it must employ at least two registered principals, one of whom must be registered as a general securities principal and one of whom must be registered as a financial and operations principal. If the firm does options business with the public, it must employ at least one registered options principal.

registered representative (RR) Associated person engaged in the investment banking or securities business. According to the NASD, this includes any individual who supervises, solicits, or conducts business in securities or who trains people to supervise, solicit, or conduct business in securities. Anyone employed by a brokerage firm who is not a principal and who is not engaged in clerical or brokerage administration is subject to registration and exam licensing as a registered representative. *Syn.* account executive; stockbroker.

registrar The independent organization or part of a corporation responsible for accounting for all of the issuer's outstanding stock and certifying that its bonds constitute legal debt.

registration by coordination A process that allows a security to be sold in a state. It is available to an issuer that files for the security's registration under the Securities Act of 1933 and files duplicates of the registration documents with the state Administrator. State registration becomes effective at the same time the federal registration statement becomes effective.

registration by filing Process that allows a security to be sold in a state. It is available to an issuer that files for the security's registration under the Securities Act of 1933, meets minimum net worth and certain other requirements, and notifies the state of this eligibility by filing certain documents with the state Administrator.

State registration becomes effective at the same time the federal registration statement does. *Syn.* notification.

registration by qualification A process that allows a security to be sold in a state. It is available to an issuer who files for the security's registration with the state Administrator, meets minimum net worth, disclosure, and other requirements and files appropriate registration fees. The state registration becomes effective when the Administrator so orders. *Syn.* qualification.

registration statement The legal document that discloses all pertinent information concerning an offering of a security and its issuer. It is submitted to the SEC in accordance with the requirements of the Securities Act of 1933, and it forms the basis of the final prospectus distributed to investors.

regressive tax A tax that takes a larger percentage of the income of low-income earners than that of high-income earners. Examples include gasoline and cigarette tax.

regular way A settlement contract that calls for delivery and payment within a standard payment period from the date of the trade. The NASD's Uniform Practice Code sets the standard payment period. The type of security being traded determines the amount of time allowed for regular way settlement.

regulated investment company An investment company to which Subchapter M of the Internal Revenue Code grants special status that allows the flow-through of tax consequences on a distribution to shareholders. If 90% of its income is passed through to the shareholders, the company is not subject to tax on this income.

Regulation T The Federal Reserve Board regulation that governs customer cash accounts and the amount of credit that brokerage firms and dealers may extend to customers for the purchase of securities. Regulation T currently sets the loan value of marginable securities at 50 percent and the payment deadline at two days beyond regular way settlement.

reinvestment privilege A service provided by most mutual funds for the automatic reinvestment of a shareholder's dividend and capital gain distributions in additional shares.

REIT *See* real estate investment trust.

restricted security An unregistered, nonexempt security acquired either directly or indirectly from the issuer, or an affiliate of the issuer, in a transaction that does not involve a public offering. *See also* holding period.

retirement account A customer account established to provide retirement funds.

return on investment (ROI) Profit or loss resulting from a security transaction, often expressed as an annual percentage rate.

revenue bond A municipal debt issue whose interest and principal are payable only from the specific earnings of an income-producing public project. *See also* double-barreled bond; general obligation bond; municipal bond; special revenue bond.

right Security representing a stockholder's entitlement to the first opportunity to purchase new shares issued by the corporation at a predetermined price (normally less than the current market price) in proportion to the number of shares already owned. Rights are issued for a short time only, after which they expire. *Syn.* subscription right; subscription right certificate.

right of accumulation A benefit offered by a mutual fund that allows the investor to qualify for reduced sales loads on additional purchases according to the fund account's total dollar value.

right of withdrawal An Investment Company Act of 1940 provision that allows an investor in a mutual fund contractual plan to terminate the plan within 45 days from the mailing date of the written notice detailing the sales charges that will apply over the plan's life. The investor is then entitled to a refund of all sales charges.

right to refund A benefit of a mutual fund front-end load plan that entitles an investor who cancels the plan within 18 months to receive the investment's current value and a refund of sales charges exceeding 15%.

rights agent Issuing corporation's agent responsible for maintaining current records of the names of rights certificate owners.

rights offering An issue of new shares of stock accompanied by the opportunity for each stockholder to maintain a proportionate ownership by purchasing additional shares in the corporation before the shares are offered to the public.

risk

1. **business or financial risk** The risk that the business in which you have invested money will not do well.

2. **credit risk** A risk that applies with debt securities (bonds). The investor has extended credit to the issuer when he buys their bonds. This is the risk that the issuer will be unable to pay the investor back.

3. **liquidity risk** The risk that an investment cannot be easily liquidated or sold.

4. **market risk** The uncertainty that a particular security may fluctuate in price solely due to investor sentiment in the market. Sometimes called systematic risk.

5. **money rate or interest rate risk** Interest rates and price have an inverse relationship for securities sold primarily for their fixed income like bonds and preferred stock. This is the risk that as interest rates rise, prices of these securities will fall.

6. **purchasing power or inflation risk** The uncertainty that a dollar will not purchase as much in the future as it does now. This risk is found in all fixed dollar securities such as bonds and fixed annuities.

7. **reinvestment risk** The risk that a purchaser of a fixed income security incurs that interest rates will be lower when the purchaser seeks to reinvest income received from the security.

rollover The transfer of funds from one qualified retirement plan to another qualified retirement plan. If this is not done within a specified time period, the funds are taxed as ordinary income.

Roth IRA Contributions are nondeductible and distributions taken for certain qualifying purposes are tax-free. Contribution limit is $4,000 per year (in 2005), but offset by contributions to a traditional IRA.

round lot A security's normal unit of trading, which is generally 100 shares of stock or five bonds.

Rule 405 NYSE rule requiring that each member organization exercise due diligence to learn the essential facts about every customer. *Syn.* know your customer rule.

S

sales charge *See* commission.

sales literature Any written material a firm distributes to customers or the public in a controlled manner (e.g., circulars, research reports, form letters, market letters, text for seminars).

sales load Amount added to a mutual fund share's net asset value to arrive at the offering price.

savings bond A government debt security that is not negotiable or transferable and that may not be used as collateral.

scheduled premium policy A variable life insurance policy under which the insurer fixes both the amount and the timing of the premium payments.

SEC *See* Securities and Exchange Commission.

secondary market The market in which securities are bought and sold subsequent to their being sold to the public for the first time.

sector fund A mutual fund whose investment objective is to capitalize on the return potential provided by investing primarily in a particular industry or sector of the economy. *Syn.* industry fund; specialized fund.

Securities Act of 1933 Federal legislation requiring the full and fair disclosure of all material information about the issuance of new securities. *Syn.* Act of 1933; Full Disclosure Act; New Issues Act; Prospectus Act; Trust in Securities Act; Truth in Securities Act.

Securities Acts Amendments of 1975 Federal legislation that established the Municipal Securities Rulemaking Board.

Securities and Exchange Commission (SEC) Commission created by Congress to regulate the securities markets and protect investors. It is composed of five commissioners appointed by the President of the United States and approved by the Senate. The SEC enforces, among other acts, the Securities Act of 1933, the Securities Exchange Act of 1934, the Trust Indenture Act of 1939, the Investment Company Act of 1940, and the Investment Advisers Act of 1940.

Securities Exchange Act of 1934 Federal legislation that established the Securities and Exchange Commission. The act aims to protect investors by regulating the exchanges, the over-the-counter market, the extension of credit by the Federal Reserve Board, broker/dealers, insider transactions, trading activities, client accounts, and net capital. *Syn.* act of 1934; Exchange Act.

Securities Investor Protection Corporation (SIPC) A nonprofit membership corporation created by an act of Congress to protect clients of brokerage firms forced into bankruptcy. Membership is composed of all brokers and dealers registered under the Securities Exchange Act of 1934, all members of national securities exchanges, and most NASD members. SIPC provides brokerage firm customers up to $500,000 coverage for cash and securities held by the firms (cash coverage is limited to $100,000).

security Other than an insurance policy or a fixed annuity, any piece of securitized paper that can be traded for value. Under the act of 1934, this includes any note, stock, bond, investment contract, debenture, certificate of interest in a profit-sharing or partnership agreement, certificate of deposit, collateral trust certificate, preorganization certificate, option on a security, or other instrument of investment commonly known as a *security*.

self-regulatory organization (SRO) One of eight organizations accountable to the SEC for the enforcement of federal securities laws and the supervision of securities practices within an assigned field of jurisdiction. For example, the NASD regulates the over-the-counter market; the Municipal Securities Rulemaking Board supervises state and municipal securities; and certain exchanges, such as the New York Stock Exchange and the Chicago Board Options Exchange, act as self-regulatory bodies to promote ethical conduct and standard trading practices.

sell To convey ownership of a security or another asset for money or value. This includes giving or delivering a security with or as a bonus for a purchase of securities, a gift of assessable stock, and selling or offering a warrant or right to purchase or subscribe to another security. Not included in the definition is a bona fide pledge or loan or a stock dividend if nothing of value is given by the stockholders for the dividend. *Syn.* sale.

selling away Associated person engaging in private securities transactions without the employing broker/dealer's knowledge and consent. Violates NASD Conduct Rules.

selling dividends (1) Illegal practice of inducing customers to buy mutual fund shares by implying that an upcoming distribution will benefit them. (2) Combining dividend and gains distributions when calculating current yield.

selling group Selected broker/dealers who contract to act as selling agents for underwriters and who are compensated by a portion of the spread called selling concession on newly issued securities. They assume no personal responsibility or financial liability to the issuer, as opposed to a syndicate member.

SEP *See* simplified employee pension plan.

separate account The account that holds funds paid by variable annuity contract holders. The funds are kept separate from the insurer's general account and are invested in a portfolio of securities that match the contract holders' objectives.

Separate Trading of Registered Interest and Principal of Securities (STRIPS) A zero-coupon bond issued and backed by the Treasury Department.

Series 6 The investment company/variable contract products limited representative license, which entitles the holder to sell mutual funds and variable annuities and is used by many firms that sell primarily insurance-related products. The Series 6 can serve as the prerequisite for the Series 26 license.

Series 7 General securities registered representative license; entitles the holder to sell all types of securities products, with the exception of commodities futures (requires Series 3). Series 7 is the most comprehensive of the NASD representative licenses and a prerequisite for most NASD principal examinations.

Series 26 The investment company/variable contract products limited principal license, which entitles the holder to supervise the sale of investment company and variable annuity products. A Series 6 or a Series 7 qualification is a prerequisite for this license.

Series 63 The Uniform Securities Agent State Law Exam, which entitles the successful candidate to sell securities and give investment advice in those states that require Series 63 registration.

Series 65 The Uniform Investment Adviser Law Exam, which entitles the successful candidate to sell securities and give investment advice in those states that require Series 65 registration.

Series EE bond A nonmarketable, interest-bearing US government savings bond issued at a discount from par. Interest on Series EE bonds is exempt from state and local taxes.

Series HH bond A nonmarketable, interest-bearing US government savings bond issued at par and purchased only by trading in Series EE bonds at maturity. Interest on Series HH bonds is exempt from state and local taxes.

settlement Completion of a trade through the delivery of a security or commodity and the payment of cash or other consideration.

settlement date Date on which ownership changes between buyer and seller. The NASD's Uniform Practice Code standardizes settlement provisions.

settlement options (variable or fixed annuity)

   1. joint and survivorship This annuity pays until the last of two parties dies. It's most commonly used for husband and wife and generally the annuitants receive the smallest payments when this option is selected.

   2. life only (straight life) This option provides that the annuitant will be paid as long as he lives. As the annuitant is assuming greater risk that he may die sooner than expected, his payout is greatest with this option.

   3. life with period certain Settlement option that allows the annuitant to receive payments for as long as he lives, but also designates a minimum guaranteed period (i.e., 10 or 15 years) for which he will receive payments. If death occurs during this guaranteed period, then payments will continue for the remaining years of the period certain to a stated beneficiary.

75-5-10 test The standard for judging whether an investment company qualifies as diversified under the Investment Company Act of 1940. Under this act, a diversified investment company must invest at least 75% of its total assets in cash, receivables, or invested securities. This 75% must be invested in such a way that no more than 5% of its total assets are invested in any one company's voting securities, and no single investment may represent ownership of more than 10% of any one company's outstanding voting securities.

share identification An accounting method that identifies the specific shares selected for liquidation in the event that an investor wishes to liquidate shares. The difference between the buying and selling prices determines the investor's tax liability.

share of beneficial interest *See* unit of beneficial interest.

short Term used to describe the selling of a security, contract, or commodity that the seller does not own (e.g., an investor who borrows shares of stock from a broker/dealer and sells them on the open market has a short position in the stock).

simplified arbitration A method of arbitration to be used when there is a small amount in dispute, no more than $25,000. This method can be used for disputes between members (simplified industry arbitration) and for disputes between a customer and a member (simplified arbitration) if the customer has agreed to arbitration.

simplified employee pension plan (SEP) A qualified retirement plan designed for employers with 25 or fewer employees. Contributions made to each employee's individual retirement account grow tax deferred until retirement. *See also* individual retirement account.

single account An account in which only one individual has control over the investments and may transact business.

single payment deferred annuity Method of purchasing an annuity in which the annuitant deposits one lump sum of money into the account and elects to have the money remain in the account and accrue tax deferred until the annuitant elects to begin the pay-out phase at a later time (deferred).

single payment immediate annuity This method of purchasing an annuity is one in which the annuitant deposits one lump sum of money into the account and elects to begin the pay-out phase immediately.

SIPC *See* Securities Investor Protection Corporation.

special deals A mutual fund underwriter's improper practice of disbursing anything of material value (more than $100) in addition to normal discounts or concessions associated with the sale or distribution of investment company shares.

special situation fund A mutual fund whose objective is to capitalize on the profit potential of corporations in nonrecurring circumstances, such as those undergoing reorganizations or being considered as takeover candidates.

specialized fund *See* sector fund.

sponsor A person who is instrumental in organizing, selling, or managing a limited partnership.

spousal account A separate individual retirement account established for a nonworking spouse. Contributions to the account made by the working spouse grow tax deferred until withdrawal.

spread In a quotation, the difference between a security's bid and ask prices.

spread load A system of sales charges for a mutual fund contractual plan. It permits a decreasing scale of sales charges, with a maximum charge of 20% in any one year and 9% over the life of the plan. Rights of withdrawal with no penalty exist for 45 days.

SRO *See* self-regulatory organization.

standby underwriting agreement An agreement between an investment banker and a corporation, whereby the banker agrees, for a negotiated fee, to purchase any or all shares offered as a subscription privilege that are not bought by the rights holders by the time the offer expires. Because this guarantees the issuer that all shares will be sold either to the rights holders or the investment banker, this is considered a form of firm commitment underwriting.

stated yield *See* nominal yield.

statutory disqualification Prohibiting a person from associating with a SRO because the person has been expelled, barred, or suspended from association with a member of an SRO; has had registration suspended, denied, or revoked by the SEC; has been the cause of someone else's suspension, barment, or revocation; has been convicted of certain crimes; or has falsified an application or a report that he must file with or on behalf of a membership organization.

statutory voting Voting procedure that permits stockholders to cast one vote per share owned for each position. The procedure tends to benefit majority stockholders.

stock certificate Written evidence of ownership in a corporation.

stock dividend *See* dividend.

stock power A standard form that duplicates the back of a stock certificate and is used for transferring the stock to the new owner's name. A separate stock power is used if a security's registered owner does not have the certificate available for signature endorsement. *Syn.* irrevocable stock power; power of substitution.

stock quote A list of representative prices bid and asked for a stock during a particular trading day. Stocks are quoted in points; one point equals $1. Stock quotes are listed in the financial press and most daily newspapers.

stock split An increase in the number of a corporation's outstanding shares, which decreases its stock's par value. The market value of the total number of shares remains the same. The proportional reductions in orders held on the books for a split stock are calculated by dividing the stock's market price by the fraction that represents the split.

stockbroker *See* registered representative.

Subchapter M The section of the Internal Revenue Code that provides special tax treatment for regulated investment companies.

subordinated debenture A debt obligation, backed by the general credit of the issuing corporation, that has claims to interest and principal subordinated to ordinary debentures and all other liabilities. *See also* debenture.

suitability Determination made by a registered representative as to whether a particular security matches a customer's objectives and financial capability. The representative must have enough information about the customer to make this judgment.

supervision System implemented by a broker/dealer to ensure that its employees and associated persons comply with the rules and regulations of the SEC, exchanges, and SROs.

syndicate A group of investment bankers formed to handle the distribution and sale of a security on behalf of the issuer. Each syndicate member is responsible for the sale and distribution of a portion of the issue. *Syn.* underwriting syndicate.

T

taxability Risk of erosion of investment income through taxation.

taxable gain The portion of a sale or distribution of mutual fund shares subject to taxation.

tax-deferred annuity *See* tax-sheltered annuity.

tax-equivalent yield Rate of return a taxable bond must earn before taxes in order to equal the tax-exempt earnings on a municipal bond. This number varies with the investor's tax bracket.

tax-exempt bond fund Mutual fund whose investment objective is to provide maximum tax-free income. Invests primarily in municipal bonds and short-term debt. *Syn.* tax-free bond fund.

tax-free bond fund *See* tax-exempt bond fund.

tax liability Amount of tax payable on earnings, usually calculated by subtracting standard and itemized deductions and personal exemptions from adjusted gross income, then multiplying by the tax rate.

tax-sheltered annuity (TSA) An insurance contract that entitles the holder to exclude all contributions from gross income in the year they are made. Tax payable on the earnings is deferred until the holder withdraws funds at retirement. TSAs are available to employees of public schools, church organizations, and other tax-exempt organizations. *Syn.* tax-deferred annuity.

tenants in common (TIC) A form of joint ownership of an account whereby a deceased tenant's fractional interest in the account is retained by his estate.

third-party account (1) A customer account for which the owner has given power of attorney to a third party. (2) A customer account opened by an adult naming a minor as beneficial owner. (3) A customer account opened for another adult. This type of account is prohibited.

time deposit Sum of money left with a bank (or borrowed from a bank and left on deposit) that the depositing customer has agreed not to withdraw for a specified time period or without a specified amount of notice.

tombstone Printed advertisement that solicits indications of interest in a securities offering. Text is limited to basic information about the offering, such as the name of the issuer, type of security, names of the underwriters, and where a prospectus is available.

trade confirmation A printed document that contains details of a transaction, including the settlement date and amount of money due from or owed to a customer. It must be sent to the customer on or before the settlement date.

trade date Date on which a securities transaction is executed.

trading authorization *See* full trading authorization; limited trading authorization.

transfer agent Person or corporation responsible for recording the names and holdings of registered security owners, seeing that certificates are signed by the appropriate corporate officers, affixing the corporate seal, and delivering securities to the new owners.

transfer and hold in safekeeping A securities buy order settlement and delivery procedure whereby the securities bought are transferred to the customer's name, but are held by the broker/dealer.

transfer and ship A securities buy order settlement and delivery procedure whereby the securities bought are transferred to the customer's name and sent to the customer.

Treasury bill A marketable US government debt security with a maturity of less than six months. T-bills are issued through a competitive bidding process at a discount from par; they have no fixed interest rate.

Treasury bond A marketable, fixed-interest US government debt security with a maturity of more than 10 years.

Treasury note A marketable, fixed-interest US government debt security with a maturity of between 1 and 10 years. *Syn.* T-note.

Treasury receipt Generic term for a zero-coupon bond issued by a brokerage firm and collateralized by the Treasury securities a custodian holds in escrow for the investor.

Treasury stock Equity securities that the issuing corporation has issued and repurchased from the public at the current market price.

trust indenture A written agreement between issuer and creditors by which the terms of a debt issue are set forth, such as rate of interest, means of payment, maturity date, terms of prior payment of principal, collateral, priorities of claims, and trustee.

trustee Person legally appointed to act on a beneficiary's behalf.

Truth in Securities Act *See* Securities Act of 1933.

TSA *See* tax-sheltered annuity.

12b-1 asset-based fees An Investment Company Act of 1940 provision that allows a mutual fund to collect a fee for the promotion or sale of or another activity connected with the distribution of its shares. The fee cannot exceed .75% of average net assets.

20-day cooling off period A period of 20 calendar days following the filing of a registration statement with the SEC, during which the SEC examines the statement for deficiencies, the issuing corporation negotiates with an underwriting syndicate for a final agreement, and the syndicate prepares for the successful distribution of the impending issue. The final day of the period is normally considered the effective date, unless otherwise stated by the SEC.

U

UGMA *See* Uniform Gifts to Minors Act.

UIT *See* unit investment trust.

underwriter An investment banker who works with an issuer to help bring a security to the market and sell it to the public.

underwriting The procedure by which investment bankers channel investment capital from investors to corporations and municipalities that are issuing securities.

underwriting spread The difference in price between the public offering price and the price an underwriter pays to the issuing corporation. The difference represents the profit available to the syndicate or selling group. *Syn.* underwriting discount; underwriting split.

unearned income Income derived from investments and other sources not related to employment services. Examples of unearned income include interest from a savings account, bond interest, and dividends from stock.

Uniform Gifts (Transfers) to Minors Act (UGMA or UTMA) Legislation that permits a gift of money or securities to be given to a minor and held in a custodial account that an adult manages for the minor's benefit. Income and capital gains transferred to a minor's name are taxed at a lower rate.

Uniform Investment Adviser Law Exam *See* Series 65.

Uniform Practice Code (UPC) The NASD policy that establishes guidelines for a brokerage firm's dealings with other brokerage firms.

Uniform Securities Act (USA) Model legislation for securities industry regulation at the state level. Each state may adopt the legislation in its entirety or it may adapt it (within limits) to suit its needs.

Uniform Securities Agent State Law Exam (USASLE) *See* Series 63.

Uniform Transfers to Minors Act (UTMA) Legislation adopted in some states that permits a gift of money or securities to be given to a minor and held in a custodial account that an adult manages for the minor's benefit until the minor reaches a certain age (not necessarily the age of majority).

unissued stock That portion of authorized stock not distributed (sold) to investors by a newly chartered corporation.

unit investment trust (UIT) An investment company that sells redeemable shares in a professionally selected portfolio of securities. It is organized under a trust indenture, not a corporate charter.

unit of beneficial interest A redeemable share in a unit investment trust, representing ownership of an undivided interest in the underlying portfolio. *Syn.* share of beneficial interest.

unit refund annuity Insurance contract in which the insurance company makes monthly payments to an annuitant over the annuitant's lifetime. If the annuitant dies before receiving an amount equal to the account's value, money remaining in the account goes to the annuitant's named beneficiary.

unrealized capital appreciation or depreciation The amount by which the market value of portfolio holdings on a given date exceeds or falls short of their cost is considered unrealized gain or loss.

unrealized gain Amount by which a security appreciates in value before it is sold. Until it is sold, the investor does not actually possess the sale proceeds.

US government and agency bond fund A mutual fund whose investment objective is to provide current income while preserving safety of capital through investing in securities backed by the US Treasury or issued by a government agency.

USA *See* Uniform Securities Act.

V

variable annuity An insurance contract in which at the end of the accumulation stage, the insurance company guarantees a minimum total payment to the annuitant. The performance of a separate account, generally invested in equity securities, determines the amount of this total payment.

variable death benefit The amount paid to a decedent's beneficiary that depends on the investment performance of an insurance company's separate account. The amount is added to any guaranteed minimum death benefit.

variable life insurance policy Insurance contract that provides financial compensation to the insured's named beneficiary if the insured dies. The insurance company guarantees payment of a minimum amount plus an additional sum according to the performance of a separate account, usually invested in equities or other high-yielding securities.

vesting (1) An ERISA guideline stipulating that an employee must be entitled to their entire retirement benefits within a certain period of time even if he no longer works for the employer. (2) The amount of time that an employee must work before retirement or before benefit plan contributions made by the employer become the employee's property without penalty. The IRS and the Employee Retirement Income Security Act of 1974 set minimum requirements for vesting in a qualified plan.

volatility The magnitude and frequency of changes in the price of a security or commodity within a given time period.

voluntary accumulation plan A mutual fund account into which the investor commits to depositing amounts on a regular basis in addition to the initial sum invested.

voluntary contribution An additional contribution an employee makes to a Keogh plan to supplement plan benefits. Contribution amount is limited to 10% of the employee's compensation. Although the contribution is not tax deductible, the resultant earnings are not subject to tax until retirement.

voting right A stockholder's right to vote for members of the BOD and on matters of corporate policy, particularly the issuance of senior securities, stock splits, and substantial changes in the corporation's business. A variation of this right is extended to variable annuity contract holders and mutual fund shareholders, who may vote on material policy issues.

W

warrant Security that gives the holder the right to purchase securities from the warrant issuer at a stipulated subscription price. Usually long-term instruments with expiration dates years in the future.

wash sale Selling a security at a loss for tax purposes and, within 30 days before or after, purchasing the same or a substantially identical security. The IRS disallows the claimed loss.

withdrawal plan Benefit offered by a mutual fund whereby a customer receives the proceeds of periodic systematic liquidation of shares in the account. The amounts received may be based on a fixed dollar amount, a fixed number of shares, a fixed percentage, or a fixed period of time.

writer The seller of an option contract. An option writer takes on the obligation to buy or sell the underlying security if and when the option buyer exercises the option. *Syn.* seller.

Y

yield Rate of return on an investment, often expressed as an annual percentage rate.

yield curve A graphic representation of the actual or projected yields of fixed-income securities in relation to their maturities.

yield to maturity (YTM) The rate of return on a bond that accounts for the difference between the bond's acquisition cost and its maturity proceeds, including interest income. *See also* bond yield.

Z

zero-coupon bond Corporate or municipal debt security traded at a deep discount from face value. The bond pays no interest, but it may be redeemed at maturity for its full face value. It may be issued at a discount or stripped of its coupons and repackaged.

Index

Numerics

1035 Exchange provision, 209
12b-1 funds, 105
12b-1 plans, 112–113
20-day cooling-off period, 175
27-H plan, 128–130
401(k) plans, 221
403(b) plans, 220–221
529 plans, 216

A

acceptance, waiver, and consent, 343, 344
accounts
    for employees of other brokers, 325
    frozen, 186
    opening, 321–326
    sales charges, 111–120
    shared, 339–340
    SIPC coverage of, 225
    statements of, 106
    types of, 125–131, 326–331
accredited investor, 174
accumulation, rights of, 276, 280
accumulation plans, 126
    contractual, 127–130
    voluntary, 126–127
accumulation units, 142
additional issues, 170
additional offerings. See additional issues, 7
adjustable-rate dividend, 15
adjustment bonds. See income bonds
advertisements
    tombstone, 176
advertising, 255–256
    generic, 258
    review and approval of, 259–260
agency issues, governmental, 57–60, 64
agent. See brokers and brokers/dealers, 34
aggressive investment strategies, 121
American depositary receipts (ADRs), 22
annuities. See also variable annuity
    payment options, 143–146
    purchasing, 142
    taxation of, 206, 209
    types of, 136
annuitization, 143, 143–144

annuity death benefit, 145
annuity units, 142
Anti-Money Laundering Rules, NASD, 350
appeal process. Code of Procedure, 345
ask price, 91
asset-to-debt ratio, 97–98
asset allocation funds, 117
assets, 5
associated persons, 195, 233–235, 238–242
    definition of, 4
assumed interest rate, 151
assumed interest rate (AIR), 143–144
authorized stock, 7
average cost basis accounting, 202

B

back-end sales load, 112, 281–282
balanced funds, 116
balanced investment strategies, 121
balance of payments, 74
balance sheet, 5
bank-grade bonds. See investment-grade bonds
banker's acceptance, 65
barring, 345
basis, 201–202, 203, 206–207, 209
bearer bonds, 34
bearish position. See short position
best efforts arrangement, 171
bid price, 91
Blend/core funds, 116
blue-skying, 169, 173, 175
blue-sky laws. See Uniform Securities Act
board of directors, 10, 101–102
bond funds, 117–118
bond quotes, 32, 35, 52–53
bonds, 31
    characteristics of, 31–33
    debt service, 39–41
    pricing of, 35
    registration of, 33–34
    types of, 38
bonus annuities, 142
book-entry bonds, 34
book value, 9
branch office, 232
breakpoints, 276, 277

breakpoint sales, 337
breakpoint sales prohibited, 278
brokerage office procedures, 184–191
broker loan rate, 73
brokers and broker/dealers, 182–183
    definition of, 4
    registration of, 193, 232
bullish position. See long position
business cycle, 69
business risk, 303

C

callable preferred stock, 18–19
callable securities, 40
callable Treasury bonds, 55
call loan rate (call money rate). See broker loan rate
call option, 28–29
call premium, 40
call risk, 40, 305–306
capital gains, 12, 124, 198, 201–202
    mutual fund distributions from, 197
capital in excess of par (capital surplus), 9
capitalization, 5
capital losses, 204
capital market, 64
capital risk, 303
carry forward, 201
cash dividends, 19
cash settlement, 185
cash value insurance. See whole life insurance
cash value of life insurance policy, 148, 151–152
censure, 345
Central Registration Depository (CRD) of NASD, 236
certificates of deposit (CDs), 65
check-writing privileges, 118
Chicago Board Options Exchange (CBOE), 28
Chinese wall, 227
churning, 329, 336
Class A mutual fund shares, 277
Class B shares, 281
Class C shares, 282
close-out transaction, 186
closed-end funds, 111

HotSheets

Investment Banker

— Assists issuer in raising capital

Stock Classifications

— Authorized—number of shares corporation is permitted to issue

— Issued—has been sold to the public

— Treasury—repurchased by corporation; no voting rights, get no dividends

— Outstanding—number of shares held by the public

— Treasury = issued – outstanding

— Outstanding = issued – Treasury

Stock Valuations

— Par—arbitrary accounting value

— Book—liquidation or net worth value

— Market—value determined by supply and demand

Preemptive Rights

— Allow shareholders to maintain proportionate interest

Voting Rights

— Directors, issuance of convertible bonds or preferred stock; not on dividend payment or amount

Dividends

— Paid quarterly

— Declaration, Ex, Record, and Payable date

Stock Splits

— Normal: more shares, less value per share, same total value before and after

— Reverse: fewer shares, more value per share, same total value before and after

Preferred Stock

— Par value = $100

— Stated (fixed) dividend rate

— Priority over common stock in liquidation and dividend payment

— Typically no voting rights

Current Yield

— Annual dividends divided by current market price

Rights

— 30–45 day duration

— Strike price below market

— Trade as a separate security

— Available to existing shareholders only; one right per share outstanding

Warrants

— Long term

— Strike price above market

— Trade as separate security; offered as sweeteners

ADRs

— No preemptive rights

— Dividends paid in dollars; declared in foreign currency

— Subject to currency or exchange risk

Investment Grade Bonds

— Baa or BBB and above, based on default risk, ability to pay interest and principal when due

Call Features

— Called by issuer when interest rates are falling; no interest paid after call
— Issuer cannot call during call protection period

Refunding

— Refinancing at a lower rate, done when interest rates are declining

Corporate Bonds

— Called funded debt (more than one year to maturity)
— Secured: mortgage, collateral trust (backed by securities), equipment trust certificates
— Unsecured: backed by full faith and credit, debentures and subordinated debentures

Bond Ratings

— Standard & Poor and Moody's rating services
— Bank (Investment) Grade: AAA (Aaa) to BBB (Bbb)
— Speculative (High Yield): BB (Bb) to C or D speculative

Bond Yields

— Current yield = annual interest ÷ current market price

Convertibles

— Convert to common shares at conversion price
— Conversion changes investment objective from income to growth
— Conversion feature benefits the investor
— Issues with lower coupon than nonconvertibles

CMOs

— Mortgage-backed pass-through certificates

— Subject to interest rate and prepayment risk

— Issued in $25,000 denominations

Money Markets

— Commercial paper: most heavily traded; corporate issue; issued at a discount, 270-day maximum maturity

— Negotiable CD: minimum face of $100,000, issued by banks

— Bankers' acceptances: time draft, letter of credit for foreign trade; 270-day maximum maturity; issued at a discount

Interest Rates

— Fed funds rate most volatile, established by market; discount rate set by FRB

Municipals

— GOs backed by taxes, revenues backed by user fees; interest is not taxable at the federal level

— IDRs may be taxable

Governments

— Bills quoted at a discount, notes and bonds in 32nds; notes/bonds can be callable, bills are not

— Treasury STRIPS are backed in full by the US government

— Treasury receipts are not directly backed

Agencies

— Ginnie Maes are backed in full by US government

— Fannie Maes and Freddie Macs are not

CMOs and REMICs

— Fully taxable monthly interest

Relationship Between Bond Prices and Yields to Maturity

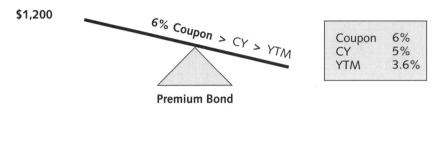

$1,200

6% Coupon > CY > YTM

Premium Bond

Coupon	6%
CY	5%
YTM	3.6%

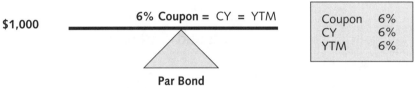

$1,000

6% Coupon = CY = YTM

Par Bond

Coupon	6%
CY	6%
YTM	6%

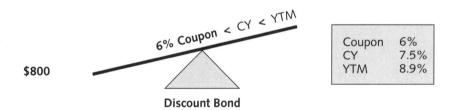

6% Coupon < CY < YTM

$800

Discount Bond

Coupon	6%
CY	7.5%
YTM	8.9%

Money Supply

— Fiscal policy: set by government through taxes and spending

— Monetary policy: set by FRB through discount rate, FOMC (most used tool), and reserve requirement (most drastic)

Currency Exchange

— Strong currency can be exchanged for more foreign currency (good for importers)

— Weak currency can be exchanged for less foreign currency (good for exporters)

PRODUCT INFORMATION: INVESTMENT COMPANY SECURITIES AND VARIABLE CONTRACTS HOTSHEET

Investment Company Act of 1940

— Defines and regulates investment companies

— Three types: FAC, UIT, management company

Open-End Company

— Mutual fund; continuous primary offering; redemption in seven calendar days; priced by formula in prospectus; fractional shares

Closed-End Company

— Trades in secondary market; issues debt and equity; fixed number of shares; sold with prospectus in IPO only

Diversified Status

— **75%** invested in other companies; maximum of **5%** in any one company; can own no more than **10%** of a target company's voting stock

— Status applies to open- and closed-end companies

Registration Requirements

— Minimum $100,000 capital; 100 investors; clearly defined investment objective

— Asset-to-debt ratio not less than 3:1 (300%)

Prohibited Investing

— No purchases on margin; no short sales; no naked options sold

— No participation in joint trading accounts

Shareholder Votes

— Change investment objective; change sales load policy; change fund classification; 12b-1 fees; board of directors

Objectives

— Growth = stock funds

— Income = bond funds, preferred stock funds

— Safety of principal = government bond funds

— Immediate liquidity = money market funds

— Aggressive growth = technology stock funds or stock funds invested in new companies, small caps

— Conservative growth = blue-chip stock funds

— Highest possible income with little concern for risk = corporate bond fund

— High tax bracket seeking income = municipal bond fund

— Income-producing stock = blue-chip stock fund, preferred stock fund, utility stock fund

— Mirror performance of the stock market overall; low expenses = index fund

Shareholder Reports

— Annual audited report; semiannual unaudited report (two reports per year total)

Sector Funds

— Minimum of 25% of assets in area of specialty; more aggressive

Money Market Funds

— No load; fixed NAV; check-writing privileges; daily interest

Performance History

— 1, 5, 10 years (or fund's life if less than 10 years)

Sales Charge %

— (POP − NAV) ÷ POP; (NASD maximum of 8.5% of POP)

POP Calculation

— NAV ÷ (100% − SC%)

$$NAV = POP - SC$$

$$\frac{NAV}{100\% - SC} = POP$$

Ex-Dividend Date

— Determined by BOD; typically business day after record date

Dollar Cost Averaging

— Produces an average cost per share that is lower than average price per share; no guarantees allowed

Contractual Plans

— Refunds:

Front-End Load Act	Spread-Load Act
— Before 45 days: NAV + 100% SC	— Before 45 days: NAV + 100% SC
— After 45 days, before 18 months: NAV + SC exceeding 15% of investment	— After 45 days: NAV only
— After 18 months: NAV only	

Variable Annuities

Fixed Annuity

— Guaranteed monthly payment

— Insurance company has investment risk

— Annuitant faces purchasing power risk

— Fixed income guaranteed for life

— Not a security

Variable Annuity

— Monthly payment dependent on separate account performance

— Investor has investment risk

— Sold with prospectus

— Can keep pace with inflation

— Variable income guaranteed for life; principal is not guaranteed

Combination Annuity

— Minimum fixed plus variable payout

Accumulation Phase

— Investor pays money to insurer to purchase accumulation units
— Units vary in value according to separate account performance

Purchase Methods

— Periodic deferred—paid in variable installments; variable payouts taken later
— Single premium immediate—lump-sum payment; payouts begin immediately; no accumulation period
— Single premium deferred—lump-sum payment; payouts taken later

Annuity Phase

— Investor receives payments from insurer
— Fixed number of annuity units, vary in value

Payout Methods

— Lump sum or random withdrawals
— Annuitization (monthly income guaranteed for life)
— Life income—no beneficiary; largest monthly payment
— Life with period certain—minimum guaranteed period
— Joint life with last survivor—annuity on two lives; smallest monthly payment

AIR

— Used to determine monthly income
— Income goes up from previous month if separate account performance is greater than AIR
— Income stays the same as previous month if separate account performance is equal to AIR
— Income falls from the previous month if separate account performance is less than the AIR

Variable Life Insurance

	Whole Life	Variable Life
Premium	Fixed	Fixed
Cash Value	Guaranteed	No guarantee
Death Benefit	Guaranteed and fixed	Minimum guaranteed, variable
Loan Privilege	100% of cash value allowed	Usually up to 90% of cash value allowed
Investment of Premiums	General account	Separate account
Investment Risk	Insurer	Policyowner
Regulation	State insurance regulations; not a security	State insurance and regulations; NASD, SEC

Contract Exchange

— 24 months to exchange variable to fixed

Policy Refunds

— Full refund within free-look period (45 days)

— First year: cash value plus excess over 30% of sales charges

— Second year: cash value plus excess over 10% of sales charges

Calculations

— Death benefit—adjusted annually

— Cash value—calculated monthly

AIR

— Death benefit fluctuates based on comparison of separate account performance to AIR

— Cash value is not affected by AIR

Voting Rights

— One vote per $100 of cash value

Loan Provision

— Minimum of 75% available after 3 years; up to maximum of 90%

SECURITIES AND TAX REGULATIONS HOTSHEET

Act of 1933

— The Paper Act

— Nonexempt issuers must file registration statements with the SEC

— Requires use of prospectus when selling new issues

— Requires full and fair disclosure of new issues

— Regulates primary market activity (issuing and underwriting)

Act of 1934

— The People and Places Act

— Regulates secondary market activity

— Created the SEC

— Registration of all representatives/firms that trade securities for the public

— Oversees exchanges and OTC market

— No security is exempt from antifraud provisions (even if exempt from 1933 registration)

Maloney Act

— Chartered the NASD as the SRO of the OTC

Investment Advisers Act of 1940

— Registration of persons who receive flat fees or percentages for giving investment advice

— At least $25 million under management

Calculating Yield

— Annual dividends ÷ POP; capital gains distributions are not included

Selling Dividends

— Prohibited practice due to tax liability

Breakpoint Sales

— Prohibited practice encouraging customer to purchase below the opportunity for a discount

Underwriters

— Corporate underwriters must be NASD members

Trading

— Listed securities are exchange traded in auction market

— Unlisted securities trade OTC; price is negotiated

— Third market is listed securities trading OTC

— Fourth market; ECNs such as INSTINET

Broker/Dealers

— Agent—Broker—Commissions

— Dealer—Principals—Markups

Settlement Dates

— Regular way: corps and munis, T+3; governments, T+1

— Cash settlement: same day

— Regulation T settlement: T+5

Frozen Accounts

— If no extension granted from SRO, 90-day freeze, amounts of less than $1,000 can be ignored

Ex-Dates

— Two business days before record date (regular way)

— Business day after record date (cash settlement and mutual funds)

— *DERP*—order of dates is declaration, ex, record, payable (D, R, and P determined by BOD; NASD determines ex-date)

— Buy before the ex-date to get the dividend in regular way settlement

Taxation of Annuities

— Monthly income: part return of cost basis, part taxable; proportion determined by ratio of cost basis to life expectancy

— Lump-sum/random withdrawals: LIFO applies; earnings withdrawn first, taxable as ordinary income; no tax on remainder because it is a return of cost basis

Regulated by

— Act of 1933; Act of 1934; Investment Company Act of 1940; Investment Advisers Act of 1940

— State insurance departments; federal insurance law

Retirement Plans
Nonqualified Plans

— Nondeductible contributions; may be discriminatory

— Examples are payroll deduction deferred compensation, Section 457

— Risk of deferred compensation is employer failure

IRAs

— Maximum contribution is $4,000 or 100% of earned income

— Additional $500 for taxpayers age 50 and above

— Spousal IRA allows $8,000 between two spouses filing joint returns, split between two accounts

— No life insurance or collectibles as contributions

— 10% penalty, plus applicable ordinary income tax, on withdrawals before age 59½

— 6% excess contribution penalty

— 50% insufficient distribution penalty (insufficient if after 70½)

— One rollover allowed each 12 months to be completed within 60 days

— Unlimited trustee to trustee transfers

SEPs

— Qualified plan that lets employers contribute money to employee IRAs

— Contribution maximum = 25% of employee salary up to $42,000 (in 2005)

— Contributions immediately vested

SIMPLEs

Money Purchase Plans

Roth IRAs

— New IRA that allows after-tax contributions, possible tax-free distributions

— Maximum contribution of $4,000 per individual, $8,000 per couple

— Additional $500 for taxpayers age 50 and above

— Does not require distributions to begin at age 70½

Coverdell Education Savings Accounts (CESAs)

— Previously known as Education IRAs

— New IRA that allows after-tax contributions for children under age 18

— Maximum contribution is $2,000 per year per child

— Tax-free distributions if funds are used for education

529 Plans

— College savings plans

— Allow for after-tax contribution with tax on earnings only at withdrawal

— Donor may be unrelated to beneficiary

Keoghs (HR-10)

— Available to self-employed persons, owners of unincorporated businesses, and professional practices

— Employees may participate if age 21 or older, employed more than 1 year, or work more than 1,000 hours per year

— Contribution limit = 100% of post-contribution income or $42,000 (in 2005), whichever is less

Self-employed 401(k)

TSAs (403(b) Plans)

— Available to employees of nonprofit organizations

— Typically funded by elective employee salary reductions; usually no cost basis

Pension Plans

— Require annual contribution

Roth 401(k)s

— Corporate plan allowing tax-free withdrawals

Defined Benefit

— Based on formula factoring age, salary, and years of service; calculated by actuary; favor older key employees

Defined Contribution

— Simpler to administer; contribution is typically a percent of salary
— 5-year income averaging available on distributions
— Benefit not predetermined

Profit-Sharing Plans

— Annual contribution not required; great investment and contribution flexibility

Withholding Rule

— 20% withholding applied to distributions from qualified plans made payable to participant

ERISA

— Protects participants in corporate (private) plans, not public plans
— Rules for funding, vesting, nondiscrimination, participation, and communication

Insider Trading Act of 1988

— Tippers and tippees are guilty
— Penalties are up to the greater of $1 million or three times profits made/losses avoided
— Broker/dealers must have written supervisory procedures

Principals

— Minimum of two per firm; manage, train, and supervise

— Approve all accounts and client transactions

Felony Conviction

— May be disqualified for 10 years (also for cash/securities misdemeanor)

Private Transactions

— Not allowed without broker/dealer's knowledge (consent required if compensated); prior written notice and disclosure of compensation required; passive investments not subject to this requirement

Gift Limit

— No more than $100 cash per person per year

MARKETING, PROSPECTING, AND SALES PRESENTATIONS HOTSHEET

Advertising and Sales Literature

— Advertising to unknown audience

— Sales Literature to known audience

— Approved by principal

— Files for 3 years

12b-1 Charges

— Distribution fee approved annually and charged quarterly; cannot be described as no-load fund if exceeds .25%

8½% Sales Charge

— Only if fund offers rights of accumulation; breakpoints

Letter of Intent

— Must be in writing; maximum 13 months; can be backdated 90 days

Conduit Theory

— IRC Subchapter M: fund is a regulated investment company if it distributes a minimum of 90% of net investment income; fund taxed only on retained earnings

Variable Contracts

— Illustrtion with 12% requires 0% growth as well

Telephone Communications

— Must keep do-not-call list

EVALUATION OF CUSTOMERS HOTSHEET

Suitability Factors

— Financial status and goals

— Risk tolerance levels

— Liquidity needs, short and long term

— Nonfinancial considerations; age, marital status, education, and employment

Investment Objectives

— Must consider primary and secondary objectives

— Growth or capital appreciation over time

— Income from dividends and interest

— Preservation of capital; maintain principal value

— Tax relief for high income investors

— Speculation; aggressive and high risk investing

— Liquidity; access to funds with little or no penalty

Business Risk

— Risk inherent in operating a business; risk that business will fail or become obsolete; nonsystematic risk

Regulatory Risk

— Risk of loss of value as a result of a change in legislation; new laws may adversely impact performance of business or taxation of investment

Call Risk

— Risk that in a declining interest rate environment, an issuer will call an outstanding bond issue that has relatively higher interest rates

Currency Risk

— Risk that exchange rates will adversely affect the value and distributions of investment in foreign securities

Credit Risk

— Risk of issuer's default causing loss of interest payments and or principal; financial risk

Liquidity Risk

— Risk that an investment cannot be converted into cash quickly and at a fair price

Timing Risk

— Risk of not purchasing or selling a security in a timely manner (due to judgment or market conditions) that generates capital gains; marketability and redeemability risk

Market Risk

— Risk overall market has on an individual security; also called systematic risk; diversification cannot reduce

Interest Rate Risk

— Risk that a security's value will decline as a result of a change in interest rates

Inflation Risk

— Also known as purchasing power risk; risk of reduction in the buying power of the dollar

Capital Risk

— Risk of loss of initial investment and accumulated income due to circumstances either related or unrelated to the issuer's financial condition; principal risk

Reinvestment Risk

— Risk of failing to secure comparable returns on new investments with funds received as proceeds from a call or principal returned to an investor due to refunding or early prepayment; prepayment risk

OPENING AND SERVICING CUSTOMER ACCOUNTS HOTSHEET

New Account Forms

— Required for all accounts

— Birth date required

— Customer signature not required for cash accounts; needed for margin accounts

— Signed by representative and approving principal

— Sent to customer within 30 days

Account Approval

— By principal, either before or promptly after the first transaction

Trading Authorization

— Limited—third party can trade only

— Full—third party can trade and withdraw cash and securities

Accounts for Other Broker/Dealer Employees

— NASD—prior written notification, duplicate confirms upon request only

Joint Accounts

— All signatures required to open

— Any party can trade

— Distributions payable to all

— Each owns undivided interest

JTWROS	TIC
— Equal ownership interest	— Unequal interests OK
— Passes to survivor(s) at death; no probate	— Passes by will to heirs, probate

Discretionary

— Authority from customer must be in writing

— Account must be approved before the first trade

— Principal must review discretionary accounts frequently for churning

— Time and price not discretionary

UGMA/UTMA

— Cash accounts only

— Minor is beneficial owner; minor's Social Security number on account

— One minor; one custodian

— No short sales; no options; no margin

— Gift tax exclusion—$11,000